Mirror on America

ESSAYS AND IMAGES
FROM POPULAR CULTURE

FIFTH EDITION

JOAN T. MIMS

ELIZABETH M. NOLLEN
West Chester University

BEDFORD/ST. MARTIN'S   Boston ◆ New York

For Bedford/St. Martin's

Senior Executive Editor: Leasa Burton
Developmental Editor: Christina Gerogiannis
Production Supervisor: Dennis J. Conroy
Marketing Manager: Molly Parke
Editorial Assistant: Mallory Moore
Project Management: DeMasi Design and Publishing Services
Photo Researcher: Martha Friedman
Permissions Manager: Kalina K. Ingham
Senior Art Director: Anna Palchik
Text Design: Tom Carling
Cover Design: Donna Lee Dennison and Billy Boardman
Cover Photo: Man Tagging a Billboard © James W. Porter/Corbis
Composition: Westchester Book Group
Printing and Binding: RR Donnelley and Sons

President: Joan E. Feinberg
Editorial Director: Denise B. Wydra
Editor in Chief: Karen S. Henry
Director of Marketing: Karen R. Soeltz
Director of Production: Susan W. Brown
Associate Director, Editorial Production: Elise S. Kaiser
Manager, Publishing Services: Andrea Cava

Library of Congress Control Number: 2011936764

Manufactured in the United States of America.

6   5   4   3   2   1
f   e   d   c   b   a

For information, write: Bedford/St. Martin's, 75 Arlington Street, Boston, MA 02116
   (617-399-4000)

ISBN: 978-0-312-66765-8 (Student edition)
ISBN: 978-0-312-66781-8 (Instructor's edition)

Acknowledgments

For Evan Paul Mims — "Promise me you'll always remember:
You're braver than you believe, and stronger than you
seem, and smarter than you think."
— Christopher Robin

For Reba Mims —Thanks for being a truly grand and much loved
role model, for so many avenues of my life.

For Patti Raines — Sister Weekends rock!

For the men and women serving in our Armed Forces —Your sacrifice
is what allows us to have a popular culture.

And, as ever, for Paul — "If you live to be 100, I hope I live to be 100 minus
a day, so I never have to live without you."
—Winnie the Pooh

J. T. M.

"When we get our hands on breast cancer, we're going to punch it,
strangle it, kick it, spit on it, choke it and pummel it until it's good and dead.
Not just horror movie dead but really, truly dead. And then we're going
to tie a pink ribbon on it."
— Susan G. Komen for the Cure advertisement

My sincere and loving thanks to all those who have helped me tie that pink
ribbon on my own breast cancer, especially to family members Dennis, Laura,
and Julia; friends like the members of my gourmet and lunch groups; and
West Chester University colleagues and students.

E. M. N.

Preface for Instructors

If popular culture is a kind of mirror that reflects our multicultural society and its values and preferences, it also forms one of the largest arenas for communication among all members of that society, irrespective of age, gender, ethnicity, or social standing. *Mirror on America: Essays and Images from Popular Culture,* Fifth Edition, gives students the context they need to understand this public dialogue and the critical thinking and writing skills necessary to participate intelligently. Composed primarily of short to medium-length, high-interest essays and striking, thought-provoking images, the text's thematic chapters present material that may already be familiar to students in new and thoughtful ways. The text guides their responses and helps them think and write critically about the popular culture surrounding them.

We turned to the subject of popular culture because, after teaching for many years, we became frustrated in our search for a reader that would at once interest and challenge students. Many writing texts underestimate students' social awareness and critical thinking capabilities. *Mirror on America* attempts to address this misconception by coupling thought-provoking editorial guidance with highly readable yet challenging selections of various types and difficulty levels including articles from popular periodicals, essays, comic strips, photographs, paintings, and advertisements.

Beginning with a student-friendly introduction, *Mirror on America* defines popular culture as "that collection of objects, people, events, and places that serves to mirror society and its members and to reflect their values and preferences." Also discussing the importance of reading and writing about popular culture, the introduction stresses that although all components of pop culture may not be of equal quality, they play a crucial role in our daily lives, as well as in our shared social history.

Eight Chapters on Popular Culture

The first chapter, "Active, Involved Reading and the Writing Process: Establishing the Connection," demonstrates the essential link between the reading and writing processes by teaching students to read thoughtfully and to recognize such fundamental issues as audience, tone, and purpose. We think that students who are able to recognize these essentials are more likely to consider them in their own writing. In this chapter we outline for students the various types of questions accompanying each selection and guide them through a sample professional essay. The second half of Chapter 1 leads students step-by-step from active reading to self-generated writing and concludes with a student paper-in-progress (from brainstorming to final draft), written in response to a professional essay. Chapter 2, "Deconstructing Media: Analyzing an Image," provides guidance on looking critically at images. Several sample images, as well as a student essay analyzing an advertisement, help students to see how they can decode visual media.

Following the initial chapters are six chapters on specific areas of popular culture. Chapters 3 and 5, titled "Define 'American': Reflections on Cultural Identity" and "How Do I Look?: How Culture Shapes Self-Image," deal with the ways popular culture affects us personally. The four remaining chapters address areas of culture that affect us in a more global sense: Chapter 4, "You Are What You Eat: American Food Culture and Traditions Around the World"; Chapter 6, "What Are You Trying to Say?: How Language Works"; Chapter 7, "Fantasies for Sale: Marketing American Culture Here and Abroad"; and Chapter 8, "Picture This: Reflecting Culture On-screen." The chapter on food is new to the fifth edition, while Chapter 8 on film has been substantially revised and now also includes lively readings on television and new media. This edition continues our focus on multiculturalism to make the text even more relevant in today's rapidly shrinking world. Each thematic chapter contains nine essays, including longer "Take the Next Step" essays that offer a bridge to the reading students are doing in their other courses.

Readable, High-Interest Selections

Like the chapter topics, selections were chosen for their currency, high interest, challenging ideas, and readability. They were also chosen with an eye to their ability to generate engaging discussion and writing activities. Selected from sources such as newspapers, magazines, webzines, and essay collections, most readings range from three to five pages—about the same length as the papers that students will be asked to write. Longer essays, labeled "Take the Next Step" and sprinkled throughout the book, offer an approachable bridge to more in-depth, academic writing, enriching students' composition experience. Well-known authors, including Stephen King and Dinaw Mengestu, write on topics such as the appeal of horror movies and the immigrant experience.

Paired selections in every chapter model effective arguments. These essays present different—often opposing—stances on a topic, offering an effective way for students to understand the issues at stake and to formulate their own arguments about them. We believe you'll find these readings will generate lively discussion in your classroom.

Striking Visuals

More accurately than other, more traditional texts, *Mirror on America,* Fifth Edition, reflects the students' world by including a wealth of images such as movie posters, paintings, advertisements, photographs, film posters, and comic strips. Every chapter opens with a dynamic and engaging image. These opening visuals are accompanied by "Analyzing the Image" questions and prompts for thinking that encourage students to approach the chapter with a critical eye. In several chapters, additional visuals accompany selected essays. These visuals are also followed by "Analyzing the Image" questions, which ask students questions about both the composition and the message of the images. The "Focusing on Yesterday, Focusing on Today" visuals and apparatus at the end of each chapter ask students to examine their current culture by comparing and contrasting it with the culture of the past.

Helpful Guidance for Students

The abundant editorial apparatus in *Mirror on America,* Fifth Edition, guides students through the discovery process by asking them carefully wrought questions and by offering them context before and after every chapter and every selection.

At the beginning of each chapter, focused activities guide students to the chapter's topic:

- "Analyzing the Image" questions accompany the chapter-opening visual to stimulate discussion or writing.

- A "Gearing Up" journal and discussion prompt asks students to reflect briefly in writing about the topic for that chapter. This feature may also be used as a homework assignment.

- A brief introduction provides valuable context for the chapter's selections and focuses students' attention more fully on the chapter's topic.

- "Collaborating" activities introduce students to major concerns of the chapter and give them a chance to exchange ideas with their classmates.

Each reading selection is preceded by relevant information and an activity to help frame students' reading:

- An informative headnote to the selection provides students with publication information for the reading and a brief biographical sketch about the selection's author.

- "Thinking Ahead" questions ask students to reflect briefly on the topic of the selection.

Accompanying many of the readings are glosses to explain contexts and terminology that might be unfamiliar to students. Six sets of questions follow each reading:

1. "Exercising Vocabulary" questions begin with a list of unfamiliar words for students to look up and incorporate into their personal vocabularies. The remaining questions ask students to derive the meaning of especially interesting words from their context and to apply and compare that meaning to usage in other contexts.

2. "Probing Content" questions call for students to engage in thoughtful discussion of the selection's subject.

3. "Considering Craft" questions require students to focus on particular techniques used by the writers to accomplish their goals.

4. The "Responding to the Writer" question asks students to reflect on some aspect of the reading and to question and comment on the writer's message while connecting it to their own experiences.

5. The "Responding to the Topic" question asks students to take a position on a topic raised in the essay.

6. The "Responding to Multiple Viewpoints" question asks students to connect two or more essays, generally from the same chapter, in significant ways.

Each chapter's set of paired readings is accompanied by "Drawing Connections" questions that ask students to compare and contrast the way the authors explain their points of view.

Each chapter concludes with "Wrapping Up" activities, including the "Focusing on Yesterday, Focusing on Today" activities discussed earlier.

- "Connecting to the Culture" questions ask students to connect ideas from the essays within or across chapters and to draw their own conclusions. These questions also ask students to reflect on personal experiences similar to those represented in the readings and to consider how their own life experiences are connected to popular culture in general.

- The section "Evaluating and Documenting Sources" at the end of the book offers concise coverage of the new 2009 MLA documentation style. This section features MLA citation models, as well as an annotation of a Web page and an exercise asking students to examine a Web source.

What's New in the Fifth Edition

TEXT SELECTIONS

To keep pace with the ever-changing rhythm of American popular culture, we have included fifty-seven compelling readings, over half of which are new. These updated readings offer wide-ranging perspectives on popular culture. For instance, an essay by Claire Suddath titled "An Open Letter to the Totally Impractical Size Chart for Women's Clothing" takes a brand new spin on an old grievance — with humor and wit to show that a critical take on something need not always be dry. In a reflective and moving essay, Daniel Akst looks at friendship — from our close relationships with our pets, to our biological need for kinship, to the family structures that often emerged among groups of gay friends during the height of the AIDS crisis — and seeks to answer an important question: Is America turning into what Akst calls "the land of loners"? And making a provocative case, Bill Mc-Kibben argues for rethinking our habits when it comes to eating meat. What he has to say is less black-and-white than one might expect.

A NEW CHAPTER ON THE CULTURE OF FOOD

Chapter 4, "You Are What You Eat: American Food Culture and Traditions Around the World," takes a sometimes serious — and occasionally humorous — look at the many influences on our food culture today. Long-standing traditions, changing norms, and new trends are all examined, from American farms, to family gatherings, to the appeal of all of those cooking shows.

MORE READING AND WRITING HELP

The fifth edition of *Mirror on America* now offers students more reading and writing help than ever. Chapter 1, "Active, Involved Reading and the Writing Process: Establishing the Connection" has been thoroughly revised. Clear for students and flexible for instructors, this chapter on reading and writing offers students the guidance they need. A new, helpfully annotated, multidraft student essay demonstrates every step of the writing process, from brainstorming to final paper. And practical, friendly explanations of each stage empower students to develop their own critical thinking, reading, and writing skills.

ENGAGING IMAGES

Because our students are highly tuned to visual information, we offer students a wide variety of vivid images — two-thirds of which are new to this edition — and ways to understand and respond to them. Chapter 2, "Deconstructing Media: Analyzing an Image," has been updated to provide students with new and interesting examples for reading and writing about visuals. A sample student paper models the kind of critical analysis students are expected to write, demonstrating that they, too, can write straightforward, thought-provoking essays for their own classes. The book's visuals have been carefully updated to focus on such contemporary cultural phenomena as gourmet food trucks, fashion advertising during difficult economic times, and the incredible popularity of teen vampire movies.

You Get More Print and Digital Choices for *Mirror on America*

Mirror on America doesn't stop with a book. Online, you'll find both free and affordable premium resources to help students get even more out of the book and your course. You'll also find convenient instructor resources, such as downloadable sample syllabi, classroom activities, and even a nationwide community of teachers. To learn more about or order any of the products below, contact your Bedford/St. Martin's sales representative, e-mail sales support (sales_support@bfwpub.com), or visit the Web site at bedfordstmartins.com.

COMPANION WEB SITE FOR *MIRROR ON AMERICA*

bedfordstmartins.com/mirror

Send students to free and open resources, choose flexible premium resources to supplement your print text, or upgrade to an expanding collection of innovative digital content.

Web links throughout the text direct students to free and open resources for *Mirror on America* that provide them with easy-to-access reference materials, visual tutorials, and support for working with sources.

- Reading quizzes for every selection in *Mirror on America*
- Five free videos of real writers from *VideoCentral*
- *TopLinks* with reliable online sources
- *Research and Documentation Online* by Diana Hacker
- *Bedford Bibliographer:* a tool for collecting source information and creating a bibliography in MLA, APA, and *Chicago* styles

VideoCentral is a growing collection of videos for the writing class that captures real-world, academic, and student writers talking about how and why they write. *VideoCentral* can be packaged with *Mirror on America* for free. An activation code is required. To order *VideoCentral* packaged with the print book, use ISBN 978-1-4576-0987-9.

Re:Writing Plus gathers all of Bedford/St. Martin's' premium digital content for composition into one online collection. It includes hundreds of model documents, the first-ever peer review game, and *VideoCentral*. *Re:Writing Plus* can be purchased separately or packaged with the print book at a significant discount. An activation code is required. To order *Re:Writing Plus* packaged with the print book, use ISBN 978-0-312-67874-6.

i•SERIES ON CD-ROM

Add more value to your text by choosing one of the following CD-ROMs, free when packaged with *Mirror on America*. This popular series presents multimedia tutorials in a flexible format—because there are things you can't do in a book. To learn more about package options or any of the products below, contact your Bedford/St. Martin's sales representative or visit bedfordstmartins.com.

ix visual exercises helps students put into practice key rhetorical and visual concepts. To order *ix visual exercises* packaged with the print book, use ISBN 978-0-31267872-2.

i-claim: visualizing argument offers a new way to see argument—with six tutorials, an illustrated glossary, and over seventy multimedia arguments. To order *i-claim: visualizing argument* packaged with the print book, use ISBN 978-0-312-67864-7.

i-cite: visualizing sources brings research to life through an animated introduction, four tutorials, and hands-on source practice. To order *i-cite: visualizing sources* packaged with the print book, use ISBN 978-0-312-67867-8.

INSTRUCTOR RESOURCES

You have a lot to do in your course. Bedford/St. Martin's wants to make it easy for you to find the support you need—and to get it quickly.

Available in print in the instructor's edition or online at bedford stmartins.com/mirror, the **instructor's manual**, *Resources for Teaching Mirror on America: Essays and Images from Popular Culture*, Fifth Edition, is designed as a practical ancillary offering additional ways to present the material effectively and exercises originating from imaginative alternatives that work well in the classroom. We do not claim to provide all the alternative teaching strategies and resources here. Instead we hope that those we do offer lead to stimulating classroom experiences.

After suggestions on strategies for teaching Chapters 1 and 2, the instructor's manual offers the following material for each additional chapter:

- A brief chapter introduction from the instructor's point of view
- A short discussion of the chapter's opening image

- Comments on "Focusing on Yesterday, Focusing on Today"
- Additional resources

For each selection, the instructor's manual offers additional apparatus:

- A brief introduction to the selection
- "Questions for Discussion"
- "Group Activities"
- "Out of Class Projects"

TeachingCentral (bedfordstmartins.com/teachingcentral) offers the entire list of Bedford/St. Martin's print and online professional resources in one place. You'll find landmark reference works, sourcebooks on pedagogical issues, award-winning collections, and practical advice for the classroom — all free for instructors.

Bedford Bits (bedfordbits.com) collects creative ideas for teaching a range of composition topics in an easily searchable blog. A community of teachers — leading scholars, authors, and editors — discuss revision, research, grammar and style, technology, peer review, and much more. Take, use, adapt, and pass the ideas around. Then, come back to the site to comment or share your own suggestion.

Bedford Coursepacks allow you to easily integrate our most popular content into your own course management system. For details, visit bedfordstmartins.com/cms.

Through class-testing many of the selections, writing suggestions, and activities in the text, we have found reading and writing about contemporary popular culture to be a highly effective means of teaching students to connect to larger cultural and discourse communities through their own reading and writing. We sincerely hope that you have equally successful classroom experiences as you use *Mirror on America: Essays and Images from Popular Culture,* Fifth Edition, with your own students.

Acknowledgments

We would like to thank Barbara Heinssen for signing this book, thus making our affiliation with Bedford/St. Martin's possible. We have found it a privilege to work with a team of highly competent people at Bedford/St. Martin's, one of the last publishing houses to truly take the time to develop its writers. We especially wish to thank Bedford's past president, Chuck Christensen; its president, Joan Feinberg; its editorial director, Denise Wydra; and its editor in chief, Karen Henry, for sharing our vision and allowing us to share it with others. Special thanks go to developmental editor Aron Keesbury for his work on the first edition. His insight, inventiveness, and general good humor made our collaboration productive and enjoyable.

Amanda Bristow, who edited the second edition, helped transform that edition into an even more relevant and usable textbook. For the third edition, we were lucky enough to benefit from the vast experience of veteran editor John Sullivan. Adam Whitehurst, the editor for the fourth edition, gave the book its exciting focus on multiculturalism. His insights into the most current topics in popular culture were invaluable.

We thank Christina Gerogiannis, the editor of the fifth edition, for her ceaseless goodwill and expert guidance as she helped us make this edition even more exciting and relevant for today's students. We appreciate her flexibility and fresh ideas, which made this project so satisfying. We are grateful to editorial assistant Mallory Moore, who helped out with the innumerable details that go into producing a textbook.

Our thanks also go to the production team, including Andrea Cava and Linda DeMasi, who skillfully engineered and guided the manuscript into book form. We also wish to recognize the hard work of Martha Friedman and Linda Finigan, who managed permissions for all of the images. Valerie Duff wrote new headnotes, updated the online reading quizzes, and provided valuable writing help with the instructor's manual. We are very grateful to Kalina Ingham and Virginia Creeden, who cleared text permissions for the book. We would also like to thank the following students for their contributions to this edition: Julia Nollen, who helped locate essays; and Marie J. Finch and Robert Yates, two extremely talented young writers who provided the student essays for Chapters 1 and 2.

We also owe a debt of gratitude to a group of people who were instrumental in the revision of this book. We thank our reviewers for their many helpful suggestions: John Tyler Blake, College of the Ozarks; Tania Darlington, Santa Fe College; Debora A. DePiero, St. Andrews Presbyterian College; Michal Eskayo, Harold Washington College; Andrea Feldman, University of Colorado at Boulder; Laurie Ferrell, South Dakota State University; Gwen K. Horsley, South Dakota State University; Sue Hum, University of Texas at San Antonio; Amanda Katz, Worcester State College; Glenn D. Klopfenstein, Passaic County Community College; Richard Marranca, Passaic County Community College; Carol McFrederick, Miami-Dade College; Erika Nanes, University of Southern California; Julie A. Ptacek-Wilkey, Northeast Community College; Vanessa L. Ruccolo, Virginia Tech; Becky Rudd, Citrus College; and Julianne White, Arizona State University.

Finally, this book never would have been written had it not been for the many students we have taught over the years in our composition classrooms. With them, we have tested many of the topics, strategies, and activities that comprise this text, and from them we have learned much of what we know about teaching writing and about popular culture today.

Introduction for Students

This is not your usual English textbook. The material focuses on reading and writing about things in your world, like television, movies, music, and technology, often called *popular culture*. Why read and write about popular culture? In order to answer this question, we first need to understand what popular culture is and why it is important.

To arrive at a working definition, we can break the term down into its two components: *popular* and *culture*. In the most general sense, *popular* means "of the people"—the common people or the population at large, not the elite or chosen few. But more often, *popular* suggests choice or preference. We usually use this term when we mean something or someone that many ordinary people prefer or value. When you think of popular culture, then, think of the People's Choice Awards as opposed to the Academy Awards.

That brings us to the second term, *culture*. Broadly defined, *culture* refers to the body of beliefs, behaviors, values, and thoughts that influence us every day. It contains not only the good, but also the bad—the high and the low. We normally associate the word *culture,* however, not with the masses—the ordinary man and woman on the street—but with the educated and financially privileged. We think of *Masterpiece* on PBS, not *American Idol.* If a person is cultured, we generally think she possesses good taste, is refined and educated, and is also probably upper class. If *popular* usually means "chosen by the common people," and *culture* is often associated with the chosen few, then what do these two seemingly contradictory terms mean when they are used together?

We may borrow the Cotton Institute slogan from television commercials to help us arrive at a working definition of popular culture: It is "the fabric of our lives." Pop culture is made up of all the objects, people, events, and places to which most of us readily relate and which comprise a society at any given time, past or present. The objects and people that are widely recognized as symbols of our culture are often referred to as cultural icons. The four components of pop culture—objects, people, events, and places—can be real or imagined. Let's look at some examples:

1. Objects as cultural icons include Barbie dolls, rap songs, television shows, films, clothing, iPods, advertisements, and even Cinderella's glass slipper.

2. People or characters as cultural icons include Michelle Obama, Mark Zuckerberg, Harry Potter, Johnny Depp, Batman, the Beatles, the Energizer Bunny, Homer Simpson, and the Aflac Duck.

3. Events, activities, or rituals in popular culture are those that large groups of people participate in or can relate to, including 9/11, the Olympics, the Super Bowl, Thanksgiving dinner, high school proms, Fourth of July fireworks, and the MTV Movie Awards.

4. Places in pop culture are settings that hold special shared meaning for many people and include shopping malls, megaplexes, amusement parks, Mount Rushmore, Las Vegas, Hollywood, the White House, and the Statue of Liberty.

These four elements of popular culture form a mirror in which each of us, as members of a common society, can see ourselves reflected as part of an interconnected, greater whole. At the same time, pop culture not only reflects our tastes and preferences at any given time, past or present, but also plays a role in determining future fads and trends. From the time we get up in the morning until the time we go to bed, and from the time we enter this world until the time we leave it, we are immersed in popular culture. We may agree that not all of its components are of the highest quality or in the best taste, but we would all have to concede that they play an integral part in our daily lives, as well as in our shared social history. Popular culture is part of what makes us all Americans.

It is important to remember that pop culture is not fixed in time. The popular or mass culture of the past may become the high or elite culture of the present, and that same elite culture may simultaneously be repopularized as it is once again embraced by the masses. Consider the case of William Shakespeare. If you read *Macbeth* or *Hamlet* in high school, you probably did not associate those difficult-to-read plays with pop culture. Remember, however, that Shakespeare's plays, much like blockbuster movies today, were extremely popular during the time they were written and enjoyed wide attendance by large, enthusiastic audiences. Shakespeare was tuned in to those audiences, which were made up of all segments of society, from the educated nobility to the illiterate "groundlings," so named because they sat or stood on the ground near the stage. Thus, during his time, Shakespeare's plays were seen as popular entertainment. It was only in later years that his plays were appropriated by learned scholars in universities who sought to analyze them word by word as they continue to do today.

Interestingly enough, as evidence of Shakespeare's popular appeal in the second half of the twentieth century and into the new millennium, entertainment moguls have sought to revitalize his plays by taking them out of the hands of university professors and giving them back to the masses. Not only serious students of Shakespeare but also people who have never read a word of his plays have been able to enjoy his works through both cinematic and live theater productions. Let's examine several of these revisionings of Shakespeare's works from the second half of the twentieth century through the present day.

You may be familiar with *West Side Story*, which recasts *Romeo and Juliet* as the story of a couple struggling to maintain a relationship against a backdrop of gang warfare in a New York City Puerto Rican neighborhood. First the story was a Broadway hit; then a film version was made which drew a much larger audience. Similarly, famed director Baz Luhrmann's 1996 cinematic version of *Romeo and Juliet*, starring Leonardo DiCaprio and Claire Danes, features tough modern gangs, a cross-dressing Mercutio, and a powerful musical score performed by contemporary artists such as Radiohead and Garbage. The 1999 Academy Awards were dominated by the Hollywood blockbuster *Shakespeare in Love*, a rollicking spoof featuring a young Shakespeare with writer's block, played by Joseph Fiennes, who is lovestruck by a beautiful woman, played by Gwyneth Paltrow. Since then, there have been several other popular reincarnations of Shakespeare classics set in contemporary America, featuring stars like Julia Stiles, Heath Ledger, Amanda Bynes, Ethan Hawke, Catherine Keener, Jet Li, and Aaliyah. These films, which target the teenage market, include *O*, a modern-day retelling of *Othello*; *10 Things I Hate about You*, based on *The Taming of the Shrew*; *She's the Man*, which adapts *Twelfth Night* to a high school setting; *Hamlet* and its satirical play-within-a-play sequel, *Hamlet 2*; and *Romeo Must Die*, yet another retelling of the classic love story *Romeo and Juliet*.

Perhaps the most exciting example of Shakespeare's reaching the masses in much the same way he did in his own day is New York City's Shakespeare in the Park series. The aptly named Public Theater, which celebrated its fiftieth anniversary in 2005, sponsors this series and provides equal accessibility to people of all ages, ethnicities, and educational and income levels. Anyone can see Shakespeare's plays for free in beautiful Central Park, and tickets or reservations are not required. The public is encouraged to attend rehearsals and even meet the actors, some of whom are Hollywood's brightest stars, such as Meryl Streep, Natalie Portman, Anne Hathaway, Philip Seymour Hoffman, Al Pacino, and Denzel Washington. Shakespeare in the Park has become not only a national, but also an international phenomenon.

Thus Shakespeare is once again finding his way back to the masses. According to the Public Theater's Web site, "The Public is an American theater in which all the country's voices, rhythms, and cultures converge." The site goes on to state that the theater is "dedicated to embracing the complexities of contemporary society and nurturing both artists and audiences," creating "a place of inclusion and a forum for ideas." This sounds a lot like the mission of popular culture studies. Since academics are already studying and writing scholarly articles on the impact of rap music, graphic novels, the Internet, films, and video games, which contemporary composers and screenwriters do you think will someday take their place alongside Shakespeare?

Popular culture, then, is that collection of objects, people, events, and places that serves to mirror society and its members and to reflect their values and preferences. By studying pop culture, you gain valuable new insights about yourself and make richer connections to all aspects of the society in which you live. Finally, we hope that you find it not only fulfilling, but also fun to read and write about popular culture, a subject with which you are intimately connected every day of your life.

Contents

1 Active, Involved Reading and the Writing Process: Establishing the Connection   1

2 Deconstructing Media: Analyzing an Image   29

3 Define "American": Reflections on Cultural Identity   42

4) You Are What You Eat: American Food Culture and Traditions Around the World   100

5) "How Do I Look?": How Culture Shapes Self-Image 157

6 What Are You Trying to Say?: How Language Works 209

7 Fantasies for Sale: Marketing American Culture Here and Abroad   265

8) Picture This: Reflecting Culture Onscreen

321

Rhetorical Table of Contents

The rhetorical strategies—analysis, argument, cause and effect, comparison and contrast, definition, description, evaluation, illustration and example, narration, and process analysis—are listed alphabetically for quick reference.

Analysis

Argument

Cause and Effect

Comparison and Contrast

Definition

Description

Evaluation

Illustration and Example

Narration

Process Analysis

Active, Involved Reading and the Writing Process
Establishing the Connection

If this is a writing course, why is there so much to read in this text? Why is reading the first thing we want to discuss with you?

It's simple, really. People who write well read often. They read to find ideas, both for what to write about and for how to write. Reading makes us think, and good writing requires thought beforehand, during, and afterward. Reading helps us identify things we'd like to model in our own work and things we'll never do, no matter what. Reading opens windows and doors to the world we share and offers mirrors in which we can look at our culture and ourselves.

Reading with a Difference

The kind of reading this discussion involves may not be the kind of reading you are used to. If you think of reading as a sit-still, passive, try-to-stay-awake-until-the-end-of-the-chapter event, you'll need to rethink. Real reading means really getting involved with the text, whether the text is song lyrics, a magazine or newspaper item, a poem, a chapter in a chemistry book, or an essay in this text. The more of your five senses you involve, the better.

GETTING INTO READING

This text includes some things that should make the reading and writing experience more manageable for you and more interesting, too. Each unit begins with an image like a photograph or an advertisement. This opening visual gives you a first glimpse of the chapter's topic and helps you begin to think about that topic. Next is the "Gearing Up" section—a journal and discussion prompt to help you reflect on your previous involvement with that chapter's topic and to get you started writing. Introductory text provides some background thoughts about the chapter and raises some questions to help you relate your own experiences to the topic for reading and discussion. Each chapter also includes a "Collaborating" opening activity that suggests questions for you and your classmates to brainstorm about together before you begin to read and discuss the individual selections.

Now you are ready to move on to the reading selections in the chapter. Each essay is introduced by a brief headnote about the selection's writer and the time and place of first publication. "Thinking Ahead" suggests a journal prompt that deals with the topic addressed by that particular reading selection. The reading selection, which may be an essay, an article, or a column from a newspaper, magazine, or Webzine, is next. Five sets of questions follow the reading selection. "Exercising Vocabulary" gives you a chance to explore the use and meaning of some especially relevant words. The first item in this set will always be a vocabulary list, which contains some words from the reading that you may find unfamiliar. Looking up definitions for these terms and writing down those definitions in your own words will help you to expand the number of words at your command when you write or read. The other questions here will challenge you to explore further the history, meaning, or usage of interesting words or phrases.

"Probing Content" asks questions about the writer's subject matter. "Considering Craft" questions ask why and how the writer has put together the selection as he or she has chosen to do. Next you'll find three questions to be used as essay prompts. The first, "Responding to the Topic," asks you to examine your own reactions, to relate how the topic affects you personally, as you respond to issues the writer has raised. The second, "Responding to the Writer," asks you to take a position on issues raised by the selection and to defend your point of view. The third, "Responding to Multiple Viewpoints," directs you to develop an essay connecting various sources from within the book. For the paired essays in each chapter, you will find one additional question set, "Drawing Connections," which asks you to compare how the authors of the paired essays make their points about similar topics.

To understand how all these parts work together, let's look at a sample essay. First, read the brief introduction to the essay's subject and author. Many readers may be tempted to skip right over this information because it isn't part of the essay, but that's a mistake. To see why, let's work with the headnote to a sample essay.

Mickey Mouse as Icon: Taking Popular Culture Seriously

BRUCE DAVID FORBES

What constitutes popular culture changes constantly, but the debate about the value of popular culture has been raging for centuries. In this article, Bruce David Forbes, a professor of religious studies at Morningside College in Sioux City, Iowa, examines a long-standing American icon, Mickey Mouse. Forbes expresses concern about the danger of dismissing popular culture as "harmless" or irrelevant and takes the reader on an in-depth journey into the world of one American icon. This article first appeared in 2003 in *Word & World,* a journal published by the Luther Seminary in Saint Paul, Minnesota.

This headnote offers several important pieces of information, such as a little background information about the author so that we can think accurately about his perspective on the topic, when and where the article first appeared, and the original intended audience. How does the information in the headnote influence your reading?

Thinking Ahead

Following our sample essay's headnote are a few sentences under the heading "Thinking Ahead." This journal and discussion prompt helps you focus your initial thoughts about the essay's subject. If you have never kept a journal before, you'll find that it's a good way to learn to transfer your thoughts and ideas to paper. Don't worry too much about grammar and spelling as you write in your journal; the important thing here is just to start writing. These journal notes may become seeds for your more formal essays later. Let's look at a sample journal prompt and one possible response for "Mickey Mouse as Icon: Taking Popular Culture Seriously."

THINKING AHEAD To what extent should we examine popular culture? Do the immediacy, relevance, and influence of popular culture make up for its frequent fluctuations and lack of academic esteem? What do we learn about ourselves when we examine popular movies, novels, celebrities, television shows, and music? How does an enduring symbol like Mickey Mouse reflect, shape, and represent American culture?

3

Now here is a journal entry written in response to this journal prompt:

It just seems too easy. If I can learn the same lessons from studying Disney characters or episodes of Grey's Anatomy that I can from reading Leo Tolstoy's novels, why would I wade through all those eight-syllable names? Who decides what's "popular," anyway? If we wait to see whether a movie or novel will stand the test of time, then it's not pop culture anymore. Mickey's been around forever, but the whole Disney corporation is about making money — selling more T-shirts and mouse ears and stuffed animals. American culture is about making big bucks. Every nobody can be an instant celebrity; all it takes to get famous is a cell phone video on Facebook or YouTube.

Remember that everyone's journal response will be different. The task of the journal prompt is to get you to think about a subject in a way that you might not have before, so the writing in your journal won't be a finished product. Your response will be just your initial ideas transferred from your head onto the paper.

Reading a Sample Essay

Once you have read the introduction to the reading selection and responded to the "Thinking Ahead" journal prompt, you are ready to read the selection itself. But reading doesn't mean you become a spectator. You don't learn about playing a sport just by watching, and you don't learn everything a text has to offer just by letting your eyes wander over the lines. That's why annotating is essential for really involved reading. Annotating means reading and marking the text with a highlighter, pencil, or pen. When you annotate, you open up a dialogue between yourself and the text. You communicate.

Here's how annotating works. Circle any unfamiliar vocabulary words so that you can look them up later. Some may be in the "Exercising Vocabulary" list, but some may not. We explain some unusual words or names, which you probably would not use in your own writing or conversation, at the bottom of the page on which they appear to help you understand what the author is trying to say; be sure to read that information. Underline or highlight important sentences, especially the *thesis*, or main idea, and the *topic sentences* for each paragraph. Mark sentences or phrases that appeal to you or seem especially well worded. Jot down questions in the margin. Draw connections between the author's experiences and your own. Put question marks by whatever you don't accept as true or just don't understand. React to what you're reading!

Here is a copy of our sample essay, "Mickey Mouse as Icon: Taking Popular Culture Seriously" with annotations. Don't worry if you would have marked different words and phrases and recorded different comments; that's fine. This is just to show you how one reader actively read and annotated this essay.

Mickey Mouse as Icon:
Taking Popular Culture Seriously

MCD's // Mickey Mouse (MM)

O ne could choose any number of "icons" as symbolic representations 1 of the dynamics and values embedded in popular culture. McDonalds' hamburgers, for example, prompt reflection upon instant gratification, mass merchandising, lifestyle and dietary shifts, family patterns, American penetration into international cultures, and much more. Marilyn Monroe's status as an icon leads to discussions of celebrity, sexuality and sensuality, gender roles, power relationships, and the role of entertainment as the standard against which everything is measured (including education and worship services). Among the obvious iconic choices, another is Mickey Mouse.

Marilyn Monroe celebrity, gender, sexuality, power, entertainment

global presence

What discussions does MM lead to?

created in 1928 —— Mickey as an icon functions on three levels of representation First 2 is the cartoon mouse himself, introduced to the world in 1928 by the artist entrepreneur Walt Disney. Russian film director Sergei Eisenstein once declared that Mickey Mouse was America's most original contribution to culture, and cultural commentator Michael Real has written that Mickey is "recognized as one of the most universal symbols in the history of humankind."[1] On this first level, we could analyze why this cartoon character has appealed to so many people, what roles he plays in cartoons and comic books, and what values he represents.

MM is universal & unforgettable

On a second level, Mickey has become a logo for a far-flung family 3 entertainment empire, no longer centered only on the mouse cartoons. This includes full-length animated movies, nature and family films, theme parks (in California, Florida, France, Japan, and soon in China), television shows like the *Mickey Mouse Club* and the various Sunday evening programs over the years, an entire Disney cable channel, and extensive Disney merchandise, found in Disney stores and almost every other kind of retail outlet one can name. Mickey has become the symbol for all of these "family-oriented" offerings.

MM present in all areas of popular culture

logo for family entertainment

On a third level, the corporation's reach has grown even wider, with 4 the acquisition of Capital Cities/ABC television in 1997. The Disney empire now includes the ABC television network, A&E, Lifetime, E!, the History Channel, ESPN, the Mighty Ducks hockey and Angels baseball franchises, real estate developments, Miramax and Touchstone movies with adult themes, and much more. While the breadth and influence of the entire corporation cannot be ignored, what has inspired the most public devotion are the Disney efforts on the first two levels, especially the animated movies, theme parks, cartoons, and related merchandise. The following brief consideration of Mickey as icon refers especially to those first two levels.

sports!

If there is any doubt about the extent of Mickey's and Disney's exposure in American culture and around the world, the statistics are overwhelming. Some miscellaneous examples: even before the corporate expansion in 1997, the Disney corporation's revenue in 1995 was $12.1 billion, and $18.7 billion in 1996. By 1999 it was $23.4 billion. *The Lion King*, one of

Revenue
$12.1 billion in 1995
$18.7 billion in 1996
$23.4 billion in 1999

[1] Christopher Finch, *The Art of Walt Disney: From Mickey Mouse to the Magic Kingdoms*, new concise edition (New York: Harry N. Abrams, 1975) 52; Michael R. Real, *Mass-Mediated Culture* (Englewood Cliffs, NJ: Prentice-Hall, 1977) 78.

Disney's most successful movies, has grossed more than one billion dollars worldwide. Orlando, Florida, with Walt Disney World as its centerpiece, has become the most popular tourist destination in the world. More than fifty million tourists visit Orlando annually, a number equal to the entire populations of California and Pennsylvania invading the Orlando area every single year. Walt Disney World has recently become the number one honeymoon destination for married couples in the United States. Approximately 100,000 people reside in Walt Disney World's on-site hotels every night.[2]

Really!

Mickey has become the trademark for all of these family-oriented enterprises, but even more, he has become an icon. In his iconic status, what themes or issues does he represent? Among many possibilities, here are two sample suggestions: 6

themes MM represents

1. Mickey Mouse as an icon of utopian dreams

What was and is the appeal of the films, theme parks, and merchandise associated with Mickey Mouse and the Disney name? Most persons first mention children, but Walt Disney and his corporate successors have been quite clear that the childhood appeal was intended for adults as well. For example, Walt Disney, in conversation with biographer Bob Thomas, said about his first theme park: "Disneyland isn't designed just for children. When does a person stop being a child? Can you say that a child is ever entirely eliminated from an adult? I believe that the right kind of entertainment can appeal to all persons, young or old."[3] Years later, Michael Eisner, the current Disney corporation CEO, also claims that Disney entertainment responds to "the child within us."[4]   7

Never!!

Speaks to the child in everyone

MM as icon uphold

Rather than focus only on children, it is more appropriate to see Disney as upholding ideals and values widely embraced by American society. Michael Real has written that "Disney's work typifies twentieth-century America's self-image and worldview much as Dante's[5] work typified Medieval Catholicism." However, it is represented in a "utopian, idealized form."[6] What kind of ideals? In the 1970s, Real administered a questionnaire to two hundred people who had spent considerable time at Disneyland in California, and when he asked what virtues were especially approved by Disney presentations, the following words were listed by multiple respondents: "kindness, honesty, truth, happiness, smile, friendliness, innocence, sweetness, generosity, sharing, creativity, thriftiness, money, industriousness, obedience, and cleanliness."[7]   8

embodies 20th C. America but still universal

MM functions as a shared experience

like what?

Disney// Dante?

feelings invoked by MM

Popular culture commentator Russel Nye, in his observations on Mickey Mouse cartoons and comic strips, has raised some related themes: 9

[2] Carl Hiaasen, *Team Rodent: How Disney Devours the World* (New York: Ballantine, 1998) 2, 6, 10; Richard E. Fogelsong, *Married to the Mouse: Walt Disney World and Orlando* (New Haven: Yale University Press, 2001) xi, 3.

[3] Bob Thomas, *Walt Disney: An American Original* (New York: Hyperion, 1994) 11.

[4] Michael Eisner, "It's a Small World After All," *NPQ: New Perspectives Quarterly* 8/4 (1991) 40–43.

[5] **Dante:** Italian poet, author of *The Inferno.*

[6] Michael R. Real, *Mass-Mediated Culture* (Englewood Cliffs: Prentice-Hall, 1977) 47.

[7] Ibid., 73

Mickey's is a child's world, safe (though occasionally scary), nonviolent, nonideological, where all the stories have happy endings. Characterization is strong and simple. . . . No Disney strip ever gave a child bad dreams or an adult anything to ponder. Mickey's whole existence is predicated on love and security for all. . . . The roots of Mickey's appeal lie in his continual reassurance that all's right with the world, that the meek will inherit, the innocent triumph. The mouse, the symbol of all that is weak, always wins in the end.[8]

lives in child's ⊕, but for adults, too

assures viewers of positivity and safety

Disney entertainment provides, for adults and children alike, a created experience that represents what many people would like the world to be: happy, innocent, simple, safe, clean, honest, and kind. Especially in the midst of the complications of our lives, it is a utopian vision for which people yearn. Instead of "utopia," in religious language we might refer to it as Eden (a golden age of the past) or paradise (the ideal that is yet to come).   10

Disney entertainment// Eden?

Disney promotes wholesome image

Even though the Disney corporation has spent much effort promoting itself as a representative of happiness and wholesome values and has received an enthusiastic response from broad segments of the American public, it has become a target for critics on all sides. Best known is the Southern Baptist boycott of Disney, initiated in 1997, as a protest against what was perceived as "gay-friendly" corporate policies and objectionable programming. From other directions, critics have complained about the subservient roles of women in Disney animated films (only partially *Look this up* ameliorated by *Pocahontas* and *Mulan*) and about racial and ethnic stereotyping. For example, one commentary on *The Lion King* summarized: 11

MM critics boycott its "gay-friendly" ideology

stereotypes perpetuated in Lion King

What they produced is a story that, on the surface, is about a lion cub who prevails in the face of adversity. But the real story of *The Lion King* is the marginalization[9] of females such as Nala and Serabi, the vilification of gays personified by Scar, the ghettoization of Blacks and Hispanics, represented by the dreaded hyenas, and the glorification of hierarchy and paternalism symbolized by Mufasa and Simba.[10]

unequal roles for men & women

look this up

generalized   In the way the Disney utopian package has been delivered, it seems to have been a largely white, middle-class American dream that has struggled to take account of the experiences of people beyond that core audience. Indeed, even some white middle-class Americans have trouble with how the dream is portrayed.   12

Whatever the criticisms, we have to understand why so many Disney fans do not want to hear them. Remember the principle articulated earlier: popular culture both shapes us and reflects us. Critics are concerned about the influence of Disney's encoded messages on our lives and understandings, but we also should ask why Mickey and Disney touch a chord *Why is MM so universal?* with so many people. Is it because the Disney experience represents a life   13

*Role of pop culture on our lives

[8] Russel Nye, *The Unembarrassed Muse: The Popular Arts in America* (New York: Dial, 1970) 233.
[9] **marginalization:** Setting aside as not significant.
[10] Gail Robertson, "Snow Whitey?" *Canadian Dimension* 32/5 (Sept/Oct 1998) 45–46. For examples of critical assessments, see Henry A. Giroux, *The Mouse That Roared: Disney and the End of Innocence* (Lanham, MD: Rowman and Littlefield, 1999), and Carl Hiaasen, *Team Rodent.*

Disney's Eden vs. other religions' ideologies

many persons yearn for, where things are happier and simpler? For persons in ministry, the appeal of Disney raises important issues. How can we take seriously these human yearnings? How does the Disney version of Eden compare with Jewish, Christian, and other religious visions? How should we respond?

2. Mickey Mouse as an icon of the commodification of culture

birth & growth of mass marketing

Today, parents complain that children's movies aren't just movies any more; [14] they always seem to be accompanied by mass marketing of toys, character bedsheets, promotions at fast-food restaurants, and more. An undisputed pioneer in such cross-marketing was Walt Disney. When the *Disneyland* television show was launched on ABC in 1954, Disney "planned to devote roughly a third of each episode to the promotion of either the park or an upcoming Disney film." He called it "total merchandising."[11] Disney also pioneered the concept of the miniseries, and his first success was Davy Crockett, "sparking television's first cult craze." Sales of coonskin caps and other Crockett merchandise surpassed $100 million in seven months, which amounted to approximately 10 percent of all domestic children's product sales at the time![12] *The Mickey Mouse Club* (1955–1959 in its original run) made celebrities of its young stars ("miniversions of Davy Crockett"), and it included more advertisements than any show up to that point—twenty-two per episode.[13] Of course, the marketing has grown ever since. Critic Henry Giroux voices the suspicion that Disney's "pretence of innocence" functions as "little more than a promotional mask that covers over its aggressive marketing techniques and influence in educating children to the virtues of becoming active consumers."[14]

generalized view of America & its ideals

Disney simply teaching kids to become consumers?

negative connotations

aggressive marketing strategy

Movie reviewer Leonard Maltin has called Disney "the merchandizing [15] king of America," and commentator Steven Stark adds,

> By weaving together the worlds of television and movies, programming and advertising, and adult programming and children's programming, Walt Disney made his TV offerings part of a seamless mesh of entertainment. Today, we are all ensnared in Walt's web.[15]

precursor to current marketing strategies

Is modern life commodified?

Walt Disney may have been a pioneer, but it is clear that such cross-merchandizing is now culturewide. A concern about this development is that all of life seems to be transformed into commodities, products to create and sell. Is this simply successful capitalism with neutral impact, or should we be concerned about corrosive effects on life experience? Just as some children prefer a sugared orange drink to fresh-squeezed orange juice, the synthetic may replace the real. Thus, Port Orleans at Walt Disney World becomes preferable to the actual city of New Orleans, and a packaged trip to Walt Disney World, something we can buy, becomes the highlight of a family's experience. Such issues invade the church as well. [16]

all negative

synthetic → real?

---

[11] Steven D. Stark, *Glued to the Set: The 60 Television Shows and Events That Made Us Who We Are Today* (New York: Delta/Dell Publishing, 1997) 71.
[12] Ibid., 73.
[13] Ibid., 74.
[14] Robertson, "Snow Whitey?" 45–46.
[15] Leonard Maltin, *The Disney Films*, 3d ed. (New York: Hyperion, 1995) 8; Stark, *Glued to the Set*, 75.

When the gospel becomes a <u>commodity</u>, a product to be <u>marketed</u>, is it changed in the process?[16]

Mickey's iconic status can lead our discussion in many directions. The point is that the entire world of popular culture, usually ignored as harmless and (innocuous) entertainment, is of immense importance and <u>worthy of critical reflection</u>—to learn about ourselves, and to respond creatively to the influences that envelop us.

MM influences pop culture. Pop culture influences us.

17

college courses?

THINKING ABOUT THE READING

After reading and annotating the piece of writing, you are ready to continue the conversation with the text, guided by several sets of questions. The first set is called "Exercising Vocabulary." The first question here encourages you to locate definitions and think about adding words to your personal spoken and written vocabulary. Following each word in parentheses is an abbreviation for the part of speech that tells how the word is used in context—*n.* for *noun, v.* for *verb, adj.* for *adjective,* or *adv.* for *adverb*—so that you'll know how you might use this word in a sentence. Next is a number in parentheses; this is the paragraph number in the essay where the word appears. This allows you to see where and how the writer has used this word. The words are purposely not defined for you; keep a vocabulary list either in your notebook or on your computer with definitions that you put into your own words after reading the dictionary definition. Don't be tempted to simply copy words from the dictionary, however. That may give you penmanship or keyboarding practice, but it won't help your personal vocabulary grow. Think about building blocks. Someone with more building blocks can build a more complete castle than someone else with fewer blocks. Words are the building blocks of essays and conversations. Read what the dictionary has to say, and write down a definition that makes sense to you. Then go back and reread the word in context to make sure your definition fits the author's intent. The objective is for you to be able to use this new word in your own conversations and writing. Our vocabulary list may not cover all the words in the selection that you find unfamiliar. Always feel free to add words you'd like to master from each essay to your list.

The next question in the "Exercising Vocabulary" set will require you to examine just a few words or phrases from the selection in close detail. You are asked to draw some conclusions and occasionally to do some detective work to arrive at a meaning for an unfamiliar word.

Here is the "Exercising Vocabulary" section for "Mickey Mouse as Icon: Taking Popular Culture Seriously." We have included working definitions that a student might supply for the vocabulary list and possible answers so that you can see how this section works.

---

[16] See R. Laurence Moore, *Selling God: American Religion in the Marketplace of Culture* (New York: Oxford University Press, 1995).

EXERCISING VOCABULARY

1. Record your own definition for each of these words.

icons (n.) (1) *Objects, persons, or places widely recognized as having great influence.*

acquisition (n.) (4) *Something gained.*

grossed (v.) (5) *Earned.*

subservient (adj.) (11) *Inferior, submissive.*

ameliorated (v.) (11) *Lessened, bettered.*

adversity (n.) (11) *Unfavorable circumstances.*

encoded (v.) (13) *Hidden, not obvious.*

seamless (adj.) (15) *Without a break.*

ensnared (v.) (15) *Trapped.*

corrosive (adj.) (16) *Damaging over time.*

synthetic (adj.) (16) *Not real.*

innocuous (adj.) (17) *Causing no harm.*

2. In paragraph 1, Forbes notes that McDonald's hamburgers may make us think about "instant gratification." What does this expression mean? How is it associated with McDonald's hamburgers and other facets of our culture?

> *Instant gratification means having our wants satisfied quickly. When we go to McDonald's, we can grab a burger and fries fast, without slowing down. We don't want to have to wait to get whatever we want. That's why we have movies on demand, TiVO to eliminate commercials, and instant music downloads to our iPods.*

3. Forbes contends that Mickey Mouse represents a "utopian" ideal. What is the origin of the word *utopian*? What values does Mickey Mouse represent that Americans would expect in a utopia?

> *Utopia was the title of a book written in 1516 by Sir Thomas More about a perfect human society. The word utopian means impossibly perfect. Americans would expect everyone in a utopia to be friendly, happy, generous, kind, law-abiding, and polite, and Mickey is all of these things.*

4. This article discusses Mickey Mouse as a symbol of the "commodification of culture." What does it mean to commodify something? How did Disney take advantage of his company's power to change marketing techniques?

> *To commodify something means to turn it into objects that can be bought and sold. Disney used children's television shows like Davy Crockett and The Mickey Mouse Club to advertise products that children would want, creating a market for things his company sold.*

The next set of questions is called "Probing Content," and these questions are designed to get you to examine closely what the writer is saying. Often a second part of the question asks you to think more deeply or to draw a conclusion. Be sure to answer all the parts of each question. You'll remember answers to some of these questions from your first reading, but for others you'll need to reread carefully. Here are "Probing Content" questions for "Mickey Mouse as Icon" with some suggested answers. Of course, you might think of equally good but different answers.

PROBING CONTENT

1. How did Mickey Mouse become "one of the most universal symbols in the history of humankind" (para. 2)? How far does Mickey's influence reach?

   Mickey Mouse is the symbol for the entire Disney empire. The unique shape of Mickey's head is everywhere — movies, toys, theme parks, and clothing. People in France, China, and Japan recognize Mickey.

2. What are some aspects of Disney's productions and corporate structure that have been criticized? What may be wrong with Disney's ideal reality?

   Disney has been criticized both for being a "gay-friendly" corporation and for vilifying gays in films, for showing women in inferior roles in animated films, and for portraying ethnic and racial stereotyping. Disney's dream world may be relevant only to some Americans.

3. Why may Mickey and Disney appeal to so many adults as well as to children? What does this appeal mean for those involved in religious ministry, like the author?

   In Mickey's world, everything is happy and safe. This is the way everyone would like life to be — no conflict, no threats, no stresses. People in the ministry may consider how the Disney paradise relates to those of many religions.

4. Why do parents think that children's movies are weighed down with too much baggage? What is that baggage?

   Today children can't just go enjoy a movie because of all the marketing attached to the movie's characters. Kids have to have the bedsheets, action figures, and other toys that go with the movie.

While the "Probing Content" questions examine what the writer has to say about the subject, the next set of questions, "Considering Craft," encourages you to find out how the writer has packaged that information. You are asked to consider the writer's purpose, audience, language and tone, sentence structure, title, introduction and conclusion, and organization—the very things you must consider when you write your own papers. Here are sample "Considering Craft" questions for "Mickey Mouse as Icon" with some possible answers.

CONSIDERING CRAFT

1. As indicated by the large number of footnotes at the bottom of the pages of this article, Forbes refers often to the work of other writers. How does his frequent inclusion of the opinions of others influence your reading of this article?

    Including all the other sources makes it seem that Forbes has really done his homework. It makes the reader more inclined to accept his point of view.

2. Why did Forbes choose Mickey Mouse as the focal point for this article? What effect does this choice have on the reader?

    Everyone knows about Mickey Mouse, so every reader will be able to appreciate what Forbes has to say. If he had chosen some other icon — maybe Lady Gaga — not everyone would be as familiar with what she represents.

3. In this article, Forbes uses two subheadings: "Mickey Mouse as an icon of utopian dreams" and "Mickey Mouse as an icon of the commodification of culture." What function do these subheadings serve?

    The subheadings help the reader to focus on the aspect of Mickey Mouse that Forbes wants to discuss in each section. There is so much information here that the reader might have trouble following Forbes's argument without the help the subheadings provide.

The final section concluding each reading selection offers three writing prompts for essay development: "Responding to the Topic," "Responding to the Writer," and "Responding to Multiple Viewpoints." Here are those writing prompts for "Mickey Mouse as Icon." One of these prompts will be developed into a sample student essay later in this chapter.

WRITING PROMPTS

Responding to the Topic   Choose a prominent cultural icon not mentioned in "Mickey Mouse as Icon" and write an essay in which you analyze how that icon symbolically represents American values and attitudes both at home and abroad.

Responding to the Writer   Forbes concludes in his essay "that the entire world of popular culture, usually ignored as harmless and innocuous entertainment, is of immense importance and worthy of critical reflection" (para. 17). Write an essay in which you offer specific examples to defend or reject Forbes's conclusion.

Responding to Multiple Viewpoints   Read this excerpt from an interview with Professor Ray Browne, a scholar famous for his pioneering efforts in popular culture studies.

Write an essay in which you explain how Bruce Forbes's essay "Mickey Mouse as Icon" illustrates Ray Browne's contention that the study of popular culture has significance for all of us.

A Conversation with Ray Browne

Americana: Why is the study of popular culture important?

Browne: For a civilization to flourish and continue, it is important that all aspects be known because up until recently they were recognized as inseparable. For example, in England and Western Europe there was no separation of "elite" and common culture until the sixteenth century, when the powerful realized that by using their power they could pull themselves "above" the so-called masses. In early America, there was less distinction between the levels of society though the Reverend Cotton Mather, though preaching to the masses, detested some of their attitudes and practices. Even Benjamin Franklin, who published for and understood the common people, thought their music very crude and detestable.

But increasingly our culture is coming to realize that the proper study of a democratic society is its democratic cultures and practices, all. Some may be more desirable and respectable, but as Lincoln might have said, some cultures are desirable to some of the people some of the time and as such they are valuable as evidence of that segment of society. This evidence is clearly visible now in the interest we are seeing among archeologists who are digging around in tombs of the dead, not looking for gold but for everyday artifacts. . . .

Americana: At the end of your biography written by Gary Hoppenstand and published in *Pioneers in Popular Culture Studies,* Hoppenstand writes, "The more things change, the more they stay the same, unless one makes a Herculean effort to interrupt the circular flow." Have things "stayed the same" for the most part or have significant changes been made in terms of academic acceptance of popular culture studies?

Browne: Pat and I have now retired and turned over further development of popular culture studies to other people. We hope our accomplishments have been substantial. During our watch, the humanities have developed from an elitist discipline to a more inclusive one. Now, all aspects of everyday life are being studied in so-called higher education. That is an opening of the door through which education should and will pass.

Within each chapter, you'll find paired selections that express two different viewpoints about a common issue. These paired selections encourage you to examine several sides of a topic and to weigh the strength of each author's position.

Now it's time to apply the ideas you have been developing while you were reading and answering questions. It's time to write about all the things you have to say.

Writing with a Difference

GETTING INTO WRITING

Writing is often not easy. There are probably a few hundred people for whom writing is as easy as bicycling is for Lance Armstrong. For most of us, though, writing is hard work. Like accurate golf shots, good writing takes practice.

For some of us, the hardest part is just getting started. There is something about blank sheets of paper or computer screens that is downright intimidating. So the first and most important thing is to put something on that paper or screen. If it loosens up your writing hand to doodle in the margins first, then doodle. But eventually (and sometime before 3 a.m. the day the paper is due), it's a good idea to get moving in the right direction.

If your creative juices are a little slow to flow, try *brainstorming*. This simply means that you commit to paper whatever ideas related to your topic pop into your head. You don't evaluate them. You just get them down on paper. You don't organize them, reflect on them, or worry about spelling correctly. You just write them down. There are several popular ways to brainstorm. Lots of people like to do *outlines*, with or without the proper Roman numerals. This method lets you list ideas vertically. Writers who think less in straight lines may want to try *clustering*, also called *webbing*. This is a lot like doodling with intent. Write your subject in the center of your blank page, and circle it. Draw lines radiating out from the center, and at the end of each line write some other words related to your subject. Each of these spokes can have words radiating from it, too. Let's return to our sample essay. If a student were brainstorming to write an essay about a popular culture icon, one web might look like the one found on page 15.

Next you will need to narrow down the wide range of potential topics you have generated. Try a "first response" paragraph that allows you to simply state what you are thinking about as a possible topic. Here's how our student framed her thoughts.

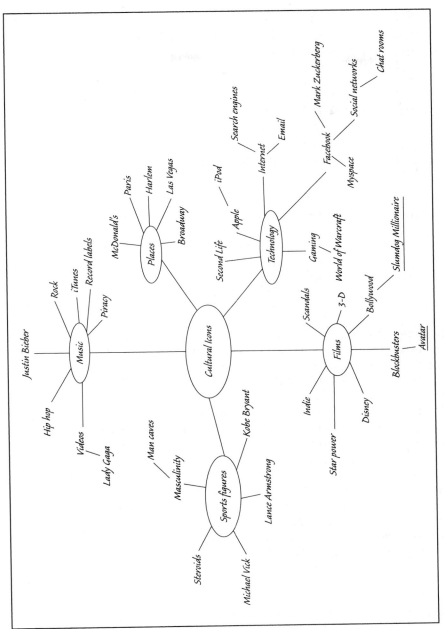

A Sample Webbing Exercise

FIRST RESPONSE

"Mickey Mouse as Icon" names McDonald's hamburgers, Marilyn Monroe, and Mickey Mouse as prominent representations of American values and attitudes. While these icons do prompt reflection on American attitudes toward instant gratification, celebrity, sexuality, obesity, etc., I think a more influential icon that has gained power throughout my lifetime is Mark Zuckerberg's Facebook. Facebook has revolutionized the way we communicate with each other as friends and family, advertisers and consumers. Like the icons mentioned in the Mickey Mouse essay, the social networking site's strategy is built on American ideals of instant gratification and fame. Facebook members in almost every country of the world create profiles with photos, interests, and contact information. Doing so allows users to create a new public identity for others to view. To Generation Y, Facebook has become synonymous with communication.

Considering Purpose, Audience, and Attitude

Before trying to impose any kind of structure or judgment on her random bursts of thought, a good writer has to consider several important things: (1) Why am I writing this paper? (2) For whom am I writing this paper? (3) What is my own attitude about this subject, and to what extent do I want this attitude reflected in the tone of my paper?

Let's think about your purpose for writing a paper. You think, "I am writing this because I am in this composition class, and the professor said to write an essay." Okay, true, but there's more to purpose than that. Are you hoping to entertain your readers? Inform them? Persuade them to take some action or change an opinion? Your answers to these questions determine how you approach your subject and develop your paper.

Something else that determines how you approach your writing is the intended audience. Who are your readers? How old are they? What are their interests? What do they already know about your topic, and what will you need to explain? Why should this group of people care about your topic? What attitudes do they already hold about this issue? The language you choose is affected by the audience that you expect to reach. An essay about rap music that you are writing for your peers won't need all the explanations that the same essay would need if you were writing it for forty-year-olds.

This is a good time to mention the level of language expected in your writing. How formal or informal should the language be? After all, you're going to be writing about popular culture. However, this does not mean that "street language" is appropriate except in situations like quoting dialogue or song lyrics. All through this first chapter, we've been focusing on popular culture as an academic subject for study, and you're taking an academic course for college credit. *Academic*, in this sense, means adhering to a certain standard or set of rules—in this case, the conventions of standard English. Maintaining academic language does not mean using large words or long sentences simply because of their length. It does mean applying everything you know about written communication to make your thoughts and ideas come across clearly and accurately to your intended audience—your peers and your professors. Slang or foreign phrases may be appropriate in some of your writing as examples or illustrations of a point, but the language of your essays should be standard English. Remember that poor writing, in this case nonstandard English, obscures thought. Good writing will go a long way toward persuading your audience that you are someone worth listening to.

Once you have determined your purpose and your audience, you are ready to determine the tone of your essay. What is your own attitude toward your subject? To what extent should your writing reflect this attitude to best achieve your purpose for the audience you have identified? Do you want to be completely serious about your subject? Will injecting some humor make your audience more receptive to your writing?

HOOKING THE READER

Once you have some ideas about why you are writing, who your audience is, and your attitude about your subject, the next step is to write a draft. How do you start? Some order has to be made of this potentially useful chaos. Good essays begin with good introductions, so we'll talk about that first. But remember: The introduction doesn't have to be written at this point. Some very good authors write the whole essay and then write the introduction last. That's fine. The introduction has to be at the beginning eventually, but no law says it has to be there in the draft. Too many good essays remain locked in the creators' heads because their writers can't think up an introduction and so never start at all.

At whatever point you are ready to write your introduction, keep in mind one essential thing: If you don't get your audience's attention right away, you lose them. Even though the students who are assigned to read your paper for peer editing will keep reading, and the professor who is paid to read it will do so, other readers need to be involved, or hooked, before they will be receptive to your viewpoint and your ideas. Advertisers figure they have only a precious few seconds to hook you as a potential customer, so they pull out all the stops to grab your attention before you flip that page in the magazine or punch that remote control. As a writer, you have to pull out all the stops to hook your readers. What really nails a reader's attention? This depends on the reader, but some tried-and-true methods work on many readers:

- You might start with a very brief story, also called an *anecdote*. We all love human interest and personal narrative. Make your readers want more information, want answers, and feel curious about what else you'll say.

- Interesting quotations make good openings, especially if they are startling or are attributed to someone famous. As quotations, though, dictionary definitions are rarely effective as introductions. Statistics can be useful if they are really amazing.

- A thought-provoking or controversial question can be a good way to get a reader's attention.

IDENTIFYING A THESIS

Besides catching your reader's attention, your introduction may perform another important task: The introduction may house your *thesis statement*. This quick but thorough statement of the main point of the paper may be the first or last sentence of the first paragraph, but it could also be the last sentence of the essay. Where the thesis is located depends on your purpose for writing, your audience, and the effect you wish to create. If you begin with one of the three attention-getters we've mentioned, you'll want to follow up your brief narrative, quotation, or question with a few general statements about your topic, gradually narrowing the focus until you reach your specific thesis, possibly at the end of the first or second paragraph. If you have identified your audience as receptive to your attitude about your subject, then you may choose to state the thesis early in your paper and follow with supporting points that will have your readers nodding in agreement. However, if your purpose is to persuade an audience that is not so like-minded, then you will want to offer convincing proof first and present your thesis later in the paper when readers have already begun to identify with your point of view.

Wherever it occurs, a good thesis can go a long way toward making your essay effective. How do you recognize or create a good thesis statement? First, a good thesis is not simply a fact. Facts don't allow for a lot of fascinating development; they just are. A good thesis expresses the writer's point of view on a topic about which more than one valid opinion exists. Your thesis must be focused. Remember that there's a difference between a subject and a thesis. A subject or topic is what the essay is about—for example, Barbie dolls. A thesis statement expresses the author's attitude about that subject: "Barbie dolls are an expression of society's misguided and demoralizing view of ideal womanhood," or "Barbie dolls are a positive influence on young girls because they indicate the wide variety of career choices available to women today." Everything in your essay must clearly relate to the development of this thesis or main idea.

SUPPORTING THE THESIS

The development of your thesis forms the body of your paper. The major points you wish to make about your thesis become the *topic sentences,* or one-sentence summaries, for various paragraphs. What information do you use for support? Where do you find this information? How much is enough, and how much is too much? Keep in mind that an important part of supporting your thesis adequately is acknowledging and then defusing the opposition's arguments.

All the support that anyone can apply to any idea fits into one of two categories: The information is gathered either from personal experience or from a source outside the self. Personal experience knowledge is whatever the writer has gathered through eyewitness encounters in which he has participated directly and personally. Outside source knowledge explains how we know everything else we know. Such outside source knowledge is often informal. We know that it would be painful to fall down a flight of stairs even though we might never have had such an experience and never looked in a medical book to see which body parts would likely be damaged.

However, such outside source knowledge may also be formal and deliberately sought, as when we look up the salaries of professional athletes in *Sports Illustrated* or schedule an interview with the football coach to talk about whether college athletes should be paid. In your writing, you may find it helpful to refer to ideas expressed in the essays in this text. In any case, you must avoid intellectual theft, called *plagiarism*. Carefully cite the source of the material you are using and put quotation marks around any words taken directly from someone else, whether they are in written or oral form and whether they are expressed in a few words or a few sentences. You can acknowledge sources by using any one of several styles of documentation. Your instructor will let you know which system to use. In the back of this book, you'll find a section called "Evaluating and Documenting Sources" that can help you determine the validity of sources and one way to document them correctly.

ORGANIZING THE CONTENT

The best way to arrange supporting details for your thesis is the one that is best for your purpose and your audience. Some essays begin with a forceful point of support on the first page, and other essays start softly and work up to a big crescendo of convincing examples or argument near the end. You might try sketching out your pieces of support in various arrangements on a sheet of paper to see which order feels most comfortable. Rarely will only one arrangement work. You are looking for whatever organization best moves along your thesis and seems most natural to you.

CONNECTING THE PIECES

The best supporting information in the world won't move your thesis forward if the parts of the paper aren't unified so that your reader can follow your train of thought. Think of the paragraphs of your essay as links in a chain: Each link must be equally strong, no link can be open-ended, and each one must be connected to the link above and the link below. Strong transitional words or phrases can smoothly carry the thesis idea and the reader from one topic sentence and one paragraph to the next one. One way to facilitate this transition process is to use words like *however, nevertheless, furthermore, consequently,* and *in addition.* Another effective transition is to identify a key word or brief phrase in the last sentence of a paragraph and then repeat that word or phrase in the first sentence of the next paragraph. Try to avoid overusing simple and obvious transitions like *first, next,* and *finally* because too many simple transitions may make your ideas seem simplistic.

ARRIVING AT A CONCLUSION

Before you know it, you're ready to arrive at your conclusion. The most important rule about conclusions is to make sure there is one. Do not simply repeat something you have already said, which may lead your readers to believe that you don't respect their intelligence. But do remember that your readers best retain whatever they read last. The conclusion is your chance to make sure the points you've raised really stick. Therefore, make sure that your main idea — your thesis — is central to your concluding paragraph. Look at how you stated the thesis earlier, and word it a little differently in your conclusion. Some of the same advice that we discussed about introductions applies here: End on a memorable note. Make your essay the one the instructor is still pondering on the ride home.

TITLING THE PAPER AND OTHER FINAL STEPS

If you haven't titled your paper already, you'll want to add a title now. A good title is not just a statement of the subject. It sheds light on which aspects of the subject are covered and how the subject is approached. Like an introduction, a good title also catches a reader's interest. Titles usually are not complete sentences.

Take time to present your paper well. You've worked hard on the ideas. Don't minimize the effect with sloppy margins, inaccurate page numbers, and other unusual printer misdeeds. Remember that your peers and your instructor are evaluating what you have produced, not your intentions.

REVISING THE PAPER

After all this work, surely the paper is ready for the instructor. Not yet. What you have now is a first draft—a fairly complete first draft, admittedly, but still a first draft. You may think it's only the not-so-good writers who go through numerous drafts, but you'd be wrong: Good writers write and rewrite and revise and rewrite. Grammar and spelling errors that seem unimportant by themselves may distract your readers from your carefully prepared chain of ideas. Thankfully, there is a logical pattern to the revising part of the writing process, too.

Start revising with the big things. It's tempting to spell-check first because it's easy and concrete, but that's a mistake for two reasons: (1) Spell-checking is editing, not revising, and (2) you may decide to delete two of the paragraphs you just spent time spell-checking. Ask yourself some hard questions. Does each paragraph contribute to the development of your thesis? If you find a paragraph that doesn't fit under that thesis umbrella, you have only two options: Delete the paragraph, or rewrite the thesis statement to make it broad enough to accommodate the additional material. Are the degree of explanation and the level of language appropriate for your audience? Does each support paragraph carry its own weight, or do some of them seem skimpy and underdeveloped? Does your essay accomplish the purpose you established?

Read the last sentence of each paragraph and the first sentence of the next paragraph. Are your transitions smooth enough? Your reader should get a sense of moving up an escalator, not a sense of being bounced down a staircase, landing with a thud on each topic sentence.

EDITING THE PAPER

Now you are ready to do some editing. Look at the sentences within each paragraph. Are fragments masquerading as sentences? This is a good time to find a quiet spot and read your essay aloud. Once two senses—sight and sound—are involved, you have twice as many opportunities to find anything that's not right yet. It's fine to run the spell-checker at this stage, but if your problem is with usage—like using *to* when you mean *too*—then the spell-checker cannot help you. It's best to keep a dictionary ready and be your own spell-checker. Be your own grammar checker, too. Even if you use a computer grammar program, don't be too quick to click Change. Keep a grammar handbook handy to consult when you are unsure about matters like usage, punctuation, and sentence structure. Remember that your instructor has office hours and that your college or university probably has a tutoring or writing center where you can get help with revising and editing.

PEER EDITING

Once you have completed your own initial revising and editing, your instructor may suggest that your class practice peer editing. No matter how good a writer you are, having someone else take a fresh look at your writing can be beneficial. Here are some steps to follow and general suggestions for specific things to evaluate when you edit a classmate's paper:

1. Read the first paragraph and stop reading. How interested are you in continuing to read? What about the introduction grabs your attention? If you wouldn't be the least bit disappointed if someone took this paper away from you right now, your classmate needs a better introduction. What can you suggest?

2. Continue reading through the first page of the paper. First write down the essay's subject, and then write down the main idea. If you can't find the thesis, make a note of that. If you are unsure of the thesis, write down what you think it might be. Take a minute now to check with the author. If you have identified the thesis correctly, that's fine. If you have identified the wrong message as the thesis, help the author clarify the main idea before you continue reading.

3. Is support for the thesis adequate? Are the examples specific enough? Detailed enough? Frequent enough? If not, make some suggestions. Is the thesis supported to your satisfaction? Why or why not?

4. What is the writer's attitude toward his subject? To what extent is the tone appropriate for the audience? How does the tone advance the writer's purpose or detract from it? When are changes in tone used appropriately or inappropriately?

5. Are there adequate transitions between sentences and paragraphs? Remember, this should feel like a smooth escalator ride. What does the writer do to make sure ideas flow smoothly throughout the paper? Can you easily follow the forward progression of the author's train of thought? If not, suggest some possible revisions.

6. Complete your reading of the essay. What about the final paragraph makes you feel a sense of completion? Is the essay finished, or does it just stop? How effective is the conclusion? What is memorable about it? What would make it stronger?

7. Review the paper now for mistakes in spelling or usage. Make a note of repetitive mistakes, and comment on any awkward points of grammar. Don't attempt to note each error. Be especially alert for the kinds of errors that disrupt the flow of a paper, like fragments, run-ons, comma splices, or sentences that don't make sense.

8. Return the paper to its author and discuss your notes. Leave your notes with the author so that he or she can use them in the final stages of revising and editing.

9. Evaluate the input you have received about your own paper. Resist the urge to be defensive. You are not obligated to make every change suggested, but you should honestly evaluate the comments and use those that seem justified to improve your work.

GAINING FROM THE EFFORT

Writing is like almost anything else: The more you practice, the better you get. We've said the same thing about reading earlier: People who read often and actively read well. The same is true of writing. For some people, writing is fun. For other people, writing is anything but fun. In either case, good writing is hard work. But perhaps no other skill except speech says so much about you to others and has so much to do with how far and how fast you will advance in your career. Writing is not just a college skill; writing is a life skill. Your willingness to better your writing ability is directly related to the impression you create, the salary you can expect to earn, and the level of advancement in life you can expect to attain.

Forget the five-paragraph boxes your writing may have been restricted to before now. Remember that formulas work well in math but cramp your style in writing. Swear off procrastination and karate-chop writer's block. There are no topics in this text that you don't already know something about. You have significant things to say. Start writing them down.

A SAMPLE STUDENT ESSAY

Here is a student essay written in response to one of the writing prompts associated with the sample essay "Mickey Mouse as Icon: Taking Popular Culture Seriously." Keep in mind that all the writing prompts can be approached from a number of different perspectives. This example reflects one student's decisions about purpose, audience, tone, and writing style. First let's look at her rough draft and some comments she's written to herself about things to expand, improve, or revise.

Responding to the Topic   Choose a prominent cultural icon not mentioned in "Mickey Mouse as Icon" and write an essay in which you analyze how that icon symbolically represents American values and attitudes both at home and abroad.

Isn't Facebook's mission statement to "make the Internet a [better] or more open place"?

From Dirty Nikes to Profit Spikes:

Mark Zuckerberg Redesigns Our Nation's Communications

Before ~~becoming~~ an American icon, Facebook was *it was* *just an* idea conceived by college sophomore Mark Zuckerberg inside the walls of a Harvard dormitory. ~~In doing so,~~ *H*e developed a site that would define a generation.

Facebook has become one of America's most popular and influential exports. *add specific statistic* *For centuries,* *typified* America has been ~~seen~~ as the land of everlasting opportunity. Facebook and the t-shirt and sneaker-wearing mastermind behind it embod~~ies~~ *y* this American spirit ~~like no other.~~

The power that fuels the American dream lies in the promise of upward social mobility: Anyone can make it to the top through hard work and ambitious motivation. This ideology stems from ~~our frontier~~ *an American* heritage *stimulated by* ~~in which~~ early settlers' ~~had to be self-sufficient. Their~~ successful departure *This* from the Establishment ~~instilled a~~ heroic optimism ~~that~~ is preserved in *just in America?* our nation's popular culture today. *P*ersonified in our national anthem, *transition needed* television, and ~~movies~~ *in films by* by *^on* hypermasculine heroes like John Wayne, Sylvester Stallone, and later geek-to-chic heroes Daniel Radcliffe, Michael Cera, and Jesse Eisenberg, ~~these men~~ *who* embody the American rags-to-riches ideal. David *One such film,* Fincher's 2010 film The Social Network *italic* chronicles Zuckerberg's rise to fame as Facebook becomes the fastest-growing website in the world. The film's modern-age hero, played by Eisenberg, follows his passion and ~~becomes~~ *defies convention?* ~~successful.~~ *Zuckerberg's character* He works hard, blows past the competition, and becomes obscenely rich while doing so. ~~In other words,~~ Facebook's story ~~is yet~~ *becomes a* ~~another~~ *cinemagraphic* manifestation of the American dream.

Another cornerstone of American values and attitudes is the *?* ~~proper~~ combination of freedom of expression and *the right to* privacy. Throughout the world, people ~~consciously and unconsciously work to define the~~ *act a particular way in hopes of influencing others'* ~~way they are perceived.~~ *perceptions.* We emphasize certain characteristics and *we* ~~through how we dress, behave, etc.~~ downplay other characteristics we consider flawed. In the job market, *first person ok?* people strive to create a personal brand by packaging themselves like an advertised product so companies can more effectively recognize their personal strengths. Business cards, clothing, and website logos ~~all~~ contribute to this

How?
TV's → persona. While this is the case in many countries, Hollywood culture
effect?   aggrandizes this ideology.

Since Facebook's inception in 2004, America's narcissism has grown

to
~~in that it~~ allow~~s~~ users to broadcast these public identities virally. On the

website, members make a public persona through what photos we upload,

who we share personal information with, and what pages we "like."

Facebook gives users the freedom to join forums and post feedback on

the user's
virtually any issue, but also protects ~~our~~ identity by offering customized

^ Each user   the
privacy settings ~~should we want it~~. ~~We can~~ adjusts ~~our~~ privacy settings so

the   the   ^   ^
that what ~~our~~ boss and girlfriend see are two entirely different pages, and
         ^   ^

a   y
thus two different representations of ~~our~~ personali~~ties~~. And because of the
                                       ^

site's growing number of members, this profile is more easily exposed to

larger audiences than any ever before. The number of people linked to on a

the number of real contacts of the person
Facebook profile is almost always larger than ~~that one would communicate~~
behind the page.
~~with in the real world.~~

to
Facebook also serves as a platform on which ~~we can freely~~ interact

with and influence political, religious, and public figures. Everyone from

Justin Bieber to Queen Elizabeth II has a Facebook page. President Obama

used the social networking site to reach out to his opponents and

supporters in what has been dubbed "The Facebook Election" of 2008,

italic
according to US News. During the presidential campaign, the site launched

its own forum for Facebook users to debate political issues. Facebook also

combined forces with TV channel ABC for election coverage and

commentary. That same year, over one million Facebook members watched

as the New Hampshire political primary candidates responded live to

questions posed by Facebook users (Wikipedia). *correct this parenthetical*
                                                 and get a valid source
Both individually and collectively, Facebook has revolutionized the way

we communicate with each other as friends and family, advertisers and

consumers, public figures and followers.

More detail needed. Strong concluding sentence needed.
→ Stress Facebook's Universal Role
   'Facebook online in every country of the world, except China, Vietnam,
   Pakistan, & 4 others
→ "Facebook" and "unfriend" listed in New Oxford American Dictionary as of 2008/2009

Now let's review her final draft.

Marie J. Finch

Professor James

English 101

October 3, 2011

From Dirty Nikes to Profit Spikes:

Mark Zuckerberg Redesigns Our Nation's Communications

Before it was an American icon, Facebook was just an idea conceived by college sophomore Mark Zuckerberg inside the walls of a Harvard dormitory. Zuckerberg sought to "make the world a more open place," but he developed a site that would define a generation (Zuckerberg). Facebook has become one of America's most popular and influential exports, with more than 500 million active users around the world (Cornish). For centuries, America has been typified as the land of everlasting opportunity. Facebook and the T-shirted, sneaker-wearing mastermind behind it reflect this American spirit.

The power that fuels the American dream lies in its promise of upward social mobility: Anyone can make it to the top with enough hard work and ambition. This heroic optimism is preserved in popular culture today, personified in our national anthem, on television, and in films. Hypermasculine heroes like Humphrey Bogart, Sylvester Stallone, and later geek-to-chic heroes Daniel Radcliffe and Michael Cera embody the American rags-to-riches ideal. One such film, David Fincher's 2010 *The Social Network,* chronicles Zuckerberg's rise to fame as Facebook becomes the fastest-growing Web site in the world. The film's modern-age hero, played by actor Jesse Eisenberg, follows his passion, works hard, blows past the competition, and becomes obscenely rich while doing so. Facebook's story becomes a cinematic manifestation of the American dream.

Another cornerstone of American values and attitudes is the combination of freedom of expression and the right to privacy. In every country, people act a particular way in hopes of influencing the public's perception of them. They emphasize certain characteristics through how they dress, behave and communicate, and downplay other characteristics they consider flawed. In the job market, people strive to create a personal brand by packaging themselves like an advertised product so companies can more effectively recognize their personal strengths. Business cards, clothing, and Web site logos all contribute to this persona. Hollywood culture aggrandizes this ideology. American televisions show public figures wearing Alexander McQueen boots with ten-inch heels and dresses designed from slabs of meat, struggling actors paying people to pose as paparazzi outside of their soon-to-be foreclosed homes, and once familiar faces almost unrecognizable after numerous Botox shots and plastic surgery procedures. From Snooki to Paris Hilton, in American culture, many celebrities are famous only because of their outrageous public personas. Since Facebook's inception in 2004, America's narcissism has grown to allow users to broadcast these public identities virally. On the Web site, members construct public personas through uploaded photos and videos, shared information, and pages tagged as "liked." Facebook gives users the freedom to join forums and post feedback on virtually any issue but also protects the user's identity by offering customized privacy settings if desired. What the boss and the girlfriend see can be two entirely different pages, and thus two vastly different representations of one personality. Because of the site's growing number of members, this profile is more easily exposed to larger audiences than ever before. In reality, the number of people associated with a particular Facebook profile is almost always larger than the number of real-world contacts of the person behind the page.

Facebook also serves as a platform on which to interact with and influence political, religious, and public figures. Everyone from Justin Bieber to Queen Elizabeth II has a Facebook page. President Obama used the social networking site to reach out to his opponents and supporters in what has been dubbed "The Facebook Election" of 2008 (Fraser). During the presidential campaign, the site launched its own forum for Facebook users to debate political issues. Facebook also combined forces with TV channel

ABC for election coverage and commentary. That same year, over one million Facebook members watched as the New Hampshire political primary candidates responded live to questions posed by Facebook users (Goldman).

Both individually and collectively, Facebook has revolutionized the way we communicate with each other as friends and family, advertisers and consumers, public figures and followers. There are now 71 countries in the world with over one million Facebook users, and 16 countries with over 10 million users ("Facebook Statistics"). The verb "unfriend" has become so widely understood that it appears in the *New Oxford American Dictionary* as its "Word of the Year" for 2009 (Stanglin). Created as a modest site for select university students, Facebook now provides a universal way to connect people across all territories, beliefs, and interests. Through Facebook, Zuckerberg has succeeded in translating the American dream into all languages.

Works Cited

Cornish, Audie. "Facebook Reaches 500 Million Milestone." *NPR*. NPR online, 24 July 2010. Web. 2 March 2011.

"Facebook Statistics by Country." *Socialbakers*. Candytech, 28 Feb. 2011. Web. 3 March 2011.

Fraser, Matthew and Soumitra Dutta. "Barack Obama and the Facebook Election." *Politics*. US News & World Report LP, 19 Nov. 2008. Web. 28 Feb. 2011.

Goldman, Russell. "Facebook Gives Snapshot of Voter Sentiment." *ABC News/ Politics*. ABC News Internet Ventures, 5 Jan. 2007. Web. 1 March 2011.

Stanglin, Douglas. "'Unfriend' is New Oxford Dictionary's Word of the Year." *USA Today*. USA Today, 17 Nov. 2009. Web. 3 March 2011.

Zuckerberg, Mark. "Basic Information." *Facebook*. Facebook, n.d. Web. 2 March 2011.

In the following chapters, you will have your own opportunities to express your ideas and practice what you've learned about the reading and writing processes.

Deconstructing Media
Analyzing an Image

2

We are a visual culture. We see thousands of visual images every day, yet we pay attention to only a few of them. Vision is our primary way of receiving information from the world around us. There is so much to see that we filter out what we don't need or what doesn't grab our immediate attention. Movie posters try to convince us to see a summertime blockbuster, magazine ads try to lure us into buying a particular product, artists and photographers try to get us to feel a certain emotion, while billboards demand our attention no matter where we turn. All visual media compete to send us their messages. The choices we make and the things we buy, even how we perceive and value ourselves, are all affected by the images that are presented to us. You'll discover as you work through this book that American popular culture relies heavily on visual representation; even music is represented visually through the use of music videos. In this text you will see a number of the kinds of visual images you encounter every day — advertisements, photographs, movie stills, and comic strips. Learning to "read" these images and discovering what responses they are intended to provoke in us is an important part of understanding our culture.

The Message of Media

Let's picture an imaginary advertisement. The woman is beautiful and graceful. The man appears wealthy and sophisticated. The white sand beach stretches wide and private; the sparkling blue water glistens cool and clear; tropical sunshine bathes the scene. The car in the foreground is a gold-colored luxury convertible. But why aren't the car's tires getting mired in the sand? Why aren't the woman's white shoulders sunburning? In reality, these might be issues you or I would have to think about, but this ad has nothing to do with reality. This is advertising — that shadow world that separates us from our money by luring us into popular mythology.

What mythology? Here's how it goes: Unpopular? Popularity is as easy as changing the brand of jeans you wear. Unsuccessful? You must drive the wrong kind of car. Unattractive? Just wear a new shade of lipstick. Misunderstood? It's not your personality; it's your poor cellular service.

We are in general a well-educated society. Why, then, are we so easily misled? Why do we buy the myths that advertising sells? We buy—and buy and buy and buy—because we desperately want the myths of advertising to be true.

For some time now, our culture has been as visual as we are verbal. We absorb images faster than our brains can process data, but the images remain imprinted in our minds. All those images influence our thoughts and the decisions we make in ways we may never have considered. From the time that we begin to learn to read, we are encouraged to recognize the power of words—to interact with a text, to weigh it for prejudice, to appreciate it with discernment. But images are as powerful as words, and they communicate ideas and impressions that we, as thinking individuals, should *question*, just as we question what we are told or what we read. How can the same skills we use to read be applied to "reading" visual images like billboards, photographs, political cartoons, drawings, paintings, and images on television, movie, smartphone, and computer screens?

ASKING THE RIGHT QUESTIONS

Effectively deconstructing media images depends on taking those images apart and asking the right questions.

- What do I see when I look at the image?
    How is color used?
    What is the significance of the layout?
    What are the relative sizes of the objects that compose the image?
- What is the role of text (any language that accompanies the image)?
- Where did I first see this image?
- Who is the target audience?
- What is the purpose of this image?
- What is its message?

The easiest questions help solve the mystery of the more difficult ones, so let's think about the obvious. What is really there to be seen when you look at the photo, the ad, or the comic strip?

TAKING THE IMAGE APART

Color   Although the images you see in this textbook are reproduced in black and white, most of the media representations around you make careful use of color. When you encounter an image, is your eye drawn to a certain spot on a page by the strength of a color, by the contrast of colors, or by the absence of color? How is color being used to catch your eye and hold your focus on a certain part of the visual?

Layout   Closely related to the use of color is the layout of objects on a page. What relationships are established by how close or how far apart objects or people are placed? What is your eye drawn to first? Sometimes the focal point will be right in the center of the ad or photo and therefore obvious to the viewer. At other times, the object the composer of the image most wants you to appreciate, the one that is central to the image's message, may be easily overlooked. Because English is read from top to bottom and left to right, we tend to look first to the upper left-hand corner of a page. That spot is often used to locate the composer's focal point. At other times the eye may come to rest at the bottom right-hand corner of a page.

Size   The relative size of the people and objects in an image may also help the designer communicate his or her message. A viewer's eye may be drawn to the largest object first, but that may not be where the message lies. To help you see how the relative size of objects can communicate a strong message, look at the photograph titled "To Have and To Hold" in this chapter (p. 33).

Text   Deciding whether a visual image should be accompanied by text or written language is another significant consideration for the photographer, artist, or ad designer. Sometimes the image may be so powerful on its own that text would be an irritating distraction. Think about the photograph of the Marines raising the flag on Iwo Jima during World War II or the shot of the three firefighters raising the flag at Ground Zero in New York City after 9/11. These images speak for themselves. When text is included, other factors have to be examined. How much text is there? Where is it located? How big is the type size? Is more than one font used? Does the text actually deliver the message? Does it enhance the message? Is part of the text a familiar slogan associated with the product, like McDonald's "I'm Lovin' It!"? Is a well-known and easily recognized logo or symbol like the Nike Swoosh part of the text? All of these considerations hinge on the importance of the text to the overall message of the visual image.

Location   To properly evaluate a visual image, the discerning viewer must know where the image appeared. Did you see this image on a billboard? On the side of a bus? In the pages of a magazine? Images in *Smithsonian* magazine will have a different purpose than those in *Maxim*. The location of a visual will help you determine the intended target audience.

Target Audience   For whom is this image intended? What are the characteristics of this target audience of viewers? What is the age range? What is their socioeconomic status? What work do they do? Where and how do they live? All this information must be taken into account by the photographer, artist, or designer if the image is to convey its intended message. For example, an ad for baby formula would most likely not hit its target audience if it were placed in *Rolling Stone,* and an ad for a jeweled navel ring in *House Beautiful* probably would not find a receptive audience.

Purpose   Every image has a purpose. If the image is an advertisement on a billboard, on a Web site, or in a magazine, the most obvious question to ask is "What is this ad for?" In today's ads, the answer isn't always readily apparent. The actual object being sold may be a tiny speck on the page or even completely absent. In the imaginary ad described earlier, the product might be the woman's alluring sundress, the man's starched khakis and sports shirt, or the convertible. Or maybe it's an ad for an exotic vacation spot. If the image is a photograph, its purpose may be to commemorate a special moment, object, or person or to illustrate an event or feeling. If the image is a comic strip, its purpose may be to entertain or to make a political or social statement through humor.

Message   "What is the purpose of this image?" may be the most obvious question to ask, but it isn't the most important one. The most important question is "What is the message of this image?" That's a very different question. This question challenges the viewer to probe beyond the obvious visual effects—color, shading, size of objects, text or lack thereof, relative placement of objects—to ferret out the message. This message always seeks to evoke a response from the viewer: Wear this, drink this, click here, think this way, feel this emotion, affirm this value. Using all the information you have assembled by answering the earlier questions, answer this one.

Now you are prepared to deconstruct or "read" the visual images that form such a large part of our popular culture.

READING VISUAL IMAGES

Let's practice with two different types of images: a photograph and a comic strip.

Look at the image on page 33 and consider some questions. What do you see in this photograph by Jean-Christian Bourcart? What event is being captured? What do the sizes and positions of the two figures indicate about their relationship? How many modern couples would find this pose an appealing one to place in their wedding albums?

How is color used?   You are seeing this photograph in black and white, but it's easy for your mind to fill in the color here—green grass and greener trees. Even in color, however, the two principal figures would be largely black and white. The white dress of the bride and the black formal wear on the groom let us know right away what event we are viewing. Here the lack of bright color works to emphasize the serious moment being captured.

To Have and To Hold

What is the significance of the layout? Think about the layout and composition of this photograph. Why did Bourcart place the couple outdoors? Perhaps he used a natural setting to reinforce the notion that a wedding is a "natural" cultural ritual. Practically speaking, this shot would have been difficult to frame indoors; the relative depth perception of the two figures is what makes the composition unique.

What is the relative size of the objects that compose the image? In this particular photo, relative size is the most important feature. Things are not equal. The groom is front and center, dominant, in control. The tiny, fragile doll bride held in his hand resembles the decorative figurine often found atop a wedding cake.

What is the role of text?   No text accompanied the original photograph. The original title in French was "Le Plus Beau Jour de la Vie," which means "the most beautiful day of one's life."

What was the original location of the image?   This photograph appeared in *Doubletake* magazine. Certainly the source is appropriate, since, after the first casual glance, the viewer's eye locks onto the two figures in their unusual pose.

Who is the target audience?   The target audience might include future brides and bridegrooms, anyone interested in photography, or an even wider group of people who are intrigued by the unusual ways that the eye conveys messages about the world and the culture around us.

What is the purpose of this image?   At first glance, this photograph may have been taken to capture an unusual image. Perhaps its intent is to preserve, in a whimsical way, one significant day in the life of a couple. Many families have albums full of wedding photos. But perhaps this photographer had something more serious in mind.

What is the message?   What is the photographer really trying to accomplish? Certainly he has chosen an off-balance approach to arrest our attention. But more is being said. Perhaps Bourcart wishes to tell us what he believes marriage offers young couples. Does he wish to make a statement about male-female relationships? On a day that seems perfect, is there an indication that life won't be "happily ever after" for this bride and groom?

Next let's work on deconstructing a very different type of visual representation, a comic strip, which appears on page 35.

What do you see when you look at this image?   With a comic strip, the viewer's eyes must travel left to right across the panels, focusing on a number of frames, each of which may offer a visual, text, or both. Often the strip's creator relies on a steady group of repeat readers who over time have learned to appreciate the personalities of the strip's characters and the subtle messages they deliver from the writer.

How is color used?   Although most strips appear in black and white in daily newspapers, many appear in color on Sundays, giving readers a chance to learn more about the characters and the strip's designer. With this particular strip, which you're seeing in black and white, the only color is in the background of each panel, which is a light green. The mouse and the monitor are both grey. Notice what happens to the mouse's eyes in the third panel and in the final one. His eyes go from little black dots to big white circles. He's having an important moment. Compare the text in these two panels.

Pearls Before Swine

What is the significance of the layout?   To some extent, the layout of a cartoon strip is prescribed: It is a series of panels. But the artist still has a great deal of flexibility with layout within the various panels. The most arresting thing about the layout here is that it never varies. From panel to panel, the mouse sits in front of the computer monitor. He's too enthralled to move except for a few upper-body gestures.

What is the relative size of the objects that compose the image?   Normally, a mouse and a computer monitor are not nearly this close to being the same size. But in this strip, they are of equal importance, and therefore, they are similar in size.

What is the role of text?   Compared to photographs, advertisements, paintings, and other forms of visual media, comic strips generally rely more heavily on text to convey their message. That is certainly true here. Except for an occasional "Ping!" from the computer, the mouse has all the lines. We'll look more closely at the text when we examine the strip's message.

What was the original location of this image?   *Pearls Before Swine* is syndicated and appears regularly in many newspapers across the country. This comic strip originally appeared on May 23, 2010.

Who is the target audience?   Although the visuals in comic strips may catch the eyes of children, most of the widely syndicated strips are not written for this audience. The message is often too subtle for children to grasp. This strip is written for savvy adult consumers who buy newspapers or read them online and who can identify with the mouse's inability to focus once Internet distractions offer their enticements.

What is the purpose of this image?   Because this is a comic strip, we expect it to be entertaining or humorous. However, in this strip, as with many contemporary comic strips like *Over the Hedge, Dilbert, Non Sequitur,* and the long-running *Doonesbury,* that is rarely the only purpose. It's amusing, but there is a punch behind the chuckle.

What is the message?   The mouse is working on a résumé, a serious task that implies job seeking. But he's distracted by the announcement of an arriving e-mail. And for the next twelve panels of the cartoon strip he chases random ideas around the Web. Near the end of the strip, he reminds himself to get back on task, but another "Ping!" (echoing the one in the second frame) immediately sets him off, down the trail to lack of accomplishment once again. The strip's creator, Stephan Pastis, who often draws himself into the strip to interact with the regular characters, portrays the Internet here as a mixed blessing at best. The implication that we have sacrificed our ability to concentrate to the wonders of the Web will ring true with most of us who have fallen prey to the "follow the link" syndrome. And who hasn't? Pastis has identified a situation with which most readers readily identify. We laugh at the mouse for being unable to concentrate, but we empathize because we *are* the mouse.

WRITING ABOUT AN IMAGE

Using these same questions we have been asking, let's see what one student has to say about decoding a third kind of media, an advertisement.

Assignment: Choose an advertisement that you believe communicates a strong message. Compose an essay in which you deconstruct the advertisement you select by addressing the questions discussed in this chapter.

Unmask Your Child's Online Identity

See Everything They Do Online

It's easy... Just press PLAY to watch a digital surveillance tape of all PC and Internet activity.

PLAY

Does Your Child Have a Secret Online Life?

The typical teenager has more than 100 chat buddies and 'friends' on MySpace and Facebook. Do you know who your children talk to online? What pictures they post and view? Are they pretending to be someone they're not?

Trust, Monitor, Protect, and Educate with Spector Pro

With Spector Pro, you'll rest easy knowing that your child is protected online with the world's most trusted monitoring software. It records everything on their computer, laptop, netbook or Mac – including chats, instant messages, emails, websites they visit, all activity on Facebook and MySpace, and much more. You can block unwanted chats and activity, and even "rewind and play" screen snapshots of everything they said and viewed on friends' profile pages – giving you total visibility into their online identity and choices they're making.

Recently awarded the 2010 Mom's Choice Award, Spector Pro gives you everything you need to ensure their safety, while helping them make smarter, safer decisions online.

SPECTOR PRO®
PC & Internet Monitoring Software

View an online demo today
www.SafeWithSpectorPro.com

Call us anytime
1.877.344.1491

Robert Yates

Professor Miller

English 101

November 16, 2011

You've Got Betrayal:

Deconstructing an Advertisement for Online Spyware

For Generation Y, Wiis and Web sites have replaced childhood pastimes like dodge ball and flashlight tag. Because the Internet offers anonymity and access to virtually anything, children are using the Internet to reach out to others, to explore their interests, and to access material that was off limits before Google. As parental concerns grow, so does the number of products on the market that claim to eradicate those concerns. This advertisement for Spector Pro, a computer-monitoring software that enables parents to review everything their children post and view on the Internet, targets worried parents by promising to answer the question: "How do I keep my children safe from the dangers lurking on the Internet?"

While flipping through the glossy pages of *MacWorld* magazine, readers are immediately struck by the startling image of a masked girl. She is pictured in the forefront of the image, staring in a zombie-like trance. Over her left shoulder, a computer monitor with an open chat-room window is clearly visible. Her mask is bright white, emblematic of purity and innocence, but tattooed with logos of popular social media Web sites like Facebook, Skype, and Chatroulette. The mask is reminiscent of Michael Myers' featureless mask, as if the logos represent a force that mars the girl's innocence.

The brightness of the mask contrasts heavily with the dark background. This ad clearly uses color and contrasts as a visual cue to the thematic significance of the mask. By literally concealing the girl's identity, the mask suggests how easily children and teens conceal their true identities online and become just another anonymous IP address on the World Wide Web. While her real eyes show through, her mouth is sealed inside the mask; the voice she expresses online may not be her own. This stark graphic guides parents to question whether their children are "pretending to be someone they're not." The anonymity of the masked girl stimulates parents' fears, encouraging them to imagine their own children's faces hidden behind the disguise.

The stark whiteness of the mask is mirrored by the lower half of the page, drawing our attention next to the prominent, clearly stated message of the advertisement, "Unmask Your Child's Online Identity." This is written in a bolded sans-serif typeface and is located in a prominent location on the page. The offer for a "free online demo" included inside a flagrant sunburst in the upper-right-hand corner provides added incentive. Its contrasting red background draws prospective customers' eyes to the right-hand side of the advertisement. The product's URL, *spectorproforparents.com,* is shown in the same patriotic hue and is also displayed prominently. While the free demo offer attracts the reader's attention, the Web site's URL beckons parents to investigate further. Spector Pro's easy-to-use method is highlighted in the box on the left-hand side. The copy is written in a "We're in this with you" tone, as if the company's employees are casual friends that parents may rely on for support through the difficult childrearing years. "Call us anytime," is certainly more personal than just providing a "1-800" helpline. The ad also includes five seals of endorsement on the left side of the page, assuring prospective buyers that experts believe consumers are making the right decision. After all, the ad boasts, this product was awarded the "2010 Mom's Choice Award."

The purpose of this advertisement is obvious—to persuade parents to invest in critically acclaimed spyware in order to monitor their children's online activity. While the purpose is clear, the debate the advertisement raises about Spector Pro's enabling parents to unethically invade their children's privacy is less transparent. New technology requires new rules for parents and children, but that does not mean that parents should exchange open communication for backhanded meddling. As Americans, our initial response is to be wary of anything that remotely suggests an invasion of privacy. But by promising that parents can "trust, monitor, protect, and educate" with Spector Pro, the ad tricks parents into overlooking the

Yates 3

potential trust issues generated by using this product. By incorporating

rhetorical hooks like "Do you know who your children talk to online?" and

"Does your child have a secret online life?" along with the image of a

zombie-like masked child, the Spector Pro ad's message is that no parent

should "rest easy" until this product is installed on every computer that

their children use.

You'll have a chance to practice your media-deconstructing skills through-out this text, from the images at the beginning of each chapter to paired images from the past and the present that bring each chapter to a close. Remember to ask yourself the questions we've identified. Look closely—and then look beyond what's on the page to see what's really being communicated.

GEARING UP TO READ IMAGES

Locate an ad, a photograph, or a cartoon strip that appeals to you. Write a brief paragraph stating your initial reaction to the image. Then de-code the image by applying the questions identified throughout this chapter. How did your initial impressions change after a careful study of the image?

COLLABORATING

1. Locate a visual image that you think communicates a significant mes-sage, and bring it to class. Working with three or four other students, discuss the images you've each chosen, and determine which one is the most effective and why. Then plan and deliver a presentation to your classmates in which your group deconstructs the image you have selected.

2. Working in a small group, assemble a collection of various types of magazines such as music, home and garden, news, sports, and fashion. Analyze the types of ads, photos, and other visuals you find to deter-mine the target audiences. How do the target audiences differ? Evaluate the match between readers of each type of magazine and the products being advertised. Discuss why the advertisers you see chose to invest their marketing dollars in that particular type of magazine. Report your conclusions in a short paper, or present them orally to the rest of the class.

Define "American"

Reflections on Cultural Identity

Analyzing the Image

The stresses of a "melting pot" culture are clearly revealed in the cover photograph from this 1999 *National Geographic.* While the mother's traditional dress reflects her heritage, the daughter's sleek jumpsuit makes a bold statement about her own cultural affiliation: "Like Mother — Not Likely!"

- What does the women's clothing say about them and their cultural identities?

- How would you interpret the facial expressions in this photo?

- What does the mother's and daughter's body language reveal about them?

Research this topic with TopLinks at bedfordstmartins.com/toplinks.

GEARING UP How would you define "American"? Think about the forces that have helped shape your sense of who you are as a person living in America today. Consider your gender, personal appearance, and ethnicity. How have these forces influenced you? How has your definition of what it means to be an American changed since you were a child?

How do I look to other people? Do I fit in? Do I want to fit in? Will I find my own place in the culture I live in? What should I call myself? Just who am I?

These are questions that all people ask themselves at some time in their lives. Many factors affect people's self-image. One is biological, such as our gender and our physical appearance. The other is cultural and is composed of two aspects: the culture of our ancestors and the larger contemporary culture that we participate in, better known as popular culture.

Cultural diversity has become a hot—and sometimes heated—topic in the United States. Should we learn about and celebrate the differences among people of different ethnicities and cultural heritages? Or should we de-emphasize those differences and concentrate on the similarities among people? Many people reject the notion that the United States is a melting pot where everyone is simply an "American." Instead, they see America as a salad bowl containing a mix of ethnicities that complement one another and that deserve to maintain their cultural identities within the larger U.S. popular culture. But can too much attention be paid to cultural diversity? Does an appreciation of other ethnic groups unite or further divide us? To what extent should those new to this country maintain their former culture?

What happens to members of minority groups when the ideals of their own culture collide with those of the dominant American popular culture? The media are gradually presenting a more accurate reflection of the actual U.S. population, as witnessed by the increasing numbers of models and actors of varying ethnicities and sexual preferences. However, many Americans still feel separated from society's mainstream because they find it difficult to relate to the majority of people who stare out at them from the pages of glossy fashion magazines or from television or movie screens. Those Americans who do not resemble society's supposed role models or live the lifestyle that the media seem to privilege can feel rejected by the mainstream.

The writers in this chapter come from diverse cultural backgrounds and reflect a wide variety of lifestyles. As these authors detail their individual struggles with cultural self-image and awareness, they encourage you to examine the richness of our country's diversity. Reading these essays will help you reflect on what goes into the continual reevaluation and reshaping of your own cultural identity as a man or woman living in the United States today.

COLLABORATING In groups of four to six students, spend fifteen to twenty minutes discussing the major cultural influences on an individual's self-image as a child and as an adolescent. Consider such influences as ethnicity, gender, sexual preference, home life, peers, teachers, and the media. Make a list of the major influences, and then discuss them as a class.

Do I Look Like Public Enemy Number One?

LORRAINE ALI

"Do I Look Like Public Enemy Number One?" is Lorraine Ali's personal account of growing up in an Arabic family in the United States and the prejudices she has faced while living an almost double life — as an American of Arab descent. Ali is a general editor and music critic at *Newsweek,* covering everything from Christian alternative rock to Latino Lone Star rap. Named 1997's Music Journalist of the Year, Ali has been a senior critic for *Rolling Stone* and a contributor to the *New York Times, GQ (Gentleman's Quarterly),* and VH-1's 2002 to 2003 series *One Hit Wonders.* Her music criticism appears in several books, including *Da Capo Best Music Writing 2001: The Year's Finest Writing on Rock, Pop, Jazz, Country, and More* (2001), edited by Nick Hornby and Ben Schafer, and *Kill Your Idols: A New Generation of Rock Writers Reconsiders the Classics* (2004), edited by Jim Derogatis and Carmél Carrillo. In 2002, she won an Excellence in Journalism award from the National Arab American Journalists Association, and in 2009 she received the Journalism Award from the New York Press Club. "Do I Look Like Public Enemy Number One?" was first published in *Mademoiselle* in 1999.

> **THINKING AHEAD**   Since the attack on America on September 11, 2001, Arab Americans have been under uncomfortable scrutiny and often unwarranted suspicion. Have terrorist actions by a radical few forever affected our ability to treat all people as the individuals they are? What repercussions will such a shift in thought have on the American way of life?

"**Y**ou're not a terrorist, are you?" That was pretty much a stock question I faced growing up. Classmates usually asked it after they heard my last name: "Ali" sounded Arabic; therefore, I must be some kind of bomb-lobbing religious fanatic with a grudge against Western society. It didn't matter that just before my Middle Eastern heritage was revealed, my friend and I might have been discussing the merits of rock versus disco, or the newest flavor of Bonne Bell Lip Smacker.[1]

I could never find the right retort; I either played along ("Yeah, and I'm going to blow up the math building first") or laughed and shrugged it off. How was I going to explain that my background meant far more than buzz words like *fanatic* and *terrorist* could say? Back in the '70s and '80s,

---

[1] **Bonne Bell Lip Smacker:** A brand of flavored lip gloss.

all Americans knew of the Middle East came from television and newspapers. "Arab" meant a contemptible composite of images: angry Palestinian refugees, irate Iranian hostage-takers, extremist leaders like Libya's Muammar al-Qaddafi or Iran's Ayatollah Khomeini, and long gas lines at home. What my limited teenage vernacular couldn't express was that an entire race of people was being judged by its most violent individuals.

Twenty years later, I'm still trying to explain. Not much has changed in   3
the '90s. In fact, now that Russia has been outmoded as Public Enemy Number One, Arabs have been promoted into that position. Whenever a disaster strikes without a clear cause, fingers point toward Islam. When an explosion downed TWA Flight 800, pundits prematurely blamed "Arab terrorists." Early coverage following the Oklahoma City bombing featured experts saying it "showed Middle Eastern traits." Over the next six days there were 150 documented hate crimes against Arab Americans; phone calls to radio talk shows demanded detainment and deportation of Middle Easterners. Last fall, *The Siege* depicted Moslems terrorizing Manhattan, and TV's *Days of Our Lives* showed a female character being kidnapped by an Arabian sultan, held hostage in a harem, and threatened with death if she didn't learn how to belly dance properly. Whatever!

My Childhood Had Nothing to Do with Belly Dancing

Defending my ethnicity has always seemed ironic to me because I consider   4
myself a fake Arab. I am half of European ancestry and half Arab, and I grew up in the suburban sprawl of Los Angeles' San Fernando Valley. My skin is pale olive rather than smooth brown like my dad's, and my eyes are green, not black like my sisters' (they got all the Arab genes). Even my name, Lorraine Mahia Ali, saves all the Arab parts for last.

I also didn't grow up Moslem, like my dad, who emigrated from Bagh-   5
dad, Iraq's capital, in 1956. In the old country he wore a galabiya (or robe), didn't eat pork, and prayed toward Mecca five times a day. To me, an American girl who wore short-shorts, ate Pop Rocks,[2] and listened to Van Halen,[3] his former life sounded like a fairy tale. The Baghdad of his childhood was an ancient city where he and his brothers swam in the Tigris River, where he did accounting on an abacus[4] in his father's tea shop, where his mother blamed his sister's polio on a neighbor's evil eye, where his entire neighborhood watched Flash Gordon[5] movies projected on the side of a bakery wall.

My father's world only started to seem real to me when I visited Iraq   6
the summer after fifth grade and stayed in his family's small stucco house. I remember feeling both completely at home and totally foreign. My sister

---

[2] **Pop Rocks:** A type of fizzy candy popular in the 1970s.
[3] **Van Halen:** A rock musical group first popular in the 1980s.
[4] **abacus:** An ancient device for calculating numbers.
[5] **Flash Gordon:** The hero of a comic book series that originated in 1934 about a space traveler battling evildoers.

Lela and I spoke to amused neighbors in shoddy sign language, sat cross-legged on the floor in our Mickey Mouse T-shirts, rolling cigarettes to sell at market for my arthritic Bedouin[6] grandma, and sang silly songs in pidgin[7] Arabic with my Uncle Brahim. Afterward, I wrote a back-to-school essay in which I referred to my grandparents as Hajia and Haja Hassan, thinking their names were the Arab equivalent of Mary Ellen and Billy Bob. "You're such a dumb-ass," said Lela. "It just means grandma and grandpa." But she was wrong too. It actually meant they had completed their Haj duty—a religious journey to Mecca in Saudi Arabia that millions of Muslims embark on each year.

At home, my American side continued to be shamefully ignorant of all   7
things Arab, but my Arab side began to notice some pretty hideous stereotypes. Saturday-morning cartoons depicted Arabs as ruthless, bumbling, and hygienically challenged. I'd glimpse grotesque illustrations of Arab leaders in my dad's paper. At the mall with my mom, we'd pass such joke items as an Arab face on a bull's-eye. She tried to explain to me that things weren't always this way, that there was a time when Americans were mesmerized by Arabia and Omar Sharif[8] made women swoon. A time when a WASP[9] girl like my mom, raised in a conservative, middle-class family, could be considered romantic and daring, not subversive, for dating my dad. In effect, my mom belonged to the last generation to think sheiks were chic.

Not so in my generation. My mother tells me that when my oldest sister   8
was five, she said to a playmate that her dad "was an Arab, but not a bad one." In elementary school, we forced smiles through taunts like, "Hey, Ali, where's your oilcan?" Teachers were even more hurtful: During roll call on her first day of junior high, Lela was made to sit through a twenty-minute lecture about the bloodshed and barbarism of Arabs toward Israel and the world. As far as I knew, Lela had never shed anyone's blood except for mine, when she punched me in the nose over a pack of Pixie Sticks.[10] But that didn't matter. As Arabs, we were guilty by association, even at the age of twelve.

By High School, I Was Beginning to Believe the Hype

It's awful to admit, but I was sometimes embarrassed by my dad.   9

I know it's every teen's job to think her parents are the most shameful   10
creatures to walk the planet, but this basic need to reject him was exacerbated by the horrible images of Arabs around me. When he drove me to school, my dad would pop in a cassette of Quran suras (recorded prayers) and recite the lines in a language I didn't understand, yet somehow the

---

[6] **Bedouin:** A tent dweller of the desert; a wanderer.
[7] **pidgin:** A simplified form of a language.
[8] **Omar Sharif:** An Egyptian actor best known for his charismatic performances in the films *Lawrence of Arabia* and *Doctor Zhivago*.
[9] **WASP:** Slang term for white Anglo-Saxon Protestant.
[10] **Pixie Sticks:** A type of powdered candy that comes in a paper straw.

twisting, weaving words sounded as natural as the whoosh of the Santa Ana winds through the dusty hills where we lived. His brown hands would rise off the steering wheel at high points of the prayer, the sun illuminating the big white moons of his fingernails. The mass of voices on tape would swell up and answer the Mezzuin[11] like a gospel congregation responding to a preacher. It was beautiful, but I still made my dad turn it down as we approached my school. I knew I'd be identified as part of a culture that America loved to hate.

My dad must have felt this, too. He spoke his native tongue only in the company of Arabic friends and never taught my sisters or me the language, something he would regret until the day he died. His background was a mystery to me. I'd pester him for answers: "Do you dream in English or Arabic?" I'd ask, while he was busy doing dad work like fixing someone's busted Schwinn[12] or putting up Christmas lights. "Oh, I don't know," he'd answer playfully. "In dreams, I can't tell the difference."   11

Outside the safety of our home, he could. He wanted respect; therefore, he felt he must act American. Though he truly loved listening to Roberta Flack[13] and wearing Adidas sweatsuits, I can't imagine he enjoyed making dinner reservations under pseudonyms like Mr. Allen. He knew that as Mr. Ali, he might never get a table.   12

Desert Storm Warning

Fifteen years later, "Ali" was still not a well-received name. We were at war with the Middle East. It was January 16, 1991, and Iraq's Saddam Hussein had just invaded Kuwait. I will never forget the night CNN's Bernard Shaw lay terrified on the floor of his Baghdad hotel as a cameraman shot footage of the brand-new war outside his window. I was twenty-six and working for a glossy music magazine called *Creem*. When the news broke that we were bombing Baghdad in an operation called Desert Storm, I went home early and sat helpless in my Hollywood apartment, crying. Before me on the TV was a man dressed in a galabiya, just like the kind my dad used to wear around the house, aiming an ancient-looking gun turret toward our space-age planes in the sky. He looked terrified, too. With every missile we fired, I watched the Baghdad I knew slip away and wondered just who was being hit. Was it Aunt Niama? My cousin Afrah?   13

Back at work, I had to put up with "funny" faxes of camels, SCUD missiles, and dead Arabs. To my colleagues, the Arabs I loved and respected were now simply targets. Outside the office, there was a virtual free-for-all of racist slogans. Arab-hating sentiment came out on bumper stickers like "Kick Their Ass and Take Their Gas." Military footage even documented our pilots joking as they bombed around fleeing civilians. They called it a turkey shoot. A turkey shoot? Those were people.   14

[11] **Mezzuin:** An Islamic cantor who sings to lead worshipers in prayer.
[12] **Schwinn:** A popular bicycle manufacturer.
[13] **Roberta Flack:** A jazz and pop singer who first gained popularity in the early 1970s.

Arabs bleed and perish just like Americans. I know, because two years   15
before we started dropping bombs on Baghdad, I watched my father die.
He did not dissolve like a cartoon character, nor defy death like a Hollywood villain. Instead, chemotherapy shrunk his 180-pound body down to
120, turned his beautiful skin from brown to ashen beige, and rendered his
opalescent[14] white fingernails a dull shade of gray. When he finally let go, I
thought he took all the secrets of my Arabness with him, all the good things
America didn't want me to know. But I look in the mirror and see my father's wide nose on my face and Hajia's think lines forming between my
brows. I also see my mom's fair skin, and her mother's high cheekbones. I
realize it's my responsibility to somehow forge an identity between dueling
cultures, to focus on the humanity, not the terror, that bridges both worlds.

EXERCISING VOCABULARY

1. Record your own definition for each of these words.

   stock (adj.) (1)
   retort (n.) (2)
   composite (n.) (2)
   outmoded (v.) (3)
   pundits (n.) (3)
   shoddy (adj.) (6)

   mesmerized (v.) (7)
   subversive (adj.) (7)
   exacerbated (v.) (10)
   pseudonyms (n.) (12)
   forge (v.) (15)

2. In paragraph 2, the author regrets "what my limited teenage vernacular couldn't express." What does *vernacular* mean? What is the purpose of a group having its own vernacular?

3. Ali states that "now that Russia has been outmoded as Public Enemy Number One, Arabs have been promoted into that position" (para. 3). What is ironic about her use of the word *promoted* in this context?

4. What does it mean to possess and to give the "evil eye"? How does Ali's inclusion of this phrase in paragraph 5 contribute to your understanding of the gap between her life and the early life of her father?

PROBING CONTENT

1. In Ali's opinion, how did television enhance the image of the "bad Arab"?

2. What elementary school experience stimulated Ali's awareness of her family's cultural heritage? How did that experience color her everyday thinking?

3. What examples does Ali provide to show how carefully she and her family tried to keep their two cultures from clashing?

---

[14] opalescent: Reflecting an iridescent light.

CONSIDERING CRAFT

1. In paragraph 5, what strong images does Ali choose to represent her American childhood? What images represent her father's childhood? How does her inclusion of these images convey the gap between her father's culture and the one in which she was raised?

2. How does Ali use her personal experience to make a broad statement about how people of one culture relate to those from a different background? How effective is this writing strategy?

WRITING PROMPTS

Responding to the Topic   Explain how Ali's phrase "dueling cultures" (para. 15) has taken on a very different meaning since this essay was first published in 1999. In light of recent events, what would you say to Ali about her effort "to focus on the humanity, not the terror" (para. 15), that bridges Middle Eastern and American cultures?

Responding to the Writer   In paragraph 8, Ali asserts that she and her family have been made "guilty by association." In an essay, identify and explore the history surrounding another cultural group that has been made "guilty by association."

Responding to Multiple Viewpoints   Write an essay in which you explore how the efforts of the teacher in "They've Got to Be Carefully Taught" (p. 51) would be received by Ali.

For a quiz on this reading, go to bedfordstmartins.com/mirror.

They've Got to Be Carefully Taught

SUSAN BRADY KONIG

This essay is one mother's humorous account of Cultural Diversity Month at her daughter's preschool. Susan Brady Konig was born in Paris, France, in 1962, but was educated in the United States. An experienced journalist, Konig has been an editor for *Seventeen* magazine, has worked as a columnist for the *New York Post,* and has written articles for such wide-ranging publications as the *Washington Post, Us, Travel & Leisure, Ladies' Home Journal,* and the *National Review.* She is currently a regular contributor to *National Review Online.* Her first book, *Why Animals Sleep So Close to the Road (and Other Lies I Tell My Children),* was published in 2005 and her most recent book, *I Wear the Maternity Pants in This Family* was published in 2007. "They've Got to Be Carefully Taught" originally appeared in the September 15, 1997, issue of the *National Review.*

THINKING AHEAD Think back to your early school days. How was the issue of cultural diversity handled? What special occasions were celebrated to highlight diversity issues? How did these events affect your own cultural awareness?

At my daughter's preschool it's time for all the children to learn that they are different from one another. Even though these kids are at that remarkable age when they are thoroughly color blind, their teachers are spending a month emphasizing race, color, and background. The little tots are being taught in no uncertain terms that their hair is different, their skin is different, and their parents come from different places. It's Cultural Diversity Month. 1

I hadn't really given much thought to the ethnic and national backgrounds of Sarah's classmates. I can guarantee that Sarah, being two and a half, gave the subject absolutely no thought. Her teachers, however, had apparently given it quite a lot of thought. They sent a letter asking each parent to contribute to the cultural-awareness effort by "providing any information and/or material regarding your family's cultural background. For example: favorite recipe or song." All well and good, unless your culture isn't diverse enough. 2

The next day I take Sarah to school and her teacher, Miss Laura, anxious to get this Cultural Diversity show on the road, begins the interrogation. 3

"Where are you and your husband from?" she cheerily demands. 4

"We're Americans," I reply—less, I must confess, out of patriotism than from sheer lack of coffee. It was barely 9:00 a.m. 5

"Yes, of course, but where are you from?" I'm beginning to feel like a   6
nightclub patron being badgered by a no-talent stand-up comic.[1]

"We're native New Yorkers."   7

"But where are your people from?"   8

"Well," I dive in with a sigh, "my family is originally Irish on both sides.   9
My husband's father was from Czechoslovakia and his mother is from the
Bronx, but her grandparents were from the Ukraine."

"Can you cook Irish?"   10

"I could bring in potatoes and beer for the whole class."   11

Miss Laura doesn't get it.   12

"Look," I say, "we're Americans. Our kids are Americans. We tell them   13
about American history and George Washington and apple pie and all that
stuff. If you want me to do something American, I can do that."

She is decidedly unexcited.   14

A few days later, she tells me that she was trying to explain to Sarah   15
that her dad is from Ireland.

"Wrong," I say, "but go on."   16

"He's not from Ireland?"   17

"No," I sigh. "He's from Queens. I'm from Ireland. I mean I'm Irish — that   18
is, my great-grandparents were. Don't get me wrong, I'm proud of my
heritage — but that's entirely beside the point. I told you we tell Sarah she's
American."

"Well, anyway," she smiles, "Sarah thinks her Daddy's from *Iceland!*   19
Isn't that cute?"

Later in the month, Miss Laura admits that her class is not quite get-   20
ting the whole skin-color thing. "I tried to show them how we all have different skin," she chuckled. Apparently, little Henry is the only one who
successfully grasped the concept. He now runs around the classroom an-
nouncing to anyone who'll listen, "I'm white!" Miss Laura asked the children what color her own skin was. (She is a light-skinned Hispanic, which
would make her skin color . . . what? Caramel? Mochaccino?[2]) The kids
opted for purple or orange. "They looked at me like I was crazy!" Miss
Laura said. I just smile.

The culmination of Cultural Diversity Month, the day when the parents   21
come into class and join their children in a glorious celebration of multicultural disparity, has arrived. As I arrive I see a large collage on the wall
depicting the earth, with all the children's names placed next to the country they are from. Next to my daughter's name it says "Ireland." I politely
remind Miss Laura that Sarah is, in fact, from America and suggest that,
by insisting otherwise, she is confusing my daughter. She reluctantly
changes Sarah's affiliation to USA. It will be the only one of its kind on the
wall.

---

[1] **stand-up comic:** A comedian who performs while standing on a stage.
[2] **mochaccino:** A frothy coffee beverage made from espresso, steamed milk, and chocolate
   syrup.

The mom from Brazil brings in a bunch of great music, and the whole   22
class is doing the samba[3] and running around in a conga line.[4] It's very
cute. Then I get up to teach the children an indigenous folk tune from the
culture of Sarah's people, passed down through the generations from her
grandparents to her parents and now to Sarah—a song called "Take Me
Out to the Ballgame." First I explain to the kids that Sarah was born right
here in New York—and that's in what country, Sarah? Sarah looks at me
and says, "France." I look at Miss Laura, who just shrugs.

I stand there in my baseball cap and sing my song. The teacher tries to   23
rush me off. I say, "Don't you want them to learn it?" They took long
enough learning to samba! I am granted permission to sing it one more
time. The kids join in on the "root, root, root" and the "1, 2, 3 strikes you're
out," but they can see their teacher isn't enthusiastic.

So now these sweet, innocent babies who thought they were all the same   24
are becoming culturally aware. Two little girls are touching each other's
hair and saying, "Your hair is blonde, just like mine." Off to one side a little
dark-haired girl stands alone, excluded. She looks confused as to what to do
next. She knows she's not blonde. Sure, all children notice these things eventually, but, thanks to the concerted efforts of their teachers, these two- and
three-year-olds are talking about things that separate rather than connect.

And Sarah only knows what she has been taught: Little Henry is white,   25
her daddy's from Iceland, and New York's in France.

EXERCISING VOCABULARY

1. Record your own definition for each of these words.

   badgered (v.) (6)   disparity (n.) (21)
   decidedly (adv.) (14)   collage (n.) (21)
   opted (v.) (20)   concerted (adj.) (24)
   culmination (n.) (21)

2. What does Konig mean when she describes the children in her daughter's class as "color blind" (para. 1)? How does this expression acquire
   additional meaning when used in the context of this essay?

3. What does Konig's description of Miss Laura's questions as an "interrogation" (para. 3) suggest about the writer's attitude toward the teacher?
   What kinds of situations or settings do you think of when you hear the
   word *interrogation*?

4. Why does the writer call "Take Me Out to the Ballgame" an "indigenous
   folk tune" (para. 22)? What does *indigenous* mean? What kinds of songs
   are usually referred to as indigenous folk tunes?

---

[3] **samba:** A Brazilian dance of African origin; also, the music for this dance.
[4] **conga line:** A Cuban dance of African origin performed by a group, usually in single file,
    involving three steps followed by a kick.

PROBING CONTENT

1. The title of this selection is derived from a Rodgers and Hammerstein song "You've Got to Be Carefully Taught" from the musical *South Pacific.* The first lines are "You've got to be taught to hate and fear. You've got to be taught from year to year. It's got to be drummed in your dear little ear. You've got to be carefully taught." Is this title, with its relationship to this popular song, appropriate for this essay? Why or why not?

2. For what reasons does the writer disagree with Miss Laura's strategy? What does she think the students are learning as a result of their classroom activities on diversity?

3. The words *American* or *Americans* are repeated four times in paragraph 13. What does the writer mean when she says that her family is American? To what else besides the geographic location of their home is she referring?

4. Describe the effect of Cultural Diversity Month on the preschool students. From Konig's description, what do the children appear to learn? What positive lessons do they fail to learn?

CONSIDERING CRAFT

1. Find several examples of the writer's use of dialogue in this essay. How does the dialogue affect your attitude about the characters?

2. Describe the writer's tone in this essay. Why does she choose this tone? What kind of response is she hoping to get from the reader as a result?

3. In paragraph 21, the author refers to events at the preschool as "a glorious celebration of multicultural disparity." What word usually appears in place of *disparity?* Why does Konig change the word?

WRITING PROMPTS

Responding to the Topic   In an essay, explore the effects that an emphasis on cultural diversity has had on life in the United States over the last twenty years.

Responding to the Writer   Write an essay in which you agree or disagree with Konig's idea that too much emphasis on cultural diversity may actually separate people of different ethnicities and cultures rather than bring them together.

Responding to Multiple Viewpoints   Compare the position on diversity that Michael Jonas takes in "The Downside of Diversity" (p. 62) with the position that Konig takes in this essay.

For a quiz on this reading, go to bedfordstmartins.com/mirror.

People Like Us

DAVID BROOKS

David Brooks is a columnist for the *New York Times* and a commentator for *The NewsHour with Jim Lehrer*. He is the author of *Bobos in Paradise: The New Upper Class and How They Got There* (2000), *On Paradise Drive: How We Live Now (and Always Have) in the Future Tense* (2004), and *The Social Animal: The Hidden Sources of Love, Character, and Achievement* (2011). In 2006, he was a visiting professor at Duke University's Terry Sanford Institute of Public Policy. "People Like Us" was first published in *The Atlantic* in 2003.

> **THINKING AHEAD** Since you've been in school, what opportunities have you had to interact with people from racial, cultural, ethnic, religious, or social backgrounds different from your own? To what extent have you taken advantage of these opportunities? Why? How has such interaction affected your ideas?
>
> **Paired Selection** Read this selection and the one that follows for two approaches to a similar topic. Then answer the "Drawing Connections" questions on p. 69.

Maybe it's time to admit the obvious. We don't really care about diversity all that much in America, even though we talk about it a great deal. Maybe somewhere in this country there is a truly diverse neighborhood in which a black Pentecostal minister lives next to a white antiglobalization activist, who lives next to an Asian short-order cook, who lives next to a professional golfer, who lives next to a postmodern-literature professor and a cardiovascular surgeon. But I have never been to or heard of that neighborhood. Instead, what I have seen all around the country is people making strenuous efforts to group themselves with people who are basically like themselves.

Human beings are capable of drawing amazingly subtle social distinctions and then shaping their lives around them. In the Washington, D.C., area Democratic lawyers tend to live in suburban Maryland, and Republican lawyers tend to live in suburban Virginia. If you asked a Democratic lawyer to move from her $750,000 house in Bethesda, Maryland, to a $750,000 house in Great Falls, Virginia, she'd look at you as if you had just asked her to buy a pickup truck with a gun rack and to shove chewing tobacco in her kid's mouth. In Manhattan the owner of a $3 million SoHo loft would feel out of place moving into a $3 million Fifth Avenue apartment. A West Hollywood interior decorator would feel dislocated if you asked him to move to Orange County. In Georgia a barista[1] from Athens would probably not fit in serving coffee in Americus.

It is a common complaint that every place is starting to look the same. But in the information age, the late writer James Chapin once told me, every place becomes more like itself. People are less often tied down to factories and mills, and they can search for places to live on the basis of cultural affinity. Once they find a town in which people share their values, they flock there, and reinforce whatever was distinctive about the town in the first place. Once Boulder, Colorado, became known as congenial to politically progressive mountain bikers, half the politically progressive mountain bikers in the country (it seems) moved there; they made the place so culturally pure that it has become practically a parody of itself.   3

But people love it. Make no mistake—we are increasing our happiness by segmenting off so rigorously. We are finding places where we are comfortable and where we feel we can flourish. But the choices we make toward that end lead to the very opposite of diversity. The United States might be a diverse nation when considered as a whole, but block by block and institution by institution it is a relatively homogeneous nation.   4

When we use the word *diversity* today, we usually mean racial integration. But even here our good intentions seem to have run into the brick wall of human nature. Over the past generation reformers have tried heroically, and in many cases successfully, to end housing discrimination. But recent patterns aren't encouraging: According to an analysis of the 2000 census data, the 1990s saw only a slight increase in the racial integration of neighborhoods in the United States. The number of middle-class and upper-middle-class African American families is rising, but for whatever reasons—racism, psychological comfort—these families tend to congregate in predominantly black neighborhoods.   5

In fact, evidence suggests that some neighborhoods become more segregated over time. New suburbs in Arizona and Nevada, for example, start out reasonably well integrated. These neighborhoods don't yet have reputations, so people choose their houses for other, mostly economic reasons. But as neighborhoods age, they develop personalities (that's where the Asians live, and that's where the Hispanics live), and segmentation occurs. It could be that in a few years the new suburbs in the Southwest will be nearly as segregated as the established ones in the Northeast and the Midwest.   6

Even though race and ethnicity run deep in American society, we should in theory be able to find areas that are at least culturally diverse. But here, too, people show few signs of being truly interested in building diverse communities. If you run a retail company and you're thinking of opening new stores, you can choose among dozens of consulting firms that are quite effective at locating your potential customers. They can do this because people with similar tastes and preferences tend to congregate by ZIP code.   7

[1] **barista:** One who is considered to have professional expertise in the preparation of coffee drinks; from the Italian for "bartender."

The most famous of these precision marketing firms is Claritas, which   8
breaks down the U.S. population into sixty-two psycho-demographic clus-
ters, based on such factors as how much money people make, what they
like to read and watch, and what products they have bought in the past.
For example, the "suburban sprawl" cluster is composed of young families
making about $41,000 a year and living in fast-growing places such as
Burnsville, Minnesota, and Bensalem, Pennsylvania. These people are almost twice as likely as other Americans to have three-way calling. They are
two and a half times as likely to buy Light n' Lively Kid Yogurt. Members
of the "towns & gowns" cluster are recent college graduates in places such
as Berkeley, California, and Gainesville, Florida. They are big consumers of
DoveBars and *Saturday Night Live.* They tend to drive small foreign cars
and to read *Rolling Stone* and *Scientific American.*

Looking through the market research, one can sometimes be amazed   9
by how efficiently people cluster—and by how predictable we all are. If you
wanted to sell imported wine, obviously you would have to find places
where rich people live. But did you know that the sixteen counties with the
greatest proportion of imported-wine drinkers are all in the same three
metropolitan areas (New York, San Francisco and Washington, D.C.)? If
you tried to open a motor-home dealership in Montgomery County, Pennsylvania, you'd probably go broke because people in this ring of the Philadelphia suburbs think RVs are kind of uncool. But if you traveled just a
short way north, to Monroe County, Pennsylvania, you would find yourself in the fifth motor-home-friendliest county in America.

Geography is not the only way we find ourselves divided from people   10
unlike us. Some of us watch Fox News, while others listen to NPR.
Some like David Letterman, and others—typically in less urban neighborhoods—like Jay Leno. Some go to charismatic[2] churches; some go to
mainstream churches. Americans tend more and more often to marry people
with education levels similar to their own and to befriend people with backgrounds similar to their own.

My favorite illustration of this latter pattern comes from the first, non-   11
controversial chapter of *The Bell Curve.* Think of your twelve closest
friends, Richard J. Herrnstein and Charles Murray write. If you had chosen
them randomly from the American population, the odds that half of your
twelve closest friends would be college graduates would be six in a thousand. The odds that half of the twelve would have advanced degrees would
be less than one in a million. Have any of your twelve closest friends graduated from Harvard, Stanford, Yale, Princeton, Caltech, MIT, Duke, Dart-
mouth, Cornell, Columbia, Chicago or Brown? If you chose your friends
randomly from the American population, the odds against your having four
or more friends from those schools would be more than a billion to one.

Many of us live in absurdly unlikely groupings because we have orga-   12
nized our lives that way.

[2] **charismatic:** Guided by the power of the Holy Spirit.

It's striking that the institutions that talk the most about diversity often   13
practice it the least. For example, no group of people sings the diversity
anthem more frequently and fervently than administrators at just such elite
universities. But elite universities are amazingly undiverse in their values,
politics and mores.[3] Professors in particular are drawn from a rather narrow
segment of the population. If faculties reflected the general population, 32
percent of professors would be registered Democrats and 31 percent would
be registered Republicans. Forty percent would be evangelical Christians.
But a recent study of several universities by the conservative Center for
the Study of Popular Culture and the American Enterprise Institute found
that roughly 90 percent of those professors in the arts and sciences who
had registered with a political party had registered Democratic. Fifty-seven
professors at Brown were found on the voter-registration rolls. Of those,
fifty-four were Democrats. Of the forty-two professors in the English, history, sociology and political-science departments, all were Democrats. The
results at Harvard, Penn State, Maryland and the University of California
at Santa Barbara were similar to the results at Brown.

What we are looking at here is human nature. People want to be around   14
others who are roughly like themselves. That's called community. It probably would be psychologically difficult for most Brown professors to share
an office with someone who was pro-life, a member of the National Rifle
Association, or an evangelical Christian. It's likely that hiring committees
would subtly—even unconsciously—screen out any such people they encountered. Republicans and evangelical Christians have sensed that they
are not welcome at places like Brown, so they don't even consider working
there. In fact, any registered Republican who contemplates a career in academia these days is both a hero and a fool. So, in a semi-self-selective pattern, brainy people with generally liberal social mores flow to academia,
and brainy people with generally conservative mores flow elsewhere.

The dream of diversity is like the dream of equality. Both are based on   15
ideals we celebrate even as we undermine them daily. (How many times
have you seen someone renounce a high-paying job or pull his child from
an elite college on the grounds that these things are bad for equality?) On
the one hand, the situation is appalling. It is appalling that Americans know
so little about one another. It is appalling that many of us are so narrow-
minded that we can't tolerate a few people with ideas significantly different
from our own. It's appalling that evangelical Christians are practically
absent from entire professions, such as academia, the media and filmmak-
ing. It's appalling that people should be content to cut themselves off from
everyone unlike themselves.

The segmentation of society means that often we don't even have argu-   16
ments across the political divide. Within their little validating communities, liberals and conservatives circulate half-truths about the supposed

[3] **mores:** Beliefs and customs of a particular group.

awfulness of the other side. These distortions are believed because it feels good to believe them.

On the other hand, there are limits to how diverse any community can   17
or should be. I've come to think that it is not useful to try to hammer diversity into every neighborhood and institution in the United States. Sure, Augusta National[4] should probably admit women, and university sociology departments should probably hire a conservative or two. It would be nice if all neighborhoods had a good mixture of ethnicities. But human nature being what it is, most places and institutions are going to remain culturally homogeneous.

It's probably better to think about diverse lives, not diverse institu-   18
tions. Human beings, if they are to live well, will have to move through a series of institutions and environments, which may be individually homogeneous but, taken together, will offer diverse experiences. It might also be a good idea to make national service a rite of passage for young people in this country: it would take them out of their narrow neighborhood segment and thrust them in with people unlike themselves. Finally, it's probably important for adults to get out of their own familiar circles. If you live in a coastal, socially liberal neighborhood, maybe you should take out a subscription to *The Door*, the evangelical humor magazine; or maybe you should visit Branson, Missouri.[5] Maybe you should stop in at a megachurch.[6] Sure, it would be superficial familiarity, but it beats the iron curtains that now separate the nation's various cultural zones.

Look around at your daily life. Are you really in touch with the broad   19
diversity of American life? Do you care?

EXERCISING VOCABULARY

1. Record your own definition for each of these words.

strenuous (adj.) (1)	congregate (v.) (5)
congenial (adj.) (3)	fervently (adv.) (13)
parody (n.) (3)	undermine (v.) (15)
segmenting (v.) (4)	appalling (adj.) (15)
homogeneous (adj.) (4)	validating (adj.) (16)

2. In paragraph 2, the author writes, "A West Hollywood interior decorator would feel dislocated" if he were asked to move to Orange County, California. With what do we usually associate the term *dislocated?* Why

---

[4] **Augusta National:** Golf club in Augusta, Georgia, that is the official site of the Masters Golf Tournament.
[5] **Branson, Missouri:** Vacation center popular with older people and featuring Las Vegas–style shows.
[6] **megachurch:** Protestant congregation with a very large number of weekly attendees, often nondenominational and generally conservative.

does Brooks choose to use that word here? How does it help to convey his message?

3. Brooks states that people "search for places to live on the basis of cultural affinity" (para. 3). Explain the term *cultural affinity*. How does this tendency affect neighborhoods and communities?

4. Who would be included in a "towns & gowns" community (para. 8)? What "gowns" are referred to here? What would the use of such an expression reveal about a community?

PROBING CONTENT

1. Explain Brooks's statement that, over time, "every place becomes more like itself" (para. 3). How does this theory relate to the idea of the American melting pot?

2. How has what Brooks refers to as "the brick wall of human nature" (para. 5) impacted social integration? What trends does Brooks see developing as a result?

3. What does Brooks maintain is lost when people relate to others like themselves? What long-term effects might this behavior create?

4. Why does Brooks support the idea of required national service? How would such a requirement benefit the country and the participating individuals?

CONSIDERING CRAFT

1. What kind of imagery is Brooks creating in paragraph 2 when he writes that "she'd look at you as if you had just asked her to buy a pickup truck with a gun rack and to shove chewing tobacco in her kid's mouth"? What point is he making? How does this language make his point?

2. In paragraph 13, Brooks focuses on a paradox at elite universities. What is a paradox? What is the paradox that Brooks notes here? How is this paradox expressed on campuses across the United States?

3. Brooks writes that national service should become "a rite of passage" (para. 18). What does this expression mean? Name some cultural rites of passage with which you are familiar. How would national service fit the definition of a rite of passage?

4. In paragraph 18, Brooks writes that even "superficial familiarity" "beats the iron curtains that now separate the nation's various cultural zones." What was the Iron Curtain? How appropriate and effective is Brooks's use of this metaphor?

WRITING PROMPTS

Responding to the Topic   Using your own experience, write an essay in response to the questions "Are you really in touch with the broad diversity of American life? Do you care?" (para. 19). Provide specific examples that support your response.

Responding to the Writer   Write an essay in which you either support or refute Brooks's assertion that "any registered Republican who contemplates a career in academia these days is both a hero and a fool" (para. 14). To obtain material for your essay, interview a number of your instructors who are willing to discuss with you their political opinions and experience as faculty at your institution.

Responding to Multiple Viewpoints   Compare Brooks's ideas about neighborhoods and their populations with those expressed by Dinaw Mengestu in "Home at Last" (p. 74).

For a quiz on this reading, go to bedfordstmartins.com/mirror.

The Downside of Diversity

MICHAEL JONAS

Michael Jonas is executive editor for *CommonWealth* magazine, published by a nonpartisan public policy think tank in Boston, Massachusetts. He also writes a weekly column on local politics for the *Boston Globe.* "The Downside of Diversity" was first published in the *Boston Globe* in August 2007. In this article, Jonas discusses research by a Harvard political scientist that challenges commonly held beliefs about the value of civic diversity.

THINKING AHEAD How beneficial do you believe diversity is to the quality of life in a community? What are the advantages of being surrounded by a very diverse population? What are the drawbacks?

Paired Selection Read this selection and the one before it for two approaches to a similar topic. Then answer the "Drawing Connections" questions on p. 69.

1   It has become increasingly popular to speak of racial and ethnic diversity as a civic strength. From multicultural festivals to pronouncements from political leaders, the message is the same: our differences make us stronger.

2   But a massive new study, based on detailed interviews of nearly thirty thousand people across America, has concluded just the opposite. Harvard political scientist Robert Putnam—famous for *Bowling Alone,* his 2000 book on declining civic engagement—has found that the greater the diversity in a community, the fewer people vote and the less they volunteer, the less they give to charity and work on community projects. In the most diverse communities, neighbors trust one another about half as much as they do in the most homogenous settings. The study, the largest ever on civic engagement in America, found that virtually all measures of civic health are lower in more diverse settings.

3   "The extent of the effect is shocking," says Scott Page, a University of Michigan political scientist.

4   The study comes at a time when the future of the American melting pot is the focus of intense political debate, from immigration to race-based admissions to schools, and it poses challenges to advocates on all sides of the issues. The study is already being cited by some conservatives as proof of the harm large-scale immigration causes to the nation's social fabric. But with demographic trends already pushing the nation inexorably toward greater diversity, the real question may yet lie ahead: how to handle the unsettling social changes that Putnam's research predicts.

"We can't ignore the findings," says Ali Noorani, executive director of   5
the Massachusetts Immigrant and Refugee Advocacy Coalition. "The big
question we have to ask ourselves is, what do we do about it; what are the
next steps?"

The study is part of a fascinating new portrait of diversity emerging from   6
recent scholarship. Diversity, it shows, makes us uncomfortable — but
discomfort, it turns out, isn't always a bad thing. Unease with differences
helps explain why teams of engineers from different cultures may be ide-
ally suited to solve a vexing problem. Culture clashes can produce a dynamic give-and-take, generating a solution that may have eluded a group
of people with more similar backgrounds and approaches. At the same
time, though, Putnam's work adds to a growing body of research indicat-
ing that more diverse populations seem to extend themselves less on behalf
of collective needs and goals.

His findings on the downsides of diversity have also posed a challenge   7
for Putnam, a liberal academic whose own values put him squarely in the
pro-diversity camp. Suddenly finding himself the bearer of bad news, Putnam has struggled with how to present his work. He gathered the initial
raw data in 2000 and issued a press release the following year outlining the
results. He then spent several years testing other possible explanations.

When he finally published a detailed scholarly analysis in June in the   8
journal *Scandinavian Political Studies,* he faced criticism for straying from
data into advocacy. His paper argues strongly that the negative effects of
diversity can be remedied and says history suggests that ethnic diversity
may eventually fade as a sharp line of social demarcation.

"Having aligned himself with the central planners intent on sustaining   9
such social engineering, Putnam concludes the facts with a stern pep talk,"
wrote conservative commentator Ilana Mercer, in a recent *Orange County
Register* op-ed[1] titled "Greater diversity equals more misery."

Putnam has long staked out ground as both a researcher and a civic   10
player, someone willing to describe social problems and then have a hand
in addressing them. He says social science should be "simultaneously rigor-
ous and relevant," meeting high research standards while also "speaking to
concerns of our fellow citizens." But on a topic as charged as ethnicity and
race, Putnam worries that many people hear only what they want to.

"It would be unfortunate if a politically correct progressivism were to   11
deny the reality of the challenge to social solidarity posed by diversity," he
writes in the new report. "It would be equally unfortunate if an ahistorical
and ethnocentric conservatism were to deny that addressing that challenge
is both feasible and desirable."

Putnam is the nation's premier guru of civic engagement. After studying   12
civic life in Italy in the 1970s and 1980s, Putnam turned his attention to the
United States, publishing an influential journal article on civic engagement

---

[1] **op-ed:** In a newspaper, a page opposite the editorials.

in 1995 that he expanded five years later into the best-selling *Bowling Alone*. The book sounded a national wake-up call on what Putnam called a sharp drop in civic connections among Americans. It won him audiences with presidents Bill Clinton and George W. Bush and made him one of the country's best known social scientists.

Putnam claims the United States has experienced a pronounced decline   13
in "social capital," a term he helped popularize. Social capital refers to the social networks—whether friendships or religious congregations or neighborhood associations—that he says are key indicators of civic well-being. When social capital is high, says Putnam, communities are better places to live. Neighborhoods are safer; people are healthier; and more citizens vote.

The results of his new study come from a survey Putnam directed   14
among residents in forty-one U.S. communities, including Boston. Residents were sorted into the four principal categories used by the U.S. Census: black, white, Hispanic, and Asian. They were asked how much they trusted their neighbors and those of each racial category, and questioned about a long list of civic attitudes and practices, including their views on local government, their involvement in community projects and their friendships. What emerged in more diverse communities was a bleak picture of civic desolation, affecting everything from political engagement to the state of social ties.

Putnam knew he had provocative findings on his hands. He worried   15
about coming under some of the same liberal attacks that greeted Daniel Patrick Moynihan's landmark 1965 report on the social costs associated with the breakdown of the black family. There is always the risk of being pilloried[2] as the bearer of "an inconvenient truth," says Putnam.

After releasing the initial results in 2001, Putnam says he spent time   16
"kicking the tires really hard" to be sure the study had it right. Putnam realized, for instance, that more diverse communities tended to be larger, have greater income ranges, higher crime rates and more mobility among their residents—all factors that could depress social capital independent of any impact ethnic diversity might have.

"People would say, 'I bet you forgot about X,'" Putnam says of the string   17
of suggestions from colleagues. "There were twenty or thirty X's."

But even after statistically taking them all into account, the connection   18
remained strong: Higher diversity meant lower social capital. In his findings, Putnam writes that those in more diverse communities tend to "distrust their neighbors, regardless of the color of their skin, to withdraw even from close friends, to expect the worst from their community and its leaders, to volunteer less, give less to charity and work on community projects less often, to register to vote less, to agitate for social reform more but have less faith that they can actually make a difference, and to huddle unhappily in front of the television."

---

[2] **pilloried:** Publicly punished or exposed to ridicule.

"People living in ethnically diverse settings appear to 'hunker   19
down'—that is, to pull in like a turtle," Putnam writes.

In documenting that hunkering down, Putnam challenged the two   20
dominant schools of thought on ethnic and racial diversity, the "contact"
theory and the "conflict" theory. Under the contact theory, more time spent
with those of other backgrounds leads to greater understanding and harmony between groups. Under the conflict theory, that proximity produces
tension and discord.

Putnam's findings reject both theories. In more diverse communities, he   21
says, there were neither great bonds formed across group lines nor heightened ethnic tensions, but a general civic malaise.[3] And in perhaps the most
surprising result of all, levels of trust were not only lower between groups
in more diverse settings but even among members of the same group.

"Diversity, at least in the short run," he writes, "seems to bring out the   22
turtle in all of us."

The overall findings may be jarring during a time when it's become   23
commonplace to sing the praises of diverse communities, but researchers in
the field say they shouldn't be.

"It's an important addition to a growing body of evidence on the chal-   24
lenges created by diversity," says Harvard economist Edward Glaeser.

In a recent study, Glaeser and colleague Alberto Alesina demonstrated   25
that roughly half the difference in social welfare spending between the
United States and Europe—Europe spends far more—can be attributed to
the greater ethnic diversity of the U.S. population. Glaeser says lower
national social welfare spending in the United States is a "macro" version
of the decreased civic engagement Putnam found in more diverse communities within the country.

Economists Matthew Kahn of UCLA and Dora Costa of MIT reviewed   26
fifteen recent studies in a 2003 paper, all of which linked diversity with
lower levels of social capital. Greater ethnic diversity was linked, for example, to lower school funding, census response rates, and trust in others.
Kahn and Costa's own research documented higher desertion rates in the
Civil War among Union Army soldiers serving in companies whose soldiers
varied more by age, occupation and birthplace.

Birds of different feathers may sometimes flock together, but they are   27
also less likely to look out for one another. "Everyone is a little self-
conscious that this is not politically correct stuff," says Kahn.

So how to explain New York, London, Rio de Janiero, Los Angeles—the   28
great melting-pot cities that drive the world's creative and financial
economies?

The image of civic lassitude dragging down more diverse communities   29
is at odds with the vigor often associated with urban centers, where ethnic
diversity is greatest. It turns out there is a flip side to the discomfort diversity

---

[3] **malaise:** Lack of a sense of well-being.

can cause. If ethnic diversity, at least in the short run, is a liability for social connectedness, a parallel line of emerging research suggests it can be a big asset when it comes to driving productivity and innovation. In high-skill workplace settings, says Scott Page, the University of Michigan political scientist, the different ways of thinking among people from different cultures can be a boon.

"Because they see the world and think about the world differently than you, that's challenging," says Page, author of *The Difference: How the Power of Diversity Creates Better Groups, Firms, Schools, and Societies.* "But by hanging out with people different than you, you're likely to get more insights. Diverse teams tend to be more productive."   30

In other words, those in more diverse communities may do more bowling alone, but the creative tensions unleashed by those differences in the workplace may vault those same places to the cutting edge of the economy and of creative culture.   31

Page calls it the "diversity paradox." He thinks the contrasting positive and negative effects of diversity can coexist in communities, but "there's got to be a limit." If civic engagement falls off too far, he says, it's easy to imagine the positive effects of diversity beginning to wane as well. "That's what's unsettling about his findings," Page says of Putnam's new work.   32

Meanwhile, by drawing a portrait of civic engagement in which more homogeneous communities seem much healthier, some of Putnam's worst fears about how his results could be used have been realized. A stream of conservative commentary has begun—from places like the Manhattan Institute and *The American Conservative*—highlighting the harm the study suggests will come from large-scale immigration. But Putnam says he's also received hundreds of complimentary e-mails laced with bigoted language. "It certainly is not pleasant when David Duke's[4] Web site hails me as the guy who found out racism is good," he says.   33

In the final quarter of his paper, Putnam puts the diversity challenge in a broader context by describing how social identity can change over time. Experience shows that social divisions can eventually give way to "more encompassing identities" that create a "new, more capacious sense of 'we,'" he writes.   34

Growing up in the 1950s in a small Midwestern town, Putnam knew the religion of virtually every member of his high school graduating class because, he says, such information was crucial to the question of "who was a possible mate or date." The importance of marrying within one's faith, he says, has largely faded since then, at least among many mainline Protestants, Catholics and Jews.   35

While acknowledging that racial and ethnic divisions may prove more stubborn, Putnam argues that such examples bode well for the long-term prospects for social capital in a multiethnic America.   36

---

[4] **David Duke:** Former Grand Wizard of the Knights of the Ku Klux Klan.

In his paper, Putnam cites the work done by Page and others, and uses   37
it to help frame his conclusion that increasing diversity in America is not
only inevitable, but ultimately valuable and enriching. As for smoothing
over the divisions that hinder civic engagement, Putnam argues that Americans can help that process along through targeted efforts. He suggests
expanding support for English-language instruction and investing in
community centers and other places that allow for "meaningful interaction
across ethnic lines."

Some critics have found his prescriptions underwhelming. And in of-   38
fering ideas for mitigating his findings, Putnam has drawn scorn for step-
ping out of the role of dispassionate researcher. "You're just supposed to tell
your peers what you found," says John Leo, senior fellow at the Manhattan
Institute, a conservative think tank. "I don't expect academics to fret about
these matters."

But fretting about the state of American civic health is exactly what   39
Putnam has spent more than a decade doing. While continuing to research
questions involving social capital, he has directed the Saguaro Seminar,
a project he started at Harvard's Kennedy School of Government that
promotes efforts throughout the country to increase civic connections in
communities.

"Social scientists are both scientists and citizens," says Alan Wolfe, di-   40
rector of the Boisi Center for Religion and American Public Life at Boston
College, who sees nothing wrong in Putnam's efforts to affect some of the
phenomena he studies.

Wolfe says what is unusual is that Putnam has published findings as a   41
social scientist that are not the ones he would have wished for as a civic
leader. There are plenty of social scientists, says Wolfe, who never produce
research results at odds with their own worldview.

"The problem too often," says Wolfe, "is people are never uncomfortable   42
about their findings."

EXERCISING VOCABULARY

1. Record your own definition for each of these words.

   homogenous (adj.) (2)   provocative (adj.) (15)
   demographic (adj.) (4)   lassitude (n.) (29)
   inexorably (adv.) (4)   wane (v.) (32)
   vexing (adj.) (6)   mitigating (adj.) (38)
   demarcation (n.) (8)

2. According to Jonas, Putnam is concerned about "an ahistorical and ethnocentric conservatism" (para. 11). How does the meaning of the word
   historical change when the prefix *a* is added? What do the two halves of
   the word *ethnocentric* mean? What is the implication when this prefix
   and suffix are combined?

3. In paragraph 12, Jonas refers to Putnam as "the nation's premier guru of civic engagement." What is a guru? Name several other individuals who have been referred to as gurus. How does Jonas justify bestowing this title on Putnam?

4. Putnam delayed releasing the final results of his study to allow himself to spend time "kicking the tires really hard" (para. 16). What does this expression mean literally, and in reference to what is it usually used? When it is used figuratively, as it is here, what does it mean?

PROBING CONTENT

1. According to Jonas, why might a culturally diverse team of experts be able to solve a problem that a team from similar backgrounds could not solve? How would Scott Page from the University of Michigan respond?

2. Based on Robert Putnam's research, what is the downside of living in a diverse community? Why may diverse communities present "a bleak picture of civic desolation" (para. 14)?

3. Explain Putman's concept of "social capital" (para. 13).

4. What is Putnam's position on the increasing diversity in America? What can Americans do to make that diversity productive?

CONSIDERING CRAFT

1. The original subtitle of this selection was "A Harvard political scientist finds that diversity hurts civic life. What happens when a liberal scholar unearths an inconvenient truth?" When you read "an inconvenient truth," what comes to mind? If Jonas is making a deliberate effort to link Putnam's research results with another very public concern, how effective is this strategy? What is that concern?

2. You may be familiar with the expression "Birds of a feather flock together." Jonas bends that saying to suit his purpose here and writes, "Birds of different feathers may sometimes flock together, but they are also less likely to look out for one another" (para. 27). What does Jonas achieve by varying the wording of an expression with which many readers will already be familiar? Does this provide greater clarity for you, or does it create confusion? In what way?

3. In this selection, Jonas delivers the majority of what many readers will perceive as "bad news" first before mitigating that bad news with hope for the future. Is this a wise pattern of organization for his content? Why or why not?

4. In paragraph 4, Jonas questions the future of "the American melting pot." What is the origin of that expression? How does its use here further Jonas's argument?

WRITING PROMPTS

Responding to the Topic   Using your personal experience, write an essay exploring the assertion that "virtually all measures of civic health are lower in more diverse settings" (para. 2).

Responding to the Writer   Robert Putnam delayed releasing the final results of his study because the results contradicted his own beliefs. Write an essay in which you support or reject Putnam's decision to share his research findings in spite of their controversial nature.

Responding to Multiple Viewpoints   Explore in an essay how David Gergen ("A Smart Exception," p. 93) would react to those who cite Robert Putnam's study as "proof of the harm large-scale immigration causes to the nation's social fabric" (para. 4, "The Downside of Diversity").

For a quiz on this reading, go to bedfordstmartins.com/mirror.

DRAWING CONNECTIONS: PAIRED SELECTIONS

1. Based on the Robert Putnam survey that Michael Jonas describes in his essay "The Downside of Diversity," how would Jonas respond to David Brooks's contention that "We don't really care about diversity all that much in America" (para. 1, "People Like Us")? Cite evidence from both essays to support the thesis and main points of your essay.

2. To what extent would David Brooks ("People Like Us") agree or disagree with Robert Putnam's contention based on his survey that "Diversity, at least in the short run, seems to bring out the turtle in all of us" (para. 22, "The Downside of Diversity" by Michael Jonas)? Write an essay in which you support your position with material from each essay.

Globalization vs. Americanization

ANDREW LAM

Andrew Lam is an editor for *New America Media* and a commentator for NPR's *All Things Considered.* Born in South Vietnam, Lam has written a book on the Vietnamese diaspora, *Perfume Dreams* (2005), which won a PEN/Beyond Margins Award. In "Globalization vs. Americanization," he argues that the spread of cultures around the world does not necessarily mean a McDonald's on every corner. The essay first appeared on the Internet news service *Alternet.*

> **THINKING AHEAD** How has living in the twenty-first century blurred the distinctions among cultures? Is national origin as fundamentally important to our sense of identity as it once was? Why or why not? What factors have most strongly impacted your own sense of cultural identity?

A friend, well traveled and educated, recently predicted the evils of globalization in very simple terms. "Everyone will be eating at McDonald's, listening to Madonna, and shopping at mega-malls," he prophesied. "It'll be absolutely awful." 1

What I told him then is that globalization is not the same as Americanization, though sometimes it's hard for Americans to make that distinction. The most crucial aspect of globalization is the psychological transformation that's affecting people everywhere. 2

Let me offer my own biography as an example. I grew up a patriotic South Vietnamese living in Vietnam during the war. I remember singing the national anthem, swearing my allegiance to the flag and promising my soul and body to protect the land and its sacred rice fields and rivers. Wide-eyed child that I was, I believed every word. 3

But then the war ended and I, along with my family (and eventually a couple of million other Vietnamese), betrayed our agrarian[1] ethos and land-bound sentiments by fleeing overseas to lead a very different life. 4

Almost three decades later, I make a living traveling between East Asia and the United States of America as an American journalist and writer. My relatives, once all concentrated in Saigon, are scattered across three continents, speaking three and four other languages, becoming citizens of several different countries. Once sedentary and communal and bound by a singular sense of geography, we are now bona fide[2] cosmopolitans who, 5

---

[1] **agrarian:** Having to do with agriculture.
[2] **bona fide:** Genuine; real.

when we get online or meet in person, still marvel at the difference between our past and our highly mobile if intricately complex present.

Yesterday my inheritance was simple—the sacred rice fields and rivers that defined who I was. Today, Paris and Hanoi and New York are no longer fantasies but my larger community, places to which I feel a strong sense of connection due to familial relationships and friendships and personal ambitions. Once great, the distances are no longer daunting but simply a matter of rescheduling. [6]

I am hardly alone. There's a transnational revolution taking place, one right beneath our very noses. The Chinese businessman in Silicon Valley[3] is constantly in touch with his Shanghai mother on a cell phone while his high-tech workers build microchips and pave the information superhighway for the rest of the world. The Mexican migrant worker moves his family back and forth, one country to the other, treating the borders as if they were mere nuisances, and the blond teenager in Idaho is making friends with the Japanese girl in Osaka in a chatroom, their friendship easily forged as if time and space and cultural barriers have been breached by their lilting modems and the blinking satellites above. [7]

The differences between my friend's view and my propositions are essentially the differences between a Disney animation and a Michael Ondaatje novel, say, *The English Patient*. Disney borrows world narratives (*Mulan* and *The Little Mermaid*) for backdrops, but it rewrites all complicated stories toward a singular outcome: happily ever after. It disembowels complexity, dismisses tragedy, forces differences into a blender and regurgitates formulaic platitudes. [8]

Ondaatje's novel, on the other hand, is a world rooted in numerous particularities. It's a world where people from dissimilar backgrounds encounter one another and are trying, by various degrees of success and failure, to connect and influence each other. And it's a world complicated by memories and ambitions and multiple connections and displacements. Its unique and rounded characters refute simplification. [9]

So McDonald's golden arches and mega-malls may be proliferating in every major metropolis across the world, but so are Thai and Vietnamese restaurants! Many other original cultures and languages and traditions continue to thrive. Think Bombay movies, Buddhist monks in Bangkok, Balinese dancers in Bali—these will not simply wash away because CNN and MTV are accessible now to the peasant in his mud hut. [10]

While there's no denying that America is the sole supreme power in this post–Cold War era, America and all things American are not the end point. As we look at the world through our own prism, we tend to forget that we ourselves have dramatically changed in an age of open systems. [11]

Koreatown in Los Angeles and Chinatown in San Francisco and the Cuban community in Miami are, after all, not places created for nostalgic purposes but vibrant and thriving ethnic enclaves. They are changing the [12]

---

[3] **Silicon Valley:** Center of the U.S. software industry, located in California.

American landscape itself—a direct challenge to the old ideas of melting pot and integration. And Islam and Buddhism are the two fastest growing religions in America.

To want to be rooted is a deep human desire, of course, but to be dis- 13
placed and uprooted, alas, is a human condition—Man's fate. All over the world, people are moving from language to language, from culture to culture, sensibility to sensibility, negotiating across time zones and continents. It's a world that resists simplification. Man's identity is in conflict, has become both the cause of pain and fear for some and the source of enormous inspiration for others. I am inclined, of course, to be on the side of the latter.

The new man's talent is the ability to overcome paralysis of the many 14
conflicting selves by finding and inventing new connections between them. He holds opposed ideas in his head without going crazy. He resists the temptation to withdraw into a small shell of separatism and fundamentalism and xenophobia. He learns instead to hear others and respect differences and, in the process, transcends paradox. He sees the world with its many dimensions simultaneously. Geography for him may be memory and logistics, but it's no longer destiny.

EXERCISING VOCABULARY

1. Record your own definition for each of these words.

   ethos (n.) (4)   platitudes (n.) (8)
   sedentary (adj.) (5)   refute (v.) (9)
   regurgitates (v.) (8)   proliferating (v.) (10)

2. Lam states that certain communities have become "ethnic enclaves" (para. 12). What is an enclave? How do these communities challenge old ideas?

3. In paragraph 14, the author notes that the "new man" refuses to fall prey to xenophobia. What is a phobia? If a person has xenophobia, what is his or her concern?

PROBING CONTENT

1. How does Lam explain globalization? How does this term differ from Americanization? Why is this distinction difficult for Americans to grasp?

2. What did people share who were "bound by a singular sense of geography" (para. 5)? What has negated this shared feeling?

3. In paragraph 7, the author discusses the "transnational revolution" happening today. What is this revolution? Why is it occurring at this point in history?

CONSIDERING CRAFT

1. Opening essays with quotations is a popular method of introduction. How well does the initial quotation in paragraph 1 set the tone for the essay that follows? Does it matter that the quotation is not from an authority or a recognized source? Why?

2. Explain what Lam means in paragraph 7 when he writes of a Chinese businessman in Silicon Valley, "His high-tech workers build microchips and pave the information superhighway for the rest of the world." How does this use of figurative language enhance Lam's writing?

3. Lam feels that Disney's view of the world "disembowels complexity, dismisses tragedy, forces differences into a blender and regurgitates formulaic platitudes" (para. 8). How does this use of figurative language, coupled with some unfamiliar words, enhance or detract from his argument?

4. In paragraphs 8 and 9, Lam compares a friend's view and his own to the difference between Disney movies and a famous author's novel. How effectively does this comparison make his point?

WRITING PROMPTS

Responding to the Topic   To what extent do you consider yourself a citizen of the world? Write an essay in which you explore your own globalization experiences or those you'd like to have in the future. Include how such experiences contribute to your sense of cultural identity.

Responding to the Writer   Lam believes that "man's identity is in conflict" as a result of globalization (para. 13). Write an essay in which you support or argue against this assertion, using both your own experience and Lam's global and psychological transformation to prove your point.

Responding to Multiple Viewpoints   Reread paragraph 13 of Andrew Lam's "Globalization vs. Americanization." In an essay, explain how Dinaw Mengestu ("Home at Last," p. 74) would respond to Lam's assertations here.

For a quiz on this reading, go to bedfordstmartins.com/mirror.

Home at Last

DINAW MENGESTU

Dinaw Mengestu immigrated from Addis Ababa, Ethiopia, to the United States as a toddler. Mengestu has written on the political/social climates in Darfur and northern Uganda for various magazines, including *Harper's, Jane,* and *Rolling Stone.* When asked how he became a writer, Mengestu responded, "I don't think most writers ever decide to write. For me, it was something that I did because I had to. It's been my way of managing and making sense of the world I live in." His first novel, *The Beautiful Things That Heaven Bears,* has been translated into more than a dozen languages. "Home at Last" originally appeared in the anthology *Brooklyn Was Mine* (2008).

> **THINKING AHEAD** "Home is the place where, when you have to go there, they have to take you in," wrote Robert Frost. And we have all heard, "Home is where the heart is." But is it? How do you define *home*? Where is home for you? Why do you identify that location (or those locations) as home?

At twenty-one I moved to Brooklyn hoping that it would be the last move I would ever make—that it would, with the gradual accumulation of time, memory, and possessions, become that place I instinctively reverted back to when asked, "So, where are you from?" I was born in Ethiopia like my parents and their parents before them, but it would be a lie to say I was from Ethiopia, having left the country when I was only two years old following a military coup and civil war, losing in the process the language and any direct memory of the family and culture I had been born into. I simply am Ethiopian, without the necessary "from" that serves as the final assurance of our identity and origin.

Since leaving Addis Ababa in 1980, I've lived in Peoria, Illinois; in a suburb of Chicago; and then finally, before moving to Brooklyn, in Washington, D.C., the de facto[1] capital of the Ethiopian immigrant. Others, I know, have moved much more often and across much greater distances. I've only known a few people, however, that have grown up with the oddly permanent feeling of having lost and abandoned a home that you never, in fact, really knew, a feeling that has nothing to do with apartments, houses, or miles, but rather the sense that no matter how far you travel, or how long you stay still, there is no place that you can always return to, no place where you fully belong. My parents, for all that they had given up by leaving Ethiopia, at least had the certainty that they had come from some place.

---

[1] **de facto:** Actual.

They knew the country's language and culture, had met outside of coffee shops along Addis's main boulevard in the early days of their relationship, and as a result, regardless of how mangled by violence Ethiopia later became, it was irrevocably and ultimately theirs. Growing up, one of my father's favorite sayings was, "Remember, you are Ethiopian," even though, of course, there was nothing for me to remember apart from the bits of nostalgia and culture my parents had imparted. What remained had less to do with the idea that I was from Ethiopia and more to do with the fact that I was not from America.

I can't say when exactly I first became aware of that feeling—that I   3
was always going to and never from—but surely I must have felt it during those first years in Peoria, with my parents, sister, and me always sitting on the edge of whatever context we were now supposed to be a part of, whether it was the all-white southern Baptist church we went to every weekend, or the nearly all-white Catholic schools my sister and I attended first in Peoria and then again in Chicago at my parents' insistence. By that point my father, haunted by the death of his brother during the revolution and the ensuing loss of the country he had always assumed he would live and die in, had taken to long evening walks that he eventually let me accompany him on. Back then he had a habit of sometimes whispering his brother's name as he walked ("Shibrew," he would mutter) or whistling the tunes of Amharic[2] songs that I had never known. He always walked with both hands firmly clasped behind his back, as if his grief, transformed into something real and physical, could be grasped and secured in the palms of his hands. That was where I first learned what it meant to lose and be alone. The lesson would be reinforced over the years whenever I caught sight of my mother sitting by herself on a Sunday afternoon, staring silently out of our living room's picture window, recalling, perhaps, her father who had died after she left, or her mother, four sisters, and one brother in Ethiopia—or else recalling nothing at all because there was no one to visit her, no one to call or see. We had been stripped bare here in America, our lives confined to small towns and urban suburbs. We had sacrificed precisely those things that can never be compensated for or repaid—parents, siblings, culture, a memory to a place that dates back more than half a generation. It's easy to see now how even as a family we were isolated from one another—my parents tied and lost to their past; my sister and I irrevocably assimilated. For years we were strangers even among ourselves.

By the time I arrived in Brooklyn I had little interest in where I actually   4
landed. I had just graduated college and had had enough of the fights and arguments about not being "black" enough, as well as the earlier fights in high school hallways and street corners that were fought for simply being black. Now it was enough, I wanted to believe, to simply be, to say I was in Brooklyn and Brooklyn was home. It wasn't until after I had signed the

[2] **Amharic:** Official language of Ethiopia.

lease on my apartment that I even learned the name of the neighborhood I had moved into: Kensington, a distinctly regal name at a price that I could afford; it was perfect, in other words, for an eager and poor writer with inflated ambitions and no sense of where he belonged.

After less than a month of living in Kensington I had covered almost   5
all of the neighborhood's streets, deliberately committing their layouts and routines to memory in a first attempt at assimilation. There was an obvious and deliberate echo to my walks, a self-conscious reenactment of my father's routine that I adopted to stave off some of my own emptiness. It wasn't just that I didn't have any deep personal relationships here, it was that I had chosen this city as the place to redefine, to ground, to secure my place in the world. If I could bind myself to Kensington physically, if I could memorize and mentally reproduce in accurate detail the various shades of the houses on a particular block, then I could stake my own claim to it, and in doing so, no one could tell me who I was or that I didn't belong.

On my early-morning walks to the F train I passed in succession a   6
Latin American restaurant and grocery store, a Chinese fish market, a Halal[3] butcher shop, followed by a series of Pakistani and Bangladeshi takeout restaurants. This cluster of restaurants on the corner of Church and Mc-Donald, I later learned, sold five-dollar plates of lamb and chicken biryani[4] in portions large enough to hold me over for a day, and in more financially desperate times, two days. Similarly, I learned that the butcher and fish shop delivery trucks arrived on most days just as I was making my way to the train. If I had time, I found it hard not to stand and stare at the refrigerated trucks with their calf and sheep carcasses dangling from hooks, or at the tanks of newly arrived bass and catfish flapping around in a shallow pool of water just deep enough to keep them alive.

It didn't take long for me to develop a fierce loyalty to Kensington, to   7
think of the neighborhood and my place in it as emblematic of a grander immigrant narrative. In response to that loyalty, I promised to host a "Kensington night" for the handful of new friends that I eventually made in the city, an evening that would have been comprised of five-dollar lamb biryani followed by two-dollar Budweisers at Denny's, the neighborhood's only full-fledged bar—a defunct Irish pub complete with terribly dim lighting and wooden booths. I never hosted a Kensington night, however, no doubt in part because I had established my own private relationship to the neighborhood, one that could never be shared with others in a single evening of cheap South Asian food and beer. I knew the hours of the call of the muezzin[5] that rang from the mosque a block away from my apartment. I heard it in my bedroom every morning, afternoon, and evening, and if I was writing when it called out, I learned that it was better to simply stop

[3] **Halal:** Arabic word meaning lawful or permitted.
[4] **biryani:** Rice-based dish with spices and sometimes meat.
[5] **muezzin:** The sound that calls Muslims to daily prayers.

and admire it. My landlord's father, an old gray-haired Chinese immigrant who spoke no English, gradually smiled at me as I came and went, just as I learned to say hello, as politely as possible, in Mandarin every time I saw him. The men behind the counters of the Bangladeshi takeout places now knew me by sight. A few, on occasion, slipped an extra dollop of vegetables or rice into my to-go container, perhaps because they worried that I wasn't eating enough. One in particular, who was roughly my age, spoke little English, and smiled wholeheartedly whenever I came in, gave me presweetened tea and free bread, a gesture that I took to be an acknowledgment that, at least for him, I had earned my own, albeit marginal, place here.

And so instead of sitting with friends in a brightly lit fluorescent restaurant with cafeteria-style service, I found myself night after night quietly walking around the neighborhood in between sporadic fits of writing. Kensington was no more beautiful by night than by day, and perhaps this very absence of grandeur allowed me to feel more at ease wandering its streets at night. The haphazard gathering of immigrants in Kensington had turned it into a place that even someone like me, haunted and conscious of race and identity at every turn, could slip and blend into. 8

Inevitably on my way home I returned to the corner of Church and McDonald with its glut of identical restaurants. On warm nights, I had found it was the perfect spot to stand and admire not only what Kensington had become with the most recent wave of migration, but what any close-knit community—whether its people came here one hundred years ago from Europe or a decade ago from Africa, Asia, or the Caribbean—has provided throughout Brooklyn's history: a second home. There, on that corner, made up of five competing South Asian restaurants of roughly equal quality, dozens of Pakistani and Bangladeshi men gathered one night after another to drink chai[6] out of paper cups. The men stood there talking for hours, huddled in factions built in part, I imagine, around restaurant loyalties. Some nights I sat in one of the restaurants and watched from a corner table with a book in hand as an artificial prop. A few of the men always stared, curious no doubt as to what I was doing there. Even though I lived in Kensington, when it came to evening gatherings like this, I was the foreigner and tourist. On other nights I ordered my own cup of tea and stood a few feet away on the edge of the sidewalk, near the subway entrance or at the bus stop, and silently stared. I had seen communal scenes like this before, especially while living in Washington, D.C., where there always seemed to be a cluster of Ethiopians, my age or older, gathered together outside coffee shops and bars all over the city, talking in Amharic with an ease and fluency that I admired and envied. They told jokes that didn't require explanation and debated arguments that were decades in the making. All of this was coupled with the familiarity and comfort of speaking in our native tongue. At any given moment, they could have told you without hesitancy where they were from. And so I had watched, hardly understanding a 9

---

[6] chai: Spiced tea.

word, hoping somehow that the simple act of association and observation was enough to draw me into the fold.

Here, then, was a similar scene, this one played out on a Brooklyn cor- 10 ner with a culture and history different from the one I had been born into, but familiar to me nonetheless. The men on that corner in Kensington, just like the people I had known throughout my life, were immigrants in the most complete sense of the word—their loyalties still firmly attached to the countries they had left one, five, or twenty years earlier. If there was one thing I admired most about them, it was that they had succeeded, at least partly, in re-creating in Brooklyn some of what they had lost when they left their countries of origin. Unlike the solitary and private walks my father and I took, each of us buried deep in thoughts that had nowhere to go, this nightly gathering of Pakistani and Bangladeshi men was a makeshift reenact-ment of home. Farther down the road from where they stood were the few remaining remnants of the neighborhood's older Jewish community—one synagogue, a kosher deli—proof, if one was ever needed, that Brooklyn is always reinventing itself, that there is room here for us all.

While the men stood outside on the corner, their numbers gradually 11 increasing until they spilled out into the street as they talked loudly among themselves, I once again played my own familiar role of quiet, jealous ob-server and secret admirer. I have no idea what those men talked about, if they discussed politics, sex, or petty complaints about work. It never mat-tered anyway. The substance of the conversations belonged to them, and I couldn't have cared less. What I had wanted and found in them, what I admired and adored about Kensington, was the assertion that we can re-build and remake ourselves and our communities over and over again, in no small part because there have always been corners in Brooklyn to do so on. I stood on that corner night after night for the most obvious of reasons—to be reminded of a way of life that persists regardless of context; to feel, however foolishly, that I too was attached to something.

EXERCISING VOCABULARY

1. Record your own definition for each of these words.

   irrevocably (adv.) (2)   dollop (n.) (7)
   assimilated (v.) (3)   sporadic (adj.) (8)
   emblematic (adj.) (7)   glut (n.) (9)
   defunct (adj.) (7)

2. Mengestu writes that the walks he took around his Kensington neigh-borhood mimicked his father's routine in an effort to "stave off" a sense of isolation and aloneness (para. 5). What does the expression "stave off" mean? What purpose did these walks serve for the author?

3. In paragraph 9, Mengestu writes that he watched his neighbors, "hoping somehow that the simple act of association and observation was enough to draw me *into the fold*." What does this idiom mean? What is the origin of this expression?

PROBING CONTENT

1. Why is it ironic that Mengestu's father often said to him, "Remember, you are Ethiopian"? How did that statement make the young man feel?

2. Why did the author and his family feel "stripped bare here in America" (para. 3)? What effect did this feeling have on relationships within his family?

3. What were Mengestu's plans for a "Kensington night" for his friends? Why did this event never take place? How did Mengestu spend his nights instead?

4. Why does the author take a book with him when he goes out at night? What role does the author play on these evenings?

CONSIDERING CRAFT

1. How appropriate is this essay's title? Why?

2. In paragraph 3, the author writes that he felt like he was "always sitting on the edge of whatever context we were now supposed to be part of." How does this metaphor capture the theme of Mengestu's essay?

3. Throughout the essay, Mengestu uses a number of words such as *Amharic, muezzin, biryani, Halal,* and *chai* that may be unfamiliar to some American readers. What effect does the use of such words have on his writing? How does the inclusion of these words affect your reading of this essay?

4. Locate two examples of highly effective descriptive language in this essay. What does this language convey to the reader? What makes its use so effective in the passages you have selected?

WRITING PROMPTS

Responding to the Topic   Choose one neighborhood where you have felt a sense of belonging or one where you would like to belong. Write an essay in which you describe this neighborhood in complete detail. Be certain to appeal to all five senses to enhance your description.

Responding to the Writer   Mengestu writes that he felt "haunted and conscious of race and identity at every turn" (para. 8). Write an essay describing a time when you felt unusually conscious of your appearance, your ethnicity, or some other aspect of your identity.

Responding to Multiple Viewpoints   In an essay, compare and contrast Dinaw Mengestu's parents' approach to adapting to life in America to the approach taken by Lorraine Ali's parents ("Do I Look Like Public Enemy Number One?" p. 45).

For a quiz on this reading, go to bedfordstmartins.com/mirror.

History Tells Hard Stories of Ethnic Clashes

Leonard Pitts Jr.

Leonard Pitts Jr., author of the novel *Before I Forget* (2009), writes for the *Miami Herald* and won the Pulitzer Prize for his commentary in 2004. A collection of his columns, *Forward From This Moment,* was published in 2009. "History Tells Hard Stories of Ethnic Clashes" first appeared in the *Miami Herald* on May 15, 2010.

> **THINKING AHEAD** Every country's history is marked by some incidents that the country's citizens would like to forget. A desire to do so may lead to what is called "revisionist history," when those who write the history books make their own determinations about what will be remembered. What dangers lie in this approach to communicating history to future generations?

History is not a Hallmark card. Sometimes, history breaks your heart. 1

I know this because I have often recounted history in this space, 2
tales of black men and women bought and sold, cheated and mistreated, maimed and lynched. And whenever I do this, I can be assured of e-mails and calls of chastisement.

I still remember one of the first, an earnest lady who pleaded with me 3
to leave this history behind. Telling such tales, she said, could not help but make black people resent white ones.

Her complaint presented a quandary. I find the same value in recount- 4
ing those stories that my former boss Bert used to find in remembering Holocaust brutalities and my friend John finds in recalling Irish suffering at British hands. Understanding the past provides context to understand the present and predict the future. Moreover, history is identity. These stories tell me who I am.

But there's a difference, isn't there? Bert's history indicts Germans in 5
Europe, John's indicts Britons in the United Kingdom. Mine indicts white people, here.

So I'm not without sympathy for people like that lady. This history 6
hurts. But is requiring me not to speak it really the best response to that hurt? Should a hard truth not be uttered for fear it might cause somebody, somewhere to resent?

Her answer, I suspect, would be yes. In that, she would be much like 7
the state of Arizona, where Gov. Jan Brewer just signed a law restricting ethnic studies courses in public schools. Having apparently decided she

had not done enough to peeve Latino voters by signing a Draconian[1] immigration bill a few days back, the governor went after a Mexican-American studies program in Tucson. But the prohibitions in the new law seem to say more about the mind-set of the governor than about any real danger posed by ethnic studies.

Specifically, the law bans classes that "promote the overthrow of the   8
United States government, promote resentment toward a race or class of people, are designed primarily for pupils of a particular ethnic group, advocate ethnic solidarity instead of the treatment of pupils as individuals." And you wonder: what sort of ethnic studies classes did *she* attend?

Is that really what people think those classes are about?   9

Worse, the restrictions are so broad, so void of legal precision, as to be   10
meaningless. How does one decide to a legal certainty whether a class is "designed primarily for pupils of a particular ethnic group"? How can one know with legal exactness whether a class will "promote resentment"?

Like the lady who called me, the governor seems to prefer that hard   11
stories not be told, that doing so detracts from American unity. As one online observer put it, "We need to focus on America instead of promoting everyone else."

The problem with that reasoning is obvious: America *is* everyone else,   12
a nation composed of other nations, a culture made of other cultures, a history built of other histories. And yes, sometimes, those histories will be hard to hear.

But silence does not make a hard story go away. Silence only makes it   13
fester, grow and, sometimes, explode.

It is in our narratives that we explain ourselves to ourselves. That's a   14
crucial matter in a nation which is, after all, bound not by common blood or ancestry, but by common fealty[2] to a set of revolutionary ideals that begins, "We hold these truths to be self-evident . . ." To those ideals have flocked men and women from every other nation on earth, each with stories of their own.

Granted, the challenge of incorporating those stories into the larger   15
American story is daunting. The governor seems to fear what kind of nation we'll be if we accept that challenge.

I fear what kind we'll be if we don't.   16

EXERCISING VOCABULARY

1. Record your own definition for each of these words.

chastisement (n.) (2)   void (adj.) (10)
quandary (n.) (4)   fester (v.) (13)
peeve (v.) (7)   daunting (adj.) (15)
prohibitions (n.) (7)

---

[1] **Draconian:** Severe, as in the strict code of laws enacted by the Athenian lawgiver Draco.
[2] **fealty:** Loyalty, faithfulness.

2. What does the word *indict* mean? In what setting is the term usually used? What does Pitts mean in paragraph 5 when he writes that his history "indicts white people, here"?

3. In paragraphs 11 and 13, Pitts describes some stories as "hard." In what sense are the lessons of history hard? Why does Pitts believe that "sometimes, those histories will be hard to hear" (para. 12)? For whom?

PROBING CONTENT

1. According to Pitts, why is understanding the past important?

2. What is the impact of the bill signed into law by Arizona governor Jan Brewer? Explain why this bill concerns Pitts.

3. Explain Pitts's contention in paragraph 12 that "America *is* everyone else."

CONSIDERING CRAFT

1. What does Pitts mean when he begins his essay by stating, "History is not a Hallmark card." Why is this an effective opening?

2. What document begins "We hold these truths to be self-evident . . ."? What does Pitts accomplish by including this quotation?

3. Read Langston Hughes's widely available poem "A Dream Deferred." Then reread paragraph 13 of Pitts's essay. How does having read this poem enhance your comprehension of Pitts's thesis? Why does Pitts choose to include words from Hughes's poem?

WRITING PROMPTS

Responding to the Topic   Write an essay in which you support or reject the statement that "history is identity." Use your own experience and the experience of others to validate your position.

Responding to the Writer   Pitts argues that it is wrong to suppress the truth because bringing it forward may cause friction, discomfort, or resentment. Choose a historical event or series of events and write an essay in which you examine the positive or negative effects of its being brought to light.

Responding to Multiple Viewpoints   Explore in an essay how Leonard Pitts might respond to the concerns Susan Konig expresses in "They've Got to Be Carefully Taught" (p. 51) about Cultural Diversity Month at her daughter's school.

For a quiz on this reading, go to bedfordstmartins.com/mirror.

America: Land of Loners?

DANIEL AKST

Daniel Akst is a contributing editor to *The Wilson Quarterly,* the journal in which "America: Land of Loners?" first appeared in 2010. Akst is the author of several books, the most recent of which is *We Have Met the Enemy: Self-Control in an Age of Excess* (2011). He has written for many magazines and periodicals including the *New York Times,* the *Wall Street Journal, Newsday,* and *Slate.*

> **THINKING AHEAD** Friendship is a persistent, timeless theme in films, books, and song lyrics. How important are friends? How did your closest friendships develop? Why, do you think, do they remain so close?

1   Science-fiction writers make the best seers. In the late 1950s far-sighted Isaac Asimov imagined a sunny planet called Solaria, on which a scant 20,000 humans dwelt on far-flung estates and visited one another only virtually, by materializing as "trimensional images"—avatars, in other words. "They live completely apart," a helpful robot explained to a visiting earthling, "and never see one another except under the most extraordinary circumstances."

2   We have not, of course, turned into Solarians here on earth, strictly limiting our numbers and shunning our fellow humans in revulsion. Yet it's hard not to see some Solarian parallels in modern life. Since Asimov wrote *The Naked Sun,* Americans have been engaged in wholesale flight from one another, decamping for suburbs and Sunbelt, splintering into ever smaller households, and conducting more and more of their relationships online, where avatars flourish. The churn rate of domestic relations is especially remarkable, and has rendered family life in the United States uniquely unstable. "No other comparable nation," the sociologist Andrew J. Cherlin observes, "has such a high level of multiple marital and cohabiting unions."

3   Oceans of ink have been spilled on these developments, yet hardly any attention is paid to the one institution—friendship—that could pick up some of the interpersonal slack. But while sizzling eros hogs the spotlight these days—sex sells, after all—too many of us overlook *philia,* the slower-burning and longer-lasting complement. That's ironic, because today "friends" are everywhere in our culture—the average Facebook user has 130—and friendship, of a diluted kind, is our most characteristic

relationship: voluntary, flexible, a "lite" alternative to the caloric meshugaas[1] of family life.

But in restricting ourselves to the thin gruel of modern friendships, we miss out on the more nourishing fare that deeper ones have to offer. Aristotle, who saw friendship as essential to human flourishing, shrewdly observed that it comes in three distinct flavors: those based on usefulness (contacts), on pleasure (drinking buddies), and on a shared pursuit of virtue — the highest form of all. True friends, he contended, are simply drawn to the goodness in one another, goodness that today we might define in terms of common passions and sensibilities.

It's possible that Aristotle took all this too seriously, but today the pendulum has swung in the opposite direction, and in our culture we take friendship — a state of strong mutual affection in which sex or kinship isn't primary — far too lightly. We're good at currying contacts and we may have lots of pals, but by falling short on Aristotle's third and most important category of friendship, we've left a hole in our lives. Now that family life is in turmoil, reinvigorating our notion of friendship — to mean something more than mere familiarity — could help fill some of the void left by disintegrating household arrangements and social connections frayed by the stubborn individualism of our times.

Friendship is uniquely suited to fill this void because, unlike matrimony or parenthood, it's available to everyone, offering concord and even intimacy without aspiring to be all-consuming. Friends do things for us that hardly anybody else can, yet ask nothing more than friendship in return (though this can be a steep price if we take friendship as seriously as we should). The genius of friendship rests firmly on its limitations, which are better understood as boundaries. Think of it as the moderate passion — constrained, yet also critical. If friendship, as hardheaded Lord Byron would have it, really is "love without his wings," we can all be grateful for its earthbound nature.

But we live now in a climate in which friends appear dispensable. While most of us wouldn't last long outside the intricate web of interdependence that supplies all our physical needs — imagine no electricity, money, or sewers — we've come to demand of ourselves truly radical levels of emotional self-sufficiency. In America today, half of adults are unmarried, and more than a quarter live alone. As Robert Putnam showed in his 2000 book *Bowling Alone,* civic involvement and private associations were on the wane at the end of the 20th century. Several years later, social scientists made headlines with a survey showing that Americans had a third fewer nonfamily confidants than two decades earlier. A quarter of us had no such confidants at all.

In a separate study, Nicholas Christakis and James Fowler, authors of *Connected: The Surprising Power of Our Social Networks and How They*

[1] **meshugaas:** Foolishness.

Shape Our Lives (2009), surveyed more than 3,000 randomly chosen Americans and found they had an average of four "close social contacts" with whom they could discuss important matters or spend free time. But only half of these contacts were solely friends; the rest were a variety of others, including spouses and children.

Here, as on so many fronts, we often buy what we need. The affluent   9
commonly hire confidants in the form of talk therapists, with whom they may maintain enduring (if remunerated) relationships conducted on a first-name basis. The number of household pets has exploded throughout the Western world, suggesting that not just dogs but cats, rats, and parakeets are often people's best friends. John Cacioppo, a University of Chicago psychologist who studies loneliness, says he's convinced that more Americans are lonely — not because we have fewer social contacts, but because the ones we have are more harried and less meaningful.

Developing meaningful friendships — having the kind of people in your   10
life who were once known as "intimates" — takes time, but too many of us are locked in what social critic Barbara Ehrenreich has called "the cult of conspicuous busyness," from which we seem to derive status and a certain perverse comfort even as it alienates us from one another. Throw in two careers and some kids, and something's got to give. The poet Kenneth Koch, whose friends included the brilliant but childless John Ashbery and Frank O'Hara, laid out the problem in verse:

> You want a social life, with friends.
> A passionate love life and as well
> To work hard every day. What's true
> Is of these three you may have two.

If time is a problem, so is space. Although Americans have been relo-   11
cating less often lately, perhaps as a result of the recession, we still move around quite a bit — for work, sunshine, retirement, or to be near family — and this process of uprooting dissolves friendships and discourages those that haven't yet formed. Few of us would turn down a tempting new job in a far-off city to stay near friends, possibly for the sensible reason that those friends might move away six months later anyway.

Divorce also takes its toll; most of us over the age of 30 are familiar   12
with the social consequences that ripple outward from a split-up, as four-somes for dinner or bridge are destroyed and friends may find themselves having to pick sides. Marital dissolution usually costs each spouse some precious connections, including in-laws who might once have been important friends.

Our longstanding reverence for self-sufficiency hasn't helped matters.   13
Ralph Waldo Emerson gave us a sharp shove down this road with his famous essay "Self-Reliance," and Cole Porter lyricized the uniquely American claustrophobia that danced off the tongues of a parade of popular crooners:

"Let me be by myself in the evenin' breeze/And listen to the murmur of the cottonwood trees/Send me off forever but I ask you please/Don't fence me in." Frontier-oriented American mythology is studded with exemplars of the lone hero, from Daniel Boone to Amelia Earhart, to say nothing of the protagonists of Hollywood westerns such as *High Noon* (1952). Male buddy films date back to Laurel and Hardy, but their profusion in the past three decades—including box-office franchises ranging from *Beverly Hills Cop* to *Harold & Kumar*—is a strong social contra-indicator, like the lavish outfits and interiors of movies made during the Great Depression. If something desirable is missing in life, people like to see it on the screen.

Friendship has also suffered from the remorseless eroticization of human relations that was bequeathed to us by Sigmund Freud. The culture stands particularly ready to sexualize men's friendships since the gay liberation movement mercifully swept away taboos against discussing same-sex relationships. In 2005 *The New York Times* laid claim to coining the term "man date" in a story—under a woman's byline—about the anxiety two straight men supposedly experience if they brave a restaurant or museum together and run the risk that people will think they are gay. The "bromance" theme, once strictly a collegiate sport among scholars scouring the letters of passionate 19th-century friends for signs of physical intimacy, has since made its way into popular culture. The pathetic state of male friendship—and the general suspicion that men who seek close friends might be looking for something more—was captured in last year's film *I Love You, Man,* in which a guy decides to get married, realizes he has no one to be his best man, and must embark on a series of "man dates" to find one.   14

The irony is that straight men could learn a thing or two from their gay brethren, as Andrew Sullivan implied in his insightful book on the AIDS crisis, *Love Undetectable: Notes on Friendship, Sex, and Survival* (1998). Often estranged from their natural families and barred from forming legally acknowledged new ones of their own, gay men, Sullivan observed, learned to rely not on the kindness of strangers but the loyalty of friends: "Insofar as friendship was an incalculable strength of homosexuals during the calamity of AIDS, it merely showed, I think, how great a loss is our culture's general underestimation of this central human virtue."   15

We make this mistake in part because we've allowed our wildly inflated view of matrimony to subsume much of the territory once occupied by friendship. Your BFF nowadays—at least until the divorce—is supposed to be your spouse, a plausible idea in this age of assortative mating, except that spouses and friends fill different needs, and cultivating some close extramarital friendships might even take some of the pressure off at home. Yet the married men I know seem overwhelmingly dependent on their wives for emotional connection, even as their wives take pleasure in friends to whom they don't happen to be wed. The Beatles' immortal lonely heart Eleanor Rigby and novelist Anita Brookner's socially isolated   16 heroines notwithstanding, the fact is that all the women I know are better at friendships — spend more time on them, take more pleasure in them, and value them more highly — than any of the straight men.

Forgive me, guys, but we are lousy at this, and while it may seem to us   17
that our casual approach is perfectly normal, in fact it's odd. Among people whose lives are more like those of our ancestors, for example, friendship is taken far more seriously. In some cultures, close friends pledge themselves to one another in bonding rituals that involve the spilling of blood. The Bangwa people in Cameroon traditionally considered friendship so important that many families assigned a best friend to a newborn right along with a spouse.

There was a time when platonic friendship was exalted — if not   18
idealized — in the West, perhaps in part because of religious paranoia about sex. The myth of Damon and Pythias and the biblical story of David and Jonathan resonated across the centuries, and in the Middle Ages knights bound themselves in ceremonies to comrades in arms. Cicero, Johann Wolfgang von Goethe, Sir Francis Bacon, Michel de Montaigne, William Wordsworth — the list of Western luminaries who have waxed rhapsodic over friendship is long enough to fill anthologies from both Norton *and* Oxford.

In the 19th century, friendship was the subject of panegyrics[2] by the   19
likes of Emerson, who wrote that "the moment we indulge our affections, the earth is metamorphosed: there is no winter and no night: all tragedies, all ennuies[3] vanish." His buddy Henry David Thoreau, lamenting that to most people a friend is simply someone who is not an enemy, declared, perhaps wishfully, "Friends do not live in harmony, merely, as some say, but in melody." Mary Wollstonecraft might have spoken for the lot when she noted that while eros is transient, "the most holy bond of society is friendship."

A grain of salt is in order: Friendship, like baseball, always seems to   20
send intellectuals off the deep end. Yet there is more biological justification for our predecessors' paeans[4] to friendship than for our modern-day tepidity. Friendship exists in all the world's cultures, likely as a result of natural selection. People have always needed allies to help out in times of trouble, raise their status, and join with them against their enemies. It doesn't seem much of a stretch to conclude that a talent for making friends would bestow an evolutionary advantage by corralling others into the project of promoting and protecting one's kids — and thereby ensuring the survival of one's genes.

If we evolved to make friends, we also evolved to tell them things.   21
Humans have an irrepressible need to divulge, and often friends can tell one another what they can't tell anyone else, a function that has come in

---

[2] **panegyrics:** Elaborate praise.
[3] **ennuies:** Feelings of boredom.
[4] **paeans:** Joyful songs of praise.

especially handy since the Protestant Reformation put so many beyond the reach of the confessional. Less grandly, trading gossip is probably one of the main reasons people evolved into such friend makers, since information (and reputation) have always been valuable—even in the evolutionary environment.

Alliances and inside dope are two of the ways people derive power from friendships, which is why tyrannies are sometimes so hostile to them. Private affiliations of all kinds are a countervailing force against the great weight of government, but Aristotle reminds us that friendship also maintains the state. Friendships, after all, entail mutual regard, respect for others, a certain amount of agreeableness, and a willingness to rise above the ties of kinship in order to knit society into a web of trust and reciprocation—qualities more likely, in a state, to produce Denmark than Iraq. 22

Living in a society of friends has many advantages. Friendship can moderate our behavior (unless, like the television mobster Tony Soprano, you happen to choose immoderate friends). Friends help us establish and maintain norms and can tell us if we're running off the rails when others don't notice, won't break the news, or lack the necessary credibility. Both our relatives and our friends, the psychologist Howard Rachlin writes, "are essential mirrors of the patterns of our behavior over long periods—mirrors of our souls. They are the magic 'mirrors on the wall' who can tell us whether this drink, this cigarette, this ice-cream sundae, this line of cocaine, is more likely to be part of a new future or an old past." 23

Indeed, the influence of friends and associates is profound. Social scientists Christakis and Fowler, working with data from the multidecade Framingham Heart Study, found that if you become obese, the odds increase by 71 percent that your same-sex friend will do likewise—a bigger impact than was measured among siblings. On the other hand, when you become happy, a friend living within a mile has a 25 percent greater chance of becoming happy as well—and even a friend of a friend has a 10 percent greater chance. Encouragingly for those who know a sourpuss or two, misery was not comparably contagious. 24

Friendship can even prolong our lives. For loneliness, the experts tell us, has to do more with the quality of our relationships than the quantity. And we now know that loneliness is associated with all sorts of problems, including depression, high blood pressure and cholesterol, Alzheimer's disease, poor diet, drug and alcohol abuse, bulimia, and suicide. Lonely people have a harder time concentrating, are more likely to divorce, and get into more conflicts with neighbors and coworkers. 25

But of course friends are not vitamins, to be taken in daily doses in hopes of cheating the Grim Reaper.[5] The real reason to prize our friends is that they help us lead good and satisfying lives, enriched by mutual understanding. This special way of knowing one another was once exalted as "sympathy," and Adam Smith described it as "changing places in fancy." As 26

[5] the Grim Reaper: Death.

Caleb Crain made plain in his excellent book *American Sympathy: Men, Friendship, and Literature in the New Nation* (2001), the 18th and 19th centuries were the heyday of sympathy, when the fervor of friends was evident in their letters as well as their comportment. Sympathy persisted in popular discourse and was studied as a scientific fact under various guises until, in the 19th century, Charles Darwin came along to replace cooperation with competition in the intellectual armament of the day.

Sympathy's long-ago advocates were onto something when they reck- 27
oned friendship one of life's highest pleasures, and they felt themselves freer than we do to revel in it. It's time for us to ease up on friending, rethink our downgrade of ex-lovers to "just" friends, and resist moving far away from everyone we know merely because it rains less elsewhere. In Asimov's vision, Solaria was a lonely planet that humans settled with the help of robots. People weren't made to live there.

EXERCISING VOCABULARY

1. Record your own definition for each of these words.

avatars (n.) (1)	scouring (v.) (14)
shunning (adj.) (2)	estranged (v.) (15)
rendered (v.) (2)	subsume (v.) (16)
currying (v.) (5)	paranoia (n.) (18)
frayed (v.) (5)	metamorphosed (v.) (19)
concord (n.) (6)	transient (adj.) (19)
dispensible (adj.) (7)	tepidity (n.) (20)
wane (n.) (7)	fervor (n.) (26)
remunerated (adj.) (9)	comportment (n.) (26)
dissolution (n.) (12)	guises (n.) (26)
exemplars (n.) (13)	

2. Akst writes that "Americans have been engaged in wholesale flight from one another, decamping for suburbs and Sunbelt" (para. 2). What is the root word for *decamping?* What is the word's original meaning? What does it mean today?

3. In paragraph 2, Akst notes the negative impact of "the *churn rate* of domestic relationships" on family life. What substance is usually churned? Explain what the author achieves by using this expression in this context.

4. In paragraph 3, the author differentiates between two kinds of affection, *eros* and *philia.* Identify the origins of these two words and explain the difference in their meanings.

5. Explain the origin of the word *platonic.* What constitutes a platonic friendship? List some examples suggested in this essay.

PROBING CONTENT

1. What parallels does Akst draw between life on the fictional planet Solaria and life on Earth?

2. According to Aristotle, what are the "three distinct flavors" of friendship? Which is the most meaningful?

3. According to University of Chicago psychologist John Cacioppo, why are more Americans lonely today than ever before? What serious problems associated with loneliness are mentioned in this essay?

4. What advantages did friendship offer in early civilizations? What are some of the modern advantages of friendships?

5. How do friendships work both for and against governments?

CONSIDERING CRAFT

1. Examine the title of this selection. How might the effect be different if the author had used a period instead of a question mark?

2. Reread the first paragraph. Why do you think Akst chooses this introduction? How well does this introduction set the stage for the essay that follows?

3. Akst often uses figurative language, like metaphor and hyperbole, to illustrate significant points in his writing: "oceans of ink have been spilled" (para. 3), "the thin gruel of modern friendships" (para. 4), friends "can tell us if we're running off the rails" (para. 23). For one of these three examples, explain what Akst means and evaluate the effectiveness of the language used to convey his point.

4. Throughout this essay, the author cites numerous other writers, both historical and contemporary. What does the author achieve by including these references?

5. Study the final paragraph of this essay. What makes this conclusion so effective?

WRITING PROMPTS

Responding to the Topic   Select a few films about friendship that you have seen and write an essay in which you compare their portrayal of friendship to the state of friendship in America today as described by Akst.

Responding to the Writer   The author deplores the "pathetic state of male friendship" (para. 14) and asserts that "all the women I know are better at friendships — spend more time on them, take more pleasure in them, and value them more highly — than any of the straight men" (para. 16). Write an essay in which you discuss your own experience to support or argue against Akst's viewpoint.

Responding to Multiple Viewpoints   Write an essay expressing how Dinaw Mengestu ("Home at Last," p. 74) would respond to Akst's ideas about loneliness.

For a quiz on this reading, go to bedfordstmartins.com/mirror.

A Smart Exception

David Gergen

In addition to being a political consultant and a senior political analyst at CNN, David Gergen is a professor of public service at the Kennedy School of Government at Harvard University. Gergen was born in North Carolina and holds degrees from Yale and Harvard University. He served as an adviser to four presidents, Democrat and Republican, and serves on the board of Teach for America. His book *Eyewitness to Power: The Essence of Leadership, Nixon to Clinton* was a *New York Times* best seller in 2000. "A Smart Exception" first appeared in *Parade* in 2010.

> **THINKING AHEAD** For some time, the United States has been embroiled in a debate about its immigration policy. How do you view the rights and responsibilities of immigrants? Should potential immigrants who are highly skilled be considered separately for legal status from those who are less skilled? Why?

1 As H. L. Mencken once observed, "There is always a well-known solution to every human problem—neat, plausible, and wrong." So often true. But when it comes to creating American jobs, there is also a partial solution that is neat, plausible, and right.

2 It lies in our immigration policies. For more than five years, Washington has wrestled so hard with the vexing problem of illegal immigration that we have forgotten how much we can gain from legal immigrants. Indeed, they can be an enormous source of vitality—and jobs.

3 Since the early days of the Republic, talented foreigners have streamed to our shores to till the soil, build industries, and turn the country into a scientific and technological powerhouse. They converted the U.S. into the first global nation, giving us adaptability, an intuitive feel for other cultures, and an innovative edge.

4 We see living proof of what they can accomplish in the lives of Sergey Brin, Jerry Yang, and Pierre Omidyar. All three came here as the children of legal immigrants and grew up with the blessings of opportunity in their adopted land. And guess what: They went on to start Google, Yahoo!, and eBay. Nor are they alone in their contributions. From 1995 to 2005, legal immigrants were CEOs or lead technologists in one of every four U.S. tech and engineering start-ups and half of those in Silicon Valley. These companies employed some 450,000 people before the recession hit.

It's now commonplace to see foreign-born students dominating U.S.   5
graduate programs in science, math, and technology. Not long ago, it was
joked that MIT stood for "Made in Taiwan." Immigrants have accounted
for 70 or so of 315 American Nobel Prize winners since 1901 and, according to one study, about half of all patents issued in the past decade.

But that flow of talent is starting to reverse course. The U.S. imposes so   6
many limits on the numbers of legal immigrants and, since 9/11, has introduced such a thicket of red tape that many who would have come here are
now staying home. Moreover, their native countries have become more alluring: By a 9 to 1 ratio, Chinese respondents to a recent survey said they
had better opportunities to start businesses in China than in the U.S. By a
2 to 1 margin, Indians said their home country provided better education
for their children.

At a time of extreme unemployment, one hears—even from the White   7
House—that it would be politically unacceptable to have a single foreigner,
even a legal immigrant, take the job of a native American. That's the wrong
way to look at the problem: Talented foreigners are job creators, not job
takers. On average, engineers from overseas are thought to create some
four to five new jobs each.

A more reasonable criticism of legal immigration is that it allows too   8
many bad actors into the country. For example, the would-be Times Square
bomber, Faisal Shahzad, was foreign-born and entered the U.S. legally. So
we do need to assure that frauds don't get through. But fear cannot allow
us to drive away some of the best brains in the world.

There are two main ways high-skilled foreigners can now gain entry to   9
the U.S.—and both are too restrictive. First, they can apply for permanent
residency, a so-called green card. The trouble is that less than 20% of the
1.1 million legal permanent residents admitted each year are highly skilled.
Second, foreigners can apply for a temporary six-year visa, the H-1B, but
the cap for those is just 85,000 a year. Far more apply than can get in, and
there are huge backlogs and long waits (as much as 20 years) for scientists
and engineers.

Strikingly, leaders on both sides of the Congressional aisle agree that   10
we should open the doors wider to skilled foreigners, but they have allowed this issue to become entangled with that of illegal immigration. This
approach to talent is loony—what *The Economist* calls a "policy of national self-sabotage."

We need to carve out "an exception for smart people," as Bill Gates has   11
put it: Split off the question of legal immigration, lift those caps, welcome
more foreign talent, and start cranking up the American job machine. That's
a solution that is neat, plausible, and right.

EXERCISING VOCABULARY

1. Record your own definition for each of these words.

    plausible (adj.) (1)   innovative (adj.) (3)
    vexing (adj.) (2)   loony (adj.) (10)
    intuitive (adj.) (3)

2. In the final paragraph, Gergen talks about "cranking up the American job machine." What does he mean? What kinds of things have to be cranked up to function? What does this language choice imply?

3. In paragraph 10, Gergen writes that the magazine *The Economist* has called our mingling the admission of skilled foreigners to the United States with the illegal immigration issue "a policy of national self-sabotage." What is sabotage? How does a nation commit "self-sabotage"?

PROBING CONTENT

1. According to the essay, what has caused some Americans to forget the positive contributions of legal immigrants? What are some of those contributions?

2. In a recent survey, what benefits of their home countries did Chinese and Indian respondents cite?

3. What are the two legal ways that highly skilled workers are now admitted to the United States? Why are these two methods insufficient?

CONSIDERING CRAFT

1. Locate the thesis in this essay and state it here. Why do you think the author chooses this location for his thesis? When is the thesis revisited? How does this benefit the essay?

2. In paragraph 6, the author refers to "a thicket of red tape." What kind of figurative language is he employing here? How does this language choice create a vivid image?

3. What does the author mean in paragraph 8 when he refers to some potential immigrants as "bad actors"? Whom does he mention as an example?

WRITING PROMPTS

Responding to the Topic   Write an essay in which you profile a public figure not mentioned in this essay who immigrated to this country and has made a significant contribution to the American economy. Describe that contribution in detail, as well as any obstacles the person may have encountered.

Responding to the Writer   Gergen's "neat, plausible, and right" solution is to "lift those caps" and "welcome more foreign talent" (para. 11). Write an essay in which you support or reject this solution.

Responding to Multiple Viewpoints   Write an essay in which you imagine how Dinaw Mengestu, author of "Home at Last" (p. 74), might react to David Gergen's solution for creating American jobs.

For a quiz on this reading, go to bedfordstmartins.com/mirror.

Wrapping Up Chapter 3

CONNECTING TO THE CULTURE

1. Think about celebrities who have helped shape your cultural identity. They might be models, sports figures, musicians, or television personalities. They might have had positive, negative, or mixed influences on you. Write an essay in which you trace the influence these people have had on your cultural identity.

2. Since you have been attending college, what new cultural influences have you experienced? Consider food, film, music, sports, language, and hobbies. Have these influences been positive, negative, or mixed? To what extent have you been influenced? In what ways have these influences changed you?

3. What influence has your particular cultural group had on the formation of your self-image? Give specific examples.

4. Imagine yourself as a current or future parent and identify some negative cultural influences on the formation of cultural identity in children. Detail how you would attempt to curb those influences.

5. What role do you think television plays in shaping and reinforcing our ideas about people of cultures or races different from our own? Cite specific examples of television shows to support your points.

Focusing on Yesterday, Focusing on Today

Amid bustling activity, masses of immigrants pour across the gangway to begin new lives in America. This 1878 illustration conveys a sense of order and process, in spite of the overflow of humanity depicted. No one appears alarmed or harried. How would you describe this scene? What tone does the artist convey? Cite some specific details to support your answer. What is the role of the policeman in the group on the left?

"Give Me Your Tired, Your Poor."

Notice the stark contrast between the 1878 illustration and this 2006 photo of a road sign located just north of the U.S.-Mexico border in San Ysidro, California. Why is there only one word on the road sign? When is this word usually used? What is the implication? What is the tone of this image? For whom is this message intended? Compare the people depicted here to those in the 1878 illustration. What do they have in common? How are their situations different?

Caution!

You Are What You Eat

4

American Food Culture and Traditions
Around the World

Analyzing the Image

 Giuseppe Arcimboldo, an Italian painter who lived from approximately 1527 to 1593, created this oil portrait of Austrian emperor Rudolf II in 1590. The work now resides at Skokloster Castle in Sweden. The work's title, *Vertumnus*, recalls the Roman god of the changing seasons, plant growth, gardens, and fruit trees. This god could change his shape at will. According to a story in Ovid's *Metamorphosis,* he used this power to gain entrance into the goddess Pomona's orchard by assuming the shape of an old woman. Once inside, Vertumnus transformed back into himself and seduced the goddess.

Arcimboldo is best known for clever portraits like this one, which reflect the growing interest in science and nature that characterized the Italian Renaissance. Art scholars have argued for Arcimboldo's influence on the Surrealist movement because of his clever designs and visual puns. One such painting, *The Cook,* appears to be the portrait of a cook, but when turned upside down, it looks like a still life depicting a sumptuous dish prepared by that cook.

- What do you first see when you look at this painting?

- On closer inspection, what do you notice about this portrait?

- Why is the subject of the portrait smiling?

- What is your reaction to the painting?

- How does this oil painting reflect the title of the chapter "You Are What You Eat"?

Research this topic with TopLinks at bedfordstmartins.com/toplinks.

GEARING UP   Think about what part food plays in your everyday life. Besides basic nourishment, what role does food serve? What decisions do you make every day about the food you eat? What influences those decisions? Where do you eat on campus? What are your favorite foods? What are your least favorite? How does that eating experience differ from eating at home? Which do you prefer? Why?

"Y ou are what you eat." This famous quotation establishes the fundamental relationship between humans and the food that nourishes them.
Those of us who are lucky enough to have never experienced hunger may
not have given much thought to the crucial role food plays in our lives.
Food not only fuels our bodies and minds; it also defines us individually
and culturally. When humankind first discovered fire, and learned to cook
food over that fire, we separated ourselves from the other animals in a unique
and lasting way. We became "cooking animals" who shared that food
around the fire and then the table or another culturally significant place like
a sports arena or a county fair. Some of our strongest memories are connected to the unique smells and tastes of certain foods and to the people
who prepared those foods. Food links generations and fosters community.
Whether that food is ceremonial like the Thanksgiving turkey or hot dogs
at the ball park, it creates and reinforces cultural memory. We carry with us
the smells and tastes of that turkey or those hot dogs throughout our lives
and associate those smells and tastes with the people who ate these foods
with us.

Even if we ourselves don't choose to spend significant amounts of time
cooking, we are fascinated with cooking. In addition to the growing number of popular "food films" from *Ratatouille* to *Julie and Julia,* and the
omnipresence of food in literature and art, there is an entire television network devoted to cooking. We know the Food Network's celebrity chefs by
name and root for our favorites as they engage in cooking challenges reminiscent of the gladiatorial battles of old. We may not try their recipes at
home, but watching these culinary alchemists transform basic or not-so-
basic ingredients into beautiful, mouthwatering masterpieces strangely fascinates and soothes us. Watching others cook seems to have taken the place
of cooking from scratch as more and more of us grab snacks at the drive-
thru or "prepare" prepackaged food at home. Is the only vestige of our origins as "cooking animals" the sight of Dad grilling on the weekend or Mom
preparing a cake from a box?

Food is also religiously, politically, and environmentally important.
Those who choose vegetarian or vegan lifestyles are making a statement
about their personal belief systems. Hindus choose not to eat beef because
the cow is sacred in their culture. PETA members advocate for a vegan lifestyle to ensure the "ethical treatment of animals." Others choose not to eat
feedlot beef because of its negative environmental impact. Many people
choose free-range or organic foods because of the threat of hormones or
pesticides. Those who seek to eliminate world hunger face an ongoing challenge. Today, many pundits speak of the "McDonaldization" of culture.
They may be discussing whether the globalization of fast food, be it the
sesame seed bun or Chinese noodles, is beneficial or harmful. Does such globalization serve to homogenize world culture or to spread the uniqueness of
different ethnic food cultures abroad? However, the term *McDonaldization* is not limited to fast food. It can refer to the Americanization of popular culture both here and abroad. For example, upscale houses that closely

resemble each other and hence reflect the lack of individuality of their owners are satirically called McMansions.

Because food plays a crucial role in your life and the lives of people around the world, it is important to reflect on that role. The readings in this chapter will help you think about the cultural significance of food for others while helping you think about the ways in which your relationship with food determines your identity.

COLLABORATING   In small groups, discuss five different holidays or special events in which food plays a major role. First, decide which holidays to discuss. You could talk about holidays like Thanksgiving or Halloween or special events like the Super Bowl or New Year's Eve. What foods are associated with those holidays or special events? Note different group members' individual responses by compiling a list. Determine how these lists reflect different personal or ethnic choices.

The Cooking Animal

MICHAEL POLLAN

Michael Pollan has written extensively about food and changes in our relationship to it with the rise of industrialization and agribusiness. Some of his best known works are *The Botany of Desire* (2001), *The Omnivore's Dilemma* (2006), and *In Defense of Food: An Eater's Manifesto* (2009). Pollan is a contributing writer to the *New York Times,* where the essay "Out of the Kitchen, Onto the Couch" appeared on July 9, 2009. "The Cooking Animal" is an excerpt from that essay. Pollan is the Knight Professor of Journalism at the University of California, Berkeley and Recipient of the 2010 Lennon-Ono Grant for Peace.

THINKING AHEAD   What do you think are the reasons that humankind developed the art of cooking? What effect has cooking had on the human race? What do you think is the future of cooking as a part of our culture?

Paired Selection   Read this selection and the one that follows for two approaches to a similar topic. Then, answer the "Drawing Connections" questions on p. 113.

The idea that cooking is a defining human activity is not a new one. In 1773, the Scottish writer James Boswell, noting that "no beast is a cook," called Homo sapiens "the cooking animal," though he might have reconsidered that definition had he been able to gaze upon the frozen-food cases at Wal-Mart. Fifty years later, in *The Physiology of Taste,* the French gastronome[1] Jean-Anthelme Brillat-Savarin claimed that cooking made us who we are; by teaching men to use fire, it had "done the most to advance the cause of civilization." More recently, the anthropologist Claude Lévi-Strauss, writing in 1964 in *The Raw and the Cooked,* found that many cultures entertained a similar view, regarding cooking as a symbolic way of distinguishing ourselves from the animals.

For Lévi-Strauss, cooking is a metaphor for the human transformation of nature into culture, but in the years since *The Raw and the Cooked,* other anthropologists have begun to take quite literally the idea that cooking is the key to our humanity. Earlier this year, Richard Wrangham, a Harvard anthropologist, published a fascinating book called *Catching Fire,* in which he argues that it was the discovery of cooking by our early ancestors — not tool-making or language or meat-eating — that made us human. By

1

2

[1] **gastronome:** A connoisseur of good food; a "foodie."

providing our primate forebears with a more energy-dense and easy-to-digest diet, cooked food altered the course of human evolution, allowing our brains to grow bigger (brains are notorious energy guzzlers) and our guts to shrink. It seems that raw food takes much more time and energy to chew and digest, which is why other primates of our size carry around substantially larger digestive tracts and spend many more of their waking hours chewing: up to six hours a day. (That's nearly as much time as Guy Fieri devotes to the activity.) Also, since cooking detoxifies many foods, it cracked open a treasure trove of nutritious calories unavailable to other animals. Freed from the need to spend our days gathering large quantities of raw food and then chewing (and chewing) it, humans could now devote their time, and their metabolic[2] resources, to other purposes, like creating a culture.

Cooking gave us not just the meal but also the occasion: the practice of eating together at an appointed time and place. This was something new under the sun, for the forager of raw food would likely have fed himself on the go and alone, like the animals. (Or, come to think of it, like the industrial eaters we've become, grazing at gas stations and skipping meals.) But sitting down to common meals, making eye contact, sharing food, all served to civilize us; "around that fire," Wrangham says, "we became tamer." 3

If cooking is as central to human identity and culture as Wrangham believes, it stands to reason that the decline of cooking in our time would have a profound effect on modern life. At the very least, you would expect that its rapid disappearance from everyday life might leave us feeling nostalgic for the sights and smells and the sociality of the cook-fire. Bobby Flay and Rachael Ray may be pushing precisely that emotional button. Interestingly, the one kind of home cooking that is actually on the rise today (according to Harry Balzer) is outdoor grilling. Chunks of animal flesh seared over an open fire: grilling is cooking at its most fundamental and explicit, the transformation of the raw into the cooked right before our eyes. It makes a certain sense that the grill would be gaining adherents at the very moment when cooking meals and eating them together is fading from the culture. (While men have hardly become equal partners in the kitchen, they are cooking more today than ever before: about 13 percent of all meals, many of them on the grill.) 4

Yet we don't crank up the barbecue every day; grilling for most people is more ceremony than routine. We seem to be well on our way to turning cooking into a form of weekend recreation, a backyard sport for which we outfit ourselves at Williams-Sonoma;[3] or a televised spectator sport we watch from the couch. Cooking's fate may be to join some of our other weekend exercises in recreational atavism:[4] camping and gardening and hunting and riding on horseback. Something in us apparently likes to be reminded of our distant origins every now and then and to celebrate whatever rough skills 5

[2] **metabolic:** Any basic process of organic functioning or operation.
[3] **Williams-Sonoma:** A high-end cooking store.
[4] **atavism:** Reversion, or throwback.

for contending with the natural world might survive in us, beneath the thin crust of 21st-century civilization.

To play at farming or foraging for food strikes us as harmless enough, perhaps because the delegating of those activities to other people in real life is something most of us are generally O.K. with. But to relegate the activity of cooking to a form of play, something that happens just on weekends or mostly on television, seems much more consequential. The fact is that not cooking may well be deleterious to our health, and there is reason to believe that the outsourcing of food preparation to corporations and 16-year-olds has already taken a toll on our physical and psychological well-being.   6

Consider some recent research on the links between cooking and dietary health. A 2003 study by a group of Harvard economists led by David Cutler found that the rise of food preparation outside the home could explain most of the increase in obesity in America. Mass production has driven down the cost of many foods, not only in terms of price but also in the amount of time required to obtain them. The French fry did not become the most popular "vegetable" in America until industry relieved us of the considerable effort needed to prepare French fries ourselves. Similarly, the mass production of cream-filled cakes, fried chicken wings and taquitos, exotically flavored chips or cheesy puffs of refined flour, has transformed all these hard-to-make-at-home foods into the sort of everyday fare you can pick up at the gas station on a whim and for less than a dollar. The fact that we no longer have to plan or even wait to enjoy these items, as we would if we were making them ourselves, makes us that much more likely to indulge impulsively.   7

Cutler and his colleagues demonstrate that as the "time cost" of food preparation has fallen, calorie consumption has gone up, particularly consumption of the sort of snack and convenience foods that are typically cooked outside the home. They found that when we don't have to cook meals, we eat more of them: as the amount of time Americans spend cooking has dropped by about half, the number of meals Americans eat in a day has climbed; since 1977, we've added approximately half a meal to our daily intake.   8

Cutler and his colleagues also surveyed cooking patterns across several cultures and found that obesity rates are inversely correlated with the amount of time spent on food preparation. The more time a nation devotes to food preparation at home, the lower its rate of obesity. In fact, the amount of time spent cooking predicts obesity rates more reliably than female participation in the labor force or income. Other research supports the idea that cooking is a better predictor of a healthful diet than social class: a 1992 study in *The Journal of the American Dietetic Association* found that poor women who routinely cooked were more likely to eat a more healthful diet than well-to-do women who did not.   9

So cooking matters—a lot. Which, when you think about it, should come as no surprise. When we let corporations do the cooking, they're bound to go heavy on sugar, fat and salt; these are three tastes we're hard-wired to   10 like, which happen to be dirt cheap to add and do a good job masking the shortcomings of processed food. And if you make special-occasion foods cheap and easy enough to eat every day, we will eat them every day. The time and work involved in cooking, as well as the delay in gratification built into the process, served as an important check on our appetite. Now that check is gone, and we're struggling to deal with the consequences.

The question is, Can we ever put the genie back into the bottle? Once it has been destroyed, can a culture of everyday cooking be rebuilt? One in which men share equally in the work? One in which the cooking shows on television once again teach people how to cook from scratch and, as Julia Child once did, actually empower them to do it?   11

Let us hope so. Because it's hard to imagine ever reforming the American way of eating or, for that matter, the American food system unless millions of Americans—women and men—are willing to make cooking a part of daily life. The path to a diet of fresher, unprocessed food, not to mention to a revitalized local-food economy, passes straight through the home kitchen.   12

But if this is a dream you find appealing, you might not want to call Harry Balzer right away to discuss it.   13

"Not going to happen," he told me. "Why? Because we're basically cheap and lazy. And besides, the skills are already lost. Who is going to teach the next generation to cook? I don't see it.   14

"We're all looking for someone else to cook for us. The next American cook is going to be the supermarket. Takeout from the supermarket, that's the future. All we need now is the drive-through supermarket."   15

Crusty as a fresh baguette,[5] Harry Balzer insists on dealing with the world, and human nature, as it really is, or at least as he finds it in the survey data he has spent the past three decades poring over. But for a brief moment, I was able to engage him in the project of imagining a slightly different reality. This took a little doing. Many of his clients—which include many of the big chain restaurants and food manufacturers—profit handsomely from the decline and fall of cooking in America; indeed, their marketing has contributed to it. Yet Balzer himself made it clear that he recognizes all that the decline of everyday cooking has cost us. So I asked him how, in an ideal world, Americans might begin to undo the damage that the modern diet of industrially prepared food has done to our health.   16

"Easy. You want Americans to eat less? I have the diet for you. It's short, and it's simple. Here's my diet plan: Cook it yourself. That's it. Eat anything you want—just as long as you're willing to cook it yourself."   17

---

[5] **baguette:** A loaf of French bread that is long and crusty.

EXERCISING VOCABULARY

1. Record your own definition for each of these words.

   primate (adj.) (2)   deleterious (adj.) (6)
   forebears (n.) (2)   whim (n.) (7)
   notorious (adj.) (2)   inversely (adv.) (9)
   detoxifies (v.) (2)   correlated (v.) (9)
   trove (n.) (2)   shortcomings (n.) (10)
   forager (n.) (3)   gratification (n.) (10)
   seared (adj.) (4)   check (n.) (10)
   explicit (adj.) (4)   poring (v.) (16)
   adherents (n.) (4)   handsomely (adv.) (16)
   relegate (v.) (6)

2. In paragraph 6, the author writes, "The fact is that not cooking may well be deleterious to our health, and there is reason to believe that the *outsourcing* of food preparation to corporations and 16-year-olds has already taken a toll on our physical and psychological well-being." What happens when a business practices outsourcing? How can food preparation be subject to outsourcing? Who are the corporations and 16-year-olds that Pollan refers to here?

3. Pollan says that human beings are "*hard-wired* to like" three tastes: "sugar, fat and salt" (para. 10). What does it mean when something is hardwired? How can tastes be hardwired?

4. In paragraph 12, the writer states, "The path to a diet of fresher, unprocessed food, not to mention to a *revitalized* local-food economy, passes straight through the home kitchen." Look up the definition of the word *revitalized.* From which root word does it come? What then is a revitalized economy?

PROBING CONTENT

1. Who were James Boswell and Jean-Anthelme Brilllat-Savarin? What did they have to say about cooking?

2. According to Lévi-Strauss and other anthropologists, what effect did cooking have on human evolution? Why?

3. What effect has the decline of cooking had on modern life? Which one kind of cooking has increased? Why?

4. Who is David Cutler? What have he and his colleagues discovered about food preparation around the world? What have they discovered about obesity?

5. How does Harry Balzer envision the role the supermarket will play in the future? How does he believe that Americans can improve their diets and their health?

CONSIDERING CRAFT

1. Find two examples where the author uses humor in his essay. How does this occasional use of humor affect the tone of this essay?

2. In his essay, Pollan liberally paraphrases the words of other people. What effect does this strategy have on your reading?

3. Find two examples of the writer's naming celebrity chefs in his essay. Why does he do this?

4. Pollan includes several interesting metaphors in his essay. For example, in paragraph 5, he compares grilling to "a backyard sport for which we outfit ourselves at Williams-Sonoma, or a televised spectator sport we watch from the couch." Find another example in which he uses a metaphor. Explain what effect this figure of speech has on your reading experience.

5. What effect does Pollan's use of expressions such as "crank up the barbecue" (para. 5) and "put the genie back in the bottle" (para. 11) have on your understanding of this essay? Why does he include them?

WRITING PROMPTS

Responding to the Topic   Write an essay in which you discuss how the invention of cooking has affected humankind. Use Pollan's essay as inspiration. Do more research on the topic by consulting the works of some of the experts he refers to in "The Cooking Animal."

Responding to the Writer   How do you react to the writer's image of the future of cooking and eating? Write an essay in which you present your own vision of our culinary future. Cite specific reasons explaining why and how you agree or disagree with the vision presented in Pollan's essay.

Responding to Multiple Viewpoints   How would Bill McKibben ("The Only Way to Have a Cow," p. 129) and Seanon Wong ("Noodles vs. Sesame Seed Buns" p. 123) react to the picture Pollan paints of the future of cooking and eating? Write an essay in which you answer this question.

For a quiz on this reading, go to bedfordsmartins.com/mirror.

An Expert's Theory of Food Television's Appeal

FRANK BRUNI

Frank Bruni was the restaurant critic for the *New York Times* from April 2004 through 2009. Before his stint as a food writer, he worked for the newspaper as a reporter in the Washington D.C. bureau and covered George W. Bush's first presidential campaign. He has published two *New York Times* best sellers: *Ambling into History,* about George W. Bush, and *Born Round,* a memoir about the author's relationship with food. He currently holds the title of "food writer at large" at the *New York Times.* This essay first appeared in *The Atlantic* in 2010.

> **THINKING AHEAD**   Do you watch cooking shows on television? If so, which shows and chefs do you especially like? What qualities of your favorite chef do you most admire? How do these shows affect your own cooking or food choices?
>
> **Paired Selection**   Read this selection and the one before it for two approaches to a similar topic. Then answer the "Drawing Connections" questions on p. 113.

At drinks with a friend the other night, the subject of *Top Chef* and other food television came up, and he remarked that his early twentysomething sons watch more than a few cooking programs, as do many of their friends. He'd overheard the discussions that attested to that. But none of these young men, he said, were home cooks. Nor did they seem to aspire to be. They just like the programs, and not solely the ones, like *Top Chef* and its imitators, that have elimination-competition suspense built into them. They like more straightforward cooking demonstrations, too.

That shouldn't really be surprising. The proliferation of food television suggests that its audience is not only huge but also varied; otherwise, there wouldn't be such a vigorous push to conceive and distribute so many food-related programs on the Food Network and on its relatively new spawn, the Cooking Channel, and on Fox (Gordon Ramsay screams some more!) and on Bravo and, well, I could keep going like this for several paragraphs. It now seems that at any hour on any day, you can choose among a half dozen shows that will let you admire (or gasp at) someone's culinary efforts and ogle the food he or she produces.

But how many of the people doing the admiring, gasping, and ogling like to cook, dream of cooking, or want to know more about the mechanics of cooking? Even if it's a majority, that still leaves a lot of non-cooks in the audience. What prompts THEM to tune into food television?

My friend has a theory I find interesting. He wonders if there's a sort of broad cultural nostalgia at work. By that he means: as fewer and fewer young people know the much-talked-about ideal of home-cooked meals and of families gathering at the table at night to eat them, do the glossy, dreamy culinary demonstrations on TV tap into, and satisfy, a kind of curiosity and longing? For these young people, does the televised cooking have the appeal of a missive[1] from a lost utopia? Is it like an artifact from a bygone era?

The lifestyle porn of food television is more often discussed in terms of aspiration: would-be home cooks with limited budgets and time watch Martha and Ina and Giada go through their fluid, calm, dexterous paces and fantasize that they can or someday will do the same. But for younger viewers, is this same lifestyle porn more of a *Little House on the Prairie* or *Leave It to Beaver* experience?

As my friend was laying out this theory for me, I remembered a conversation a year ago with a recent college grad working for a glossy men's magazine. He wasn't a big home cook. He wasn't a big restaurantgoer. He didn't have the money to make those things happen, and beyond that, his culinary curiosity wasn't all that keen.

But he was a committed fan of *The Barefoot Contessa* on TV. Why? He just loved Ina's kitchen. He just loved the idea that he was in there, with her, watching her cook, presumably for him. It pleased him. Lulled him.

This leads me to one of my own theories about the popularity of food television among those who don't cook. When many people turn on the television set, as opposed to picking up a book or doing something more interactive, they're looking for a passive, mind-resting experience. They want something that doesn't require close attention, the way a twisty plot might. Something akin to visual music. Something ambient, in a way.

Much food television gives them that. It's a banquet of colorful, seductive, and familiar images, presented rhythmically, with a soundtrack of oohs and aahs.

I don't watch a lot of it, but when I do happen to turn to a cooking program [I] then get distracted. I sometimes lose any active awareness of it and don't even remember, for hours, that it or the cooking programs that follow it are on. I don't change the channel. I sit at the nearby computer while, just 12 feet away, chops are being grilled and vegetables sautéed and potatoes mashed. Is this footage not so much exhorting me to the stove or priming my appetite but, in some corner of my brain, simply putting me at peace?

[1] **missive:** A message.

EXERCISING VOCABULARY

1. Record your own definition for each of these words.

   attested (v.) (1)
   aspire (v.) (1)
   proliferation (n.) (2)
   vigorous (adj.) (2)
   ogle (v.) (2)
   utopia (n.) (4)
   artifact (n.) (4)
   aspiration (n.) (5)

   dexterous (adj.) (5)
   lulled (v.) (7)
   akin (adj.) (8)
   ambient (adj.) (8)
   sautéed (v.) (10)
   exhorting (v.) (10)
   priming (v.) (10)

2. In paragraph 2, Bruni refers to the Cooking Channel as the "spawn" of the Food Network. What does the word *spawn* mean? In which other contexts is this word used? What is the connotation of this word?

3. The author asks the following question about food television: "But for younger viewers, is this same lifestyle porn more of a *Little House on the Prairie* or *Leave It to Beaver* experience?" (para. 5). Why does the writer call food TV "lifestyle porn"? What lifestyle do the two shows *Little House on the Prairie* and *Leave It to Beaver* represent?

PROBING CONTENT

1. How big is the audience for food shows on television? Who makes up this audience?

2. According to the author's friend, why do non-cooks watch cooking shows? What vacancy in the viewers' lives do these shows fill?

3. What is Bruni's theory about the popularity of food shows with those who don't cook? What exactly appeals to these audience members?

CONSIDERING CRAFT

1. Reread the title of this essay. How does this title influence your reading of this article? Why do you think the author chose this title?

2. Bruni names several specific food shows and celebrity chefs in his essay. What is the effect of this writing strategy on your reading?

3. The author asks numerous questions in this essay. Find three of his questions and explain their function in the essay.

WRITING PROMPTS

Responding to the Topic   Think of the kind of cooking show you would like to see on television. Then write a detailed proposal for this program including the title, the premise of the show, its stars, the set, the desired time slot and channel, and the target audience. Make your proposal as detailed and persuasive as possible.

Responding to the Writer   Write an essay in which you argue for or against Bruni's reasons for cooking shows' popularity. Use examples to strengthen your argument.

Responding to Multiple Viewpoints   How would Connie Schultz ("Heat, Tray, Love," p. 114) respond to the idea of "cultural nostalgia" that Bruni mentions in paragraph 4 to explain the popularity of food TV?

For a quiz on this reading, go to bedfordstmartins.com/mirror.

DRAWING CONNECTIONS: PAIRED SELECTIONS

1. Frank Bruni calls food TV "lifestyle porn" (para. 6) and questions whether "televised cooking" is "like an artifact from a bygone era"? How would Michael Pollan respond to this idea?

2. Michael Pollan writes about some of the harmful effects that the decline in cooking can have on the human body while Frank Bruni writes about the potentially beneficial effects of food TV. Which author's viewpoint do you find more convincing? Why?

Heat, Tray, Love

CONNIE SCHULTZ

Connie Schultz is a Pulitzer Prize–winning journalist and columnist for the *Cleveland Plain Dealer*. Her books include . . . *and His Lovely Wife: A Memoir from the Woman Beside the Man* (2007) and *Life Happens: And Other Unavoidable Truths* (2006). Schultz also writes a column called "Back Page" for *Parade* magazine, where her essay "Heat, Tray, Love" was published in 2010.

> **THINKING AHEAD**   Have there been meals with family or friends that were especially memorable for you? Why? What dishes did they include? What was eventful about those meals in addition to the food?

I magine my horror when one of my friends told me recently that she had 1 no childhood memory of eating TV dinners.

"Wait a minute," I said. "You mean you never had thinly sliced pieces 2 of turkey smothered in gravy resting on two scoops of cornbread dressing, with baked apples for dessert?"

"Um, noooo," she said slowly, raising a cautious eyebrow. 3

"Well, surely you had the choicest three parts of golden-brown chicken 4 that went from stove to tabletop in just 25 minutes."

"Did that come with peas and carrots?" she asked. 5

"Yes!" 6

"Nope," she said, sighing. "Never had it. Mother was opposed." 7

I'll bet she was. I've always known there were too many highballs and 8 not enough Schlitz in that family. My poor friend. I am so grateful for my privileged upbringing in a working-class family. In our house, a TV dinner wasn't just a meal—it was an event.

Oh, the unrivaled joy that leapt from the heart of the child I used to be 9 whenever that ridge of aluminum prevented a triangle of peas from mingling with the triangle of mashed potatoes. I was no more than 6 the first time I laid eyes on that miracle meal of metal and meat. Family lore has it that I softly chanted my brand-new word: Salisbury . . . Salisbury . . . Salisbury. . . .

Alas, it wasn't always so. While my mother was raised to believe that 10 good wives always cooked from scratch, she didn't really enjoy cooking all that much. It bored her. She was big on adventure, though, and always game for the next new thing. She was the first mom in our neighborhood, for example, to wear a disposable paper dress. Oh, how the Tsk-Tsk Chorus of the Ladies Church Guild chirped about that one.

As for the TV dinners, we'll never know which came first: the rumor   11
that a mom three doors down had already served not one but two kinds of the no-work-no-mess partitioned meals, or the ads that promised piping-hot meat loaf and mixed vegetables simmering in their own seasoned sauce. Mom never revealed what put her over the top. All I remember is that fateful day in first grade when Mom took the lunch pail from my father as he walked through the door and announced, "Chuck, we're having TV dinners tonight." Dad shrugged, we cheered, and a family ritual was born.

It wasn't long before we all had our own TV tray tables. Dad surprised   12
Mom with a set from Sears, Roebuck. They had metal legs and pictures of autumn leaves on the plastic table tops, which Mom pointed out when it was her turn to host the Canasta Club.[1]

"Chuck always knows what I like," she said, patting the back of her bee-   13
hive.[2] "Fall's my favorite season, you know."

Oh, how the envy flowed from the women in that room. Thick as rich   14
brown gravy, it was, the kind that smothered the turkey but never touched that little square of cranberries.

EXERCISING VOCABULARY

1. Record your own definition for each of these words.

   unrivaled (adj.) (9)
   partitioned (adj.) (11)
   fateful (adj.) (11)

2. In paragraph 10, the author writes, "Oh, how the Tsk-Tsk Chorus of the Ladies Guild chirped about that one." What kind of animal chirps? Why does the writer say that these ladies "chirped"?

PROBING CONTENT

1. Why was a TV dinner an "event" in Schultz's family? How old was she when she ate her first TV dinner? What was her reaction?

2. What did the author's father buy for her mother? How did their design increase the value of the gift?

---

[1] **Canasta Club:** A group of people who meet to play a card game called canasta.
[2] **beehive:** A 1960s hairstyle in which the hair is piled on top of the head in the shape of a beehive.

CONSIDERING CRAFT

1. The title is a play on words. What phrase does it recall? Where has the original phrase been used?

2. The author includes dialogue in this essay. What is the effect of its inclusion on both the tone of the essay and on your reading?

3. In paragraph 8, the writer states that she's "always known there were too many highballs and not enough Schlitz" in her friend's family. What tone is the author using here? What does this description imply about her friend's family?

WRITING PROMPTS

Responding to the Topic   Do some research on the TV dinner. Use print or Web resources and consider conducting some interviews to aid in your research. Then write an essay in which you analyze why the TV dinner is an icon of American culture.

Responding to the Writer   What kind of meal qualifies as an "event" or "ritual" in your household? Write an essay in which you describe this meal. What do you eat? Who prepares it? How and where is it served? Who participates? What significance is associated with this meal?

Responding to Multiple Viewpoints   Food evokes strong memories in people. Using "Heat, Tray, Love" and Julie Dash's "Rice Culture" (p. 138) as models, write an essay about one of your fondest memories involving food and family or friends. Make sure to include sensory details.

For a quiz on this reading, go to bedfordstmartins.com/mirror.

Custom-Made

Tara Parker-Pope

Tara Parker-Pope is a health columnist for the *New York Times,* where she maintains a blog on health entitled *Well.* Before that, she wrote a weekly health column for the *Wall Street Journal.* She is the author of *Cigarettes: Anatomy of an Industry from Seed to Smoke* (2001). "Custom-Made" was first published in the *Wall Street Journal Europe* on September 30, 1996. In this essay, Parker-Pope takes us on a fascinating trip around the world and behind the scenes where marketing decisions are made to see what's hot and what's not about American favorites.

> **THINKING AHEAD** What is the strangest food or combination of foods you have ever tasted? Why did you eat this? Where were you? What did you learn from the experience? What foods would you like to try that you have never tasted? Why?

P ity the poor Domino's Pizza Inc. delivery man. 1

In Britain, customers don't like the idea of him knocking on their 2 doors—they think it's rude. In Japan, houses aren't numbered sequentially—finding an address means searching among rows of houses numbered willy-nilly.[1] And in Kuwait, pizza is more likely to be delivered to a waiting limousine than to someone's front door.

"We honestly believe we have the best pizza delivery system in the 3 world," says Gary McCausland, managing director of Domino's international division. "But delivering pizza isn't the same all over the world."

And neither is making cars, selling soap, or packaging toilet paper. Inter- 4 national marketers have found that just because a product plays in Peoria, that doesn't mean it will be a hit in Helsinki.

To satisfy local tastes, products ranging from Heinz ketchup to Cheetos 5 chips are tweaked, reformulated, and reflavored. Fast-food companies such as McDonald's Corp., popular for the "sameness" they offer all over the world, have discovered that to succeed, they also need to offer some local appeal—selling beer in Germany and adding British Cadbury chocolate sticks to their ice-cream cones in England.

The result is a delicate balancing act for international marketers: How 6 does a company exploit the economies of scale that can be gained by global marketing while at the same time making its products appeal to local tastes?

The answer: Be flexible, even when it means changing a tried-and-true 7 recipe, even when consumer preferences, like Häagen-Dazs green tea ice cream, sound awful to the Western palate.

---

[1] willy-nilly: In random order.

"It's a dilemma we all live with every day," says Nick Harding, H. J.   8
Heinz Co.'s managing director for Northern Europe. Heinz varies the recipe of its famous ketchup in different markets, selling a less-sweet version
in Belgium and Holland, for instance, because consumers there use ketchup
as a pasta sauce (and mayonnaise on french fries). "We're looking for the
economies from globalizing our ideas, but we want to maintain the differences necessary for local markets," says Mr. Harding.

For those who don't heed such advice, the costs are high. U.S. auto   9
makers, for instance, have done poorly in Japan, at least in part because
they failed to adapt. Until recently, most didn't bother even to put steering
wheels on the right, as is the standard in Japan. While some American makers are beginning to conform, European companies such as Volkswagen
AG, Daimler-Benz AG, and Bayerische Motoren Werke AG did it much
sooner, and have done far better in the Japanese market as a result.

For Domino's, the balancing act has meant maintaining the same basic   10
pizza delivery system world-wide—and then teaming up with local franchisers[2] to tailor the system to each country's needs. In Japan, detailed wall
maps, three times larger than those used in its stores elsewhere, help delivery
people find the proper address despite the odd street numbering system.

In Iceland, where much of the population doesn't have phone service,   11
Domino's has teamed with a Reykjavik drive-in movie theater to gain access to consumers. Customers craving a reindeer-sausage pizza (a popular
flavor there) flash their turn signal, and a theater employee brings them a
cellular phone to order a pizza, which is then delivered to the car.

Local Domino's managers have developed new pizza flavors, including   12
mayo jaga (mayonnaise and potato) in Tokyo and pickled ginger in India.
The company, which now has 1,160 stores in 46 countries, is currently trying to develop a nonbeef pepperoni topping for its stores in India.

When Pillsbury Co., a unit of Britain's Grand Metropolitan PLC, wanted   13
to begin marketing its Green Giant brand vegetables outside the United
States, it decided to start with canned sweet corn, a basic product unlikely
to require any flavor changes across international markets. But to Pillsbury's surprise, the product still was subject to local influences. Instead of
being eaten as a hot side dish, the French add it to salad and eat it cold. In
Britain, corn is used as a sandwich and pizza topping. In Japan, school children gobble down canned corn as an after-school treat. And in Korea, the
sweet corn is sprinkled over ice cream.

So Green Giant tailored its advertising to different markets. Spots show   14
corn kernels falling off a cob into salads and pastas, or topping an ice-cream
sundae.

"Initially we thought it would be used the same as in the United States,"   15
says Stephen Moss, vice president, strategy and development, for Green

---

[2] **franchisers:** People who pay for the right to use a company's name and to market its
products.

Giant. "But we've found there are very different uses for corn all over the world."

And Green Giant has faced some cultural hurdles in its race to foreign markets. Although vegetables are a significant part of the Asian diet, Green Giant discovered that Japanese mothers, in particular, take pride in the time they take to prepare a family meal and saw frozen vegetables as an unwelcome shortcut. "Along with the convenience comes a little bit of guilt," says Mr. Moss.

The solution? Convince moms that using frozen vegetables gives them the opportunity to prepare their families' favorite foods more often. To that end, Green Giant focused on a frozen mixture of julienned[3] carrots and burdock root, a traditional favorite root vegetable that requires several hours of tedious preparation.

The company also has introduced individual seasoned vegetable servings for school lunch boxes, with such flavors as sesame-seasoned lotus root. Although fresh vegetables still dominate the market, Green Giant says its strategy is starting to show results, and frozen varieties now account for half the vegetable company's sales in Japan.

The drive for localization has been taken to extremes in some cases: Cheetos, the bright orange and cheesy-tasting chip brand of PepsiCo Inc.'s Frito-Lay unit, are cheeseless in China. The reason? Chinese consumers generally don't like cheese, in part because many of them are lactose-intolerant.[4] So Cheetos tested such flavors as Peking duck, fried egg, and even dog to tempt the palates of Chinese.

Ultimately, says Tom Kuthy, vice president of marketing for PepsiCo Foods International's Asia-Pacific operations, the company picked a butter flavor, called American cream, and an Asianized barbecue flavor called Japanese steak. Last year, Frito rolled out its third flavor, seafood.

In addition to changing the taste, the company also packaged Cheetos in a 15-gram size priced at one yuan, about 12 cents, so that even kids with little spending money can afford them.

The bottom line: These efforts to adapt to the local market have paid off. Mr. Kuthy estimates that close to 300 million packages of Cheetos have been sold since they were introduced two years ago in Guangzhou. Cheetos are now available in Shanghai and Beijing as well.

Frito isn't through trying to adapt. Now the company is introducing a 33-gram pack for two yuan. Mr. Kuthy also is considering more flavors, but dog won't be one of them. "Yes, we tested the concept, but it was never made into a product," he says. "Its performance was mediocre."

Other PepsiCo units have followed with their own flavor variations. In Thailand, Pizza Hut has a tom yam-flavored pizza based on the spices of the traditional Thai soup. In Singapore, you can get a KFC Zinger chicken

[3] **julienned:** Sliced into thin strips.
[4] **lactose-intolerant:** Unable to properly digest lactose, the sugar in milk and certain other dairy products.

burger that is hot and spicy with Asia's ubiquitous chili. The Singaporean pizza at Pizza Hut comes with ground beef, green peppers, and chili. Elsewhere in Asia, pizzas come in flavors such as Mongolian, with pork, chili, and garlic; salmon, with a creamy lobster sauce; and Satay, with grilled chicken and beef.

Coming up with the right flavor combinations for international consumers isn't easy. Part of the challenge is building relationships with customers in far-flung markets. For years, the founders of Ben & Jerry's Homemade Inc. had relied on friends, co-workers, and their own taste buds to concoct such unusual ice-cream flavors as Chunky Monkey and Cherry Garcia.   25

But introducing their ice cream abroad, by definition, meant losing that close connection with their customers that made them successful. "For Ben and me, since we've grown up in the United States, our customers were people like us, and the flavors we made appealed to us," says co-founder Jerry Greenfield, scooping ice cream at a media event in the Royal Albert Hall in London. "I don't think we have the same seat-of-the-pants feel for places like England. It's a different culture."   26

As a result, one of the company's most popular flavors in the United States, Chocolate Chip Cookie Dough, flopped in Britain. The nostalgia quotient of the ice cream, vanilla-flavored with chunks of raw cookie dough, was simply lost on the Brits, who historically haven't eaten chocolate-chip cookies. "People didn't grow up in this country sneaking raw cookie-dough batter from Mom," says Mr. Greenfield.   27

The solution? Hold a contest to concoct a quintessential British ice cream. After reviewing hundreds of entries, including Choc Ness Monster and Cream Victoria, the company in July introduced Cool Britannia, a combination of vanilla ice cream, strawberries, and chocolate-covered Scottish shortbread. (The company plans to sell Cool Britannia in the United States eventually.)   28

And in a stab at building a quirky relationship with Brits, the duo opted for a publicity stunt when Britain's beef crisis meant farmers were left with herds of cattle that couldn't be sold at market. Ben & Jerry's creative solution: Use the cows to advertise. The company's logo was draped across the backs of grazing cattle, and the stunt made the front page of major London newspapers.   29

The company has just begun selling ice cream in France but isn't sure whether the company will try contests for a French flavor in that market. One reason: It's unclear whether Ben & Jerry's wry humor, amusing to the Brits, will be understood by the laconic French. "We're going to try to get more in touch, more comfortable with the feel of the French market first," says Mr. Greenfield.   30

But for every success story, there have been a slew of global marketing mistakes. In Japan, consumer-products marketer Procter & Gamble Co. made several stumbles when it first entered the market in the early 1970s.   31

The company thought its thicker, more-absorbent Pampers diapers in big packs like those favored in America would be big sellers in Japan. But   32

Japanese women change their babies twice as often as Americans and prefer thin diapers. Moreover, they often have tiny apartments and no room to store huge diaper packs.

The company adapted by making thinner diapers packaged in smaller 33 bags. Because the company shifted gears quickly, Procter & Gamble is now one of the largest and most successful consumer-goods companies in Japan, with more than $1 billion in annual sales and market leadership in several categories.

EXERCISING VOCABULARY

1. Record your own definition for each of these words.

   sequentially (adv.) (2)   quintessential (adj.) (28)
   tweaked (v.) (5)   quirky (adj.) (29)
   globalizing (v.) (8)   laconic (adj.) (30)
   ubiquitous (adj.) (24)   slew (n.) (31)
   concoct (v.) (28)

2. According to the article, Ben & Jerry's Chocolate Chip Cookie Dough ice cream failed to appeal to the British because in England that flavor has no "nostalgia quotient" (para. 27). What does the word *nostalgia* mean? What other foods have a high nostalgia value for Americans? Why is this true?

3. What does the verb *opted* mean in paragraph 29? In answering, consider what the noun *option* means.

PROBING CONTENT

1. According to Parker-Pope, why must companies custom-market American products to suit the tastes of international consumers?

2. Choose one of the author's examples and discuss the changes made to the product to market it in another country. Explain why the effort failed or succeeded.

3. Not only are the ingredients in American products often varied for international markets, but sometimes whole products are put to entirely different uses outside the United States. What examples does Parker-Pope give of such products?

4. What kind of pizza topping is Domino's trying to develop for its Indian market? Why would such a product sell in India?

CONSIDERING CRAFT

1. This essay first appeared in the World Business section of the *Wall Street Journal Europe.* Knowing this, how might you characterize Parker-Pope's audience? Why would this essay also appeal to readers outside that audience?

2. Why does this author need to provide specific examples of marketing campaigns or custom-made products? How do you think Parker-Pope determined how many examples to use?

3. How does the writer use the example in the final paragraph to create a satisfying conclusion? How else might the author have ended this essay?

WRITING PROMPTS

Responding to the Topic   Write an essay in which you consider your food choices. How open are you to including foods from other countries in your diet? Would you Americanize certain dishes, or would you eat them in the same way they are prepared in their native countries?

Responding to the Writer   To what extent should foods and food packaging and services be adapted for foreign consumers? What are the advantages? What are the disadvantages?

Responding to Multiple Viewpoints   In her essay "Custom-Made," Parker-Pope writes, "Part of the challenge [of global marketing] is building relationships with customers in far-flung markets" (para. 25). Do some research on a highly successful global advertising campaign, such as the one conducted by McDonald's. Then using what you have learned from that research and from the readings in this chapter, write an essay in which you detail one such successful worldwide campaign and the reasons for its success.

For a quiz on this reading, go to bedfordstmartins.com/mirror.

Noodles vs. Sesame Seed Buns

SEANON WONG

Seanon Wong is a graduate student at the University of Southern California studying political science and international relations. He has a certificate from Johns Hopkins University–Nanjing University Center for Chinese and American Studies, and a BA and MA from the University of Chicago. This essay has been excerpted from "What's in a Dumpling? The Chinese Fast Food Industry and the Spread of Indigenous Cultures under Globalization," which appeared in the winter 2006 issue of the *Stanford Journal of East Asian Affairs.*

THINKING AHEAD Think about the fast food that you or your friends eat. What kinds of fast food do you eat? How much of it is inspired by foreign cuisines? How much does the origin of the fast food affect your choices?

C onsidering the omnipresence of McDonald's, KFC and Pizza Hut, American fast food has been a revolutionary force in China's everyday culture. They have yet to become the most popular dining locations, however. Indigenous cultures, including culinary traditions, are on the rise in China. Paradoxically, globalization is responsible for their revival.

The evolution of Hong Kong's culinary scene offers an ideal starting point for discussion, since the city has been on the forefront of global integration for a much longer time than mainland China. As American fast food chains have boomed in Hong Kong over the last three decades, the demand for fast food—American or otherwise—has grown even faster. Currently, Hong Kong ranks first in the world for frequency of fast food consumption. Over 60 percent of the city's denizens[1] eat at take-away restaurants at least once a week, compared to only 41 percent and 35 percent in mainland China and the United States respectively.[2] Hong Kong's fast food industry, nevertheless, is dominated by Chinese companies such as Café de Coral, Fairwood and Maxim. Chinese dishes accounted for over 70 percent of fast food supplied in Hong Kong in 2002.

Just as India underwent a trend of "fast-foodization" as it joined the global economy, the success of Café de Coral in Hong Kong epitomized the mass commoditization of Chinese cuisines. Before the company was established in 1969, Hong Kong already had a long history of eating out. Café de Coral, however, was among the first to put Chinese food into large-scale

---

[1] **denizens:** Inhabitants.
[2] ACNielsen, *Consumers in Asia Pacific—Our Fast Food/Take Away Consumption Habits,* 2nd Half, 2004.

production and consumption. Its initial strategy was simple: "It moved Hong Kong's street foods indoors, to a clean, well-lighted cafeteria that offered instant services and moderate prices . . . ,"[3] and business expanded steadily thereafter. Ironically, the real boost for Café de Coral came when the Golden Arches arrived in 1975. According to Michael Chan, the company's current chairman, "McDonald's landing . . . inspired [Café de Coral's] confidence in self-service catering."[4] In the late-1970s, Café de Coral started using television commercials for mass advertising, and learning from McDonald's production model, established its first central food processing plant. Café de Coral is now Hong Kong's largest supplier of fast food.

Recently, Café de Coral extended its ambition beyond Hong Kong. The   4
company's mission is to become "a distinguished corporation in the food and catering industry as the world's largest Chinese quick service restaurant group. . . . "[5] In 2000, it acquired Manchu Wok, Canada's largest Chinese fast food supplier and second largest in the United States. With over 200 restaurants throughout North America and the number rising constantly, Café de Coral prides itself "as a menu innovator specializing in fast and fresh Chinese cuisine, ranging in style from Cantonese to Szechwan." Chan boasts that eventually, "Chinese [food] will displace the burger and the pizza." The future of fast food, as *The Economist* predicts, "may be congee,[6] tofu and roast duck."[7]

The recent flourish of local fast food restaurants in mainland China is   5
reminiscent of Hong Kong's experience, as challenges posed by American fast food since the late-1980s have compelled many Chinese restaurateurs to react and innovate. It was against this backdrop of foreign competition that the genesis of Chinese fast food occurred. The industry's nascent phase—which lasted until the early-1990s—was marked by constant attempts by local entrepreneurs to imitate their foreign challengers. Numerous copycat restaurants, with names such as "McDuck's," "Mcdonald's" and "Modormal's," appeared in the major cities. Most of them have posed little threat to the Western fast food giants. One outstanding exception, however, is Ronghuaji, or "Glorious China Chicken."

Ronghuaji was founded in 1989 after two Shanghai entrepreneurs were   6
inspired by KFC's business model. Since its inception, emulating KFC has been Ronghuaji's *modus operandi*.[8] Franchises were set up in downtown Beijing and Shanghai, usually right next to existing KFC restaurants, selling chicken products prepared with a wide variety of Chinese recipes. Although all of its Beijing outlets failed to be consistently profitable and eventually

---

[3] James L. Watson, "McDonald's in Hong Kong: Consumerism, Dietary Change, and the Rise of a Children's Culture," in *Golden Arches East: McDonald's in East Asia,* ed. James L. Watson (Stanford: Stanford UP, 1997), 81.

[4] Café de Coral company profile, Hong Kong Chamber of Commerce, available online at <www.chamber.org.hk/info/member_a_week/member_profile.asp?id=80>

[5] Company website, <www.cafedecoral.com>

[6] **congee:** Rice soup with flavorings.

[7] "Fast Chinese Cuisine: Junk Food?," *The Economist,* December 7, 2002.

[8] **modus operandi:** Latin for "mode of operation."

went out of business, Ronghuaji's moment of success "demonstrated that Chinese entrepreneurs could employ Western technology and create an industry with 'Chinese characteristics.'"[9]

Throughout the 1990s, Chinese entrepreneurs learned that reinvention   7
of Chinese cuisine in the form of fast food—rather than blind imitation of foreign recipes—provided a better path to business success. Alarmed by the popularity of the American chains, the Chinese government promulgated state policy in 1996 to foster a local fast food industry.[10] As Yan observes, the "fast-food fever" jump-started by the Western restaurants in Beijing "has given restaurant frequenters a stronger consumer consciousness and has created a Chinese notion of fast food and an associated culture."[11] By the end of 1996, over 800 local fast food companies were doing business in China, operating over 4,000 restaurants. The annual revenue was over RMB40 billion,[12] accounting for one-fifth of the catering industry's total revenue. By 1999, annual revenue surged to RMB75 billion, 20 percent higher than the previous year, and accounted for one-third of the industry's total. The growth rate for fast food was 7 percent higher than the average growth rate of the catering industry as a whole. Furthermore, contrary to the myth of foreign domination, Chinese-style fast food occupied a much larger portion of the market. As of 2002, four out of five fast food operators are Chinese restaurants. Business turnover of fast food restaurants serving Western dishes in 2000 accounted for only one-third of the industry's total volume.[13]

The extraordinary growth of the Chinese fast food market is the direct   8
result of rising consumerism. As in Café de Coral's success in Hong Kong, however, the real impetus to growth was the introduction of fast food management to aspiring Chinese entrepreneurs. Several of the industry's leading figures were former employees of McDonald's and KFC—an experience which equipped them with Western management concepts and techniques. The success of their business owed much to their ability to combine "modern methods of preparation and hygiene with traditional Chinese cuisine. . . . " Beijing's most famous restaurant, Quanjude Roast Duck Restaurant, even sent its management team to McDonald's in 1993. A year later, it introduced its own roast duck fast food.[14]

An important business concept that helped Chinese chains to prolifer-   9
ate is franchising. Today, nearly all fast food restaurants in China publicize

---

[9] Eriberto P. Lozada Jr., "Globalized Childhood?: Kentucky Fried Chicken in Beijing," in *Feeding China's Little Emperors: Food, Children, and Social Change*, ed. Jun Jing (Stanford: Stanford UP, 2000), 125.

[10] Yunxiang Yan, "Of Hamburger and Social Space: Consuming McDonald's in Beijing," in *The Consumer Revolution in Urban China*, ed. Deborah S. Davis (Berkeley and Los Angeles: U of California P, 2000), 207.

[11] Ibid., 201.

[12] RMB40 billion: The Renminbi, abbreviated RMB, is the official currency of the People's Republic of China.

[13] *Fast Food Market Report* (Friedl Business Information, 2002).

[14] Yunxiang Yan, "McDonald's in Beijing: The Localization of Americana," in *Golden Arches East: McDonald's in East Asia*, ed. James L. Watson (Stanford: Stanford UP, 1997), 74–75.

telephone hotlines for franchise information. With the friendly denomination of *jiameng rexian* (literally, "the hotline to join the league") these numbers are usually posted in prominent places, such as restaurant entrances. For instance, in 1996, Daniang Dumplings was merely a community restaurant in Changzhou in Jiangsu province with only six employees selling arguably the most prototypical of northern Chinese food—*shuijiao* (boiled dumplings). Within the next nine years, it expanded into an empire of over 150 franchises throughout the country and as far as Indonesia and Australia.

The phenomenal success of Café de Coral, Daniang Dumplings and others is of great significance not only to the preservation of Chinese culinary cultures at home, but also their influence abroad. When a new restaurant is established in a foreign territory, not only is its food consumed, but its associated culture is also propagated among the host community. The case of Mongolian hotpot illustrates how a culture that was once found in a restricted geographical region can spread through market expansion. In the past, Mongolian hotpot was found mostly in northern China; it was considered an exotic cuisine even to Chinese of other regions. In the past six years, however, Xiaofeiyang—a chain enterprise started at the turn of the century with just one outlet in Inner Mongolia—transformed hotpot into a regular repast[15] throughout the country. Today, the chain owns franchises in as far south as Guangdong and Hong Kong—the geographical opposite of the cuisine's origin in China. It has an aggressive plan to expand overseas, with outlets already set up in North America.   10

Another remarkable example is Malan Hand-Pulled Noodles. The company opened its first restaurant in 1993, serving traditional dishes from northwestern China in a fast food setting. By the end of 2002 it had multiplied into 436 outlets nationwide. By 2004, it had expanded outside of China, into Singapore, Western Europe, and California.[16] On the opening day of its first restaurant in the United States, company manager Frank Wang declared that by "inheriting the essence of traditional beef noodles, and maintaining the original taste of Chinese food culture, Malan Noodle achieves further development by applying the modern fast food concept, thus making the national snack flourish."[17]   11

Conclusion

The primary lesson one can learn from the thriving Chinese fast food sector is that globalization is facilitating the spread of cultural diversity, rather than—as the word *globalization* so misleadingly suggests—a tendency towards cultural homogeneity. The opening up of Chinese society cultivated a population curious about outside ideas, values and cultures. A taste for foreign lifestyle, however, is not the same as cultural submission. As the   12

---

[15] **repast:** A meal.
[16] Malan Noodle Corporate Website, "Introduction," <http://www.malan.com.cn/introduce_en.htm>
[17] Malan Noodle Corporate Website, "Grand Opening of Malan Noodle Outlet Restaurant in Monterey Park, USA," <http://www.malan.com.cn/news/73147200312264325_en.htm>

Chinese learned to become "modern," globalization also nurtured a class of outward-looking entrepreneurs who extracted elements of Chinese culture and combined them with modern business management to compete in the global economy.

The arguments presented in this article serve to rectify the misconception of cultural homogenization that underpinned intellectual exchanges in the past. The case of Chinese culinary cultures, however, represents only the tip of the iceberg of China's contribution to global cultural trends. Other areas of Chinese traditions are also experiencing a revival. The production, research and development of Chinese medicine, for example, have been modernized; its practice is gaining wide acceptance in many Western countries. Various types of *qigong*—the Chinese art of self-healing that combines meditation and body movements—are also proliferating. To truly understand the fate of indigenous cultures under globalization, analysts should pay more attention to China as a cultural emitter, rather than simply labeling it a passive follower of a purported global culture. 13

EXERCISING VOCABULARY

1. Record your own definition for each of these words.

   omnipresence (n.) (1)   promulgated (v.) (7)
   indigenous (adj.) (1)   foster (v.) (7)
   paradoxically (adv.) (1)   surged (v.) (7)
   epitomized (v.) (3)   impetus (n.) (8)
   commoditization (n.) (3)   aspiring (adj.) (8)
   catering (n.) (3)   hygiene (n.) (8)
   innovator (n.) (4)   proliferate (v.) (9)
   displace (v.) (4)   franchising (n.) (9)
   reminiscent (adj.) (5)   prototypical (adj.) (9)
   innovate (v.) (5)   propagated (v.) (10)
   nascent (adj.) (5)   flourish (v.) (11)
   entrepeneurs (n.) (5)   extracted (v.) (12)
   inception (n.) (6)   rectify (v.) (13)
   emulating (n.) (6)   emitter (n.) (13)

2. In paragraph 5, Wong writes, "It was against this *backdrop* of foreign competition that the genesis of Chinese fast food occurred." In which context is the word *backdrop* generally used? Then what does the phrase "backdrop of foreign competition" mean?

3. The writer states, "The primary lesson one can learn from the thriving Chinese fast food sector is that globalization is facilitating the spread of cultural diversity, rather than — as the word *globalization* so misleadingly suggests — a tendency towards cultural *homogeneity*" (para. 12). Look up the word *homogeneity*. Which two parts make up this word? What then does homogeneity mean in this context?

PROBING CONTENT

1. What is Café de Coral? What is ironic about its success? What impact did it have on the fast food industry in Hong Kong?

2. What role did Ronghuaji or "Glorious China Chicken" play in the development of the fast food market in mainland China? On which business example was Ronghuaji modeled?

3. In what way are Chinese restaurant franchises important in China and abroad? Name one restaurant that sent its management team to McDonald's for training.

4. What does the globalization of Chinese fast food spread besides exposure to the food itself? How is the Mongolian hotpot an example of this kind of globalization?

CONSIDERING CRAFT

1. This essay, written by a PhD candidate at USC, first appeared in an academic publication called *Greater China.* How is the language used in this essay different from what you might read in a newspaper or magazine?

2. How does the inclusion of endnotes affect your reading experience?

3. How does the use of extended examples of restaurant chains and specific dishes add to the essay?

4. Find two places in the essay where the author quotes other people. How does this writing strategy function in the essay?

WRITING PROMPTS

Responding to the Topic   Visit your local mall. Examine the different fast food establishments in the food court there. How many have been influenced by a foreign cuisine? Note the different items on the menu. Try to interview the people who work there to discover which food items are the most popular. Then write an essay in which you describe the kind of fast food experience one would have at this mall.

Responding to the Writer   To what extent do you agree with the writer's main argument as stated in the conclusion? In your essay, make sure to use specific examples to defend your stance.

Responding to Multiple Viewpoints   How would Michael Pollan ("The Cooking Animal," p. 104) respond to Seanon Wong's essay? How would Pollan feel about Chinese fast food?

For a quiz on this reading, go to bedfordstmartins.com/mirror.

The Only Way to Have a Cow

BILL MCKIBBEN

Bill McKibben, a scholar-in-residence at Middlebury College, Vermont, is an environmentalist and the author of many books including *Earth, Deep Economy,* and *Hope, Human and Wild.* His work has been published in the *New York Times, The Atlantic, Harper's, Orion, Mother Jones,* the *New York Review of Books, Granta, Rolling Stone,* and *Outside.* He is also a board member and contributor to *Grist* magazine. In 2010 the *Boston Globe* called him "probably the nation's leading environmentalist" and *Time* magazine described him as "the world's best green journalist." The following essay, "The Only Way to Have a Cow," appeared in the March/April 2010 issue of *Orion.*

> **THINKING AHEAD** Are you a vegetarian or have you ever thought about giving up meat or other animal products? Why or why not?

May I say—somewhat defensively—that I haven't cooked red meat in many years? That I haven't visited a McDonald's since college? That if you asked me how I like my steak, I'd say I don't really remember? I'm not a moral abstainer—I'll eat meat when poor people in distant places offer it to me, especially when they're proud to do so and I'd be an ass to say no. But in everyday life, for a series of reasons that began with the dietary scruples of the woman I chose to marry, hamburgers just don't come into play.

I begin this way because I plan to wade into one of the most impassioned fracases now underway on the planet—to meat or not to meat—and I want to establish that I Do Not Have A Cow In This Fight. In recent years vegetarians and vegans have upped their attack on the consumption of animal flesh, pointing out not only that it's disgusting (read Jonathan Safran Foer's new book [*Eating Animals*]) but also a major cause of climate change. The numbers range from 18 percent of the world's greenhouse gas emissions to—in one recent study that was quickly discredited—51 percent. Whatever the exact figure, suffice it to say it's high: there's the carbon that comes from cutting down the forest to start the farm, and from the fertilizer and diesel fuel it takes to grow the corn, there's the truck exhaust from shipping cows hither and yon, and most of all the methane[1] that emanates from the cows themselves (95 percent of it from the front end, not the hind, and these millions of feedlot cows would prefer if you used the word *eructate* in place of *belch*). This news has led to an almost endless

---

[1] **methane:** A colorless, odorless gas.

series of statistical calculations: going vegan is 50 percent more effective in reducing greenhouse gas emissions than switching to a hybrid car, according to a University of Chicago study; the UN Food and Agriculture Organization finds that a half pound of ground beef has the same effect on climate change as driving an SUV ten miles. It has led to a lot of political statements: the British health secretary last fall called on Englishmen to cut their beefeating by dropping at least a sausage a week from their diets, and Paul McCartney has declared that "the biggest change anyone could make in their own lifestyle to help the environment would be to become vegetarian." It has even led to the marketing of a men's flip-flop called the Stop Global Warming Toepeeka that's made along entirely vegan lines.

Industrial livestock production is essentially indefensible—ethically, ecologically, and otherwise. We now use an enormous percentage of our arable land to grow corn that we feed to cows who stand in feedlots and eructate until they are slaughtered in a variety of gross ways and lodge in our ever-larger abdomens. And the fact that the product of this exercise "tastes good" sounds pretty lame as an excuse. There are technofixes—engineering the corn feed so it produces less methane, or giving the cows shots so they eructate less violently. But this type of tailpipe fix only works around the edges, and with the planet warming fast that's not enough. We should simply stop eating factory-farmed meat, and the effects on climate change would be but one of the many benefits. 3

Still, even once you've made that commitment, there's a nagging ecological question that's just now being raised. It goes like this: long before humans had figured out the whole cow thing, nature had its own herds of hoofed ungulates.[2] Big herds of big animals—perhaps 60 million bison ranging across North America, and maybe 100 million antelope. That's considerably more than the number of cows now resident in these United States. These were noble creatures, but uncouth—*eructate* hadn't been coined yet. They really did just belch. So why weren't they filling the atmosphere with methane? Why wasn't their manure giving off great quantities of atmosphere-altering gas? 4

The answer, so far as we can tell, is both interesting and potentially radical in its implications. These old-school ungulates weren't all that different in their plumbing—they were methane factories with legs too. But they used those legs for something. They didn't stand still in feedlots waiting for corn, and they didn't stand still in big western federal allotments overgrazing the same tender grass. They didn't stand still at all. Maybe they would have enjoyed stationary life, but like teenagers in a small town, they were continually moved along by their own version of the police: wolves. And big cats. And eventually Indians. By predators. 5

As they moved, they kept eating grass and dropping manure. Or, as soil scientists would put it, they grazed the same perennials once or twice a

[2] **ungulates:** Animals with hooves.

year to "convert aboveground biomass to dung and urine." Then dung beetles buried the results in the soil, nurturing the grass to grow back. These grasslands covered places that don't get much rain—the Southwest and the Plains, Australia, Africa, much of Asia. And all that grass-land sequestered stupendous amounts of carbon and methane from out of the atmosphere—recent preliminary research indicates that methane-loving bacteria in healthy soils will sequester more of the gas in a day than cows supported by the same area will emit in a year.

We're flat out of predators in most parts of the world, and it's hard to 7 imagine, in the short time that we have to deal with climate change, ending the eating of meat and returning the herds of buffalo and packs of wolves to all the necessary spots. It's marginally easier to imagine mimicking those systems with cows. The key technology here is the single-strand electric fence—you move your herd or your flock once or twice a day from one small pasture to the next, forcing them to eat everything that's growing there but moving them along before they graze all the good stuff down to bare ground. Now their manure isn't a problem that fills a cesspool, but a key part of making the system work. Done right, some studies suggest, this method of raising cattle could put much of the atmosphere's oversupply of greenhouse gases back in the soil inside half a century. That means shifting from feedlot farming to rotational grazing is one of the few changes we could make that's on the same scale as the problem of global warming. It won't do away with the need for radically cutting emissions, but it could help get the car exhaust you emitted back in high school out of the atmosphere.

Oh, and grass-fed beef is apparently much better for you—full of Omega 8 3s, like sardines that moo. Better yet, it's going to be more expensive, because you can't automate the process the same way you can feedlot agriculture. You need the guy to move the fence every afternoon. (That's why about a billion of our fellow humans currently make their livings as herders of one kind or another—some of them use slingshots, or dogs, or shepherd's crooks,[3] or horses instead of electric fence, but the principle is the same.) More expensive, in this case, as in many others, is good; we'd end up eating meat the way most of the world does—as a condiment, a flavor, an ingredient, not an entrée.

I doubt McDonald's will be in favor. I doubt Paul McCartney will be 9 in favor. It doesn't get rid of the essential dilemma of killing something and then putting it in your mouth. But it's possible that the atmosphere would be in favor, and that's worth putting down your fork and thinking about.

---

[3] **crooks:** Staffs, hooked at one end, used for herding sheep.

EXERCISING VOCABULARY

1. Record your own definition for each of these words.

   abstainer (n.) (1)
   scruples (n.) (1)
   wade (v.) (2)
   fracases (n.) (2)
   discredited (v.) (2)
   suffice (v.) (2)
   emanates (v.) (2)
   indefensible (adj.) (3)

   arable (adj.) (3)
   uncouth (adj.) (4)
   sequestered (v.) (6)
   stupendous (adj.) (6)
   emit (v.) (6)
   marginally (adv.) (7)
   rotational (adj.) (7)
   condiment (n.) (8)

2. Explain the difference between the eating practices of vegetarians and those of vegans.

3. What is the concept of rotational grazing? What "rotates" in this practice?

PROBING CONTENT

1. Is Bill McKibben a strict vegetarian? Why or why not? What led him to consider not eating red meat?

2. According to the author, what effect do vegetarianism and veganism have on climate change?

3. Historically, what role did predators play? How has that role changed in modern times?

4. According to McKibben, what are the advantages of grass-fed beef over feedlot beef?

CONSIDERING CRAFT

1. The title of this essay is a play on words. What does the phrase "to have a cow" normally mean? What does the phrase mean in this essay?

2. Why does McKibben begin his essay with a series of questions followed by a brief personal anecdote? How effective is this writing strategy for an introduction?

3. The author includes some interesting metaphors and similes in this essay. Reread paragraphs 5 and 9. Find two examples of these figures of speech. Explain how they function in the essay.

4. The writer includes some informal phrases in his essay. Locate two or three. How does their inclusion affect your reading?

WRITING PROMPTS

Responding to the Topic   In an essay, argue for or against a vegetarian or vegan lifestyle. Consider the benefits and disadvantages both to society and to the individual.

Responding to the Writer   In paragraph 8, Bill McKibben imagines a time in the future in which Americans would "end up eating meat the way most of the world does — as a condiment, a flavor, an ingredient, not an entrée." Write an essay in which you examine the likelihood of McKibben's vision ever being realized in the United States. You may wish to conduct interviews with friends and family to support your argument.

Responding to Multiple Viewpoints   How would Seanon Wong ("Noodles vs. Sesame Seed Buns," p. 123), who argues against "cultural homogenization" (para. 13), respond to McKibben's argument against feedlot beef?

For a quiz on this reading, go to bedfordstmartins.com/mirror.

Analyzing the Image

Pooch Café

BY PAUL GILLIGAN

Pooch Café is a nationally syndicated comic strip drawn by Paul Gilligan that chronicles the interaction between a dog and his owner. This strip appeared on September 26, 2010. In it, as in "The Only Way to Have a Cow" by Bill McKibben, the topic of vegetarianism comes to the fore.

- What is the dog's reaction to his owner's explanation of tofu?

- What is unique about the dog's appearance and his vocabulary?

- What is the dog doing in the last frame? Why?

- What does this comic strip have in common with Bill McKibben's essay "The Only Way to Have a Cow," in addition to the broad topic of vegetarianism?

Research this topic with TopLinks at bedfordstmartins.com/toplinks.

Food Traditions: The Thread That Links Generations

BONNY WOLF

Bonny Wolf is a National Public Radio commentator. She contributes monthly food essays to NPR's *Weekend Edition Sunday* and is the editor of *Kitchen Window,* NPR's online food column. Wolf has been a working journalist for over thirty years. She is a reporter, editor, and food critic at multiple newspapers, as well as author of *Talking with My Mouth Full,* a collection of essays and recipes. Wolf was also the speechwriter to Secretaries of Agriculture Mike Epsy and Dan Glickman. Wolf currently lives in Washington, D.C. This essay is a transcript of a radio broadcast that took place on December 3, 2006.

> **THINKING AHEAD** Think about times when food has made you feel especially connected to members of your family or to your friends. What role did food play in these feelings of connectedness? Are there particular foods that evoke these feelings? Why?

Andrea Seabrook, host: Many of us will spend as much time in the kitchen as in the office between now and New Year's—steaming figgy pudding, roasting chestnuts by an open fire. Okay, maybe just microwaving water for hot chocolate. But as we do, we'll tell our children about how our mothers cooked and baked for us. Food is a great connector, as *Weekend Edition* food commentator Bonny Wolf has been hearing from people she's met on her recent book tour.

Bonny Wolf:

It's primal. Foods evoke incredibly strong memories and feelings, and never more so than at the holidays. If your parents served roast goose or Yorkshire pudding at Christmas, you probably will too. Ditto: potato latkes[1] and [brisket][2] for Hanukah. Food imprinting is strong. A woman in Baltimore told me her husband still makes his grandfather's brown bread in tin cans, just like his grandfather did.

Sometimes we repeat family food patterns and don't even know why. In Chicago, Debbie said her friend always cuts one end off a roast before cooking because that's what her mother did. Her mother did it that way because her mother did. So one day she asked her grandmother why she cut the end off and her grandmother replied, because it wouldn't fit in the pan.

---

[1] **potato latkes:** In Jewish cuisine, a pancake, especially one made of grated potato.
[2] **brisket:** A slow roasted beef dish containing vegetables and tomatoes served during Hanukah celebrations.

Food binds families together, keeps generations connected and creates 3
community. And the foods we remember are a big part of our identity. They tell us who we are and where we came from.

Tom grew up in western Pennsylvania with a grandfather who smoked 4
his own sausage and a great-grandmother who was never out of an apron and made pies he still longs for after 50 years. He says nothing makes him feel better than running into someone who shares his memories of blackberry stew with dumplings and string beans with ham.

We cook and eat to connect with family and friends, to mark the sea- 5
sons and celebrate important events. And as we all know, we cook and eat for comfort.

Debbie is a hospice[3] nurse. She once volunteered at a home hospice 6
where cooking family-style meals for patients was central to their care. Families and patients wandered in and out of the kitchen telling stories and offering recipes. Sometimes they cried. Sometimes they laughed.

One patient who had little time left had one request. He couldn't eat 7
but he wanted liver and onions one more time. So they fried up a big pan-full, put it on a plate and set in front of him to see and smell. They even cut up a tiny piece to put on his tongue. Debbie said his smile, as he closed his eyes and savored the smell and taste, is one of her fondest memories, because on a holiday, or any day, food is a simple act of love and connections.

EXERCISING VOCABULARY

1. Record your own definition for each of these words.

   primal (adj.) (1)
   evoke (v.) (1)
   savored (v.) (7)

2. Wolf states, "Food imprinting is strong" (para. 1). What does the word *imprinting* mean when it is used in the context of the animal kingdom? What then is food imprinting?

PROBING CONTENT

1. How are food and family connected? Describe Tom's favorite food memory. Why does Tom sense an immediate connection with those who share certain food memories?

2. What does Debbie do for a living? What is her favorite career memory? Why?

---

[3] **hospice:** Of or related to end-of-life care.

CONSIDERING CRAFT

1. In which ways does this transcript of a radio broadcast differ from a traditional essay? How does experiencing this genre affect you as a reader?

2. In this interview, Wolf gives specific examples of individuals' relationships with food. What effect does this writing strategy have?

WRITING PROMPTS

Responding to the Topic   Interview a friend or family member about his or her food traditions. With the interviewee's permission, record the interview. Then transcribe that interview using "Food Traditions" as a model.

Responding to the Writer   Write an essay in which you describe a particular meal that several generations of your family shared. Make sure to describe in detail the food, the table, the family members and their reaction to the food, the dialogue at the table, and the particular occasion that prompted this meal.

Responding to Multiple Viewpoints   How would Julia Alvarez ("Picky Eater," p. 143) respond to Wolf's claim in "Food Traditions" that those traditions are "the thread that links generations"?

For a quiz on this reading, go to bedfordstmartins.com/mirror.

Rice Culture

JULIE DASH

Julie Dash, born in New York City, is a filmmaker whose 1991 film *Daughters of the Dust* received much acclaim. The film focuses on a family of Gullahs described by Dash as "descendents of African captives that worked the low country and sea islands that stretch out along the coastlines of both South Carolina and Georgia." Dash also worked on a Grammy-nominated music video for Tracy Chapman and wrote and directed a segment for the HBO anthology *Subway Stories,* produced by Rosie Perez and Jonathan Demme. Her essay "Rice Culture" was anthologized in Arlene Voski Avakian's book *Through the Kitchen Window: Women Explore the Intimate Meanings of Food and Cooking* (1998).

> **THINKING AHEAD**   What special food defines your family? How so? Where did the recipe for this dish originate? How long has your family been cooking this recipe? Which family members prepare this dish?

I come from a family of rice eaters, a home where Uncle Ben was never invited to dinner. Uncle Ben's converted rice is not rice—it's "like rice." Kind of like what German *spritzal*[1] is to elbow macaroni and cheese. Kind of like rice in a bag. If my great Aunt Gertie had lived long enough to see rice in a perforated plastic bag being tossed around a pot of boiling water—she would not have lived to the age ninety-nine. Aunt Gertie, the doyenne[2] cook in our family, would have folded her apron in disgust and given up her title. My family is seriously radical about the cooking and serving of rice. We don't do bags floating in water. We don't do converted rice. In my house, Rice-a-Roni is totally unacceptable.

We come from South Carolina, a region where rice has always been an issue. We come from a long line of Geechees. We are the descendants of African captives that worked the low country and sea islands that stretch out along the coastlines of both South Carolina and Georgia. Geechees, or Gullahs as we are called by anthropologists, are rice eaters of the highest order. Some of our older family members, like Aunt Gertie, would have a serving of rice with *every* meal. For breakfast they would eat rice with milk, butter, and sugar; lunch was anything over rice. Dinner could include macaroni and cheese or any other starchy foods, but there would always

1

2

---

[1] *spritzal:* A German noodle dish.
[2] **doyenne:** The senior female member of a group.

be a serving of rice as well. Call it tradition, call it courage, call it what you may, the bottom line is Geechees gotta have it!

Before we were rice eaters we were rice planters and harvesters.   3

For centuries rice was cultivated along Africa's coastal regions, especially in the Senegal-Gambia region. During America's peculiar institution of slavery, that same Senegal-Gambia region of Africa supplied nearly 20 percent of all the slaves imported to South Carolina.   4

In 1685, Captain John Thurbar piloted one of many slave ships from Africa to South Carolina. Stashed among his human cargo was a bag of Golden Madagascar rice seeds. According to historians, Thurbar left a bushel of those seeds with his friend, a Dr. Woodward, when he reached Charleston, South Carolina. In the years that followed, the South Carolinian African captives played a major role in establishing a powerful rice culture in the antebellum South. Their labor and early technological knowledge of cultivating this difficult crop led to a rice aristocracy among southern planters long before cotton was King.   5

Carolina rice became renowned because of its superior quality compared with all other varieties of rice throughout the world.   6

Some 209 years after Captain Thurbar dropped off his cargo on Market Street, Gertrude Prunella Dash was born in Charleston, South Carolina. Born in 1894, Gertrude would become my Aunt Gertie.   7

Gertrude began her early education at Mrs. Saunder's School and the Avery Institute in Charleston. Gertrude believed in careful preparation. She had a love for music which led to studies as far away as New York's Columbia University and the Julliard School of Music. When she returned home, Gertrude Prunella Dash became the supervisor of music for the county of Charleston, for "Colored." She taught music, she married and raised three children, and she cooked. During those cooking, cleaning, toddler years, she became Aunt Gertie. Aunt Gertie was an exacting woman who brought the sensibilities of music and preparedness into her kitchen. She was a great cook. One of her specialties was Red Rice, a spicy dish made with onions, bell peppers, and bacon.   8

Like every other child in her community, Gertrude Prunella Dash learned the basics of rice preparation early. A ritual of scrubbing the grain, boiling, but *never* stirring (you shake the pot), and steaming till each kernel "stood on its own." Gertrude was taught to never, ever, use a colander to steam rice—she learned to do it by measurement. The ratio is—as it's always been—two parts water to one part rice.   9

To grow up a Geechee is to grow up tossed around the school of hard knocks. There was a lot of love in my family; on weekends we would all get together for big family meals. My family loved to eat good food, take photographs, smoke cigarettes with one eye closed, tell wild stories and argue. Everyone could cook, the men, women, and children. It was unheard of not to be able to "throw down" in the kitchen.   10

You never wanted to make any mistakes around my family because they would never let you forget it. I made a mistake when I was about ten.   11

They never let me forget it. *I tried to stir a pot of Red Rice after it had started boiling!* To make matters worse, it happened on a Sunday. As far as Aunt Gertie was concerned, I was "too old for that kind of nonsense." A dozen Geechees, family members, rushed into the kitchen to take a look at me. I was still standing there with a big spoon in my hand. Looking like a fool. Laughing, some of my uncles wanted me to reenact the scene. Why hadn't my mother warned me? It was then I remembered that everyone always laughed at my mother's rice. Now they were laughing at me. I was forgiven because I had been born in New York and my mother had been born in the Piedmont section of South Carolina so that probably had something to do with my recklessness. Learning through humiliation and fear is certainly not the best way to acquire knowledge—but you damn sure never forget it! To this day I cannot put a spoon in a pot of rice that is cooking.

Like so many born of a South Carolina heritage, rice was more than just a staple food for Aunt Gertie. Rice was a way of life. Rice had been in her family for more than three hundred years—it was a science and art form. Aunt Gertie had a vested interest in a boiling pot of rice, and she taught us all that she knew, all that she recollected. 12

Before cooking, Aunt Gertie would wash her rice, really scrub it in a bowl of water until all the water was clear. Sometimes she would change the scrubbing water up to ten times! That's if you want each kernel to absorb her special red sauce! Every kernel of rice was scrubbed to a shiny translucence. When she was a child, they would use the cloudy rice water to starch their clothes. 13

Today as I stand over a bowl of cold water and rice, scrubbing, I feel Aunt Gertie watching me. Checking on me. Perhaps behind her the old souls are watching all of us, checking on the seeds that they have planted. 14

Aunt Gertie's Red Rice

1 cup South Carolina white rice (do not use converted rice)

2 cups water

1 clove garlic

½ cup chopped onions

½ cup chopped bell peppers

1 6-ounce can tomato paste

5 strips bacon (or smoked turkey)

¼ cup vegetable oil

1. Place rice in a large bowl of water and scrub it between your hands. Keep changing water until it is clear of starch. Pour off water.
2. Use a deep, heavy pot with a lid. Cook bacon or, if you prefer, smoked turkey with ¼ cup of vegetable oil in the bottom of the pot.

3. Add onions, peppers, garlic, and cook until they are done.

4. Add tomato paste mixed with 2 cups of water. When sauce begins to boil, add rice. Use a fork to make sure rice is evenly distributed in tomato sauce. Never stir rice once it begins to boil: "Never put a spoon in rice that's cooking." When rice begins to boil, lower the heat.

5. Wrap a wet brown paper bag around the lid of the pot and cover. Slow-cook. "Every grain must stand on its own. Every grain must be red." Slow-cook until rice absorbs all of the sauce. Red Rice tastes even better the next day.

EXERCISING VOCABULARY

1. Record your own definition for each of these words.

   perforated (adj.) (1)
   anthropologists (n.) (2)
   stashed (v.) (5)
   renowned (adj.) (6)
   exacting (adj.) (8)
   sensibilities (n.) (8)

   colander (n.) (9)
   reenact (v.) (11)
   vested (adj.) (12)
   recollected (v.) (12)
   translucence (n.) (13)

2. Dash states emphatically that her family does not cook or eat "converted rice." With what activity is the word *converted* usually associated? What happens to rice that has been converted?

3. In paragraph 5, Dash writes, "the South Carolinian African captives played a major role in establishing a powerful rice culture in the antebellum South." Break the word *antebellum* into its two parts. What does *ante* mean? What does *bellum* mean? Then what does the term *antebellum* mean in Dash's sentence? To what time period does it refer?

4. The author writes that "rice was much more than a staple food for Aunt Gertie" (para. 12). What is a food staple? What kinds of food might be considered staples? How do staples relate to other kinds of food?

PROBING CONTENT

1. Who is Uncle Ben? Why was he never a guest in the author's house?

2. What part of the United States does Dash come from? From which people is she a descendant? What would a typical breakfast, lunch, and dinner be like in her home?

3. Who was Aunt Gertie? What kind of woman was she? What kind of cook was she?

4. What culinary mistake did Dash make when she was a little girl? What were the repercussions of her error?

CONSIDERING CRAFT

1. What is unique about the third paragraph of the essay? How does this paragraph relate to the rest of the essay?

2. Why does the author include historical information in her essay? Why is it important to her topic?

3. In paragraph 10, Dash remarks, "To grow up a Geechee is to grow up tossed around the school of hard knocks." What does this colorful metaphor mean? Give an example from the essay.

4. Find a sentence in the essay that is italicized, and take note of the punctuation mark that ends the sentence. What effect does this italicized sentence have on your reading of the rest of the essay?

WRITING PROMPTS

Responding to the Topic   Do some research on the food culture of an ethnic group other than your own. Then write an essay in which you analyze that culture. Consider answering questions like these: Which foods are staples of this culture? Which foods have particular ceremonial status? What characterizes the eating habits of this ethnic group? How much food is cooked from scratch and how much is bought already prepared? What culinary customs are observed by this group?

Responding to the Writer   Think about why the author included the recipe for Aunt Gertie's Red Rice in her essay. Then select your family's favorite recipe and write an essay that explains its importance to you and other family members. Model your essay on "Rice Culture."

Responding to Multiple Viewpoints   Write an essay in which you discuss the ways food binds together family and/or friends. Use Dash's "Rice Culture," Bonny Wolf's "Food Traditions" (p. 135), and Connie Schultz's "Heat, Tray, Love" (p. 114) as models for your work. Make sure to give examples and to use sensory detail in your essay. You may also wish to use dialogue to enliven your writing.

For a quiz on this reading, go to bedfordstmartins.com/mirror.

Picky Eater

JULIA ALVAREZ

Julia Alvarez was born in New York, spent some of her childhood in the Dominican Republic, and then returned to the United States at the age of ten.
She is a well-known writer of novels, essays, and poetry; she is perhaps
best known for the novels *How the Garcia Girls Lost Their Accents* (1991)
and *In the Time of the Butterflies* (1994). Her nonfiction book *Once Upon
a Quinceañera* (2007) deals in part with her experience of growing up
transplanted in the United States. Alvarez teaches at Middlebury College
in Vermont.

> **THINKING AHEAD** How adventurous an eater are you?
> What kinds of different foods have you eaten? What kinds of food
> have you refused to eat? Why? What are the advantages of trying
> new foods? When you travel, how likely are you to try new dishes?

I met my husband in my late thirties and when we were beginning to date   1
I was surprised by his preoccupation with food. "Can we go out to dinner?" was, I believe, the second or third sentence out of his mouth. That
first date we ate at a local restaurant, or I should say, he ate and talked, and
I talked and picked at my food. "Didn't you like your stir-fry?" he asked
me when the waitress removed my half-eaten meal.

"Sure, it was okay," I said, surprised at this non sequitur.[1] We had been   2
talking about India, where he had recently done volunteer surgery. I hadn't
given the food a thought—except in ordering it. Being a picky eater, my one
criterion for food was: Is it something I might eat? Once it met that standard, then it was okay, nothing to think or talk too much about.

Mostly, if I was eating out, I didn't expect food to taste all that good.   3
This was a carryover from my childhood in a big Dominican family in
which the women prided themselves on the fact that nobody could put a
meal on the table like they could put a meal on a table. You went out for
the special purpose of seeing and being seen by your friends and neighbors, but you never went out to have a good meal. For that, you stayed
home or went over to a relative's house where you could be sure that the
food was going to be prepared correctly—that is, hygienically—and taste
delicious.

Perhaps this bias had to do with the fact that I grew up in the 1950s in   4
a small underdeveloped country where there were very few tourists and,
therefore, few eating establishments that catered to pleasure dining. The

---

[1] **non sequitur:** A statement having little or no relevance to what preceded it.

common *comedores* were no-nonsense, one-room eating places for work-ers, mostly male, who all ate the same "plate of the day" on long tables, with small sinks and towels in a corner for washing their hands, and tooth-picks for cleaning out their teeth when they were done. Little stands on the street sold fried *pastelitos* or *frío-frío* in paper cones or chunks of *raspa-dura* wrapped in palm leaves, treats I was never allowed to taste.

Eating *en la calle* was strictly forbidden in my family. We came home   5
from school at noon for the main dinner meal. On long trips into the inte-rior to visit Papi's family, we carried everything we might need on the way, including water. It was dangerous to eat out: You could get very sick and die from eating foods that had gone bad or been fixed by people who had diseases you could catch. In fact, the minute any of us children com-plained we didn't feel right, the first question asked of our nursemaids was, "Did they eat anything on the street?"

My mother and aunts were extremely careful about food preparation.   6
Had the vegetables been properly peeled and boiled so that no *microbios* were left lodged in the skins? Was the lettuce washed in filtered water? Since electricity, and therefore refrigeration, were not dependable, was the meat fresh or had it been left to lie around? During certain seasons in the Tropics, some kinds of fish carry toxins—so that had to be taken into ac-count as well. Had the milk been pasteurized? Had tarantulas gotten into the sugar or red ants into the cocoa powder? To get a healthy meal on the table seemed to be an enterprise laden with mythic dangers—no wonder a street vendor couldn't be trusted.

In short, I cannot remember ever eating out at a restaurant before com-   7
ing to live in this country. The one exception was La Cremita, the ice cream shop that had recently opened up near the hospital. On Sundays, after we'd accompanied him on his rounds, my father took my sisters and me to La Cremita where we picked out one small scoop apiece of our favorite *he-lado*. "Don't tell your mother," my father would say. I don't know if he was worried that my mother would accuse him of ruining our appetites before the big Sunday afternoon meal at my grandparents' house or if he was afraid she would fuss at him for exposing us to who-knows-what *micro-bios* the owners might have put into those big vats of pistachio or coconut or mango ice cream.

But even when we ate perfectly good, perfectly healthy food at home,   8
my sisters and I were picky eaters. I remember long postmeal scenes, sitting in front of a plate of cold food that I had to finish. One "solution" my mother came up with was a disgusting milk drink, which she called *engrudo,* a name still synonymous in our extended family with my mother's strict-ness. Whatever my sisters and I left on our plates was ground up and put in a mixer with milk. This tall glass of greenish-brown liquid was then placed before us at the table. We were given a deadline: five minutes, ten minutes. (It seemed hours.) At the end of that time if we had not drunk up our *en-grudos,* we were marched off to our rooms to do time until my father came home.

I have to say in my mother's defense that my sisters and I were very 9
skinny and not always healthy. One sister had a heart ailment. Another had
polio as a young child. I myself lost most of my hair at age three from a
mysterious malady. The doctors finally diagnosed it as "stress." (Probably
from having to drink *engrudos*!) My mother worried herself sick (literally,
bad migraines) that her children would not make it through childhood. In
a country where infant mortality was shockingly high, this was not an ir-
rational worry. Of course, most of these young deaths tended to be among
the poor who lacked proper nutrition and medical care. Still, in my father's
own family, only one of his first ten siblings survived into adulthood.

And so childhood meals at home were battlegrounds. And even if you 10
won the dinner battle, refusing to clean your plate or drink your *engrudo*,
you inevitably lost the war. When Papi came home, noneaters got shots.
This is not as sinister as it sounds: The shots, it turns out, were "vitamin
shots," B_{12} and liver, which really were for "our own good." But to this day,
every time I go to the doctor and have to have blood drawn, I feel a vague
sense that I am being punished for not taking better care of myself.

Once we came to this country, the tradition of family meals stopped 11
altogether. We were suddenly too busy to eat together as a family. Break-
fasts were catch-as-catch-can before running down the six or seven blocks
to school. We kept forgetting our lunches, so Mami finally gave up and
doled out[2] lunch money to buy what we wanted. What we wanted was the
"junk food" we had never before been allowed to eat. My sisters and I
started putting on weight. I think we all gained five or ten pounds that
first year. Suddenly I had leg and thigh and arm muscles I could flex! But
what good were they when there were no cousins to show them off to? As
for dinner — now that Papi was working so hard and got home late at
night, we couldn't have this meal together, either. My sisters and I ate earlier, whenever the food was done. When Papi got home he ate alone in the
kitchen, my mother standing by the stove warming up a pot of this or that
for him.

In a few years, when my father's practice was doing better, he started 12
coming home in time to join us for dinner. Actually he had shifted his hours
around so that, instead of staying at the office late at night, he opened at
five-thirty in the morning. This way his patients, many of them Latinos
with jobs in *factorías,* could see the doctor before going to work on the
first shift. Since Papi had to get up at four-thirty, so he could dress, have
breakfast, and drive the half hour or so to Brooklyn, we ate dinner the
minute he got home. As soon as he finished eating, my father would go
upstairs and get ready for bed.

My mother and my sisters and I stayed behind at the table, Mami eat- 13
ing her Hershey bars — she'd pack in two or three a night, but then put
Sweet 'n Low in her *cafecito!* Now that her daughters were in the full,
feisty bloom of adolescent health, she no longer worried over our eating

[2] **doled out:** Distributed.

habits or got insulted if we didn't eat her cooking. She had brought up a maid from the island to do the housework, so she could spend the day helping Papi out at his *oficina*. Lunch was take-out from a little bodega[3] down the street. It was safe to eat out now. This was America. People could be put in jail for fixing your food without a hair net or serving you something rotten that made you sick to your stomach.

The family plan had always been to go back home once the dictatorship had been toppled. But after Trujillo's assassination in 1961, politics on the island remained so unstable that my parents decided to stay "for now." My sisters and I were shipped off to boarding school, where meals again became fraught with performance pressures. We ate at assigned tables, with a teacher, a senior hostess, and six other girls. The point was to practice "conversational skills" while also learning to politely eat the worst food in the world. Everything seemed boiled to bland overdoneness. And the worst part of it was that, as in childhood, we had to eat a little serving of everything, unless we had a medical excuse. My father, who was still as much of a spoiler as back in his La Cremita days, agreed to let me fill in the infirmary form that asked if we had any special allergies or needs. I put down that I was allergic to mayonnaise, brussels sprouts, and most meats. No one, thank God, challenged me.   14

In college, in the height of the sixties, I finally achieved liberation from monitored eating. Students had to be on the meal plan, unless they had special dietary needs. A group of my friends applied to cook their own macrobiotic[4] meals in a college house kitchen, and I joined them. I soon discovered vegetarianism was a picky eater's godsend. You could be fussy *and* highminded. Most meats were on my inedible list already, and mayonnaise was out for macrobiotics, who couldn't eat eggs. As for brussels spouts, they were an establishment vegetable like parsnips or cauliflower, something our parents might eat as an accompaniment to their meat.   15

All through my twenties and thirties as a mostly single woman, my idea of a meal was cheese and crackers or a salad with anything else I had lying around thrown in. I don't think I ever used the oven in my many rentals, except when the heat wasn't working. As for cooking, I could "fix" a meal, i.e., wash lettuce, open a can, or melt cheese on something in a frying pan, but that was about the extent of it. The transformations and alchemy recorded in cookbooks were as mysterious to me as a chemistry lab assignment. Besides, once I got a soufflé or a lasagna out of the oven, what was I supposed to do with it? Eat it all by myself? No, I'd rather take a package of crackers and a hunk of cheese with me in my knapsack to work. For an appetizer, why not a cigarette, and for dessert, some gum?   16

---

[3] **bodega:** Small neighborhood grocery store.
[4] **macrobiotic:** Refers to a dietary regimen that involves eating grains as a staple food supplemented with other foods, such as vegetables and beans, and avoids the use of highly processed or refined foods.

When I had friends over, a meal was never the context. Some other pre-   17
text was—listening to music, reading a new poetry book together, drinking
a cup of coffee or a bottle of wine, munching on some more cheese and
crackers. I'd clear off the dining table, which I had been using as my desk,
to hold this feast of bottles and boxes and packages and ashtrays.

Had I had a family I would no doubt have learned how to cook per-   18
suasive, tasty meals my children would eat. I would have worried about
nutrition. I would have learned to knit the family together with food and
talk. But just for myself, I couldn't be bothered. Cooking took time. Food
cost money. I was too busy running around, earning a living, moving from
job to low-paying job. Sometimes I lived in boarding houses where I didn't
even have access to a kitchen. I grew as thin in my twenties and thirties as
I had been as a child. My mother began to worry again about my eating.
Maybe I had a touch of that anorexia disease American girls were increasingly getting.

"No," I protested, shades of *engrudo* lurking in my head. I preferred to   19
think of myself as a picky eater. But probably all these bad eating habits
and attitudes are "kissing cousins." Eating is dislodged from its nurturing
purpose and becomes a metaphor for some struggle or other. My own experience with food had always been fraught with performance or punishment pressures. No wonder I didn't enjoy it, didn't want to deal with it,
didn't want to cook it or even serve it. (My one waitressing job lasted less
than a week. I kept forgetting what people had ordered and bringing them
the wrong things.)

Of course, there was a way in which my whole apprehensive approach   20
to food fell right in with the American obsession with diets and fear of
food additives and weight gain. As a child I had never heard of diets, except as something that people who were ill were put on. It was true that
women sometimes said they were watching their figure, but it was vain and
rude to stick to a diet when someone had gone to the trouble of putting
some tasty dish on the table before you. The story is still told of my coquettish[5] great-grandmother who was always watching her "little waist."
She would resolve to keep a strict diet—only one meal per day—but then,
approaching the table, she would invariably be tempted by an appetizing
dish. "Well," she'd say, "I'm going to have lunch but I'll skip supper." At
supper, she again couldn't resist what was on the table. "Well," she'd say,
"I'm going to have a little supper, but I'll skip breakfast." By the time she
died in her nineties, she owed hundreds upon hundreds of skipped meals.

And so when at thirty-nine I married a doctor who was very involved   21
with food and food preparation, I seemed to be returning to the scene of
earlier emotional traumas to settle some score or exorcise some demon. A
divorced father with two teenage daughters, my new husband had learned

---

[5] coquettish: Flirty.

to cook out of necessity. Since his boyhood on a farm in Nebraska, he had always been involved in growing food, but the responsibility of being a single parent to two girls had turned him into a chef. Enter: one picky eater.

"What would you like to eat tonight?" my husband would ask me over the phone when he called me at lunch from his office. "I don't know," I'd say. Did I really have to make up my mind now about what I was going to eat in seven or eight hours? 22

With all this food planning and preparation going on around me I started to worry that I was not pulling my share. One night I announced that I thought we should each make dinner every other night. My husband looked worried. The one time I had invited him over to my house for dinner before we were married, I had served him a salad with bottled dressing and a side plate of fried onions and tofu squirted with chili sauce. This is a story my husband likes to tell a lot. I am always aggrieved that he forgets the dinner rolls, which I bought at the Grand Union bakery, something I would normally not do, since I much preferred crackers as "the bread" with my dinner. 23

But he liked doing the nightly cooking, he explained. It was his way to relax after a day at the office. Why not just help him out? I could do the shopping, which he didn't like to do. It turned out that he had to be very specific about what he put on the list or I would get "the wrong thing": baking powder instead of baking soda, margarine instead of butter. "You're so picky!" I would say, not always immediately aware of the irony. One stick of yellow grease was so much like another. 24

I also helped with making dinner, though he gave me so little to do beyond washing the lettuce and keeping him company while he did the rest that I began to suspect he didn't trust me even to help. Finally, we agreed that I would be in charge of making the desserts. For months we had brownies, which were really quite good when I remembered to put the sugar in. 25

Meals, which had been something I did while doing something else, now took up big blocks of time, especially on Sundays, when Bill's parents came over for dinner. First, we had soup, and then when we were done with the soup, several platters made the rounds, and then there was dessert. Then coffee. During all these courses there was much talk about what we were eating and other memorable variations of what was on the table. If you were to take one of those pies statisticians use to show percentages and were to cut out a serving that would represent how much of the time we talked about food, I would say you'd have to cut yourself at least half the pie, and probably a second serving before the night was over. It took so long to eat! 26

True, when I was a young girl, the weekly dinners in my grandparents' house were long, lingering family affairs, but that was true only for the adults. Once we children got through the chore of finishing what was on 27 our plates, we would be excused to go play in the garden while the grown-ups droned on over their everlasting courses and *cafecitos*. (No *engrudos* when we ate at somebody else's house!)

But now I was one of those adults at the table of a family that was obviously bound together, not at the hip, but the belly. Traditionally my husband's people have been farmers, intimately connected with food—growing it, serving it, preserving it, preparing it. As we lingered at the table, I listened, not understanding at first what the fuss was about. What was the difference between a Sungold tomato and a Big Boy? Why was sweet corn better than regular corn? What was the difference between a Yukon Gold and a baking potato? What did it mean when they said raspberries were "setting on"? And how come the second crop was always bigger, juicier? 28

Eventually I realized that if I ate slowly and kept my ears opened, I could learn a lot. I also started to taste the food, instead of swallowing it, and slowly I developed new criteria—not just would I eat it or not. Did the flavors work together? Was the polenta bland or the bread chewy enough? As my own cooking repertoire expanded beyond brownies, I discovered the wonderful pleasure of transforming a pile of ingredients into a recipe that nurtured and sometimes delighted the people I love. It was akin to writing a poem, after all. 29

Now, eight years into sharing our table, my husband and I have developed a fair and equitable cooking arrangement. I am in charge of certain recipes—and not just desserts. I've even learned to cook certain meats for him and his parents, though I still don't eat them. For holidays, when the house is humming with beaters, hissing with steamers, beeping with oven timers, I feel the pulse of happiness whose center is the kitchen. 30

But I admit that years of picky eating don't vanish overnight. I still worry when we go out if there will be anything in the category of things-I-eat. There are still times when I come back from the kitchen and spy my husband and his family gathered at the table, talking away about the difference between this week's crust and last week's crust or how you can get the peak in those whipped potatoes or individual grains in the rice, and I wonder if I belong here. Will I ever stop feeling as if I've wandered into one of those Norman Rockwell scenes of a family sitting around a table laden with platters and pies? But each time I've put down what I had in my hands—my contribution to the feast—and looked around, I've found a place set for me at the table. 31

EXERCISING VOCABULARY

1. Record your own definition for each of these words.

   criterion (n.) (2)   toxins (n.) (6)
   hygienically (adv.) (3)   enterprise (n.) (6)
   bias (n.) (4)   laden (adj.) (6)

fraught (adj.) (14)
spoiler (n.) (14)
inedible (adj.) (15)
mythic (adj.) (6)
synonymous (adj.) (8)
malady (n.) (9)
mortality (n.) (9)
inevitably (adv.) (10)
flex (v.) (11)
feisty (adj.) (13)
toppled (v.) (14)

pretext (n.) (17)
anorexia (n.) (18)
invariably (adv.) (20)
traumas (n.) (21)
exorcise (v.) (21)
aggrieved (adj.) (23)
irony (n.) (24)
droned (v.) (27)
lingered (v.) (28)
akin (adj.) (29)
equitable (adj.) (30)

2. In paragraph 4, Alvarez writes, "Perhaps this bias had to do with the fact that I grew up in the 1950s in a small underdeveloped country where there were very few tourists and, therefore, few eating establishment that *catered* to pleasure dining." What is usually catered? What does the word *catered* mean in this sentence?

3. What is alchemy? How can alchemy be practiced in the kitchen?

4. The author writes, "As my own cooking *repertoire* expanded beyond brownies, I discovered the wonderful pleasure of transforming a pile of ingredients into a recipe that nurtured and sometimes delighted the people I love" (para. 29). What is a repertoire? Who usually has a repertoire? What is a "cooking repertoire"?

PROBING CONTENT

1. Describe the author's childhood meals at home. Why were they like this?

2. During Alvarez's twenties and thirties, what was her relationship with food? What kinds of meals did she eat and serve to her friends?

3. How did Alvarez and her husband divide culinary duties? How well did this work?

4. How did Alvarez's in-laws relate to food? What influence did this eventually have on her?

CONSIDERING CRAFT

1. Alvarez begins her essay with an anecdote about her husband. How does she end her essay? How effective is this framing strategy given the topic of her essay?

2. The author includes the names of several foreign dishes and does not translate many of them. How does this color her essay? How does this affect your reading?

3. In paragraph 29, the author compares cooking to a poem. What is this figure of speech called? What does Alvarez mean by this comparison?

4. Reread the final sentence of the essay. What does Alvarez mean in both a literal and a figurative sense when she says, "I've found a place set for me at the table"?

WRITING PROMPTS

Responding to the Topic　Write an essay in which you describe your childhood meals at home and at school. You may choose to write either an expository essay or a narrative essay in which you include dialogue and description.

Responding to the Writer　In an essay, either defend or argue against the writer's decision to be a "picky eater." Consider the impact of this decision on other people and how refusing to eat certain foods in certain situations could be interpreted as impolite or even insulting.

Responding to Multiple Viewpoints　How would Bonny Wolf ("Food Traditions," p. 135) and Julie Dash ("Rice Culture," p. 138) address Alvarez's approach to cooking and eating? What would Wolf and Dash say about why Alvarez never "learned to knit the family together with food and talk" (para. 18) as they did and what she missed by not doing so?

For a quiz on this reading, go to bedfordstmartins.com/mirror.

Freedom from Want

Norman Rockwell's art for the *Saturday Evening Post* has long been considered a staple of American popular culture. This New England artist rendered the everyday moments that have defined our society, catching our humanity and our frailty in a way that everyone can relate to and few other artists can match. In this iconic 1943 painting, *Freedom from Want,* Rockwell captures a moment familiar to many Americans, the extended family gathered around the table celebrating Thanksgiving. The song lyrics "Over the river and through the woods to Grandmother's house we go" may come to mind as we seem to be invited into this happy gathering by the smiling figures around the table.

- What do you first see when you look at *Freedom from Want*?
- Why is the layout of this painting important?
- What is the significance of the title *Freedom from Want*?
- What is the mood of the people pictured here?
- Why are two of the people looking directly at the viewer?

Research this topic with TopLinks at bedfordstmartins.com/toplinks.

Focusing on Yesterday, Focusing on Today

Rosie's Diner, located in Rockford, Michigan, provides an example of pure Americana. This 1992 photograph of Rosie's, a 1950s-style diner, includes a 1956 Ford Fairlane Victoria. The first recorded diner was actually a horse-drawn wagon from which Walter Scott sold hot food to employees of the *Providence Journal* in Providence, Rhode Island, in 1872. However, what we recognize as traditional diners were once railroad dining cars. When these dining cars were "retired," they were converted into the restaurants known today as diners. These establishments were located near train stations or train tracks and served simple, inexpensive food, often twenty-four hours a day. Customers sat on stools at a counter and sometimes in booths. Diners have become so iconic that they are depicted in famous paintings like Norman Rockwell's *The Runaway* and Dennis Hopper's *Nighthawks,* on television shows like *Happy Days,* and in movies like *Diner.* Once found mostly in the Northeast, diners now abound throughout the United States. The most traditional ones, dating from the 1950s, feature stainless steel and neon exteriors like Rosie's and recall the old rail cars that inspired them. Diners are places where people meet to grab a full breakfast or a burger and fries or where they go to be alone to sip a cup of coffee and eat a slice of apple pie.

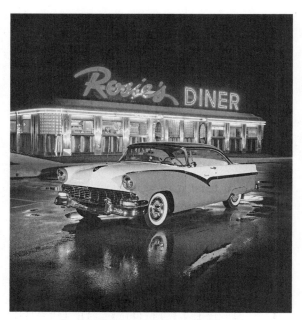

Let's All Meet at Rosie's Diner!

This gourmet lunch truck, Le Paris Creperie, located on First Street in Austin, Texas, has certain affinities with the diners of old. However, it also has its differences. In Austin, as in many American cities, the lunch wagon scene has gone decidedly upscale. This particular lunch truck is an Airstream trailer run by Bobby and Juine Abraham, an engineer and a nurse. The large menu board on the front of the trailer offers sixteen different varieties of crêpes, the thin French pancakes served as main dishes or as desserts, depending on the filling; prices range from $5.00 to $7.00. Benches nestling under trees provide a shady spot to relax while eating. Background music wafts from a stereo system.

- Compare and contrast Le Paris Creperie and Rosie's Diner. Consider appearance, clientele, and the food served.
- How would the eating experience differ at each of these establishments?
- Which diner would you prefer to frequent? Why?

Fine Dining à la Airstream

CONNECTING TO THE CULTURE

1. Food has become an important theme in film, as well as in television. Some examples are *Babette's Feast, Soul Food, Like Water for Chocolate, Chocolat, Ratatouille, Julie and Julia,* and *Eat, Pray, Love.* Pick one film that you admire in which food is a significant factor, and write an analysis of that film. Focus on the importance of food in the movie and the role it plays.

2. Read a short story whose main theme is centered around food. For example, you might choose Truman Capote's "A Christmas Memory" or T. C. Boyle's "Carnal Knowledge." Then write an essay in which you focus on the relationship of the characters to food.

3. Search the Web for examples of paintings or drawings that feature food or eating. You might also visit a museum to find such examples. These might be traditional paintings, like Hopper's *Nighthawks* or Norman's Rockwell's *Freedom from Want,* or less traditional works like those actually created from real food, generally called "food art." Then do some research on the artist. Choose a specific work, and write an analysis of it.

4. Page through magazines, or watch television for an hour. Note the advertisements that feature a food product or eating establishment. As you watch the ads, take notes on the advertising strategies that are used. Then write an ad parody based on one of these print or television ads, or you may write a parody based on your own original food product or restaurant.

5. Read several restaurant reviews in a newspaper or on the Web. Then go to one restaurant about which you have read reviews. Note the location, the service, the menu, the atmosphere, the prices, and the food choices and quality. Write your own review based on your experience at that restaurant.

Analyzing the Image

Examine this contemporary advertisement for Body Mod of Boston, a Massachusetts "piercing, branding, & scarification" parlor. For some, to express oneself today requires more than wardrobe enhancement; it requires body modification.

- Why did the ad designer choose to use the split image?

- What function does the text in this ad serve?

- Why are so many people today exploring fashion trends beyond clothing, like piercing or tattooing?

Research this topic with TopLinks at bedfordstmartins.com/toplinks.

GEARING UP Think about the forces that have shaped the image you project to the world. Make a list of the major influences on your personal style. These might include people you know, television and movie actors, fashion models, makeover shows, advertisements, magazines, Web sites, or even music videos. Then think about specific times during your teen years when you were satisfied or dissatisfied with the way you appeared to others. Why did you feel the way you did? How did these feelings affect you? To what extent do you still feel the effects today?

We are aware of how we look to others from the time we are toddlers. "What a pretty little girl" or "What a big strong boy" echoes in our ears and in our minds. At an early age, we begin to realize that there are very specific feminine and masculine ideals of beauty and behavior. Although these may be somewhat culture-specific, all Americans, regardless of ethnicity, quickly discover that the dominant ideal is represented by young, attractive men or women with toned bodies, winning personalities, and a great sense of style. Think about the Abercrombie & Fitch models frolicking on the beach, the famous faces selling Revlon cosmetics, or the curvaceous Victoria's Secret models lounging in sexy lingerie. Think, too, of the movie stars, television actors, and sports stars you watch and have possibly come to idolize. Do you feel that their good looks and confidence often contribute substantially to their success? Hasn't research shown that attractive people have an edge over those judged less attractive when all other attributes are equal? Is it an accident that the great majority of American presidents have been more than six feet tall and that tall men are more successful than short men in the world of business? Even in the virtual world, it is rare to find overweight avatars.

Most of us never have and never will look like these "beautiful" people. Luckily, for many of us, our appearance does not become a major lifelong obsession. Though we may have grown up playing with Barbie or Ken (in their WASP or ethnic versions), we didn't grow up thinking we had to look like them or like the contestants on *America's Next Top Model* or the star of *The Bachelor.* Even though most people find the teenage years difficult because that is when we begin to discover who we are, we generally grow into fairly confident adults who are comfortable in our own skins. Most of us have decided to make the most of our good features and to downplay or simply live with the less-than-perfect ones.

For some people, however, the search for the perfect look becomes a distracting, even life-threatening, obsession. In an effort to improve the bodies they were born with or to reverse the march of time, men and women alike have succumbed to some form of makeover madness like fad diets and exercise programs, steroids and liposuction, Botox and collagen injections, and extreme body modification and cosmetic surgery. In this chapter, you will read selections by a variety of authors about their own struggles with or reflections on self-image. Some of the essays are humorous, and some are serious. All, however, should make you reflect on not only the image you see in the mirror every morning, but also the image you want others to see. Additionally, these readings should encourage you to reflect on those cultural influences that have helped shape who you are, how you see yourself, and how others see you.

> **COLLABORATING**   In groups of four to six students, discuss the following question: What makes people attractive? Brainstorm a list of ten attributes for men and ten for women. Then study your lists to determine how many of these qualities relate to body image and how many to behavior. Share your observations with the rest of the class.

The "Modern Primitives"

JOHN LEO

This essay by John Leo first appeared in the July 31, 1995, edition of *U.S. News & World Report*. Leo, whose weekly column appeared in *U.S. News & World Report* and 150 newspapers from 1988 to 1995, has also written for the *New York Times* and *Time* magazine and is the author of *Two Steps Ahead of the Thought Police* (1998) and *Incorrect Thoughts: Notes on Our Wayward Culture* (2000). He is now a writer and contributing editor for the Manhattan Institute's *City Journal*. "The 'Modern Primitives'" examines the renewed popularity of body modification.

> **THINKING AHEAD** When you think of body modification like piercing or tattooing, who comes to mind? A friend? A movie star? A musician? A gang member? What image do you have of people with piercings or tattoos? Do you have a piercing or tattoo, or have you considered getting one? What was your motivation? What effect did you want to achieve? What reactions did your piercing or tattoo elicit from other people?

The days when body piercers could draw stares by wearing multiple earrings and a nose stud are long gone. We are now in the late baroque phase[1] of self-penetration. Metal rings and bars hang from eyebrows, noses, nipples, lips, chins, cheeks, navels and (for that coveted neo-Frankenstein[2] look) from the side of the neck. 1

"If it sticks out, pierce it" is the motto, and so they do, with special attention to genitals. Some of the same middle-class folks who decry genital mutilation in Africa are paying to have needles driven through the scrotum, the labia, the clitoris, or the head or the shaft of the penis. Many genital piercings have their own names, such as the ampallang or the Prince Albert. (Don't ask.) 2

And, in most cases, the body heals without damage, though some women who have had their nipples pierced report damage to the breast's milk ducts, and some men who have been Prince Alberted no longer urinate in quite the same way. 3

What is going on here? Well, the mainstreaming-of-deviancy thesis naturally springs to mind. The piercings of nipples and genitals arose in the 4

---

[1] **late baroque phase:** A period of ornate, richly ornamented decoration.
[2] **Frankenstein:** Refers to an unnamed monster created from parts of dead bodies by Dr. Victor Frankenstein in Mary Shelley's 1818 novel *Frankenstein, or The Modern Prometheus.*

homosexual sadomasochistic[3] culture of the West Coast. The Gauntlet, founded in Los Angeles in 1975, mostly to do master and slave piercings, now has three shops around the country that are about as controversial as Elizabeth Arden[4] salons. Rumbling through the biker culture and punk, piercing gradually shed its outlaw image and was mass marketed to the impressionable by music videos, rock stars and models.

The nasty, aggressive edge of piercing is still there, but now it is coated   5 in happy talk (it's just body decoration, like any other) and a New Age[5]-y rationale (we are becoming more centered, reclaiming our bodies in an anti-body culture). Various new pagans, witches and New Agers see piercing as symbolic of unspecified spiritual transformation. One way or another, as Guy Trebay writes in the *Village Voice*, "You will never find anyone on the piercing scene who thinks of what he's doing as pathological."

The yearning to irritate parents and shock the middle class seems to rank   6 high as a motive for getting punctured repeatedly. Some ask for dramatic piercings to enhance sexual pleasure, to seem daring or fashionable, to express rage, or to forge a group identity. Some think of it as an ordeal that serves as a rite of passage, like ritual suspension of Indian males from hooks in their chests.

Piercing is part of the broader "body modification" movement, which   7 includes tattooing, corsetry, branding and scarring by knife. It's a sign of the times that the more bizarre expressions of this movement keep pushing into the mainstream. The current issue of *Spin* magazine features a hair-raising photo of a woman carving little rivers of blood into another woman's back. "Piercing is like toothbrushing now," one of the cutters told *Spin*. "It's why cutting is becoming popular." Slicing someone's back is a violent act. But one of the cutters has a bland justification: People want to be cut "for adorn-ment, or as a test of endurance, or as a sacrifice toward a transformation." Later on we read that "women are reclaiming their bodies from a culture that has commodified starvation and faux sex." One cuttee says: "It creates intimacy. My scars are emotional centers, signs of a life lived."

But most of us achieve intimacy, or at least search for it, without a knife   8 in hand. The truth seems to be that the sadomasochistic instinct is being repo-sitioned to look spiritually high-toned. Many people have found that S&M[6] play "is a way of opening up the body-spirit connection," the high priest of the body modification movement, Fakir Musafar, said in one interview.

Musafar, who has corseted his waist down to nineteen inches and morti-   9 fied his flesh with all kinds of blades, hooks and pins, calls the mostly twen-tyish people in the body modification movement "the modern primitives."

[3] **sadomasochistic:** Relating to the association of sexual pleasure with the inflicting and receiving of pain.
[4] **Elizabeth Arden:** A company that produces beauty products and owns beauty spas.
[5] **New Age:** A spiritual movement that stresses the unity and practice of all belief systems despite their differences.
[6] **S&M:** Sadomasochistic.

This is another side of the movement: the conscious attempt to repudiate Western norms and values by adopting the marks and rings of primitive cultures. In some cases this is expressed by tusks worn in the nose or by stretching and exaggerating holes in the earlobe or nipple.

Not everyone who pierces a nipple or wears a tongue stud is buying   10
into this, but something like a new primitivism seems to be emerging in body modification, as in other areas of American life. It plugs into a wider dissatisfaction with traditional Western rationality, logic and sexual norms, as well as anger at the impact of Western technology on the natural environment and anger at the state of American political and social life.

Two sympathetic analysts say: "Amidst an almost universal feeling of   11
powerlessness to 'change the world,' individuals are changing what they have power over: their own bodies. . . . By giving visible expression to unknown desires and latent obsessions welling up from within, individuals can provoke change."

Probably not. Cultural crisis can't really be dealt with by letting loose   12
our personal obsessions and marking up our bodies. But the rapid spread of this movement is yet another sign that the crisis is here.

EXERCISING VOCABULARY

1. Record your own definition for each of these words.

decry (v.) (2)	commodified (v.) (7)
deviancy (n.) (4)	faux (adj.) (7)
rationale (n.) (5)	mortified (v.) (9)
centered (adj.) (5)	repudiate (v.) (9)
reclaiming (v.) (5)	latent (adj.) (11)
pathological (adj.) (5)	welling (v.) (11)
bland (adj.) (7)	

2. In paragraph 1, Leo speaks of "that coveted neo-Frankenstein look." What does the verb *to covet* mean? What then does the word *coveted* mean? What does the prefix *neo* mean? Describe a neo-Frankenstein look.

3. Paragraph 4 refers to "the mainstreaming-of-deviancy thesis." What does the verb *to mainstream* mean? How can you apply that meaning of *mainstream* to Leo's phrase?

PROBING CONTENT

1. In what cultures or among what groups of people did body piercing first become popular in the United States? What was its significance?

2. Explain the broader movement of which, according to Leo, body piercing is a part.

3. Before Leo explains what he means by the "new primitivism" (para. 10), he offers several other motives for body modification. What are these?

4. How effectively does the writer think body modification deals with "cultural crisis" (para. 12)? Why is this true?

CONSIDERING CRAFT

1. The title is an oxymoron, or a phrase made up of seeming opposites. Explain how people with tattoos or body piercings can be both modern and primitive.

2. Why does Leo mention several other motives for body modification and then dismiss them in favor of the idea that "a new primitivism" (para. 10) is the major motive?

3. What effect do Leo's many graphic examples of body modification have on you? Why does he include them?

4. Describe the writer's attitude toward his subject. What is the tone of this essay? How difficult is the vocabulary? Based on this information, for what audience do you think Leo is writing?

WRITING PROMPTS

Responding to the Topic   You probably know several people who have body piercings or tattoos, and you might have them yourself. What were their or your motives for these body modifications? What images did they or you want to project? Did these body modifications produce the anticipated results?

Responding to the Writer   In paragraph 10, Leo claims that "a new primitivism" "plugs into a wider dissatisfaction with traditional Western rationality, logic and sexual norms, as well as anger at the impact of Western technology on the natural environment and anger at the state of American political and social life." Respond to this statement in an essay. Be sure to provide specific examples.

Responding to Multiple Viewpoints   John Leo quotes "two sympathetic analysts" as saying, "Amidst an almost universal feeling of powerlessness to 'change the world,' individuals are changing what they have power over: their own bodies . . ." (para. 11). Write an essay in which you imagine how Dan Barden ("My New Nose," p. 181) would respond to this quotation.

For a quiz on this reading, go to bedfordstmartins.com/mirror.

My Inner Shrimp

GARRY TRUDEAU

GarryTrudeau's humorous essay "My Inner Shrimp" examines the impact of body image on the fragile self-esteem of a teenager. Trudeau is well known for his comic strip *Doonesbury,* for which he won a Pulitzer Prize in 1975. He has contributed articles to *The New Yorker, The New Republic, Harper's,* the *Washington Post, Time,* and the *New York Times.* "My Inner Shrimp" first appeared in the *New York Times Magazine* on March 31, 1997.

> **THINKING AHEAD**   Describe a time when you were dissatisfied with the way you looked, when your "inner" and "outer" body image were at odds. How did this affect you?

For the rest of my days, I shall be a recovering short person. Even from   1
my lofty perch of something over six feet (as if I don't know within a micron), I have the soul of a shrimp. I feel the pain of the diminutive, irrespective of whether they feel it themselves, because my visit to the planet of the teenage midgets was harrowing, humiliating, and extended. I even perceive my last-minute escape to have been flukish,[1] somehow unearned — as if the Commissioner of Growth Spurts had been an old classmate of my father.

My most recent reminder of all this came the afternoon I went hunt-   2
ing for a new office. I had noticed a building under construction in my neighborhood — a brick warren[2] of duplexes, with wide, westerly-facing windows, promising ideal light for a working studio. When I was ushered into the model unit, my pulse quickened: The soaring, twenty-two-foot living room walls were gloriously aglow with the remains of the day. I bonded immediately.

Almost as an afterthought, I ascended the staircase to inspect the loft,   3
ducking as I entered the bedroom. To my great surprise, I stayed ducked: The room was a little more than six feet in height. While my head technically cleared the ceiling, the effect was excruciatingly oppressive. This certainly wasn't a space I wanted to spend any time in, much less take out a mortgage on.

Puzzled, I wandered down to the sales office and asked if there were   4
any other units to look at. No, replied a resolutely unpleasant receptionist, it was the last one. Besides, they were all exactly alike.

"Are you aware of how low the bedroom ceilings are?" I asked.   5

[1] **flukish:** Accidental; by chance.
[2] **warren:** A mazelike place where one could easily become lost.

She shot me an evil look. "Of course we are," she snapped. "There   6
were some problems with the building codes. The architect knows all about
the ceilings.

"He's not an idiot, you know," she added, perfectly anticipating my next   7
question.

She abruptly turned away, but it was too late. She'd just confirmed that   8
a major New York developer, working with a fully licensed architect, had
knowingly created an entire twelve-story apartment building virtually unin-
habitable by anyone of even average height. It was an exclusive highrise for
shorties.

Once I knew that, of course, I couldn't stay away. For days thereafter,   9
as I walked to work, some perverse, unreasoning force would draw me back
to the building. But it wasn't just the absurdity, the stone silliness of its
design that had me in its grip; it was something far more compelling. Like
some haunted veteran come again to an ancient battlefield, I was revisiting
my perilous past.

When I was fourteen, I was the third-smallest in a high school class of   10
one hundred boys, routinely mistaken for a sixth grader. My first week of
school, I was drafted into a contingent of students ignominiously dubbed
the "Midgets," so grouped by taller boys presumably so they could taunt us
with more perfect efficiency. Inexplicably, some of my fellow Midgets refused to be diminished by the experience, but I retreated into self-pity. I sent
away for a book on how to grow tall, and committed to memory its tips on
overcoming one's genetic destiny—or at least making the most of a regret-
table situation. The book cited historical figures who had gone the latter
route—Alexander the Great, Caesar, Napoleon (the mind involuntarily
added Hitler). Strategies for stretching the limbs were suggested—hanging
from door frames, sleeping on your back, doing assorted floor exercises—all
of which I incorporated into my daily routine (get up, brush teeth, hang
from door frame). I also learned the importance of meeting girls early in the
day, when, the book assured me, my rested spine rendered me perceptibly
taller.

For six years, my condition persisted; I grew, but at nowhere near the   11
rate of my peers. I perceived other problems as ancillary, and loaded up the
stature issue with freight shipped in daily from every corner of my life. Lack
of athletic success, all absence of a social life, the inevitable run-ins with
bullies—all could be attributed to the missing inches. The night I found
myself sobbing in my father's arms was the low point; we both knew it was
one problem he couldn't fix.

Of course what we couldn't have known was that he and my mother   12
already had. They had given me a delayed developmental timetable. In my
seventeenth year, I miraculously shot up six inches, just in time for graduation and a fresh start. I was, in the space of a few months, reborn—and I
made the most of it. Which is to say that thereafter, all of life's disappointments, reversals, and calamities still arrived on schedule—but blissfully free
of subtext.

Once you stop being the butt, of course, any problem recedes, if only   13
to give way to a new one. And yet the impact of being literally looked down
on, of being *made* to feel small, is forever. It teaches you how to stretch,
how to survive the scorn of others for things that are beyond your control.
Not growing forces you to grow up fast.

Sometimes I think I'd like to return to a high-school reunion to sur-   14
prise my classmates. Not that they didn't know me when I finally started
catching up. They did, but I doubt they'd remember. Adolescent hierarchies
have a way of enduring; I'm sure I am still recalled as the Midget I myself
have never really left behind.

Of course, if I'm going to show up, it'll have to be soon. I'm starting to   15
shrink.

EXERCISING VOCABULARY

1. Record your own definition for each of these words.

   diminutive (adj.) (1)   compelling (adj.) (9)
   harrowing (adj.) (1)   contingent (n.) (10)
   ascended (v.) (3)   ignominiously (adv.) (10)
   excruciatingly (adv.) (3)   taunt (v.) (10)
   resolutely (adv.) (4)   ancillary (adj.) (11)
   perverse (adj.) (9)   calamities (n.) (12)

2. In the opening sentence, Trudeau refers to himself as a "recovering short person." What type of person do you usually think of when you hear the word *recovering?* How does the author's word choice prepare you for the subject of this essay?

3. In paragraph 12, Trudeau explains that when he was seventeen, "all of life's disappointments, reversals, and calamities still arrived on schedule — but blissfully free of subtext." What is a subtext? What is the subtext to which the author is referring in this sentence?

4. Trudeau states that "adolescent hierarchies have a way of enduring" (para. 14). What is a hierarchy? Give an example. What does he mean when he refers to adolescent hierarchies? Give some examples from your own experience to explain your response.

PROBING CONTENT

1. What effect did the author's visit to the new apartment building have on him? Why did it affect him this way?

2. What problem did Trudeau have in high school? How did he react to the nickname he was given? How did his reaction differ from that of others with the same problem? How did he attempt to overcome this problem?

3. What happened when Trudeau was seventeen? How did this affect his outlook on life?

4. Has Trudeau completely overcome his high school anxiety? Support your response with material from his essay.

CONSIDERING CRAFT

1. Trudeau is a well-known cartoonist. Describe his tone in this essay. How does he use humor to drive home his argument? Refer to several specific examples, including the title.

2. In paragraph 9, the author describes himself as a "haunted veteran come again to an ancient battlefield, . . . revisiting my perilous past." Examine this comparison. What kind of figure of speech is it? How effective is its use here?

3. Trudeau's use of irony often enhances his writing. In paragraph 10, he writes, "some of my fellow Midgets refused to be diminished by the experience." How is this statement ironic? What effect does he achieve by using irony here?

WRITING PROMPTS

Responding to the Topic   How do you respond to Trudeau's obsession with his "inner shrimp"? Do you empathize with him? If so, why? Or do you think he makes too much of his problem, especially because many will say that he should have grown out of it? In your response, make sure to include any personal experiences that have influenced your thinking.

Responding to the Writer   Trudeau believes that "height matters." Write an essay in which you argue for or against this idea. Include numerous specific examples.

Responding to Multiple Viewpoints   Trudeau ("My Inner Shrimp"), Dan Barden ("My New Nose," p. 181), Alice Walker ("Beauty: When the Other Dancer Is the Self," p. 193), and Grace Suh ("The Eye of the Beholder," p. 187) all write about physical features that made them feel different or "other." To what extent has society in the past decade become more accepting of difference? Consider the role of the media (television, film, newspaper and magazine stories, and the Internet) when forming your response.

For a quiz on this reading, go to bedfordstmartins.com/mirror.

Venus Envy

PATRICIA MCLAUGHLIN

Patricia McLaughlin's column "Ask Patsy" has appeared on TotalWoman.com since its launch in April 2000. Her syndicated style column appears in more than two hundred newspapers nationwide. She has also published feature stories and essays in the *Washington Post, Mirabella, The American Scholar,* the *New York Times Magazine,* and *Rolling Stone.* In this essay, first published in the *Philadelphia Inquirer Magazine* on November 5, 1995, McLaughlin draws candid and often humorous parallels with women's long-standing worries about their looks.

> **THINKING AHEAD** How much does gender influence people's concern with their personal appearance? Which specific things about appearance most concern men? Which things most concern women? Compare the amount of time you think men and women devote to looking their best.

It used to be that what mattered in life was how women looked and what men did—which, to many women and other right-thinking people, didn't seem fair. Now, thanks to the efforts of feminists (and a lot of social and economic factors beyond their control) what women do matters more.

Meanwhile, in a development that's almost enough to make you believe in the Great Seesaw of Being, how men look is also beginning to carry more weight. Men are having plastic surgery to get rid of their love handles[1] and tighten their eye bags and beef up their chins and flatten their bellies and even (major wince) bulk up their penises. They're dyeing their hair to hide the gray. They're buying magazines to find out how to lose those pesky last five pounds.

Naturally, women who always envied the way men never had to suffer to be beautiful think they're making a big mistake. (What next: too-small shoes with vertiginous heels?) But maybe they don't exactly have a choice.

The key to how men feel about how they look, says Michael Pertschuk, who's writing a book about it, is social expectation: What do they think folks expect them to look like? And how far do folks expect them to go to look that way?

You think of anorexia and bulimia as disorders that strike teenage girls, but men get them, too—not many, but "a bit more" than used to, according to Pertschuk, a psychiatrist who sees patients (including men) with eating

---

[1] **love handles:** Excess fat around the waist; also called a spare tire.

disorders. Because eating disorders virtually always start with a "normal" desire to lose weight and look slimmer, the increase among men suggests that men are worrying about their looks more than they used to.

Pertschuk has also worked with the dermatologists and plastic surgeons 6 at the Center for Human Appearance at the University of Pennsylvania to screen candidates for cosmetic surgery, and he says "there are certainly more male plastic surgery patients," which suggests the same thing: "It's become more culturally accepted or expected for men to be concerned about their appearance."

And no wonder, when you look at the media. Stephen Perrine, articles 7 editor at *Men's Health,* a magazine that in the last six years has built a circulation as big as *Esquire*'s and *GQ*'s put together, says the mass media "in the last five to seven years has really changed the way it portrays men." Whether you look at Calvin Klein's[2] underwear ads or that Diet Coke commercial where the girls in the office ogle the shirtless construction hunk, "men are more and more portrayed as sex objects. So they're feeling the way women have for many, many years: 'Oh, that's what's expected of me? That's what I'm supposed to look like?'" And they—some of them, anyway—rush to live up to those expectations.

Which—wouldn't you know?—turns out to be a heck of a lot easier for 8 them than it ever was for women: "It's easier for men to change their bodies," Perrine says, "easier to build muscle, easier to burn fat." Besides, the male physical ideal is more realistic to begin with: A man "who's healthy and works out . . . will look like Ken, but a woman can exercise till she's dead, and she's not going to look like Barbie," Perrine says.

Ken? Is that really what women want? 9

Maybe some women. Me, I get all weak in the knees when I see a guy 10 running a vacuum, or unloading a dishwasher without being asked. Not that Calvin Klein is ever going to advertise his underwear on a cute guy with a nice big electric broom.

But what women want isn't the point. 11

Used to be, Pertschuk says, men who had plastic surgery said they were 12 doing it for their careers: They wouldn't get promoted if they looked old and fat and tired. Now they say the same thing women do: "I want to feel better about myself." In other words, they look at their love handles or eye bags or pot bellies or saggy chins and feel inadequate and ugly and unworthy, just the way women have been feeling all along about their hips, stomachs, thighs, breasts, wrinkles, etc.

That's new: For more men, self-regard has come to hinge not just on 13 what they do, but on what they see in the mirror. And it's easier to change that than the values that make them feel bad about it.

[2] **Calvin Klein:** An American fashion designer known for his classic style.

EXERCISING VOCABULARY

1. Record your own definition for each of these words.

   wince (n.) (2)
   vertiginous (adj.) (3)
   ogle (v.) (7)

2. What does the adjective *pesky* (para. 2) mean? This word sounds like the noun *pest.* What characteristics do pests and pesky things share? In what way could the last five pounds of a diet be pesky?

3. Check your definition for *vertiginous.* Using that definition as a starting point, explain what a person who suffers from vertigo fears. How does the phrase "too-small shoes with vertiginous heels" (para. 3) relate to what McLaughlin is saying here?

PROBING CONTENT

1. According to McLaughlin, what three changes in men's behavior show that they are worrying more about their looks than they used to? How are these changes a reaction to what is happening in our society?

2. Why does McLaughlin say that it is easier for men to conform to a cultural ideal than it is for women? Where do these cultural ideals come from?

3. According to Michael Pertschuk, why did men in the past say they were altering their appearance by such methods as plastic surgery? How have the reasons men give for having plastic surgery changed? What does this change indicate about our culture?

CONSIDERING CRAFT

1. Who is Venus? How does knowing who she is help you understand the deliberate play on words in this essay's title?

2. How do McLaughlin's quotations from Michael Pertschuk and Stephen Perrine help make her point? If she wanted to use other sources, what would she gain by quoting them directly instead of just summing up their opinions?

3. What is the effect of having paragraphs 9 and 11 each be only one sentence long? What makes this strategy successful?

4. In her conclusion, McLaughlin restates her thesis. How does this kind of conclusion benefit the reader? How does it benefit the writer?

WRITING PROMPTS

Responding to the Topic   Based on your personal experience and your knowledge of the opposite sex, to what extent do you believe that men and women agonize about personal appearance and are willing to suffer for it? Write an essay in which you answer these questions.

Responding to the Writer   McLaughlin argues that men are now more concerned than ever before with their appearance. Write an essay in which you agree or disagree with her position. Make sure to provide specific examples.

Responding to Multiple Viewpoints   Write an essay in which you compare the way plastic surgeons are portrayed in McLaughlin's "Venus Envy" and Dan Barden's "My New Nose," (p. 181). Use examples from both texts.

For a quiz on this reading, go to bedfordstmartins.com/mirror.

100% Indian Hair

TANZILA AHMED

Tanzila Ahmed is an activist, writer, and founder of South Asian American Voting Youth, a national nonprofit organization that encourages political participation. Her essays have appeared on the Web sites *Wiretap* and *Pop & Politics,* where "100% Indian Hair" appeared in February 2006. She graduated from the University of Southern California and currently lives in Los Angeles.

> **THINKING AHEAD** Many of the products you use and the fashions you wear originate in other cultures. How much thought have you given to this reality? Reflect on an occasion when you or someone you know has adopted a look borrowed from another culture. What were the reasons for adopting this look? Describe the reactions to this new look.

E very time I drive down La Brea here in L.A., I always do a double take 1 when I cross Pico. There is this huge red sign in front of a store in a strip mall that says, "100% Indian Hair." As a South Asian woman, I find this sign ridiculously strange and wonder just what exactly would happen if I walked into the store. Would they turn me away? Would they kidnap me into the back room for a hair hijacking? Should I start collecting the hair out of my drain and bring it in for some extra money to pay for grad school? What is it about my kind of hair that makes beauty shops so excited about advertising that they have "100% Indian Hair"?

I am reminded of a former African American co-worker of mine every 2 time I think of hair weaves. I remember the first time she told me she was getting hair extensions in her hair, how she was so excited and ecstatically told me, "I'm paying more money for my extensions because it's real human hair!"

I was mortified. "Whose human hair is it?!?!" 3

She thought about it for a minute. "You know, I don't know. I just know 4 it's human hair."

I was seriously grossed out by this thought. I likened it to using old nail 5 clippings and gluing them onto someone else's nail. You see, in the process of getting hair extensions, one gets long strands of hair, sometimes fake, sometimes real. These strands are then placed into people's hair to give the appearance of longer, fuller hair overnight. The hair can be braided in, glued in, sewed in, or clamped in. People pay a lot of money to get this hair placed into their own. But the thing that they don't know is where this human hair comes from.

Why Indian hair? Because our hair is the best. No, for real, that's what the research shows. Indian hair is thicker than European hair and thinner than Chinese hair. Once treated, it is less prone to breaking. The best kind of hair is long and untreated, with all the cuticles[1] in the same direction. It is collected in plaits.[2] Where, oh where, can you find such hair?   6

Well, the Web research shows that plaits of hair in India are cut off for weddings or offered to a god at religious temples. This hair is then collected by "hair factories" that buy it for 15 rupees (25 cents) per gram. This one hair retailer based out of Chennai says, "Indian women donate their hair as an offering to their god as a sign of modesty. It is their understanding that it will be sold by the monks for a substantial sum of money that will be used to finance schools, hospitals and other publicly favored facilities."   7

I have some serious problems believing this. First of all, I don't remember an Indian wedding I've attended or a Bollywood[3] movie I've seen where the hair was cut off the women. Secondly, women in India are ridiculously vain about their hair and will spend hours going through the ritual of soaking their hair in warm coconut oil and shampooing twice. A woman would have to be desperate and really in need of the 15 rupees per gram to cut her hair. Thirdly, supposing that women cut off their hair at the temple as an offering to a god, I'm not so sure that they'd be happy in knowing that their hair is really going around the world to be [woven] into someone's hair for $50 a plait.   8

OK, here comes the speech. The thing that disturbs me about the whole hair trade is the "south corrupts the south" mentality; that is, women of color in the United States are the ones benefiting from the exploitation of women of color in South Asia. How can women consciously get human hair [woven] into their own without knowing where the hair came from? Or that it came from the exploitation of other women of color? It's the same way people of color will go to Wal-Mart to buy their clothes without consciously thinking of the people of color who created the clothes in sweatshops. Where's the solidarity, people?   9

I'm all about looking good and spending the money on making that happen. I'm also totally aware that I have cream of the crop hair that is the envy of all, and whatever I say will be met with, "What do you care? You have 100 percent Indian hair." I also understand that there is a whole culture of getting hair weaves that I am not a part of, and that by telling people not to get hair weaves anymore I am inflicting my cultural values on theirs. I get it. But I do think that, as one woman of color to another woman of color, it is important to know the truth about 100 percent human hair, that this hair was actually alive and had a life before it entered into a weave.   10

As for me, I'm going to start collecting the hair off my pillow and see if I can make some money with my 100 percent Indian hair.   11

---

[1] **cuticles:** The outermost layers of hair shafts that overlap like shingles.
[2] **plaits:** Braids of hair.
[3] **Bollywood:** The name given to Indian film; a combination of Bombay and Hollywood.

EXERCISING VOCABULARY

1. Record your own definition for each of these words.

   ecstatically (adv.) (2)
   mortified (adj.) (3)
   exploitation (n.) (9)

2. What are sweatshops (para. 9)? How does the term *sweatshop* reflect the working conditions within? Who usually works in sweatshops? How much do they get paid? In which areas are sweatshops located?

3. What does the word *solidarity* mean (para. 9)? How does its prefix reflect its meaning? Name some groups of people who feel a sense of solidarity.

4. What does the expression "the cream of the crop" mean (para. 10)? Where did this term originate?

PROBING CONTENT

1. What does Ahmed's coworker say about her new weave? How does the author respond to this comment?

2. What does a hair retailer from Chennai claim about its product? Why does the writer find it difficult to believe these claims?

3. Describe what Ahmed means by "the 'south corrupts the south' mentality" (para. 9). What does she think of this kind of thinking?

4. What does the writer mean when she says that she is "inflicting [her] cultural values" on other people (para. 10)? Which people is she speaking of? How does this make her feel?

CONSIDERING CRAFT

1. Ahmed poses four questions in the first paragraph of her essay. Why does she do this? How does this strategy affect the reader's approach to this essay?

2. Find each appearance of the phrase "100% Indian Hair" in the essay. Describe its effect each time it is used. Why is this placement of the title phrase important?

3. In paragraph 9, Ahmed writes, "OK, here comes the speech." What does she mean by this? How effective is this transition?

4. Describe the writer's tone in the final paragraph of the essay. Why does she adopt this tone? How does it affect your reading?

WRITING PROMPTS

Responding to the Topic   Ahmed asks us to consider the social and political implications of fashion and urges us to think about the real people behind those fashion trends. Write an essay in which you explore a fashion trend that originated in a culture different from your own. Consider questions such as the following: Who inspired this look? Who created it? Why has this fashion trend been so popular? Who wears it? Have there been any controversies surrounding this fashion trend? Why?

Responding to the Writer   In her essay, Ahmed writes that she is aware that she is "inflicting [her] cultural values" on others when she tells them not to get hair weaves (para. 10). Write an essay in which you agree or disagree with her statement. Examine whether fashion reflects cultural values and whether people have the right to tell others how to look. Make sure to cite specific examples in your writing.

Responding to Multiple Viewpoints   How would Grace Suh ("The Eye of the Beholder," p. 187) and John Leo ("The 'Modern Primitives,'" p. 160) respond to Ahmed's social concerns in her essay "100% Indian Hair"? What would they think of "the speech" she gives in paragraph 9 when she speaks of what she terms "the 'south corrupts the south' mentality"?

For a quiz on this reading, go to bedfordstmartins.com/mirror.

Identity in a Virtual World

MICHELLE JANA CHAN

Michelle Jana Chan is a travel writer for the *Financial Times, Condé Nast Traveler,* and the *Daily Telegraph.* She also has her own travel show on the BBC, *Insider Guide,* and she founded a travel publishing company that produces guides for weekend travelers. "Identity in a Virtual World" appeared on CNN.com on June 14, 2007.

> **THINKING AHEAD** Online alter egos are called avatars. Do you have or would you like to have an avatar? Why? What would your avatar look like? Would it be human or nonhuman? What would be its gender, its name, its race, and its age? Why would you make these choices when you create your avatar?

There's more to someone's identity than a Social Security number, passport photo and set of fingerprints, but it's difficult to define exactly what else it is. Is it what the public sees or the inner self? Some would argue that virtual identity is a truer reflection of self than someone's image in the real world. 1

Photographer Robbie Cooper has studied the relationship between gamers' real and online identities, taking photographs of the two images for the book he co-authored, *Alter Ego: Avatars and Their Creators.* Cooper fuses together real portraits and virtual images of dozens of gamers and investigated if people's digital representations in role-playing environments were an echo of their true selves. 2

Cooper says it was initially tough to get people to volunteer for the book, which essentially took the mask off the character. "It was extremely difficult going to chat rooms and trying to persuade people I was really a photographer and doing this project," he explains. "But then I posted Web pages on fan sites associated with certain games, asking people to apply with a picture of themselves and their avatar and I was quite surprised. We were getting fifty e-mails a day." 3

He confesses he doesn't completely understand why some people came forward, especially when they highlighted how much they enjoyed the anonymity of the online world. "It's a bit ironic," Cooper says. "There was a professor who teaches public policy and law at Seoul University in South Korea. In the game world, he plays a little girl and he said he wanted to maintain the illusion, yet he's sitting there posing for my book. My feeling about it is you might create a character and enjoy the anonymity of it at first, but that character then becomes a bigger part of your life." 4

Who's Who?

In a virtual world, online identity is potentially much more flexible than real   5
identity, allowing easily changes in race, class, gender, age, socio-economic
background and even species. It offers freer self-definition, including multiple
identities and shared identity, within worlds lacking behavior guidelines or
prescribed etiquette.

Cooper says, if there was a general trend, the online identities people   6
chose were "less ordinary" than their real selves. "In the virtual world, they
either had more powers or better looks. I tried hard to find someone who
deliberately played a fat avatar and I couldn't find anyone—although apparently they do exist. It does seem like in almost every case, the avatar is
bigger, better, faster, it can fly, it has abilities the person doesn't have in the
real world."

Nick Yee studies immersive virtual reality[1] at Stanford University, Cali-   7
fornia, and says there are measurable trends in character creation. "One of
my studies showed that introverts generally describe their avatars as idealized versions of themselves," Yee says. "Another observation is that in games
where people can gender-bend, men are much more likely to than females."

But Yee concedes there's not necessarily a deep psychological reason for   8
everything. "It could be that it's harder for men to explore different gender
roles in real life. But the most common reasons I hear from men are that
female avatars are treated better in games, that they are more often given
free gifts, and if they are going to stare at a character for twenty hours a
week, they would rather look at a female!"

Blurring the Lines

Studies do suggest virtual environments can be a way of expressing a differ-   9
ent side of personalities or escaping the social constraints of real life. But Yee
says, even though online characters are not bound by rules, they tend to self-
regulate how they look and often mirror human behavior in the real world.

"I've found the more flexibility there is," Yee says, "the more limita-   10
tions come in. Take Second Life.[2] It's a place where you can get away from
your first life, but it ends up looking exactly like suburban America. Second Life bores me because it feels like my backyard."

As Cooper was taking photos for the book *Alter Ego,* co-author Tracy   11
Spaight was conducting interviews of the subjects. Spaight agrees that human characteristics and behavior patterns are present throughout the virtual world. "We bring a lot of ourselves into the game space, the appropriate
norms, what's considered proper and not proper," Spaight says. "I mean, if
you just got up and logged off from the game, if you didn't wave or bow or
say goodbye, that would be rude."

---

[1] **immersive virtual reality:** A hypothetical future technology in which the virtual and real
    worlds will be indistinguishable to the user.
[2] **Second Life:** A popular video game that allows its players to live in an alternate universe.

Yee says he can be scared or sickened by what he sees in the online   12
world. "When we have all the freedom that we could want, what's strange is
how much we insist on being in bodies that we're used to and spend time
doing suburban activities like shopping," he says. "In the virtual world, we
even exaggerate the superficiality of what we're used to, like stereotypical
female anatomies. That's what really fascinates me about these worlds. They
trap us even more."

EXERCISING VOCABULARY

1. Record your own definition for each of these words.

   anonymity (n.) (4)   introverts (n.) (7)
   prescribed (adj.) (5)   concedes (v.) (8)
   etiquette (n.) (5)

2. What does it mean to "gender-bend" (para. 7)? With whom do we associate this term? What is its connotative meaning?

3. In her essay, Chan cites a book entitled *Alter Ego.* What does the term
   mean? Why is the title particularly fitting, given the book's subtitle?

4. In paragraph 11, Chan speaks of appropriate "norms." What is a norm?
   List other words that share the prefix *norm.* Give several examples of
   behavioral norms in the game space.

PROBING CONTENT

1. According to the essay, how can an online identity be more "flexible"
   than real identity? How do avatars usually differ from their real-life
   counterparts? Provide specifics in your response.

2. What effect does the lack of rules have on the virtual world and its inhabitants? Why?

3. According to Chan, why do men often choose female avatars for themselves?

4. Nick Yee states that virtual worlds "trap us even more" (para. 12). More
   than what? In what ways?

CONSIDERING CRAFT

1. In paragraph 2, Chan describes Robbie Cooper's experiment to discover
   whether people's avatars were "an echo of their true selves." How can
   an online identity echo a real one?

2. Chan writes that Cooper said that at first it was difficult to persuade the
   subjects in his experiment to take "the mask off the character" (para. 3).

Why does Chan use the word *mask*? To what kind of a mask is she referring? How effective is her word choice here?

3. In most of her essay, Chan summarizes and quotes from the findings of other people. Why did she make this choice? In what way does this help or hinder her in getting her own ideas across?

4. In paragraph 9, Chan suggests that we are attracted to virtual reality because in it we can evade "the social constraints of real life." What are some of these constraints? Why would we choose to avoid them?

WRITING PROMPTS

Responding to the Topic If you could live in a virtual world, would you? Write an essay in which you detail the advantages and the disadvantages of shedding the life you now lead for a virtual one.

Responding to the Writer Nick Yee argues that the virtual identities that some people adopt "trap" them in identities very similar to their "real-world" ones (para. 12). Write an essay in which you agree or disagree with his opinion. Make sure to cite specific examples from your own experience or that of others.

Responding to Multiple Viewpoints Dan Barden (p. 181), Alice Walker (p. 193), and Garry Trudeau (p. 164) all struggle with personal identity. What kinds of avatars might these authors have created before they came to terms with their personal images? Describe these avatars in detail, including what they might look like and how they might act.

For a quiz on this reading, go to bedfordstmartins.com/mirror.

Analyzing the Image

Me and My Avatar

This "split-screen" photograph is one of three that accompanied Michelle Jana Chan's essay "Identity in a Virtual World." The photo first appeared in *Alter Ego,* a book written by Robbie Cooper and discussed by Chan in her essay. Pictured here are South Korean gamer Choi Seang Rak, professor of law at Seoul University, and his avatar Uroo Ahs.

- Compare the two parts of the photograph. How are they different? How are they similar?

- What surprises you about the avatar that Choi Seang Rak created for himself? What image is he trying to portray through Uroo Ahs?

- How does the layout of the photograph mirror the idea of an alter ego or a split personality? How effective is this visual composition?

- How does seeing this photograph affect your reading? Pay particular attention to paragraph 4 in which Chan discusses Robbie Cooper's impression of Choi Seang Rak and Uroo Ahs.

Research this topic with TopLinks at bedfordstmartins.com/toplinks.

My New Nose

DAN BARDEN

Dan Barden's fiction and essays have appeared in *GQ* (*Gentlemen's Quarterly*), *Details,* and various literary magazines. His first long work, *John Wayne: A Novel,* was published in 1998. He is currently an associate professor at Butler University in Indianapolis, where he teaches creative writing and fiction writing. In "My New Nose," which appeared in *GQ* magazine in May 2002, Barden takes a humorous but candid journey "to the center of his face."

> **THINKING AHEAD** What do you think of men who have cosmetic surgery to improve their looks? How does your response compare to your opinion of women who have cosmetic surgery?

Until several months ago, I had a thuggish nose. It looked like I got hit 1
real hard. Collapsed in the middle, it leaned a lot toward the left. It made people think I was tougher than I was, or aiming to be. Once, in a bar in San Francisco, an old drunk asked me if I'd been a boxer. When I lied and said yes, he told me I must have lost a lot. That's the sort of nose I had.

I got it from a run-in with a surgeon who was supposed to correct a 2
deviated septum, which made my breathing difficult. But the operation was botched, and I came out looking like a prizefighter. That operation — when I was 19 — was the most pain I've ever experienced, hands down. Months later I found that my breathing had only gotten worse.

Eventually, I made peace with my nose. I found that I *liked* looking like 3
a thug. The nose turned me into the kind of Irish Catholic guy who might fit in at the squad room on *NYPD Blue*. Without the nose, I came to think, I might have been just another guy who missed the boat to blandly handsome by about twenty minutes. I believed my nose was my destiny — my dark, Irish, bar-fighting heritage somehow rising to the surface of my face. It didn't matter that I'd never been in a fistfight. The nose was a projection of who I might have been if I weren't, in fact, me. I was almost convinced I *was* the nose. I don't know how many times I've puffed up my chest in front of some fellow who could easily crush me, thereby avoiding a fight. That was the nose talking.

But then a few things happened that I think of as the beginning of the 4
end of the old nose. I married a good woman. I started — brace yourself — wearing loafers. I shaved my goatee. It was at that point that I started to wonder, What if I wanted to pretend to be something other than what I always thought I should be? I watch way too many movies, and I began to worry about the distinction between a character actor and a leading man. Most guys with faces like mine are character actors. What if I wanted to be

a lead? When I say *lead*, I don't mean being out there fighting for the spot-light. I mean leading the way leading men do, almost invisibly. John Wayne used to say that being a lead was less fun than people thought: Everybody else got to show off, and he had to stand there, alone, at the center of it all. Being a lead is like being the straight man—the fellow who stands around and lets everyone else do their shtick.

My old nose was my shtick, a song and dance I did for years. I wanted to drop it all and lead, for once. I wanted to be so out in front of things that I became invisible.   5

So I decided to get a nose job. Rhinoplasty. The big fix. I made an ap-pointment with a cosmetic surgeon, telling him the precise sort of nose I wanted. Neurotically, I explained to him the difference between an "Irish" nose and a "Caucasian" nose. I can't believe I said that. The bottom line was that I didn't want a perfect little Anglican nose, but one that fit my rangy[1] face. I had walked around for twenty years with a sponge of meat above my mouth, but I was terrified of a perfect nose.   6

The surgery went smoothly this time. I had no real pain, just an un-pleasant swollen feeling. As I recovered, I wondered, floating in the Vicodin[2] clouds, whether I had betrayed some cosmic rule by changing my flesh. A friend, talking about his wife's plastic surgery, once told me that our bodies were nothing more than vehicles for our souls. He asked me whether I would live my whole life in the same dented car just because I was born in it. Well, maybe I should. Even if I could, did I have the *right* to try to change myself from a character actor into a lead?   7

It was a week or so before I could see the thing. My doctor snipped at some sutures, removed the splint and told me that my new nose had carti-lage from one of my ears. I kept him talking for a while to postpone the moment of truth. After he removed the cowl, he held up a mirror—just like in the movies—and I was amazed by the absolute straightness of the thing though it was a little bulbous at the end, the way my ancestors would want it. It was, indeed, a leading man's nose.   8

In some ways, the new nose is bigger than the old nose, but this time like the prow of a ship that cuts through the world more neatly. As my nose settled (and I began to breathe through it as well as my doctor promised I would), I noticed something: I stopped looking at the nose, almost as soon as it arrived. It immediately stopped being the focus of my face—it disap-peared as a concern to me. My doctor put it best: "It's not that it's aestheti-cally such a better nose," he said, "but trauma is no longer the first thing someone thinks [of] when they look at your face."   9

Something else happened as I got used to the nose: I could feel my per-sona shifting. It was a little scary. Actually, it felt like I was shifting in the direction of *not* having a persona. This felt weirdly powerful. I was no longer looking at my nose but at the absence of two decades of built-up defenses.   10

[1] **rangy:** With ample room.
[2] **Vicodin:** A pain-killing medication.

Psychologically, my nose had become the emblem for all that held me   11
back, and I had had to deal with it. Some people will tell you that's an inside
job. Years of psychotherapy, spiritual growth—blah, blah, blah. Of course,
they're right, but I believe rhinoplasty can also be a kind of spiritual growth.
It has taught me how to be, or how to begin to be, self-effacing—the man
who can lead and disappear at the same time. Certainly, it has helped me
physically. After I settled into my new nose, I suddenly yearned to get into
shape. I'd been swimming before the operation, but after the surgery it just
kicked in. My stroke became this thing of beauty. Part of the reason I'm
swimming, I'm sure, is vanity—I want a nice body to go with my nice
face—but it's also more mystical than that. I feel like I'm being charmed
back to some state before anything went wrong, before [the] trauma. I'm
starting over, in a way, but no one's looking at my face.

I saw my doctor again recently. He's a great man—both a technician   12
and an artist—and people should write poems about him, the way Yeats
wrote poems about Byzantine[3] goldsmiths. Who has more to say about the
turn of this century than a man who gives people new faces?

When I tried to explain to him the way I feel about my new nose, he   13
talked about a "fixation on structure," how the service he provides is often
to eliminate the structure and therefore the fixation. I would have thought
this a load of crap if it weren't now the story of my life.

In the same conversation, he also reminded me of the nineteenth-   14
century fondness for dueling scars, which I had totally forgotten about.
Once upon a time, when men dueled, it was so fashionable to have saber
scars on your face that some men actually faked them. Maybe that's what
happened to me. I'm just glad I don't need to fake it anymore.

EXERCISING VOCABULARY

1. Record your own definition for each of these words.

   cowl (n.) (8)   emblem (n.) (11)
   bulbous (adj.) (8)   self-effacing (adj.) (11)
   aesthetically (adv.) (9)   fixation (n.) (13)
   persona (n.) (10)

2. What does the idiomatic expression "missed the boat" mean (para. 3)?
   How might the writer have "missed the boat to blandly handsome"
   (para. 3)? How does the word *blandly* qualify the word *handsome* here?

3. In paragraph 4, Barden writes, "Being a lead is like being the straight
   man — the fellow who stands around and lets everyone else do their
   shtick." In what context do you normally hear the terms *lead, straight*

---

[3] **Byzantine:** Relating to the ornate painting and decorative style developed during the Byzantine empire.

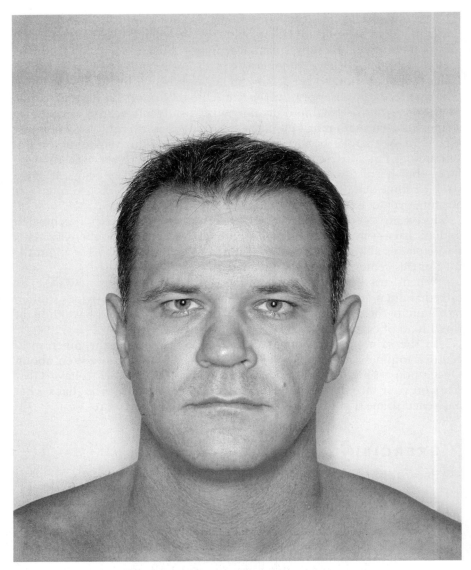

Losing the Trauma: The Author Before and After Surgery

man, and *shtick*? What is a straight man? What is shtick? What do these terms mean as they are used in the essay?

PROBING CONTENT

1. What does Barden mean when he says that "my nose had become the emblem for all that held me back" (para. 11)?

2. How does the author describe what his nose looked like before surgery? What specific words does he use and why?

3. Describe what happened to make Barden consider "the beginning of the end of the old nose" (para. 4). What impact did the old nose have on his self-image?

4. How does the author react to his "new nose" directly after surgery? How does his reaction change later on? Why?

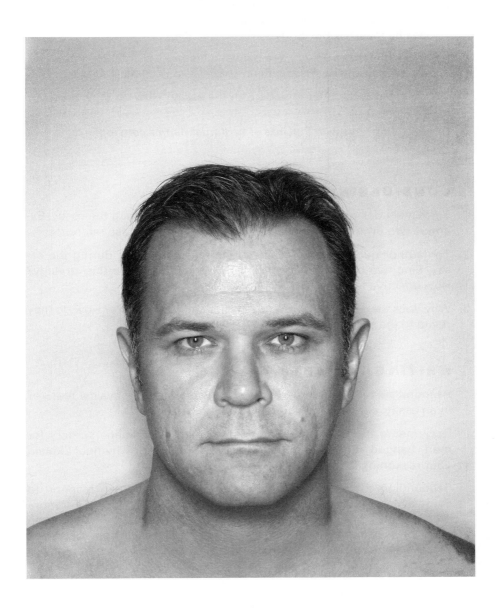

Analyzing the Image

A large picture of the author with a bandaged face takes up most of the first page of Barden's article as it originally appeared in *GQ*. The two photographs shown on pp. 184–85 appeared on the second page of the article and were much smaller than the first image. The caption accompanying these two visuals in the original article reads "Losing the Trauma: The Author Before and After Surgery."

- Where does Barden mention "trauma" in the essay? What exactly does he mean by the term?

- What differences do you see between his *before* and *after* shots? How significant are these differences?

- Why include the photographs with the essay? How do they affect your reading?

Research this topic with TopLinks at bedfordstmartins.com/toplinks.

CONSIDERING CRAFT

1. Barden alludes to actors and acting several times during the essay. Examine two or three examples. Why does he include these references?

2. The author quotes his cosmetic surgeon several times during the essay. Find two or three examples. Why does Barden use this strategy? How effective is it?

3. Why does the essay end with a discussion of dueling scars? How do they relate to the subject of the essay?

WRITING PROMPTS

Responding to the Topic   What is your least favorite physical feature? In an essay, explain why you feel the way you do.

Responding to the Writer   Has your opinion of cosmetic surgery for men changed after reading "My New Nose"? Why or why not? Explain your reasoning in an essay.

Responding to Multiple Viewpoints   How would Barden respond to Patricia McLaughlin's final assertion in "Venus Envy" (p. 168): "For more men, self-regard has come to hinge not just on what they do, but on what they see in the mirror. And it's easier to change that than the values that make them feel bad about it" (para. 13)?

For a quiz on this reading, go to bedfordstmartins.com/mirror.

The Eye of the Beholder

GRACE SUH

Grace Suh is a native of Seoul, Korea, but she was raised in Wisconsin and Chicago. She works as an editor and writing coach in New York City. Her work has appeared in the *New York Times, Smock* magazine, and the *Asian Pacific American Journal.* She has been awarded fellowships by the Overbrook Foundation and the Edward F. Albee Foundation. This essay appears in *Echoes: New Korean American Writings* (2003), edited by Elaine H. Kim and Laura Hyun Yi Kang. By reading Suh's description of her makeover, which first appeared in *A Magazine* in 1992, we become passengers on her journey to selfhood.

> **THINKING AHEAD**   Reflect on a time when you did something solely to fit in with a certain group. What was the outcome? To what extent did your efforts achieve the desired effect?
>
> Paired Selection   Read this selection and the one that follows for two approaches to a similar topic. Then answer the "Drawing Connections" questions on p. 201.

Several summers ago, on one of those endless August evenings when the sun hangs suspended just above the horizon, I made up my mind to become beautiful. 1

It happened as I walked by one of those mirrored glass-clad office towers and caught a glimpse of my reflection out of the corner of my eye. The glass on this particular building was green, which might have accounted for the sickly tone of my complexion, but there was no explaining away the limp, ragged hair; the dark circles under my eyes; the facial blemishes; the shapeless, wrinkled clothes. The overall effect—the whole being greater than the sum of its parts—was one of stark ugliness. 2

I'd come home from college having renounced bourgeois suburban values, like hygiene and grooming. Now, home for the summer, I washed my hair and changed clothes only when I felt like it, and spent most of my time sitting on the lawn eating mini rice cakes and Snickers[1] and reading dogeared[2] back issues of *National Geographic.* 3

But that painfully epiphanous day, standing there on the hot sidewalk, I suddenly understood what my mother had been gently hinting these past months: I was no longer just plain, no longer merely unattractive. No, I had broken the Unsightliness Barrier. I was now UGLY, and aggressively so. 4

[1] **Snickers:** A candy bar.
[2] **dogeared:** With page corners turned down.

And so, in an unusual exertion of will, I resolved to fight back against ⁵
the forces of entropy.[3] I envisioned it as reclamation work, like scything
down a lawn that has grown into meadow, or restoring a damaged fresco.[4]
For the first time in ages, I felt elated and hopeful. I nearly sprinted into the
nearby Neiman Marcus. As I entered the cool, hushed, dimly lit first floor
and saw the gleaming counters lined with vials of magical balm, the priestesses of beauty in their sacred smocks, and the glossy photographic icons of
the goddesses themselves—Paulina, Linda, Cindy, Vendella—in a wild, reckless burst of inspiration I thought to myself, Heck, why just okay? Why not
BEAUTIFUL?

At the Estée Lauder[5] counter, I spied a polished, middle-aged woman ⁶
who I hoped might be less imperious than the aloof amazons at the Chanel
counter.

"Could I help you?" the woman (I thought of her as "Estée") asked. ⁷

"Yes," I blurted. "I look terrible. I need a complete makeover—skin, face, ⁸
everything."

After a wordless scrutiny of my face, she motioned [to] me to sit down ⁹
and began. She cleansed my skin with a bright blue mud masque and clear,
tingling astringent and then applied a film of moisturizer, working extra
amounts into the rough patches. Under the soft pressure of her fingers, I
began to relax. From my perch, I happily took in the dizzying, colorful
swirl of beautiful women and products all around me. I breathed in the bil-
lows of perfume that wafted through the air. I whispered the names of
products under my breath like a healing mantra:[6] cooling eye gel, gentle
exfoliant,[7] nighttime neck area reenergizer, moisture recharging intensifier,
ultra-hydrating complex, emulsifying[8] immunage. I felt immersed in femininity, intoxicated by beauty.

I was flooded with gratitude at the patience and determination with ¹⁰
which Estée toiled away at my face, painting on swaths of lip gloss, blush,
and foundation. She was not working in vain, I vowed, as I sucked in my
cheeks on her command. I would buy all these products. I would use them
every day. I studied her gleaming, polished features—her lacquered nails,
the glittering mosaic of her eyeshadow, the complex red shimmer of her
mouth, her flawless, dewy skin—and tried to imagine myself as impecca-
bly groomed as she.

Estée's voice interrupted my reverie, telling me to blot my lips. I stuck ¹¹
the tissue into my mouth and clamped down, watching myself in the mirror. My skin was a blankly even shade of pale, my cheeks and lips glaringly
bright in contrast. My face had a strange plastic sheen, like a mannequin's.
I grimaced as Estée applied the second lipstick coat: Was this right? Didn't

---

[3] **entropy:** In physics, the tendency of things to move toward disorder.
[4] **fresco:** A painting that is created on wet plaster.
[5] **Estée Lauder:** A manufacturer of expensive cosmetics.
[6] **mantra:** A secret word chanted repeatedly in prayer or incantation.
[7] **exfoliant:** A mixture that causes peeling off in layers.
[8] **emulsifying:** Making a suspension of two liquids that do not mix, such as oil and water.

I look kind of—fake? But she smiled back at me, clearly pleased with her work. I was ashamed of myself: Well, what did I expect? It wasn't like she had anything great to start with.

"Now," she announced, "Time for the biggie—Eyes." 12

"Oh. Well, actually, I want to look good and everything, but, I mean, 13 I'm sure you could tell, I'm not really into a complicated beauty routine." My voice faded into a faint giggle.

"So?" Estée snapped. 14

"Sooo." I tried again, "I've never really used eye makeup, except, you 15 know, for a little mascara sometimes, and I don't really feel comfortable—"

Estée was firm. "Well, the fact is that the eyes are the windows of the 16 face. They're the focal point. An eye routine doesn't have to be complicated, but it's important to emphasize the eyes with some color, or they'll look washed out."

I certainly didn't want that. I leaned back again in my chair and closed 17 my eyes.

Estée explained as she went: "I'm covering your lids with this cham- 18 pagne color. It's a real versatile base, 'cause it goes with almost any other color you put on top of it." I felt the velvety pad of the applicator sweep over my lids in a soothing rhythm.

"Now, being an Oriental, you don't have a lid fold, so I'm going to 19 draw one with this charcoal shadow. Then, I fill in below the line with a lighter charcoal color with a bit of blue in it—frosted midnight—and then above it, on the outsides of your lids, I'm going to apply this plum color. There. Hold on a minute. Okay. Open up."

I stared at the face in the mirror, at my eyes. The drawn-on fold and dark, 20 heavy shadows distorted and reproportioned my whole face. Not one of the features in the mirror was recognizable, not the waxy white skin or the re-drawn crimson lips or the sharp, deep cheekbones, and especially, not the eyes. I felt negated; I had been blotted out and another face drawn in my place. I looked up at Estée, and in that moment I hated her. "I look terrible," I said.

Her back stiffened. "What do you mean?" she demanded. 21

"Hideous. I don't even look human. Look at my eyes. You can't even see 22 me!" My voice was hoarse.

She looked. After a moment, she straightened up again, "Well, I'll admit, 23 the eyeshadow doesn't look great." She began to put away the pencils and brushes. "But at least now you have an eyelid."

I told myself that she was a pathetic, middle-aged woman with a boring 24 job and a meaningless life. I had my whole life before me. All she had was the newest Richard Chamberlain[9] miniseries.

But it didn't matter. The fact of the matter was that she was pretty, and 25 I was not. Her blue eyes were recessed in an intricate pattern of folds and hollows. Mine bulged out.

---

[9] **Richard Chamberlain:** An actor who starred in the television program *Dr. Kildare* in the 1960s and in the television miniseries *Shogun* and *The Thorn Birds* in the 1980s.

I bought the skincare system and the foundation and the blush and the   26
lip liner pencil and the lipstick and the primer and the eyeliner and the eye-
shadows—all four colors. The stuff filled a bag the size of a shoebox. It cost
a lot. Estée handed me my receipt with a flourish, and I told her, "Thank
you."

In the mezzanine[10]-level washroom, I set my bag down on the counter   27
and scrubbed my face with water and slimy pink soap from the dispenser. I
splashed my face with cold water until it felt tight, and dried my raw skin
with brown paper towels that scratched.

As the sun sank into the Chicago skyline, I boarded the Burlington   28
Northern Commuter[11] for home and found a seat in the corner. I set the
shopping bag down beside me, and heaped its gilt boxes and frosted glass
bottles into my lap. Looking out the window, I saw that night had fallen.
Instead of trees and backyard fences I saw my profile—the same reflection,
I realized, that I'd seen hours ago in the side of the green glass office building. I did have eyelids, of course. Just not a fold. I wasn't pretty. But I was
familiar and comforting. I was myself.

The next stop was mine. I arranged the things carefully back in the rec-   29
tangular bag, large bottles of toner and moisturizer first, then the short cylinders of masque and scrub and powder, small bottles of foundation and
primer, the little logs of pencils and lipstick, then the flat boxed compacts of
blush and eyeshadow. The packages fit around each other cleverly, like
pieces in a puzzle. The conductor called out, "Fairview Avenue," and I stood
up. Hurrying down the aisle, I looked back once at the neatly packed bag
on the seat behind me, and jumped out just as the doors were closing shut.

EXERCISING VOCABULARY

1. Record your own definition for each of these words.

   stark (adj.) (2)   scrutiny (n.) (9)
   renounced (v.) (3)   wafted (v.) (9)
   bourgeois (adj.) (3)   reverie (n.) (11)
   icons (n.) (5)   mannequin (n.) (11)
   imperious (adj.) (6)   distorted (v.) (20)
   aloof (adj.) (6)   recessed (v.) (25)

2. What is an epiphany? How is Suh's day of beauty "painfully epiphanous"
   (para. 4)?

3. In paragraph 4, Suh says that she "had broken the Unsightliness Barrier." In the fields of science and engineering, what other barrier can be
   broken? Why does the writer choose this image?

---

[10] **mezzanine:** A low-ceilinged story between two main stories of a building.
[11] **Burlington Northern Commuter:** A commuter train that ran from Chicago to the city's
    northern suburbs.

4. Suh refers to famous models in paragraph 5 as "goddesses" and to their pictures as "icons." How are these two words used in a religious sense? How does that affect your reading of this paragraph?

PROBING CONTENT

1. What causes Suh to get a makeover? What feelings lead her to make this decision?

2. On which facial feature does Estée focus? What is the significance of this? What does it say about Estée's ideas about beauty?

3. What is the writer's reaction to the makeover? Whom does she think she looks like now?

4. What causes Suh to leave the makeup behind her on the commuter train? What does she feel like after she does this?

5. What lesson do you think Suh learns from her experience at Neiman Marcus?

CONSIDERING CRAFT

1. Of what common saying does the title of the essay remind you? How does this saying relate to the general message of the essay?

2. How does Suh's tone or attitude change as she begins to describe the cosmetic counters at Neiman Marcus? Why does it change? Why does Suh call the saleswomen "priestesses of beauty" (para. 5)? What does this indicate about her opinion of them? Of American culture as a whole?

3. Reread paragraphs 9 and 10, in which Suh uses many examples of specialized language, or jargon, from the beauty industry — including "exfoliant," "ultra-hydrating complex," and "emulsifying immunage." What is the effect of Suh's use of such language? Describe in detail how she communicates her "reverie" in these paragraphs.

4. The saleswoman calls Suh "an Oriental" (para. 19). What does Suh achieve by using this word? What is the difference between this term and the currently more culturally acceptable term "Asian American"?

5. Reread the dialogue in paragraphs 12 through 16. What effect does this exchange have on your understanding of the essay's message?

WRITING PROMPTS

Responding to the Topic   Have you or a person you know ever had a makeover or considered having one? Have you ever watched a television show that featured a makeover? Write an essay in which you describe one of these scenarios and its outcome.

Responding to the Writer   As a Korean American, Suh details her struggle to conform to a Western ideal of beauty. Write an essay in which you argue the pros and cons of adopting a mainstream look.

Responding to Multiple Viewpoints   John Leo ("The 'Modern Primitives,'" p. 160) and Dan Barden ("My New Nose," p. 181) present examples of the difficult decisions some people make that affect the ways in which others perceive them. Write an essay in which you examine the reasons people might decide to make significant changes in their appearance or behavior. Explore how these changes might affect the way others perceive them. Use material from these two essays to support your ideas.

For a quiz on this reading, go to bedfordstmartins.com/mirror.

Beauty: When the Other Dancer Is the Self

ALICE WALKER

Alice Walker was born in 1944 in Georgia, the youngest of eight children. She is best known for her novel *The Color Purple* (1982), which in 1983 won both the Pulitzer Prize for Fiction and the National Book Award. In 1985, it was made into a film which was nominated for eleven Academy Awards. In 2005, *The Color Purple* was adapted as a Broadway musical produced by Oprah Winfrey. A prolific and varied writer, Walker has produced eight novels, three collections of short stories, numerous volumes of poetry, and three collections of essays. Her work has been included in many anthologies. In 2002, she published an update of her early work *Langston Hughes, American Poet,* a biography for children. Her most recent novel, *Now Is the Time to Open Your Heart,* was published in 2004, and in 2010 she published a memoir entitled *The Chicken Chronicles.* "Beauty: When the Other Dancer Is the Self" first appeared in her essay collection *In Search of Our Mothers' Gardens: Womanist Prose* (1983). It has become an iconic description of one amazing woman's struggle to accept herself — flaws and all.

THINKING AHEAD Think of a time when you or someone you know — a friend or a fictional character — suffered a disfiguring or debilitating injury. What was the person's response to this injury? How did that response change over time?

Paired Selection Read this selection and the one before it for two approaches to a similar topic. Then answer the "Drawing Connections" questions on p. 201.

It is a bright summer day in 1947. My father, a fat, funny man with beautiful eyes and a subversive wit, is trying to decide which of his eight children he will take with him to the county fair. My mother, of course, will not go. She is knocked out[1] from getting most of us ready: I hold my neck stiff against the pressure of her knuckles as she hastily completes the braiding and then beribboning of my hair. 1

My father is the driver for the rich old white lady up the road. Her name is Miss Mey. She owns all the land for miles around, as well as the house in which we live. All I remember about her is that she once offered 2

---

[1] **knocked out:** Fatigued; tired out; exhausted.

to pay my mother thirty-five cents for cleaning her house, raking up piles of her magnolia leaves, and washing her family's clothes, and that my mother—she of no money, eight children, and a chronic earache—refused it. But I do not think of this in 1947. I am two and a half years old. I want to go everywhere my daddy goes. I am excited at the prospect of riding in a car. Someone has told me fairs are fun. That there is room in the car for only three of us doesn't faze me at all. Whirling happily in my starchy frock, showing off my biscuit-polished[2] patent-leather[3] shoes and lavender socks, tossing my head in a way that makes my ribbons bounce, I stand, hands on hips, before my father. "Take me, Daddy," I say with assurance, "I'm the prettiest!"

Later, it does not surprise me to find myself in Miss Mey's shiny black   3
car, sharing the back seat with the other lucky ones. Does not surprise me that I thoroughly enjoy the fair. At home that night I tell the unlucky ones all I can remember about the merry-go-round,[4] the man who eats live chickens, and the teddy bears, until they say: that's enough, baby Alice. Shut up now, and go to sleep.

It is Easter Sunday, 1950. I am dressed in a green, flocked,[5] scalloped-hem   4
dress (handmade by my adoring sister, Ruth) that has its own smooth satin petticoat and tiny hot-pink roses tucked into each scallop. My shoes, new T-strap patent leather, again highly biscuit-polished. I am six years old and have learned one of the longest Easter speeches to be heard that day, totally unlike the speech I said when I was two: "Easter lilies/pure and white/blossom in/the morning light." When I rise to give my speech I do so on a great wave of love and pride and expectation. People in the church stop rustling their new crinolines.[6] They seem to hold their breath. I can tell they admire my dress, but it is my spirit, bordering on sassiness (womanishness), they secretly applaud.

"That girl's a little *mess*," they whisper to each other, pleased.   5

Naturally I say my speech without stammer or pause, unlike those who   6
stutter, stammer, or, worst of all, forget. This is before the word "beautiful" exists in people's vocabulary, but "Oh, isn't she the *cutest* thing!" frequently floats my way. "And got so much sense!" they gratefully add . . . for which thoughtful addition I thank them to this day.

It was great fun being cute. But then, one day, it ended.   7

I am eight years old and a tomboy.[7] I have a cowboy hat, cowboy boots,   8
checkered shirt and pants, all red. My playmates are my brothers, two and

---

[2] **biscuit-polished:** Greased with a biscuit and made shiny.
[3] **patent-leather:** Leather with a hard, shiny surface.
[4] **merry-go-round:** An amusement park ride featuring brightly colored animals to sit on; a carousel.
[5] **flocked:** Having a raised velvety pattern.
[6] **crinolines:** Stiff petticoats designed to make a skirt stand out.
[7] **tomboy:** A young girl who enjoys vigorous activities traditionally associated with males.

four years older than I. Their colors are black and green, the only difference in the way we are dressed. On Saturday nights we all go to the picture show, even my mother; Westerns are her favorite kind of movie. Back home, "on the ranch," we pretend we are Tom Mix,[8] Hopalong Cassidy,[9] Lash LaRue[10] (we've even named one of our dogs Lash LaRue); we chase each other for hours rustling cattle, being outlaws, delivering damsels from distress. Then my parents decide to buy my brothers guns. These are not "real" guns. They shoot "BBs," copper pellets my brothers say will kill birds. Because I am a girl, I do not get a gun. Instantly I am relegated to the position of Indian. Now there appears a great distance between us. They shoot and shoot at everything with their new guns. I try to keep up with my bow and arrows.

One day while I am standing on top of our makeshift "garage"—pieces of tin nailed across some poles—holding my bow and arrow and looking out toward the fields, I feel an incredible blow in my right eye. I look down just in time to see my brother lower his gun.   9

Both brothers rush to my side. My eye stings, and I cover it with my hand. "If you tell," they say, "we will get a whipping. You don't want that to happen, do you?" I do not. "Here is a piece of wire," says the older brother, picking it up from the roof; "say you stepped on one end of it and the other flew up and hit you." The pain is beginning to start. "Yes," I say. "Yes, I will say that is what happened." If I do not say this is what happened, I know my brothers will find ways to make me wish I had. But now I will say anything that gets me to my mother.   10

Confronted by our parents we stick to the lie agreed upon. They place me on a bench on the porch and I close my left eye while they examine the right. There is a tree growing from underneath the porch that climbs past the railing to the roof. It is the last thing my right eye sees. I watch as its trunk, its branches, and then its leaves are blotted out by the rising blood.   11

I am in shock. First there is intense fever, which my father tries to break using lily leaves bound around my head. Then there are chills: my mother tries to get me to eat soup. Eventually, I do not know how, my parents learn what has happened. A week after the "accident" they take me to see a doctor. "Why did you wait so long to come?" he asks, looking into my eye and shaking his head. "Eyes are sympathetic," he says. "If one is blind, the other will likely become blind too."   12

This comment of the doctor's terrifies me. But it is really how I look that bothers me most. Where the BB pellet struck there is a glob of whitish scar tissue, a hideous cataract, on my eye. Now when I stare at people—a favorite pastime, up to now—they will stare back. Not at the "cute" little girl, but at her scar. For six years I do not stare at anyone, because I do not raise my head.   13

---

[8] **Tom Mix:** An actor in 1930s Western films.
[9] **Hopalong Cassidy:** An actor in Western films and television series from the 1930s through the 1950s.
[10] **Lash LaRue:** An actor in Western films in the 1940s, known as the King of the Bullwhip.

Years later, in the throes[11] of a mid-life crisis, I ask my mother and sister   14
whether I changed after the "accident." "No," they say, puzzled. "What do
you mean?"

What do I mean?   15

I am eight, and, for the first time, doing poorly in school, where I have   16
been something of a whiz since I was four. We have just moved to the place
where the "accident" occurred. We do not know any of the people around
us because this is a different county. The only time I see the friends I knew
is when we go back to our old church. The new school is the former state
penitentiary. It is a large stone building, cold and drafty, crammed to over-
flowing with boisterous, ill-disciplined children. On the third floor there is
a huge circular imprint of some partition that has been torn out.

"What used to be here?" I ask a sullen girl next to me on our way past   17
it to lunch.

"The electric chair," says she.   18

At night I have nightmares about the electric chair, and about all the   19
people reputedly "fried" in it. I am afraid of the school, where all the students seem to be budding criminals.

"What's the matter with your eye?" they ask, critically.   20

When I don't answer (I cannot decide whether it was an "accident" or   21
not), they shove me, insist on a fight.

My brother, the one who created the story about the wire, comes to my   22
rescue. But then brags so much about "protecting" me, I become sick.

After months of torture at the school, my parents decide to send me   23
back to our old community, to my old school. I live with my grandparents
and the teacher they board. But there is no room for Phoebe, my cat. By the
time my grandparents decide there *is* room, and I ask for my cat, she cannot be found. Miss Yarborough, the boarding teacher, takes me under her
wing, and begins to teach me to play the piano. But soon she marries an
African—a "prince," she says—and is whisked away to his continent.

At my old school there is at least one teacher who loves me. She is the   24
teacher who "knew me before I was born" and bought my first baby
clothes. It is she who makes life bearable. It is her presence that finally
helps me turn on the one child at the school who continually calls me "one-
eyed bitch." One day I simply grab him by his coat and beat him until I am
satisfied. It is my teacher who tells me my mother is ill.

My mother is lying in bed in the middle of the day, something I have never   25
seen. She is in too much pain to speak. She has an abscess in her ear. I stand
looking down on her, knowing that if she dies, I cannot live. She is being
treated with warm oils and hot bricks held against her cheek. Finally a doctor comes. But I must go back to my grandparents' house. The weeks pass
but I am hardly aware of it. All I know is that my mother might die, my

---

[11] **throes:** Difficult or painful struggles.

father is not so jolly, my brothers still have their guns, and I am the one sent away from home.

"You did not change," they say.   26

Did I imagine the anguish of never looking up?   27

I am twelve. When relatives come to visit I hide in my room. My cousin   28
Brenda, just my age, whose father works in the post office and whose mother is a nurse, comes to find me. "Hello," she says. And then she asks, looking at my recent school picture, which I did not want taken, and on which the "glob," as I think of it, is clearly visible, "You still can't see out of that eye?"

"No," I say, and flop back on the bed over my book.   29

That night, as I do almost every night, I abuse my eye. I rant and rave   30
at it, in front of the mirror. I plead with it to clear up before morning. I tell it I hate and despise it. I do not pray for sight. I pray for beauty.

"You did not change," they say.   31

I am fourteen and baby-sitting for my brother Bill, who lives in Boston. He   32
is my favorite brother and there is a strong bond between us. Understanding my feelings of shame and ugliness he and his wife take me to a local hospital, where the "glob" is removed by a doctor named O. Henry. There is still a small bluish crater where the scar tissue was, but the ugly white stuff is gone. Almost immediately I become a different person from the girl who does not raise her head. Or so I think. Now that I've raised my head I win the boyfriend of my dreams. Now that I've raised my head I have plenty of friends. Now that I've raised my head classwork comes from my lips as faultlessly as Easter speeches did, and I leave high school as valedictorian,[12] most popular student, and *queen,* hardly believing my luck. Ironically, the girl who was voted most beautiful in our class (and was) was later shot twice through the chest by a male companion, using a "real" gun, while she was pregnant. But that's another story in itself. Or is it?

"You did not change," they say.   33

It is now thirty years since the "accident." A beautiful journalist comes to   34
visit and to interview me. She is going to write a cover story for her magazine that focuses on my latest book. "Decide how you want to look on the cover," she says. "Glamorous, or whatever."

Never mind "glamorous," it is the "whatever" that I hear. Suddenly all   35
I can think of is whether I will get enough sleep the night before the photography session: if I don't, my eye will be tired and wander, as blind eyes will.

At night in bed with my lover I think up reasons why I should not ap-   36
pear on the cover of a magazine. "My meanest critics will say I've sold out," I say. "My family will not realize I write scandalous books."

---

[12] **valedictorian:** The student who has the highest rank in his or her class and delivers the graduation speech.

"But what's the real reason you don't want to do this?" he asks.   37

"Because in all probability," I say in a rush, "my eye won't be straight."   38

"It will be straight enough," he says. Then, "Besides, I thought you'd   39
made your peace with that."

And I suddenly remember that I have.   40

I remember: 41

I am talking to my brother Jimmy, asking if he remembers anything   42
unusual about the day I was shot. He does not know I consider that day
the last time my father, with his sweet home remedy of cool lily leaves,
chose me, and that I suffered and raged inside because of this. "Well," he
says, "all I remember is standing by the side of the highway with Daddy,
trying to flag down[13] a car. A white man stopped, but when Daddy said he
needed somebody to take his little girl to the doctor, he drove off."

I remember: 43

I am in the desert for the first time. I fall totally in love with it. I am so   44
overwhelmed by its beauty, I confront for the first time, consciously, the
meaning of the doctor's words years ago: "Eyes are sympathetic. If one is
blind, the other will likely become blind too." I realize I have dashed about
the world madly, looking at this, looking at that, storing up images against
the fading of the light. *But I might have missed seeing the desert!* The
shock of that possibility—and gratitude for over twenty-five years of
sight—sends me literally to my knees. Poem after poem comes—which is
perhaps how poets pray.

On Sight

I am so thankful I have seen
The Desert
And the creatures in the desert
And the desert Itself.

The desert has its own moon
Which I have seen
With my own eye.
There is no flag on it.
Trees of the desert have arms
All of which are always up
That is because the moon is up
The sun is up
Also the sky
The stars
Clouds
None with flags.

[13] **flag down:** To signal to stop.

If there *were* flags, I doubt
the trees would point.
Would you?

But mostly, I remember this: 45

I am twenty-seven, and my baby daughter is almost three. Since her   46
birth I have worried about her discovery that her mother's eyes are different from other people's. Will she be embarrassed? I think. What will she
say? Every day she watches a television program called *Big Blue Marble*. It
begins with a picture of the earth as it appears from the moon. It is bluish,
a little battered-looking, but full of light, with whitish clouds swirling
around it. Every time I see it I weep with love, as if it is a picture of Grandma's house. One day when I am putting Rebecca down for her nap, she
suddenly focuses on my eye. Something inside me cringes, gets ready to try
to protect myself. All children are cruel about physical differences, I know
from experience, and that they don't always mean to be is another matter.
I assume Rebecca will be the same.

But no-o-o-o. She studies my face intently as we stand, her inside and   47
me outside her crib. She even holds my face maternally between her dim-
pled little hands. Then, looking every bit as serious and lawyerlike as her
father, she says, as if it may just possibly have slipped my attention:
"Mommy, there's a *world* in your eye." (As in, "Don't be alarmed, or do anything crazy.") And then, gently, but with great interest: "Mommy, where
did you *get* that world in your eye?"

For the most part, the pain left then. (So what, if my brothers grew up   48
to buy even more powerful pellet guns for their sons and to carry real guns
themselves. So what, if a young "Morehouse man"[14] once nearly fell off the
steps of Trevor Arnett Library because he thought my eyes were blue.) Crying and laughing I ran to the bathroom, while Rebecca mumbled and sang
herself off to sleep. Yes indeed, I realized, looking into the mirror. There
was a world in my eye. And I saw that it was possible to love it: that in fact,
for all it had taught me of shame and anger and inner vision, I *did* love it.
Even to see it drifting out of orbit in boredom, or rolling up out of fatigue,
not to mention floating back at attention in excitement (bearing witness, a
friend has called it), deeply suitable to my personality, and even characteristic
of me.

That night I dream I am dancing to Stevie Wonder's[15] song "Always"   49
(the name of the song is really "As," but I hear it as "Always"). As I dance,
whirling and joyous, happier than I've ever been in my life, another bright-
faced dancer joins me. We dance and kiss each other and hold each other

---

[14] **Morehouse man:** A student at Morehouse College, Atlanta, Georgia, the only all-male,
historically black institution of higher learning in the United States.
[15] **Stevie Wonder:** An African American singer, pianist, and songwriter who is blind.

through the night. The other dancer has obviously come through all right, as I have done. She is beautiful, whole and free. And she is also me.

EXERCISING VOCABULARY

1. Record your own definition for each of these words.

   faze (v.) (2)   penitentiary (n.) (16)
   sassiness (n.) (4)   sullen (adj.) (17)
   relegated (v.) (8)   crater (n.) (32)
   makeshift (adj.) (9)   scandalous (adj.) (36)
   cataract (n.) (13)   dashed (v.) (44)

2. In paragraphs 12 and 44, Walker quotes her doctor as saying, "Eyes are sympathetic. If one is blind, the other will likely become blind too." In what other context do we generally use the word *sympathetic?* What does it mean?

3. Walker writes that "Miss Yarborough, the boarding teacher, takes me under her wing" (para. 23). What does it mean to offer someone board? What is the situation of the boarding teacher? What does it mean to take someone under one's wing? Where does this image originate?

PROBING CONTENT

1. What happens that causes Walker to stop being "cute" (para. 7)? What role do her brothers play in this incident?

2. Describe the author before the "accident." What are her outstanding characteristics? How does she relate to those around her?

3. Describe Walker after the accident. How does she change both physically and psychologically?

4. When does Walker begin to regain her confidence? What role does her brother Bill play in this?

5. In paragraph 47, Rebecca says, "Mommy, there's a *world* in your eye." What does the child mean? Where does Rebecca get this idea? How does the child's reaction affect her mother?

CONSIDERING CRAFT

1. What is the significance of the title? Why does Walker choose a dance metaphor?

2. Why does Walker insert the poem "On Sight" within her essay (para. 44)? How does this affect your reading?

3. Why does the author repeat certain phrases throughout the essay? Find two or three examples and discuss their use in the essay.

4. Examine several examples of achronological order in Walker's essay. Why do you think she chooses to present her narrative in this manner?

WRITING PROMPTS

Responding to the Topic   Think about people with a physical disability whom you have known personally or have seen on television or in the movies. Write an essay in which you describe how they dealt with their condition and your reaction to them.

Responding to the Writer   Walker's essay details her struggle to come to terms with her physical difference and to finally see herself as beautiful. Children and their reactions to her eye play a significant role in her struggle with self-image. Write an essay in which you argue that children play either a primarily positive or a primarily negative role in the formation of others' perceptions of themselves.

Responding to Multiple Viewpoints   Both Walker and Dan Barden ("My New Nose," p. 181) detail the epiphanies they experienced concerning their self-image in their essays. Compare their experiences. How are they similar? How are they different?

For a quiz on this reading, go to bedfordstmartins.com/mirror.

DRAWING CONNECTIONS: PAIRED SELECTIONS

1. How does the saying "Beauty is in the eye of the beholder" apply to Grace Suh's "The Eye of the Beholder" (p. 187) and Walker's "Beauty: When the Other Dancer Is the Self"? Write an essay in which you answer this question by using examples from both essays.

2. In the final paragraph of her essay, Walker describes the dancer as "beautiful, whole and free" and adds that "she is also me." How do the adjectives Walker uses to describe her new self-image apply to Grace Suh in "The Eye of the Beholder"?

3. In both Walker's and Grace Suh's essays, a woman's eye plays a central role. Consider the lessons that both Walker and Suh learned about themselves and about others. Also explore the importance of societal and cultural pressures on both women's struggle to become comfortable with their personal images.

An Open Letter to the Totally Impractical Size Chart for Women's Clothing

CLAIRE SUDDATH

Claire Suddath graduated from Vanderbilt University in 2004 and spent three years writing for the alternative weekly *Nashville Scene* after graduation. She attended Columbia University's Graduate School of Journalism and is currently a writer for *Time* magazine, where she discusses music, pop culture, and social media. This essay originally appeared in the *McSweeney's* column "Open Letters to People or Entities Who are Unlikely to Respond" in 2005.

> **THINKING AHEAD**   What do you find frustrating about buying clothing? How much attention do you pay to sizes? Do you try things on at the store or wait until you're at home? Do you buy clothing online? Why or why not?

AN OPEN LETTER TO THE TOTALLY IMPRACTICAL SIZE CHART FOR WOMEN'S CLOTHING.

1

May 26, 2005

Dear Totally Impractical Size Chart for Women's Clothing,

2

I've been dealing with you for nearly 12 years, since that summer in junior high when I skyrocketed to atmospheric heights, head and shoulders above my classmates, and the clothing in the kids' section of the department store no longer fit my long legs and gangly arms. My mother took me to your side of the store, and, for a moment, I felt mature, womanly, the kind of mystical feminine that one only sees in movies. I was one step closer to being an adult. I was happy. And then I tried on your clothes.

3

Everything I tried on I had to try on in threes. For years, I've been carting trilogies of skirts and pants into the dressing room, armfuls at a time, because I have no idea what size I wear. I can make an approximation, but that "size" ranges between three of your numbers, depending on the store, because these sizes don't actually mean anything. I'm an 8, but an 8 of what? Inches? Feet? Joules, the numeric value describing the relation between heat and mechanical work that I used in my high-school physics class and then never again? Is that it?

4

Why can't you just use inches, like the male size chart? Why is that too hard? Do you think women will feel paranoid if we suddenly go from single- to double-digit numbers? We already have to convert in our heads whenever we buy clothes that come from any other country except America.

You have wasted hours of my life, Totally Impractical Size Chart for Women's Clothing. Women spend days each year standing in dressing rooms, one hand on the mirror, the other tugging on a pair of jeans, trying to force them up because, damn it, the label says they're their size. And don't think that women are the only ones hassled. Men spend a good amount of time dealing with your repercussions, too. If we have to buy a pair of pants that are a size larger than what we normally wear, you can bet we're going to go home cranky. When the men watch television with us that evening, we will notice them staring a little too longingly at Courtney Cox or Jessica Alba, and we will pick a fight. "You think she's pretty?" we will say. "Yeah," the men will reply. "Is she prettier than me?" The men will take a split second too long to respond, and we will say, "Oh! I see how it is!" When the men finally get the words out, when they finally say, "No, honey. You're pretty, too. And besides, Jessica Alba looks nothing like you," we will interpret that to mean "because you're a fat cow," and then we will cry.

See the pain and suffering you have caused? If only you were a sensible size chart, one using inches, or even centimeters, the world would be a better place. Women wouldn't have to carry pant triplets into the dressing rooms, and couples wouldn't fight over Jessica Alba on television. We could direct our attention to more important things, like world peace. But because of you, we still have war and violence. I hope you're happy.

Claire Suddath
Nashville, Tennessee

EXERCISING VOCABULARY

1. Record your own definition for each of these words.

   gangly (adj.) (3)   repercussions (n.) (6)
   trilogies (n.) (4)   longingly (adv.) (6)

2. Suddath describes her feeling as "the kind of mystical feminine that one only sees in movies" (para. 2). What does the word *mystical* mean? Then what would "mystical feminine" mean? Name some movies to which you think this description might apply.

3. In paragraph 4, the writer says that "for years, I've been carting trilogies of skirts and pants into the dressing room. . . ." What function does a cart serve? Then what does "carting" mean?

PROBING CONTENT

1. To whom does Suddath address her letter? How long has she been interacting with the addressee? Describe her first interaction.

2. How does the author want the addressee to change? Why?

3. How does the addressee create problems for men? How does the way women appear on television affect the way men treat their female companions?

4. What kind of "pain and suffering" has the addressee caused? What would women have more time for if the addressee would be "sensible" (para. 7)?

CONSIDERING CRAFT

1. This essay is written in the form of a letter to an object instead of a person. How effective is this strategy?

2. In paragraph 3, the author states that in junior high, she "skyrocketed to atmospheric heights." What does she mean? How is her description an example of overstatement? Is it an effective strategy? Locate another example of overstatement used for effect in this letter.

WRITING PROMPTS

Responding to the Topic   Using Suddath's letter as a model, pick an object that annoys you. Write a letter to that thing, airing your complaints and suggesting beneficial changes. Make sure that your arguments are clear and well conceived.

Responding to the Writer   Write an essay in which you argue that the author is or is not complaining too much about the sizing of women's clothing. State your reasons in a convincing manner by including examples from your personal experience.

Responding to Multiple Viewpoints   In an essay, explore how Garry Trudeau ("My Inner Shrimp," p. 164) would react to Suddath's problems with growing up and confronting the "Totally Impractical Size Chart for Women's Clothing."

For a quiz on this reading, go to bedfordstmartins.com/mirror.

Analyzing the Image

Cathy by Cathy Guisewite

"What should I wear?" Millions of women ask themselves this every day. For the luckless Cathy of cartoon fame, this is just one of her multitude of problems. Cathy is an Everywoman with whom many women can empathize. In this 2010 comic strip, Cathy faces the denim dilemma.

- What does the salesperson declare to Cathy about jeans? Is she correct? Why? What is ironic about her use of the words *liberated* and *free*?

- What is Cathy's reaction? Why?

- What do you see in the final frame? Why is this frame more than twice as large as the others?

- Why is the second salesperson introduced in the final frame? How do her words summarize the message of the cartoon?

Research this topic with TopLinks at bedfordstmartins.com/toplinks.

Wrapping Up Chapter 5

Focusing on Yesterday, Focusing on Today

Blue jeans are arguably the most iconic piece of clothing in American history. Although denim overalls were originally made in the 1870s for working men like cowboys, miners, and lumberjacks, blue jeans are now worn by men, women, and children around the world. Available at all price points and in a wide variety of styles, denim jeans are a staple of most Americans' wardrobes. Levi Strauss & Co., based in San Francisco, made jeans strictly for workwear purposes until the 1930s, when they were adopted as sportswear during the Dude Ranch craze and vacationing easterners brought the pants with their patented rivets back home. Jeans gained further popularity during World War II, when they were worn by people working for the war effort. Then they really came into their own in the 1950s and 1960s, when rebellious youth subcultures adopted them. The rest is history. Of all the jean brands out there, Levi's, with its readily recognizable red tag, leads the pack.

Here are two advertisements for Levi's jeans. One dates from the 1950s and was originally printed in color, while the other is a contemporary ad from the very successful "Go Forth" campaign. It originally printed black and white with the exception of the red Levi's logo and features the campaign's trademark quotation. What do the two advertisements have in common? How do they differ? Explain the message of the text in each visual. What does that message say about the people featured? What messages

Courtesy Levi Strauss & Co. Archives.

Even Ladies Can Wear Levi's!

RESOURCES FOR TEACHING

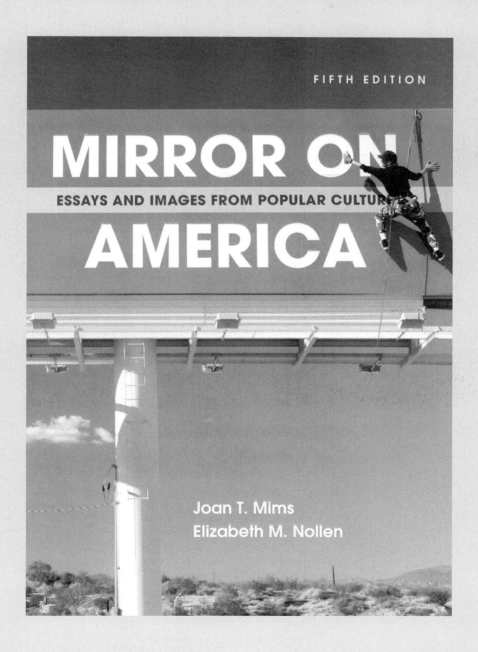

FIFTH EDITION

MIRROR ON

ESSAYS AND IMAGES FROM POPULAR CULTURE

AMERICA

Joan T. Mims

Elizabeth M. Nollen

Resources for Teaching
Mirror on America

ESSAYS AND IMAGES
FROM POPULAR CULTURE

FIFTH EDITION

JOAN T. MIMS

ELIZABETH M. NOLLEN
West Chester University

BEDFORD/ST. MARTIN'S   Boston ♦ New York

Instructors who have adopted *Mirror on America: Essays and Images from Popular Culture,* **Fifth Edition,** as a textbook for a course are authorized to duplicate portions of this manual for their students.

Manufactured in the United States of America.

6   5   4   3   2   1
f   e   d   c   b   a

For information, write: Bedford/St. Martin's, 75 Arlington Street, Boston, MA 02116   (617-399-4000)

ISBN: 978-0-312-66782-5

Preface

WHY USE THIS MANUAL?

Most instructor's manuals languish in bottom desk drawers, never seeing the light of day unless the textbook authors have included something so perplexing in the text itself that professors resort to the manual in desperation. Those types of instructor's manuals are a waste of trees. We don't use them, either. This isn't that kind of instructor's manual.

Our goal is to share with you some of our ideas about how we teach these essays and about how to make *Mirror on America*, Fifth Edition work well for you and your students. Don't expect to find answers to life's great mysteries in these pages. Do expect to find some expanded suggestions about ways to apply what the textbook offers. Don't expect to find ideas that are better than your own best instincts and experience. Do expect to find ideas that can shed new light on tried-and-true practices and open up pathways to some new ones. Don't expect to find discussions of pedagogical theory. Do expect to find ways to develop that theory in action in the classroom.

Students in composition courses at all levels, beginning with developmental students, are just that—developing. Their challenges with writing may not be due to a lower skill level or to high school instruction that did not focus on composition. We believe that composition students often do not write as well as they might because they may not yet have explored the world of writing in response to their own interests and knowledge. Listen to your students in the cafeteria lines, in the bookstore, and around campus. They have plenty to say. But they may not realize that the arguments they make to a friend to justify their preference for rap-rock or hip hop music can form the basis for a competent essay on trends in music culture. They are perfectly capable of complex critical thinking if we are willing to let them begin with content that inhabits their sphere of concern. That's what this textbook is about—moving writing into our students' real world.

NOTE TO ESL INSTRUCTORS

Having taught non-native speakers, we know that their first concern is not to be able to write the perfect English sentence. Their immediate objective is to participate in the conversations swirling around them. This textbook can help you develop students' English skills in composition and thought and give them a chance to explore American culture. We see this as a perfect blending of students' desires with your mandate as an instructor—of form fitting function. The essays in *Mirror on America* offer students occasion to talk and think critically about music, technology, and movies, while glosses help define American pop culture terminology that may be unfamiliar to them. We have found that by the time that students are asked to write about what they've read, they have so many ideas to express that the words fairly jump onto the pages. Once you are past the familiar complaint, "I haven't got anything to say about this subject that anyone would want to read," you are free to concentrate on the other things that make English grammar and syntax a challenge for non-native—and native—speakers.

Contents

6 What Are You Trying to Say?: How Language Works 45

8 Picture This: Reflecting Culture Onscreen   71

Active, Involved Reading and the Writing Process

1

Establishing the Connection

The first chapter of *Mirror on America*, Fifth Edition, and the Preface for Instructors identify the pedagogical philosophy of the text. For the student, this initial chapter with the Introduction for Students cement the bond between reading and writing, establish the connection between this course and "real life," and preview all the whys and wherefores of the structure of the book.

TEACHING STRATEGIES

The most important strategy for teaching this text is to teach Chapters 1 and 2 first. The other chapters are designed to be taught in almost any order that fits interests and schedules without losing any vital connectivity, but Chapters 1 and 2 are unique.

Let's think about Chapter 1 first. We suggest working through the first sample essay "Mickey Mouse as Icon: Taking Popular Culture Seriously" (text p. 5) with students just as you would work through the other essays throughout the text; the only difference here is that possible answers have been included for the questions about the reading. You may want to begin by taking a close look at the headnote to the sample essay, emphasizing why skipping introductions may be like missing the first five minutes of a movie. Move on to the journal prompt ("Thinking Ahead"), and take time to allay any fears that students may have about journaling: A journal is generally not graded for content or mechanics, and no one but you will see their entries. For the vocabulary words ("Exercising Vocabulary"), emphasize that the intent is to increase one's own vocabulary, not to practice penmanship by copying from a dictionary. Spend some time discussing the merits of annotating while reading; this practice can become a valuable skill for students to develop as they prepare material for other courses, too. Take every opportunity to relate what you are teaching to practical application beyond your classroom.

Encourage students to discuss the essay and the subjects that it suggests in as broad a context as possible. The goal is for students to think critically about the selection and to share and support their ideas in class. Then, when it's time for them to write, they will be raring to go. You may want to preview the three types of questions ("Writing Prompts") that follow each essay in the book to emphasize the different focus of each set, as Chapter 1 points out. Ask students if they agree or disagree with the student answers provided. Emphasize that many of the questions that they will be asked have more than one possible correct response or call for a student's opinion; each student should feel free to offer his or her own interpretation, as long as the answer offered can be supported by the text of the essay just read. In "Responding to the Writer," students are encouraged to develop their own response to something the writer has articulated. Beginning to propose a well-reasoned argument lays the groundwork for a full-length essay with a credibly argued thesis.

The second half of Chapter 1 shifts the focus from reading to writing. How much time you devote to this coverage of the writing process will depend on your sense of your students' level of experience. Certainly you and your students will want to clarify the audience for the essays that they will be writing and spend some time reviewing how purpose and tone (attitude) color writing. As we recommend for the first half of Chapter 1, "Getting into Reading," we encourage you to cover each subtopic under "Getting into Writing," letting your students' responses to your questions tell you when and where they need more help with particular aspects of the writing process.

New to this edition is the student paper-in-progress, "From Dirty Nikes to Profit Spikes: Mark Zuckerberg Redesigns Our Nation's Communication" (text p. 23). The essay is presented in two versions: the first an annotated draft that discusses necessary revisions and the second a final draft that incorporates those suggested changes. We suggest asking students to dissect the student essay—have them comment on the changes made to the draft, and see if they have anything they would add or suggest to further improve the draft.

The peer editing process near the end of Chapter 1 (text p. 22) can easily be applied by your class to the sample student essay, a teaching strategy that may make students more comfortable with their role as peer editors when the time comes to analyze each other's work. This also can be a meaningful group activity, of which there are many in the student edition of this text and in this manual. You may want to divide the class into twos or threes and assign each group one or more items from the peer review to complete. This provides a friendly introduction to peer review and to group responsibility for an assignment.

We've organized the material in Chapter 1 to show the relationship between active reading and good writing and also to introduce students to the book's activities. This way when they tackle the various reading and writing projects on their own, they can approach each task with a better understanding of the assignments' goals and of what they can accomplish by actively engaging in them. It is our hope that time spent in Chapter 1 will help to make students more observant readers and more eager writers for all the chapters to follow—and beyond.

ADDITIONAL RESOURCES

1. To supplement Chapter 1 with more detailed coverage of the writing process, you may want to refer to *The Bedford Handbook*, Eighth Edition, by Diana Hacker and Nancy Sommers.

2. Throughout the course, we encourage you to supplement the text with newspapers, magazines, television, radio, movies, and Web sources. To help persuade students that this course relates to the real world outside the classroom, bring in real-world materials. These commentaries repre-

sent a variety of perspectives, as well as questions and suggestions for pursuing more deeply the issues that are raised in the essays. You can also refer your students to the numerous articles available in past editions of *Newsweek* (www.newsweek.com), *Time* (www.time.com), or *Salon* (www.salon.com) that devote whole sections to different perspectives on popular culture topics.

2 Deconstructing Media

Analyzing an Image

Just as Chapter 1 moves students step-by-step through the analysis of text, Chapter 2 offers a step-by-step guide to "reading" visual images. Because our culture is highly visual, your students will think that they are already quite alert to the images around them. Chapter 2 is all about moving them beyond the obvious.

The questions that we have provided for students to ask as they examine an advertisement or a photograph break down what might appear to be a daunting task into easily manageable, practical parts. As the chapter says, it's all about asking—and answering—the right questions.

As in Chapter 1, we have included samples—a photograph called "To Have and to Hold" (text p. 33) and a *Pearls Before Swine* cartoon strip (text p. 35)—and we have included answers for the questions that we ask about these two images. Remind students that the answers we include represent one person's responses; their own responses may be different but equally valid, as long as their answers can be authenticated by the image.

Next, Chapter 2 includes an advertisement called "Unmask Your Child's Online Identity" (text p. 38) and a student's essay decoding that ad, which he has titled "You've Got Betrayal: Deconstructing an Advertisement for Online Spyware." This student essay offers a good opportunity to practice the peer editing strategies explained in Chapter 1.

Finally, we've included a suggestion for a practice essay and several collaborating exercises to allow students to become more comfortable with the deconstruction process. By the end of Chapter 2, students should feel ready to approach analytically the ads, photos, cartoons, paintings, and other media images in the chapters of this text and in the world around them.

Define "American"

Reflections on Cultural Identity

3

In this chapter, a variety of authors from diverse backgrounds relate their own struggles with cultural identity in a country that often favors an Anglo ideal. Students may be surprised to learn that certain "looks" are favored not only by the larger society but also within individual families. They will also discover that individual cultural heritages—which determine the customs we follow, the foods we eat, the holidays we celebrate, the ways we define ourselves, and even the clothes we wear—may also conflict with the larger American popular culture around us. Cultural identity makes people unique, and it can either divide or unite the members of society. Many students will find themselves—or a kindred spirit—reflected in the essays that follow.

"Like Mother—Not Likely!" (p. 42)

This *National Geographic* cover graphically reflects the degree of separation that Lorraine Ali longed for when growing up as she tried to move away from her heritage to be fully Americanized. Ask students to examine posture, dress, and facial expression in this photograph to ascertain just how similar, yet different these two generations appear.

Do I Look Like Public Enemy Number One? (p. 45)

LORRAINE ALI

When Lorraine Ali's essay was first published in 1999, she probably could not have imagined the firestorm in which Arab Americans would find themselves after the events of September 11, 2001. Her title has unwittingly become ironic. Arab Americans are detained at airport security checkpoints and questioned vigorously about their daily activities. How do your students feel about individuals who are deemed "guilty by association"? What strategies can they suggest as we struggle to maintain fairness toward all Americans? To what extent are the many responsible for the actions of a few?

TEACHING STRATEGIES

Questions for Discussion

1. Explore with students how stereotypes become culturally embedded. How can stereotypes be displaced? Ask students if they have known members of a stereotyped group who didn't fit the widely accepted image.

2. Discuss with students the idea of "racial profiling." In light of recent crimes or acts of terrorism, do law enforcement officials have the right to

give members of certain ethnic, racial, gender, or cultural groups closer scrutiny than others? What are the benefits and risks of such policies?

3. Although we have moved further from September 11, 2001, there is still major debate about whether America's borders should be open to immigrants. Recently, Congress has discussed enacting even stricter restraints on immigration. What do students think about the future of such potential legislation? What would be the advantages and disadvantages of further restricting immigration into America?

Group Activities

1. In paragraph 8 of her essay, Ali writes, "As Arabs, we were guilty by association, even at the age of twelve." Divide students into small groups to identify and discuss other groups of people living in the United States who have suffered "guilt by association." What circumstances caused them to be perceived as guilty? Has the negative image been displaced? How? If the guilty image persists, why is this so?

2. Have students work in pairs to list the groups of students who populated their high schools (punks, jocks, gang members, goths, nerds). What attributes were associated with members of each group? What were the liabilities and compensations of belonging to each group? How easy was it to shift from one group to another? Move students into groups of four to compare their ideas.

Out of Class Projects

1. Have students research what they believe to be the unfair treatment of a group of people living in the United States and build a case for that group's vindication. The students should conduct Internet and/or library research and also interview members of the cultural, racial, or ethnic group they have selected. Students may then present their case to their classmates.

2. Ask students to gather at least ten images of members of one ethnic, racial, or cultural group from magazines and newspapers or from the Internet. They may also use television or movie excerpts. Then have them design a visual presentation using their images to demonstrate how that group is portrayed. The finished product might be a video, a collage, or any other type of visual art.

They've Got to Be Carefully Taught
(p. 51)
SUSAN BRADY KONIG

Did your students attend multicultural celebrations at their schools when they were in elementary, middle, or high school? If so, what did they think of them? Perhaps they considered these celebrations to be fun, educational, or simply a good excuse to sample some tasty food and to get out of classes. They may not have analyzed the benefits or drawbacks of these activities. This essay provides a good springboard for discussion about cultural diversity as Konig presents one viewpoint with plenty of humor.

TEACHING STRATEGIES

Questions for Discussion

1. What do your students know or remember about how different religious and ethnic holidays were celebrated in their elementary and middle schools? What made these celebrations fun? Educational? Controversial?

2. Ask students how their families celebrate their heritage. What special customs do they observe? Are special clothes, music, or foods associated with these celebrations?

Group Activities

1. Divide the class into small groups. Have students share a description of a family cultural artifact (such as a menorah, a kinara, a dream catcher, a Santa Lucia wreath, or a crèche) with other members of the group. Ask students to explain to the group the significance of the artifact.

2. Have students work in small groups and tell each other something about their cultural identity. The students might explain, for example, where their ancestors lived and if their family emigrated, when they came to this country and why they left their homeland.

Out of Class Projects

1. Have students arrange to visit a local elementary or middle school during a multicultural celebration or visit a neighborhood or community celebration. What was celebrated, and how? Have students share their findings with the class.

2. Ask your class to watch a movie that deals with an ethnicity different from their own — for example, *Kite Runner, Eat Drink Man Woman, The Namesake, Bend It Like Beckham, Winter's Bone The Joy Luck Club, A Thousand Acres, Beloved, My Big Fat Greek Wedding, Smoke Signals*, or *Slumdog Millionaire*. Ask students to take notes on and analyze the characters, their interactions, and their cultural traditions. Allow them to share their observations with the class, using short film clips to enhance their presentations.

People Like Us (p. 55)
DAVID BROOKS

In America, we're used to hearing analogies that compare our society to a "melting pot," and we're accustomed to hearing diversity championed as a cultural idea. Conservative columnist David Brooks argues differently. Brooks cites several studies that find that, when given the option, most people seek to surround themselves with those of similar racial, ethnic, and socioeconomic backgrounds. Rather than condemning this behavior, Brooks argues that forcing diversity creates the opposite of community and that ultimately diversity is more about choosing to experience things outside one's comfort zone than it is about continually living in a heterogeneous neighborhood.

TEACHING STRATEGIES

Questions for Discussion

1. Brooks uses categorizations from the marketing firm Claritas to identify different sects in American life. Do your students think that consumer habits may be the best way to categorize Americans — more so than ethnicity, religion, or geography? Why or why not?

2. In what ways (if any) do your students think that they lead "diverse lives"? How has experiencing another culture shaped their perceptions?

Group Activities

1. In groups, have your students consider what everyone in the class has in common that led them to be at this school right now. What is their collective demographic?

2. As an ad team, have each group formulate one product that students would buy and market it to classmates based on the demographic profile created in Group Activity 1.

Out of Class Projects

1. Brooks writes, "It's striking that the institutions that talk the most about diversity often practice it the least" (para. 13). By reading and discussing this essay, your students are talking quite a bit about diversity. Ask them to research your academic institution and identify its stance on diversity, including its specific strategies for implementing diversity. Is your institution practicing the diversity that it talks about?

2. Brooks ends his essay by challenging his reader: "Look around at your daily life. Are you really in touch with the broad diversity of American life?" (para. 19). Ask students to keep a record for one day of the number of people and institutions that they interact with that are "different" from them. Ask them to define the differences and briefly discuss their findings.

The Downside of Diversity (p. 62)

MICHAEL JONAS

In this essay, Michael Jonas looks at a study written by acclaimed sociologist Robert Putnam that concludes that more diverse communities have less civic involvement, findings that run contrary to the common American belief that diversity strengthens communities. Jonas examines possible actions that might be taken from data that is explosive to the mission of multiculturalism.

TEACHING STRATEGIES

Questions for Discussion

1. What feels more comfortable for your students—a culturally heterogeneous or homogeneous environment? Ask them to examine the reasons for their responses. What factors play a part in their comfort or discomfort?

2. Some individuals contend that there is a discrepancy between what people want and what is good for them. Do you agree or disagree with this sentiment? How would this idea relate to the article?

Group Activities

1. In groups, have your students consider a hypothetical situation in which they are leaders in a community with a substantial amount of diversity (you may choose to assign a local neighborhood or town for each group). As the leaders of their community, ask students to design an action plan that will bring residents together. Encourage them to be creative in their plans. Each group may present its plan to the class.

2. In his article, Jonas quotes Scott Page: "[B]y hanging out with people different than you, you're likely to get more insights. Diverse teams tend to be more productive" (para. 30). To test this idea, assign one person in each group to take notes on team dynamics. Which teams seem to be the most productive in brainstorming and planning? Who dominates the group and who supports? How do people who rarely interact socially work together in a work environment? Have each team's reporter present its findings to the class after the "action plan" presentations.

Out of Class Projects

1. Direct students to use television and the Internet to research conservative and liberal media outlets and to compare their coverage of a diversity issue such as immigration. They should examine the belief system that is behind each point of view and the ways that Jonas's research could help or hurt these perspectives.

2. Have students interview a leader in their own community about the issue of community involvement and diversity. Ask them to transcribe the interview and present their subjects' perspectives in class.

Globalization vs. Americanization (p. 70)
ANDREW LAM

Andrew Lam's essay is a definition piece that explains the concepts of globalization and Americanization. Lam argues that most Americans perceive these terms to mean the same thing and that we have negative feelings about globalization because of the popular misconception that it means the unchecked spread of American culture and businesses throughout the world, which most of us perceive to be a threat to cultural preservation. Instead, Lam sees globalization as a consequence of the ways that many cultures are connecting to share information and respective cultures.

TEACHING STRATEGIES

Questions for Discussion

1. The author quotes his friend as saying "Everyone will be eating at McDonald's, listening to Madonna, and shopping at mega-malls. . . . It'll be absolutely awful" (para. 1). Ask the class if this will happen and if it did, whether it would be absolutely awful. Why or why not?

2. Ask students if they think that they could live without the influence of other cultures, even if they wanted to. Discuss if and how this could be done and what limitations this would present.

Group Activities

1. Have students form small groups and choose one well-known Disney movie. Instruct them to reimagine the story in a way that is more realistic and complicated (more in the style of a Michael Ondaatje novel, to use Lam's example). Ask each group to rewrite a scene from the Disney movie, assign parts, and perform the scene in front of the class.

2. Lam concludes his essay by writing that "Geography for [the new man] may be memory and logistics, but it's no longer destiny." In groups, have students research a current figure that could be considered a "new man" (or woman). This could be a politician, a musician, a CEO, or any public person. Using the Internet, have students gather material about this person's life and present it to the class.

Out of Class Projects

1. Have students write a short personal essay answering these questions: "Where is home for you or your family? How do geographies of your

past inform your memory, sense of patriotism, consumer habits, and so on?"

2. Ask students to keep a journal for a week, documenting everything that they buy. They should then determine the cultural origin of each product and construct a graph that visually communicates this information. Allow time in class for students to present their findings.

Home at Last (p. 74)
Dinaw Mengestu

When people ask Dinaw Mengestu where he is from, he can answer either Ethiopia (where he was born) or the United States (where he has lived since the age of two), yet neither answer feels correct. The question of home is often a complicated one for an immigrant, especially if he or she faces barriers of race, culture, religion, or other factors within the adopted community. For Mengestu, home is Brooklyn, New York, in a neighborhood "emblematic of a grander immigrant narrative," where people are not simply from America or Ethiopia, and identities can continually be formed.

TEACHING STRATEGIES

Questions for Discussion

1. Mengestu was twenty-one when he moved to Brooklyn. Ask students if they have yet felt completely at home anywhere. If they have, where is that place they consider home? If they have not, do they have a sense of where they might one day feel at home?

2. Do students feel any loyalty to or identification with the country from which their parents, great-grandparents, or distant ancestors emigrated?

Group Activities

1. Ask students, in small groups, to consider Mengestu's statement about what his family sacrificed when they moved to the United States. He says they lost "parents, siblings, culture, a memory to a place that dates back more than half a generation" (para. 3) Do students know about any sacrifices of that kind made by their families? What sort of circumstances would require them to give up such important things? Can they imagine anything similar potentially happening in their own lives?

2. Mengestu describes his Peoria, Illinois, home as having an "all-white southern Baptist church" and a "nearly all-white Catholic school" that his family was part of, but never felt assimilated into. Have students brainstorm ideas about what sort of community support these institutions might be able offer people like Mengestu and his family, who feel separated from them by race, culture, language, experience, and possibly other aspects.

What can students come up with that might be helpful to a family like Mengestu's? Ask each group to share its conclusions.

Out of Class Projects

1. In this essay, there is a detailed description of a Kensington neighborhood, and Mengestu writes that Brooklyn is always reinventing itself. Ask students to describe their own neighborhoods. Have them look around for clues to the different people and ethnicities that make up the neighborhood.

2. Are there organizations in the United States (beyond federal immigration and naturalization services) that help immigrants or refugees assimilate into a new culture? Have students conduct phone, periodical, and/or Internet research to answer that question. What did they learn about where people can find support when they enter this country? What kinds of support might immigrants be seeking?

History Tells Hard Stories of Ethnic Clashes (p. 81)
LEONARD PITTS JR.

Leonard Pitts Jr. reminds us that even difficult stories must be told . . . and retold. As he argues the need to write freely on historical events, he takes note of a recent Arizona law that restricts ethnic studies courses in public schools. This law bans the teaching of any ethnic studies classes that might stir resentment, "advocate ethnic solidarity," or create related controversy; the restriction, he notes, is worded in very broad terms. How, Pitts asks, are we to interpret such restrictions? Do laws like these help students in some way or hurt their perceptions of a shared history by shutting down important discussions?

TEACHING STRATEGIES

Questions for Discussion

1. Have students ever taken an ethnic studies course? What did the course cover? What did they learn?

2. Students should ask themselves about the idea of American unity mentioned by Pitts. How do they respond to this quotation that he takes issue with: "We need to focus on America instead of promoting everyone else" (para. 11). Who is "America" in that statement and who is "everyone else?" Is the person being quoted different from or the same as the woman mentioned in the beginning of the essay, in terms of reasoning and outlook?

Group Activities

1. In groups, ask students to list events in history that involved the oppression of one ethnic group by another. Once lists are assembled, encourage them to outline a course that would teach about an event on the list and involve the ethnic group's history. Would their course be breaking the law in Arizona? Discuss as a class.

2. Pair students. Ask one student to take the part of a writer or teacher dealing with a difficult historical time or event. The history of African American men and women in the United States, the plight of Jews during the Holocaust, and the history of the Irish fighting against the British presence in Northern Ireland are examples from the essay, and can be used. Ask the other student to assume the role of someone (like the woman in the beginning of Pitts's essay) who wishes that the history could be left alone. Both students should take notes about why they might want to talk or write about the history or might want to bury the history before they engage in discussion.

Out of Class Projects

1. Students should peruse their college/university catalogues to find classes that address ethnic studies and ethnic struggle. Are the courses offered to everyone? Why are these courses important, or why not? In a short paper, have students explain the value (or lack thereof) of such courses to higher education.

2. Students may develop a class on ethnic studies, draft a syllabus, and include some class information: goals, possible materials, and requirements. Then they should check their proposal against the information about the course ban in Arizona. Does their class do any of the things that are forbidden by the law? Why or why not?

America: Land of Loners? (p. 84)
DANIEL AKST

Daniel Akst exhorts Americans to "rediscover the value of friendship," noting that they have gone from relying on others and benefiting from close yet nonsexual relationships with friends to leading lonelier, less satisfying lives. He catalogues the reasons for the decline of friendships and the cost—real, physical, and psychological—it exacts on humans. Akst reminds us of the reasons friendship was so important from an evolutionary standpoint, and makes it clear that we lose something of our humanity—become more robotic—without true friends.

TEACHING STRATEGIES

Questions for Discussion

1. Akst points out that the friendships people have now are often superficial, eroticized, or dispensable. Ask students how "modern friendships" differ from the friendships Akst says are truly beneficial.

2. Do students have best friends? Who are they? Are students' friendships with their best friends made of the stuff Akst describes, or do they fall short when held against his criteria for a lasting and valuable friendship?

Group Activities

1. In pairs, ask students to reminisce about a childhood friend. What qualities did that person have that made him or her so important? What important memories does the student have of time with that friend? Ask each pair to consider whether this particular friendship matches Akst's description of friendship.

2. In groups, ask students to consider various ways people are more isolated now than perhaps twenty to fifty years ago. Have them go further back in history. How were people more reliant on each other one hundred years ago than today? Is the converse true? Groups should compile lists, discuss, and then present findings to the class.

Out of Class Projects

1. Facebook has been revolutionary in its ability to keep people in touch with each other and allows a space for "friendship" in a fast-paced, largely electronic world. After examining a list of Facebook "friends," ask students to consider who on the list is a true friend (one who can be relied on and who offers support or "sympathy").

2. Many different books dealing with friendship are referenced in this essay. Ask students to read either *Solaris*; *Friendship, Sex, and Survival*; or *American Sympathy: Men, Friendship, and Literature in the New Nation* and then write a report on the book with an eye toward what the work says about friendship and what it means to be human.

A Smart Exception (p. 93)
DAVID GERGEN

Sergey Brin, Jerry Yang, and Pierre Omidyar are three immigrants held up as shining examples of children of U.S. immigrants who grew up to be successful, creative entrepreneurs. Brin, Yang, and Omidyar are the creative forces behind Google, Yahoo!, and eBay. Writer David Gergen calls attention in his essay to immigrant achievement, hoping to persuade others that by reforming

America's approach toward immigration, this country will give foreign talent a better chance to blossom in American soil.

TEACHING STRATEGIES

Questions for Discussion

1. Gergen points out that from this country's beginnings, many of the innovative thinkers in the United States have been immigrants. We are, in fact, a country of immigrants. Find out what students know about their own family's immigration background. How long ago did their forerunners arrive in the United States? Is their immigration history recent or from long ago?

2. How do students perceive the current U.S. immigration laws? Are our requirements too strict? Too loose? Where do they agree with Gergen's argument about the laws and where do they differ? If they do agree with his stance, is it because they believe changing the laws will attract more foreign talent, or do they think the laws should be changed for other reasons?

Group Activities

1. Gergen writes, "Since the early days of the Republic, talented foreigners have streamed to our shores to till the soil, build industries, and turn the country into a scientific and technological powerhouse" (para. 3). Immigrants are responsible both for creative output and for the fulfillment of much menial daily work in our country. Ask students to reflect, in groups, on why their own ancestors (or recent family) came to the United States. What did they hope to achieve here? What work did they end up doing?

2. The entry of "would-be Times Square bomber, Faisal Shahzad," into the country is mentioned in this essay as an example of why some are unsure of how stringent immigration law should be. How do students respond to that criticism? Gergen says, "fear cannot allow us to drive away" talent from this country (para. 8). In a post-9/11 world, are immigrants people to be feared? Ask students to write a list of reasons why immigration law should be reconsidered or rewritten. Ask them to consider, as they discuss, whether the structure of immigration law should be based on an emotional response to a person, event, or projections about the future.

Out of Class Projects

1. Have students interview a business owner or employer to discover his or her feelings about hiring immigrants for work. Has the person ever hired someone who was a legal (or illegal) immigrant? What was the employer's experience with that worker, or those workers? Did he/she/they over- or underperform natural-born citizens who were part of the same organization? Does the employer feel, as business owners or people with the

power to employ others, that they hold any prejudices about hiring immigrants? Does the employer believe the U.S. immigration laws should change to enhance the workforce? Students may use the questions listed above in their interviews, but ask them to come up with a full page of questions (to include some of their own) before they conduct the interview.

2. Allow students to choose one of the three men mentioned in the essay as an example of immigrant success and have them write a profile of his life. They should do research on the man's childhood and its perceived influence on his career choices, talent, and persistence. Research can be done on the Internet, from books, from current magazines, or other library sources, and all sources should be cited.

Focusing on Yesterday, Focusing on Today
"Give Me Your Tired, Your Poor." (p. 98)

This illustration of a group of immigrants from 1878 is likely indicative of what students associate with Ellis Island and the flood of immigration that took place in nineteenth-century America. Have your students analyze the scene in the illustration, and ask them how they think it relates to the current immigration policies in the United States. You can note that most of the immigrants in the photo look relatively happy, there is a feeling of order to the scene, and the police officers are helping the immigrants with their luggage.

Caution! (p. 99)

This photograph of a highway sign near the U.S. border in Mexico is a stark contrast to the 1878 illustration. Ask your students what they think the sign is trying to convey, and if it has any other implications than its intended warning. Have them compare the family depicted in the sign to the families shown in the 1878 illustration. You may also want to discuss the different ideas on immigration that these two images represent, and perhaps even how the word *immigration* has evolved in meaning, especially in the United States.

ADDITIONAL RESOURCES

1. For some thought-provoking poems that explore cultural identity, read the following works: "Queens, 1963" by Julia Alvarez; "Green Chile," by Jimmy Santiago Baca; "Ellis Island" by Joseph Bruchac; "Indian Movie, New Jersey" by Chitra Divakaruni; "Negro" and "I, Too" by Langston Hughes; "AmeRícan" by Tato Laviera; "The English Are So Nice!" by D. H. Lawrence; "Telephone Conversation" by Wole Soyinka; and "Recipe" by Janice Murikitani.

2. For articles on cultural identity, see "Race Is Over" by Stanley Crouch, *New York Times Magazine*, September 29, 1996, and "The Good Daughter" by Caroline Hwang, *Newsweek*, September 21, 1998.

3. Lewis Lapham's article "Is There an American Tribe," which appeared in the January 1992 issue of *Harper's Magazine*, explores the question of how to define *American*. He asks whether the growing trend to place an adjective like "gay," "native," "female," or "black" runs counter to the American democratic ideal.

4. Mary C. Curtis's article in the *Charlotte Observer* (Charlotte, North Carolina, May 17, 2004), "Pop Culture Fostering Arab Discrimination," is a good resource and has interesting ties to Chapter 8 as it discusses negative portrayals of Arabs in the 1994 James Cameron movie *True Lies* and in an early version of Disney's *Aladdin*. The last line reads, "In life or the movies, when you treat someone as less than human, that's what you become."

4 You Are What You Eat

American Food Culture and Traditions Around the World

Food is something that every culture has in common, and as stated in the chapter, "it defines us individually and culturally." From food in popular culture to the globalization of certain foods, this chapter explores how pervasive food and the cultural analysis of food has recently become. How do your students think about food? Is it simply a necessity, or does it play a larger role in their lives? The essays in this chapter range from nostalgic, in Connie Shultz's *Heat, Tray, Love*, to economic, in Seanon Wong's *Noodles vs. Sesame Seed Buns*, but they are all prime examples of the way food not only defines our lives but also, to a certain extent, dictates them.

Vertumnus (p. 100)

Some students may be familiar with Giuseppe Archimboldo's work, and *Vertumnus* is a striking example of his portraits that also lends itself to the cultural importance of food. You may want to bring a color version of the image to class to show your students so they can see the minute details in the painting. Your students may be surprised that this is such an old painting, as it does display many modern elements. Ask your students about their views on the cultural importance of food, and how they think they may be defined by food. If they were to create a similar portrait of themselves, what types of food would that portrait represent? How would their food portrait reflect their individual cultural background?

The Cooking Animal (p. 104)
Michael Pollan

In this essay, Michael Pollan remembers Julia Child and her cooking show *The French Chef*. When he compares Child's show to the cooking shows proliferating on television today, he comes across some real differences. The differences cause him to reflect on whether today's cooking shows are truly devoted to the art of cooking—and then he tries to determine what they do in fact impart to us about food and its preparation.

TEACHING STRATEGIES

Questions for Discussion

1. Why do people enjoy watching others cook on television? Ask students to explain the difference, as Pollan explains it, between Julia Child's show and the cooking shows of today.

2. Discuss the skill involved in cooking. Ask students why we might not want to lose it.

Group Activities

1. In groups, ask students to discuss when they are more interested in and/ or inclined to prepare a meal and when they are more likely to opt for fast or prepared foods. Do students believe there is an interest in a return to the slow preparation of meals or is fast food an inevitable fact of modern life?

2. Put students into groups and ask them to consider each argument in "The Cooking Animal," taking notes during their discussion. "The Cooking Animal" is an excerpt from a longer Pollan article in which he states that "cooking strikes a deep emotional chord in us." (The full article is "Out of the Kitchen, Onto the Couch," *New York Times*, July 29, 2009.) Present this quote to students and ask if arguments in the excerpt support this claim and whether or not they agree with the class. Have groups share their opinions with the class.

Out of Class Projects

1. The movie *Julie and Julia* offers one depiction of Julia Child. Students can watch the movie and then describe, based on the film, the appeal of her approach to cooking for American housewives.

2. Pollan notes that the ads on the Food Network do not "hawk kitchen appliances or ingredients (unless you count A.1. steak sauce)," but instead "push the usual supermarket cart of edible foodlike substances." Have students watch an hour of the Food Network, compiling a list of ads they see as they watch, to see if Pollan's assessment of its advertising is correct.

An Expert's Theory of Food Television's Appeal (p. 110)
FRANK BRUNI

As Bruni mentions in his essay, food television is everywhere. There are multiple channels that carry nothing but food- and cooking-based programming, even though the number of home-cooked meals appears to be in decline. Have a discussion with your students about their experiences with cooking—were they taught how to cook when they were younger? Did they have family meals or anyone in their household who cooked often? Does this affect whether or not they watch food television?

TEACHING STRATEGIES

Questions for Discussion

1. Bruni makes the argument that television is not always about entertainment, but about relaxation. Discuss with students what they think the purpose of television has become, and whether Bruni's theory applies to other TV programs. Is there a difference between being actively engaged with a television show, and simply observing it?

2. Bruni's friend offers a theory that food television is about nostalgia, and poses the question, "Do the glossy, dreamy culinary demonstrations on TV tap into, and satisfy, a kind of curiosity and longing" (para. 4)? Explore this idea of nostalgia with your students and ask where else in popular culture this idea permeates. Is our culture nostalgic? If so, why do your students think it is appealing?

Group Activities

1. Divide students into small groups and have them create a list of cooking shows that they have watched or heard about. How many of these shows fall under the category of competition cooking shows—like *Top Chef*—and how many are demonstration shows—like *Barefoot Contessa*? What conclusions can students draw about Bruni's theory from these lists?

2. In small groups, have students discuss their favorite foods and the foods they grew up on. Were these store bought or home cooked? Then ask students what types of food television, if any, appeal to them. Do they see any correlations between their favorite foods and the types of cooking shows they would be interested in watching? If your students are not at all interested in cooking shows, have them discuss with their group why they are not intrigued by the trend.

Out of Class Projects

1. Have students choose two cooking shows, one competition and one demonstration, to research. How is each show presented in advertisements? What network do the shows appear on? If possible, have students find the television ratings for the shows—how many people watch them? What are the shows themselves like? How are the sets, camera angles, lighting, and pacing different in the two categories? Have students present their findings to the class.

2. Ask students to watch a cooking show that they have never seen before, preferably for a style of cooking that they are not familiar with. Have them respond to the episode in a short essay, explaining whether they found the show appealing, and why. Would they consider cooking any of the food featured? Why or why not?

Heat, Tray, Love (p. 114)
CONNIE SCHULTZ

Connie Schultz turns her nose up at current health trends or any arguments about the importance of home-cooked meals in this article, which venerates the frozen TV dinner. Influenced by her childhood memories of eating these dinners with her family, she insists on the integrity of the TV dinners of years past. For her, they not only represent her childhood meals but also her family's approach to life.

TEACHING STRATEGIES

Questions for Discussion

1. Do students have any memories of something their family might have used as a "shortcut," either at mealtimes or in other areas of family life? Did these shortcuts cause mixed feelings about the way things could or should be done? Are the memories positive or negative?

2. Why would TV dinners be considered "the next new thing" for Schultz's mother? How is her mom a trailblazer or adventurer of sorts? How do you understand Schultz's comparison between frozen dinners and a disposable paper dress?

Group Activities

1. Ask students whether they remember eating frozen dinners as a child. Divide them into small groups based on who ate prepared foods regularly and who usually had meals cooked from scratch. Groups should discuss their current eating habits. Did the meals they ate as children have any effect on how they prepare their food and eat now?

2. The assumption is made in Schultz's essay that she ate TV dinners because her family was of the working class. Break students into small groups and ask them to prepare a short essay in which they discuss what effect having more or less money, or being of a certain "class," has on a family's food choices. Are children in working-class families more likely to eat TV dinners or the modern equivalent? Are children in more affluent, or "white collar," homes more likely to eat dinners made from scratch? Why or why not?

Out of Class Projects

1. The TV dinner craze, which began with the Salisbury steak–peas–potatoes meal described in this essay, blossomed into a culinary phenomenon that now includes meals for those watching their weight, frozen pizzas of every style and topping, and ethnic foods from all parts of the globe. Ask students to do some research in their local supermarkets and on the Internet and then compare the TV dinners of the 1950s and 1960s to the TV dinners of today.

2. Ask students to imagine the Schultz family's lifestyle. What were the women of the day wearing? What sort of occupations did they hold? Are student descriptions based strictly on the essay or some knowledge of the time period. Ask students to consider what the family might have watched on television as they ate their meals. How do television shows today compare with the sort of things the Schultz family would have watched? What clues does Schultz give about the atmosphere surrounding her childhood, and what comparisons can students make about that world and the one of today?

Custom-Made (p. 117)
TARA PARKER-POPE

This clever title reflects Tara Parker-Pope's interest in the way that American culture has invaded the culture and customs of other nations. Students are likely to be intrigued—and occasionally repelled—by the variations on American favorites that exist outside our territorial boundaries and sometimes outside our definition of good taste, too.

TEACHING STRATEGIES

Questions for Discussion

1. Why are American foods, jeans, T-shirts, and other uniquely American items popular abroad? Even in countries where American foreign policy is unpopular, American movies and clothing are still much in demand. What do Americans seem to have that attracts people in other countries? How accurate is the idea that many people elsewhere have about America? What perpetuates this stereotypical view?

2. What does it take for a new food item to become a hit in the United States? What adaptations have to be made for Americans to accept a traditionally "foreign" food? Name some foods popular in other countries that have become popular here. With what age groups are these foods popular?

Group Activities

1. Ask students to divide into small groups and to choose one traditionally American food (not hamburgers) and one foreign country. Ask them to plan a campaign to introduce this food into the diet of people who live in that country. Students should detail the specific ways that they would advertise the new product, explaining what consumer population they would try to reach and any changes that they might have to make to the product to make it more palatable to non-American consumers. What considerations would be most important in selling the product? What obstacles would need to be overcome to sell this food item in the country selected?

2. Ask students to work in small groups to make a list of five foods that have been introduced into the United States from other countries within the last five to ten years. Students should then design eight survey questions about these new food products, including the following: Have you tried any of these foods? Which ones? Where did you try them? Why did you decide to try them? How did they taste to you? Have students add any other questions that their group wants to ask. Then ask each group member to ask ten friends these questions and report back to the group with the answers. Each group will then discuss the data gathered and prepare a report to present to the class summarizing their findings.

Out of Class Projects

1. Ask your class to choose an item that is not originally American (sushi, futons, or MINI Coopers, for example) and then to conduct some research on the Internet and in the library to learn what the origin of the item is, when it was introduced in the United States, why it became popular here, who first introduced it, what advertising campaigns were used, and what kind of success (or lack of success) it has had in this country. Ask students to share their findings with the class. Encourage your class to include visuals with their final presentations.

2. Have students research a traditionally American business or product that has been tweaked for a foreign market. Suggestions might include Euro-Disney, Hong Kong Disneyland (see pages 52–53 of *Time*, July 18, 2005), McDonald's, Burger King, or Kentucky Fried Chicken. Students should learn what adaptations have been made to bridge the cultural gaps and how successful the transactions have been both for new consumers and for the company involved. Allow class time for students to report their findings.

Noodles vs. Sesame Seed Buns (p. 123)
Seanon Wong

Globalization can be seen as a blessing or a curse in terms of what it does to a regional or national culture. In this essay, Wong makes the case that traditional Chinese cultures are actually enhanced by the rise of Chinese fast food and its global dissemination. Whether students believe that Chinese fast food equals a championing of cultural diversity is open for debate. One does discover how the food and culture of this particular region has begun to cope with and stand up to the domination of Western fast food.

TEACHING STRATEGIES

Questions for Discussion

1. For many students, the "McWorld" is the only one they've ever known. Ask students whether they have ever traveled to a country (or a part of

the United States) that has been free of most Western food chains. If they have, ask them to speak about the experience. If they have not, ask them to consider and speak about what they might be missing.

2. Based on what Wong has said, do the Chinese people seem opposed to globalization? What clues can students point to that show the acceptance or rejection of globalization? What about signs of ambivalence?

Group Activities

1. Ask students to review the selection titled "Noodles vs. Sesame Seed Buns" in small groups. Have them outline the points being made, and then ask each group to develop plans for its own fast food chain (the culture it seeks to promote can be Chinese or that of another non-European country). Students should provide a bit of background on their chain and present their ideas about menu, ambience, and clientele to the class.

2. Divide students into two groups—one that represents the interests of globalization (and students should be prepared to explain which aspects of globalization they are representing), and one that represents insular indigenous cultures which prefer to remain distinct. Get a debate going between them, with an eye to Wong's statement that "the primary lesson one can learn from the thriving Chinese fast food sector is that globalization is facilitating the spread of cultural diversity, rather than . . . a tendency towards cultural homogeneity" (para. 12).

Out of Class Projects

1. Have students do some research on one of the Chinese fast food restaurants mentioned in this essay. What can they learn about it beyond what Wong chooses to impart? Does the restaurant have a Web site? Ask students to describe the restaurant and its food to the best of their ability, based on the research they have done. How does it compare with other Chinese restaurants? With Western restaurants?

2. Have students ever visited an American fast food restaurant in another country? Ask students to write a short personal essay about the country they visited and the effect that patronizing an "American" restaurant had on their experience of the "indigenous" culture.

The Only Way to Have a Cow (p. 129)
BILL McKIBBEN

Bill McKibben offers a solution to the dilemma of those who are carnivores but who worry about global warming—eat, but make sure the cows are moving and eating grass. McKibben reminds us of the history of herding cattle, and how herding methods used to help strike an ecological balance instead of creating climate change. Both the fast food industry and strict vegetarians will have to come to terms his argument; although his point of view doesn't help either cause, his call to a return to rotational grazing may indeed be the answer that people on Earth's rapidly warming surface should contemplate.

TEACHING STRATEGIES

Questions for Discussion

1. After reading McKibben's essay, students should consider the methods that were once used to raise herds and hunt big game in this country. Do they believe that such methods can work once again, on any scale? Why or why not?

2. "I doubt McDonald's will be in favor," McKibben writes of his position on how to raise cattle for consumption. "I doubt Paul McCartney will be in favor." Divide the class into two groups: one taking McDonald's and the fast food industry's position, the other taking the position of McCartney and strict vegetarians. Have each brainstorm their group's view of the essay's argument and write a speech that outlines the difficulties this position presents.

Group Activities

1. Divide students into groups, and ask them to consider various ways people are trying to combat global warming. They may research any new information on climate change or radical changes in human behavior/ business practices currently being implemented. They may also consider what still needs to be done or is being ignored in the fight to stop climate change. Have the groups present their findings to the class.

2. In small groups, ask students to discuss the information McKibben presents about how meat is raised to be eaten in modern society, and their own feelings about eating meat. Ask them to try to find at least one fact about modern food production in the essay that surprised them. Were any of the arguments against eating meat something students could relate to? Did the essay change their perception of the food they eat in any way?

Out of Class Projects

1. Have students do Internet research to find data that illustrates the difference between the agribusiness of today's farming versus the smaller family-owned farms that used to predominate in this country. Then have them write a brief essay that argues the value of one method or the other, and carefully cites all of their sources.

2. Ask students to gather five to ten articles from magazines, newspapers, and the Internet (from a combination of these three media and not all from one source) about global warming and current farming practices or society's eating habits. Then have them outline points from their articles and explain how they relate to the points McKibben brings out in his essay.

Pooch Café (p. 134)

This *Pooch Café* comic strip shows two different sides to the vegetarian argument. The strip questions the necessity of vegetarian products like processed tofu burgers because they seem to have many of the negative characteristics that are usually assigned to meat. Students may disagree strongly with this cartoon, especially if they are vegetarian. Have students explore the idea that Bill McKibbon presents in "How Not to Have a Cow," which is that not all meat is necessarily bad. How can this idea be applied to a vegetarian diet, and how does it relate back to the comic strip?

Food Traditions: The Thread That Links Generations (p. 135)
Bonny Wolf

Weekend Edition food commentator Bonny Wolf has written a book called *Talking with My Mouth Full*, a collection of essays that explores the communal and cultural aspects of food. In this NPR interview, Wolf explains the premise of her book and introduces the audience to some of the "characters" in her book. For each person, his or her connection to certain foods strongly shapes family relationships and has a fundamental influence on his or her experience of life events.

TEACHING STRATEGIES

Questions for Discussion

1. In class discussion, try to determine when students believe our relationship with food begins. Do they think food continues to have an influence over them as they move out of childhood? In what way?

2. Have students consider how food preparation differs from one cultural group to another, and in fact, from individual to individual. How do students experience food's impact on their identity? Have they ever noted that their family prepares the same foods differently from another? Ask them to elaborate on these differences.

Group Activities

1. Wolf names many reasons for eating: hunger, comfort, celebration, and so on. Divide the class into small groups and ask students to list all the reasons we eat. In a class discussion, go over the reasons they have come up with and try to sort them out in terms of importance.

2. When do we eat alone, and when do we eat socially? Again, ask students to come up with reasons we might dine alone or with others. As a class, rank these in order of importance (for eating solo or with others) and notice when the lists overlap in any way. Also take note of when eating one way or the other happens for very distinct reasons.

Out of Class Projects

1. Wolf recounts the story of a hospice nurse who made home-cooked meals for patients in her care. The effect on families and patients was striking; the preparation of food elicited many stories and emotions. Have students write a brief essay about a food from childhood that has stayed with them because of the feeling it left them with and the story it brings to mind.

2. Direct students to the broadcast of this interview with Bonny Wolf at www.npr.org/templates/story/story.php?storyId=6572685. Have them write about the experience of listening to it versus reading it. Did they prefer reading the interview or hearing it? Why?

Rice Culture (p. 138)
Julie Dash

Julie Dash refers to her family as "rice eaters" when the truth of the matter is that they are the best of the "rice cookers." This skill derives from their history as rice planters and harvesters—as slaves. From generation to generation, her people passed down the way to perfect each rice dish. Dash has immortalized this act in her essay, reminding readers of her Aunt Gertie's history, of the expectations of her community, and of Dash's own desire to impart the lessons she has learned.

TEACHING STRATEGIES

Questions for Discussion

1. Ask students if they cook. Do they think of cooking as a science or art form as Dash does? Why or why not?

2. Different crops or foods are important to different nations, regions, and ethnic groups. Ask students to explain in their own words why rice is so important to the Geechees. Others in South Carolina might not feel that rice has the same importance to them.

Group Activities

1. Ask students to discuss among themselves what foods they remember their parents preparing and why they think those foods stand out in their memories. Is there a particular dish that reminds them of their heritage? Groups should present their findings to the class.

2. In groups of three or four have students consider how we learn skills or traditions as children. Who are our teachers? How is information shared when our learning doesn't happen in a classroom? Is there any truth to Dash's statement: "Learning through humiliation and fear is certainly not

the best way to acquire knowledge—but you damn sure never forget it!" (para. 11). In what other ways do we learn?

Out of Class Projects

1. Have students interview a family member about a food or recipe that is somehow important to the family. Extra research on the subject matter can be conducted once the interview is complete. Students should write a short personal essay that explains the significance of the food based on their interview and any relevant research or stories they wish to add. They should include a recipe, if possible.

2. The Geechees are a relatively unknown people in the United States, although they have their own language and a well-preserved heritage, and they once contributed greatly to the culture of South Carolina. Ask students to research the Geechee, or Gullah, people. They should draw some conclusions from their research about why so few people know about the Geechees, and about how they have managed to preserve their culture and traditions.

Picky Eater (p. 143)
Julia Alvarez

For Julia Alvarez, going out to dinner does not offer the same pleasures that it does for many of us. Alvarez can point to various things about meals that have created tension in her family; in this essay, she charts the changes that have occurred in her feelings about food now that she's married to a man who likes to cook, and eat, and talk about meals. As she points out, background has much to do with whether one shies away from food or embraces it. Her own pickiness might be cultural, due to her experience "in the 1950s in a small underdeveloped country where there were very few tourists and, therefore, few eating establishments that catered to pleasure dining" (para. 4), or psychological, because childhood meals were "fraught with performance or punishment pressures" (para. 19).

TEACHING STRATEGIES

Questions for Discussion

1. Have students ever been afraid to eat a food because of safety issues, as Alvarez was afraid to eat foods in her homeland? If so, can they articulate that fear and its effect on their overall enjoyment of food? Did it have a notable impact? Do they think Alvarez's early fears about the safety of eating certain foods played into her eating habits overall?

2. Alvarez chronicles her relationship with food from childhood to early adulthood to now. Have students' relationships to food changed over the years? What influences any changes (or not) in that relationship?

Group Activities

1. Some people enjoy food and the social aspects of eating. Others do not, or learn those aspects over time. Ask students in small groups to align themselves with Alvarez or her husband in terms of their appreciation of food. They should discuss how they are more like one or the other.

2. Hunger is primal, and one's immediate relationship with one's mother usually revolves around food. Pair up students and ask them to debate whether Alvarez's mother used food as a way to nurture her daughters. If the relationship of the family to food wasn't one of nurture, what was it? Ask pairs to share any of their insights with the class.

Out of Class Projects

1. Julia Alvarez is a prolific writer of poetry, novels, and essays. Direct students to other works by Alvarez and ask them to read at least one. Have students write a short paper about her choice of subject matter, style, or tone using the essay "Picky Eater" and the work they have chosen as examples.

2. Ask students to find images in ads in current media that are suggestive about individuals and families and food. What do these ads tell them to think about families and their relationship to food? Ask students to write a brief essay about the picture they are given about relationships and food using various advertisements as research.

Freedom from Want (p. 152)

Some of your students will be familiar with Norman Rockwell's iconic American paintings. Bring in color reproductions of *Freedom from Want* and some of his other works to spark class discussion. Ask your students what image of that famous American holiday, Thanksgiving, is being presented. How does it compare with their own celebrations?

Focusing on Yesterday, Focusing on Today
Let's All Meet at Rosie's Diner! (p. 154)

Most of your students will probably be familiar with the 1950s diner, especially since popular nationwide chains like Johnny Rocket's have adopted the theme. Although this photograph was taken fairly recently, it is a nostalgic image with strong 1950s connotations. Ask students what they associate with diners of this kind—what type of food is served? What is the atmosphere like? Why are diners like these so ingrained in American pop culture?

Fine Dining à la Airstream (p. 155)

The gourmet food truck trend has become wildly popular within the last few years, serving a much different clientele than the food trucks and diners of the past. Ask students if they have ever eaten from a food truck—what was the experience like? Why might this type of restaurant be coming into fashion now? *Time* also has an article and photo essay on gourmet food trucks entitled "Gourmet On the Go: Good Food Goes Trucking" by Joel Stein (March 29, 2010) and the Food Network airs a successful reality competition show called *The Great Food Truck Race*.

ADDITIONAL RESOURCES

1. In 2006, Michael Pollan kept a regular blog on the *New York Times* Web site. With entries like "My Letter to Whole Foods" and "Food from a Farm Near You," Pollan further explores modern issues in food consumption. You can find the blog at http://pollan.blogs.nytimes.com.

2. Food writing has become one of the most popular topics for bloggers. For some popular food blogs, which incorporate beautiful photography alongside food writing and recipes, try Pen & Fork (penandfork.com), Aapplemint (aapplemint.com), Matt Bites (mattbites.com), and Serious Eats (seriouseats.com).

3. Anthony Bourdain is best known for his sometimes outrageous food and travel show *No Reservations*, but he is also the author of many books and articles, which take a more humorous look at the world of food. A prime example of a Bourdain essay is "Don't Eat before Reading This," which appeared in *The New Yorker* on April 19, 1999.

4. *Sunset* magazine often publishes brief and helpful articles on food, such as "10 Worst Food Trends" (July 2011), and the blog One-Block Diet (oneblockdiet.sunset.com) follows several contributing food writers and editors as they try their hand at local, sustainable eating.

5. For an interesting discussion of the American fast food invasion of France, especially McDonald's (which the French have dubbed McDo's), see *A Goose in Toulouse: And Other Culinary Adventures in France* by Mort Rosenblum (North Point Press, 2000). This works well with Tara Parker-Pope's "Custom-Made."

"How Do I Look?"
How Culture Shapes Self-Image

5

How many of your students really believe that "beauty is in the eye of the beholder" or that "beauty is only skin deep"? Many would admit that they spend more time, thought, and money on their own physical appearance than they need to or might even wish to. And it is no wonder that they do so when their reflection may differ from the faces that they see on television and computer screens, in magazines, and in the movies. Have any of your students gone to unusual lengths to alter their body image? Some alterations are only "skin-deep" like body art, while others are much more insidious like drug abuse and eating disorders. Although cultural influence on self-image is an inherently serious issue, you will find a variety of approaches to this topic in this chapter. They range from a consideration of physical identity in the online world, to a candid and sometimes humorous Patricia McLaughlin essay in which she decries the increase in cosmetic surgery among men saying: "Ken? Is that really what women want? Maybe some women. Me, I get all weak in the knees when I see a guy running a vacuum, or unloading a dishwasher without being asked. Not that Calvin Klein is ever going to advertise his underwear on a cute guy with a nice big electric broom." As your students reflect on the different viewpoints offered in this chapter, they may come to a new understanding of the pervasive influence of popular culture on self-image and may even reevaluate their own.

Body Mod of Boston (p. 157)

Ask your students to read John Leo's "The 'Modern Primitives' " before they read this visual to enhance the discussion. What are students' gut reactions to this advertisement? Ask them to analyze their reactions and to consider the following questions: Why does the advertiser use what many would consider an extreme example of body modification? In what ways is this an effective advertisement? How does the ad make use of strategies of comparison and contrast? Why is the shop called Body Mod of Boston? Are the young men in the photograph simply making a fashion statement?

The "Modern Primitives" (p. 160)
John Leo

Students are likely to enjoy this fascinating treatment of a subject that probably intrigues many of them—body modification. Most students have pierced their ears, and many have additional piercings and tattoos. They are probably aware of the message that they wish to send through their own body fashion, but they may be unaware of the larger implications of the widespread body modification phenomenon as explored by John Leo in this thoughtful essay.

TEACHING STRATEGIES

Questions for Discussion

1. Ask your students whether they or their friends have modified their bodies with tattoos or piercings. What kind of body art do they have? Why did they decide to have it done, and how did their parents and friends react? Have they experienced any second thoughts about their body modifications? Why or why not?

2. What celebrities can your students think of who have modified their bodies with tattoos or piercings? Angelina Jolie, Eminem, and Tommy Lee are examples. What images do students believe that these stars are trying to project?

Group Activities

1. Divide the class into small groups. Have each group member interview five acquaintances who have gotten tattoos or piercings. Each student should have a prepared list of five questions to ask each interviewee. Group members should then reconvene and collate their findings before presenting their results to the class. They may also wish to add information about their own body modifications and reasons for them.

2. Divide the class into groups of three or four students. Have each group research the body modification rituals or practices of a particular culture (like a Native American tribe) or subculture (like motorcycle gangs). Students may use interviews, site visits, libraries, or the Web to conduct their research. Have students share their findings in a formal presentation in which each group member takes part or submits his or her results in written form.

Out of Class Projects

1. Ask your class to survey the campus for as many unique fashion statements as they can find. Describe each fashion statement in detail in a notebook. What do students think that the fashion is "stating"? These notes can then be transformed into an oral presentation or an essay.

2. Have students make arrangements to visit a tattoo or piercing parlor and interview the body artist about his or her clientele and the latest trends in body modification. Students should examine the different kinds of body art that are available and find out about their cost and any possible risks. If it is impossible or uncomfortable for students to make a site visit, have them do research in the library or on the Web about body art. Students may present their findings orally to the class or in writing.

My Inner Shrimp (p. 164)

GARRY TRUDEAU

Many of your students will relate to this confessional essay by well-known humorist Garry Trudeau. Most of us have at least one physical characteristic that we have wished we could change at some time in our lives (see also Dan Barden's "My New Nose," which appears later in this chapter). Traditional college-age students are still coming to terms with their self-images, both outwardly and inwardly. Try to take the class's pulse after students have read Trudeau's essay. Find out what his words said to them about their own inner selves.

TEACHING STRATEGIES

Questions for Discussion

1. Ask students to compare the pressure to conform to a cultural norm of beauty in the high school and college years. Does this pressure lessen or intensify? How did they react to this pressure in the past? How do they expect to handle it in the future? Tell the class to pay attention to any differences in responses from male and female students.

2. Most recent presidents of the United States have been taller than six feet. Reports have also shown that tall, attractive men do better in the world of business. Ask your students whether this is just coincidence or whether other forces are at work.

Group Activities

1. In small groups have students come up with as many films or television shows as they can think of that feature characters whose body image differs from the cultural norm. Tell the group to pick three of these characters to present to the class. Students should describe these characters, explain how these characters view themselves, and discuss how other characters react to them.

2. Divide the class into small groups. Direct students to list as many social and professional situations as they can in which height is or could be an issue. Have groups share their lists with the class.

Out of Class Projects

1. Have students research a court case in which someone sued over loss of position, recognition, or promotion due to a physical characteristic that was perceived as detrimental. Tell students to use the library's periodical resources as well as the Internet for their research. They should include all relevant aspects of the case as well as its current status.

2. Tell students to conduct interviews with ten students outside of class. Tell your class to prepare a series of questions concerning the interviewees'

attitudes about height and the ways that it is perceived in our society. Students should summarize their findings for the class.

Venus Envy (p. 168)
PATRICIA MCLAUGHLIN

Patricia McLaughlin writes that, according to *Men's Health* editor Stephen Perrine, mass media "in the last five to seven years has really changed the way it portrays men" (para. 7). Do your students remember the TV commercial that showed female office workers rushing to a window to gawk at a construction worker removing his T-shirt and sipping a Diet Coke? If not, they are no doubt familiar with the Calvin Klein underwear ads that McLaughlin refers to as evidence of the "Great Seesaw of Being"—the idea that men are becoming more aware of their appearance, believing that the way they look really counts and perhaps even defines them, and they are willing to do whatever it takes to improve on what they have, as demonstrated in "My New Nose."

TEACHING STRATEGIES

Questions for Discussion

1. What dictates our society's standards for acceptable male appearance? Is regarding men as sex objects just an example of "turnabout is fair play"? What evidence do you see of this trend in movies, music videos, television ads, and television shows? What does it say about women's increasing influence on the business world (and their status as consumers) that more ads are showing what advertisers believe are women's preferences?

2. What role has television played in determining what McLaughlin argues is men's increasing emphasis on their looks? Which shows and actors are currently setting the standard for looks for men? For women? Which commercials focus particularly on looks? What role do movies and the influence of Hollywood play in setting standards of female and male beauty? What does all this emphasis on physical appearance indicate about our society's values?

Group Activities

1. Divide the class into small same-gender groups. Ask the women to make two lists—the top five qualities that they believe men look for in a partner and the top five qualities that women look for in a partner. Ask the men to make two lists—the top five qualities that they believe women look for in a partner and the top five qualities men look for in a partner. Ask each group to send a representative to the board to list its ideas about what men look for in partners. How accurately did the women predict what the men said? Ask each group to list on the board what women look for in partners. How accurately did the men predict what the women said?

Point out similarities and differences in these lists. Discuss what the results say about our level of gender communication or lack of it.

2. In small groups have students discuss the pressures on men and women to "measure up" physically. What standard was the goal in high school? In college? What image is the right one, and who determines what's "right"? How much does physical appearance affect life choices, like potential jobs, making friends, and finding a partner? How might our society shift away from its emphasis on a physical standard to measure value and worth? What conditions would be required for this to occur?

Out of Class Projects

1. Ask students to go to a newsstand or bookstore and survey the magazines dealing with men's health and physical appearance. If possible, have students discuss with the owner or a salesperson whether the store has increased the number of such magazines that it carries over the last several years. What topics are most popular in these publications? Ask students to select several of these magazines for a closer look. What can students deduce about the age, social status, and interests of potential readers from skimming the magazines' articles?

2. Ask your class to investigate, with the help of the computer searches available in the library, the recent most popular types of elective plastic surgery for men and for women. Who tends to spend more and on what kinds of physical alterations? In what areas of the United States is plastic surgery most popular? How might students characterize those who spend money on elective plastic surgery?

100% Indian Hair (p. 172)
Tanzila Ahmed

In this essay, Tanzila Ahmed raises questions about the cultural significance of Indian hair, examining how hair that is often cut off under unexplained circumstances often makes its way to America to be used in hair weaves. In the context of America's obsession with beauty and self-image, Ahmed wonders how women can be uninterested in the origin of the hair, and compares this to the lack of interest that people show toward the plight of sweatshop laborers.

TEACHING STRATEGIES

Questions for Discussion

1. Do your students think that the "solidarity" that Ahmed calls for is important among women of color? Why or why not?

2. Ask the class why Ahmed is "grossed out" by the thought of using human hair in weaves. What are your students' opinions about this?

Group Activities

1. In her essay, the author writes about Americans who shop at Wal-Mart "to buy their clothes without consciously thinking of the people of color who created the clothes in sweatshops" (para 9). Break the class into two groups, and ask each group to research the various policies and practices of the store chain. Conduct a classroom debate with one side defending American Wal-Mart shoppers and one side condemning them.

2. Ask your students if their ethnicity is associated with a certain physical attribute. Have them discuss how they would feel if an aspect of their culture was mass marketed. Create a piece of advertising for another cultural attribute that has the same impact as "100% Indian Hair."

Out of Class Projects

1. Have students investigate the truth about Indian hair. They should research the production of human hair pieces and decide whether the truth matches up to the story that Ahmed found on the Internet about Indian women cutting their hair "as an offering to their god as a sign of modesty" (para. 7).

2. Hair weaves are just one way that some Americans try to enhance beauty artificially. Ask students to find an image of a celebrity and label all of his or her artificial enhancements. Ask them if it is possible to find an image of a celebrity who has no artificial enhancements and what the possible implications might be.

Identity in a Virtual World (p. 176)
MICHELLE JANA CHAN

When we think about self-image, we often think about the ways in which society has shaped us. However, online worlds and role-playing games offer an opportunity for us to think about the ways that we would "remake" ourselves if we had the freedom to do so. Michelle Jana Chan looks at the work of photographer Robbie Cooper, whose book *Alter Ego: Avatars and Their Creators* presents side-by-side portraits of people and the online characters that they have created. How would your students look if they were able to create new versions of themselves online? Why would they make changes to their physical appearances or personality traits?

TEACHING STRATEGIES

Questions for Discussion

1. Ask students to consider the following quote from photographer Robbie Cooper: "[Y]ou might create a character and enjoy the anonymity of it at first, but that character then becomes a bigger part of your life" (para. 4). What does this imply about individuals with avatars?

2. Have students discuss whether they think that someone completely satisfied with their life would take part in virtual worlds. Why or why not?

Group Activities

1. Divide students into groups, and ask them to consider whether the criminal justice system has a right to discipline a person whose avatar displays consistently violent behavior in a virtual community. Research the rules of online communities, and search for example cases. Each group will then present its findings to the class.

2. Reinventing identity is a strong theme in many literary and film classics. In small groups, ask students to discuss the human impulse to "start over" and decide if it is something that they can relate to in their own lives.

Out of Class Projects

1. Using magazine clippings, drawings, or any media that they prefer, students should create a superhero self-portrait. They can give themselves whatevert physical and nonphysical characteristics they like (they can give themselves eagle's wings if that's what they please). They can present their self-portraits to the class and explain the choices that they made.

2. Ask students to do some research into virtual online communities and multiplayer games. They should contact a member of one of these communities and do an e-mail interview with them about the issues in Chan's article.

Me and My Avatar (p. 180)

This portrait by Robbie Cooper appears in his book *Alter Ego: Avatars and Their Creators* (published by Chris Boot, 2007) and is mentioned in Chan's article. It shows the stark differences between South Korean professor Choi Seang Rak and his schoolgirl avatar Uroo Ahs. Ask your students to discuss the differences between these images. Do they find it strange that an adult man would want to play an online game as a girl? Why? You might want to try obtaining a copy of Cooper's book. One interesting exercise would involve showing students each portrait separately and seeing whether they can correctly pair people with their avatars.

My New Nose (p. 181)
Dan Barden

This essay offers a unique look at the growing trend among men to opt for cosmetic surgery. Dan Barden's frank analysis of his reasons to "journey to the center of his face" and his reactions to that journey will probably surprise students. His many references to television and film provide interesting links with essays in Chapter 8.

TEACHING STRATEGIES

Questions for Discussion

1. Ask students what they know about the boom in cosmetic surgery for men. Where did they acquire their information? What do they think of this trend?

2. Do your students think that men will ever be as open and candid about changing their appearance as some women are? Will men brag about inviting their favorite doctor and friends to a Botox party? Will male athletes ever chat about thigh implants in the locker room? Have students defend their responses.

Group Activities

1. Break the class into small mixed-gender groups. Instruct students to share their views on cosmetic surgery for the opposite sex. How would they advise friends or family members who wanted to surgically enhance their looks? How would their advice for the opposite sex compare to the advice they would offer members of their own gender?

2. Tell your students to bring magazine advertisements for cosmetic surgical procedures targeted at men to class and to prepare a brief presentation on their ads. Break the class into groups of five or six students. Allow enough time for students to present their ads to the other members of their group. Then direct each group to analyze the ads' strategies to hook potential patients/consumers and to pick the most effective ad. They will then present this advertisement to the rest of the class.

Out of Class Projects

1. Have students research a particular cosmetic surgical procedure. Students should find out exactly what the procedure entails, how popular it is, and how the numbers of men and women undergoing this procedure compare. Class members should then report their findings to the class.

2. Instruct students to interview ten students (five men and five women) who are not in your class about their views on cosmetic surgery for men. Students should prepare at least ten interview questions and take careful notes during and immediately following their interviews. Have them summarize their findings and report on them briefly in class.

Losing the Trauma: The Author Before and After Surgery (pp. 184–185)

Although students may not at first see any striking differences between these two photos, encourage them to look closely and discern the subtle transformation that has taken place. Have them point to specific passages in the essay that refer to the author's "old" and "new" noses. Encourage your class to decode the title "Losing the Trauma."

The Eye of the Beholder (p. 187)
GRACE SUH

Television talk shows and fashion magazines devote entire segments and many glossy pages to makeovers, and many students have probably responded to the promise of a more appealing image to present to the world. What is at the basis of the desire to make one's self over? Do your students embrace the notion of "making over," or like Grace Suh—who writes, "I wasn't pretty. But I was familiar and comforting. I was myself" (para. 28)—do they ultimately reject the pressure to conform to or imitate the societal ideal and value themselves as they are? This essay is interesting to relate to Alice Walker's "Beauty: When the Other Dancer Is the Self."

TEACHING STRATEGIES

Questions for Discussion

1. What do your students think of the prevalence of makeover segments on talk shows? Why do many people volunteer for them? Why are these segments popular? Would your students volunteer for one of these makeovers? What would they hope to gain from the experience?

2. Ask your class to think of and discuss examples of fashion looks that have crossed ethnic boundaries into the mainstream, for example, cornrow braids and hair beads or Mehndi (the East Indian art of skin decoration). Does this "crossing over" affect that fashion's cultural significance? If so, how?

Group Activities

1. Form small groups, and ask students to share their experiences (or those of a friend) with makeovers or with trying to make some other drastic change in their looks. Why did they do what they did? Were they pleased with the results?

2. Ask your students to work in small groups to discuss an "epiphanous" moment like Suh's when they came to a realization about their sense of who they are. What did they realize? How did this realization change their outlook on life?

Out of Class Projects

1. Have your class find other advertisements for beauty products that feature models of different ethnicities. Ask students to pick out three of the most interesting ads to analyze for class.

2. Ask students to do some library or Internet research on beauty ideals in other cultures or in America in the past. Students should pick one country, one ethnic group, or one time period. How do these ideals differ from ours today? Ask students to report their findings to the class.

Beauty: When the Other Dancer Is the Self (p. 193)
ALICE WALKER

This classic essay allows you to introduce the topic of physical disability, a topic that is crucial to any discussion of body image, but that too often is ignored. Alice Walker's moving and poetic description of her journey to self-acceptance as a beautiful black woman, mother, and writer brings into question those seemingly shallow quests for the perfect body that take up so much air time and space in magazines.

TEACHING STRATEGIES

Questions for Discussion

1. Ask students what other works they have read by Alice Walker. Pick one or two that provide an interesting comparison with this essay, and assign one or both for the class to read. Provide several questions to direct class discussion.

2. Discuss how this essay differs from other narrative essays that your students have read. Ask students how they react to the repeated phrases or refrains, to the poem "On Sight," and to the achronological ordering of the essay.

Group Activities

1. Divide the class into small groups. Instruct each group to think of as many films as they can that deal with the topic of physical disability. Ask the group to discuss questions like the following: How is the disabled character treated in the film? What is his or her disability? To what extent does he or she triumph over the disability? What does the movie teach us?

2. Alice Walker's daughter Rebecca proved to be a great inspiration to her without even knowing it. In small groups, discuss how people can be influential in other people's lives without intending to be. Examples can come from real life, films, or readings.

Out of Class Projects

1. Have students research their university's policy on students with disabilities. They may consult the university Web site or conduct personal, telephone, or e-mail interviews with campus personnel who deal with accommodations. They may also interview students or professors who

have dealt with disabilities. Students should remember that this is a sensitive issue and that confidentiality is mandated by law.

2. Tell your students to research cosmetic surgery among African Americans or another ethnic group. How does it compare to cosmetic surgery among white Americans? Which procedures are performed and how often? How do the reasons for cosmetic surgery compare between white and nonwhite groups?

An Open Letter to the Totally Impractical Size Chart for Women's Clothing (p. 202)
CLAIRE SUDDATH

Claire Suddath's open letter for *McSweeney's* exposes the difficulty of shopping in the women's clothing section. Why, she asks, is there no reasonable way to determine one's size (as found in the male size chart, for example)? These sizes, she complains, simply don't make sense and add to the stress of trying to dress in a world in which women are often told to make a "totally impractical size" their ideal. Her very reasonable essay exposes some of the unreasonableness of American fashion.

TEACHING STRATEGIES

Questions for Discussion

1. Ask students why they think women's dress sizes are not based on inches or a more concrete method of measurement. Do women's clothing sizes mean anything? Do men also have the same difficulties determining their size that Suddath mentions here for women? Note any differences between men and women's responses.

2. Suddath notes that the boyfriends and husbands of women frustrated by their clothing sizes will be caught looking "a little too longingly at Courteney Cox or Jessica Alba," leading to general strife (para. 6). Do you think it is a coincidence that these women are the ones the men are watching on television? What do Cox and Alba have to do with Suddath's anger about the impracticality of the size chart for women's clothing?

Group Activities

1. Divide the class into small groups. Have each group write an open letter concerning an issue they have strong personal feelings about. Ask students to pay attention to the tone of Suddath's letter and imitate it in some way. After each group presents its letter, discuss as a class how each group letter was like or unlike the Suddath letter.

2. In small groups, ask students to come up with film, television, and music stars who might be the type to incite jealousy among women who can't find clothes that fit. Would any of these stars have difficulty finding the

right clothes size? Why or why not? Students should explain why normal-sized women would experience the phrase "X looks nothing like you" to mean "because you're a fat cow," as Suddath does in the essay.

Out of Class Projects

1. Ask students to conduct interviews with ten students outside of class. Before the interview, students should prepare a series of questions about how the interviewees experiences clothing ads, whether they like shopping for clothes, whether finding the right size clothing is difficult, and how they feel society influences self-perception and what clothing people buy. A report should be written after all interviews that summarizes the findings. Students should make note of whether or not responses were influenced by gender.

2. Have students look at popular magazines that target a female audience, examining both article content (taking particular note of fashion articles) and advertisements. What images are used to promote fashion trends? What sort of language is used in articles about clothing and appearance?

Cathy by Cathy Guisewite (p. 205)

This *Cathy* comic strip illustrates the absurdity surrounding women's clothing. Students can relate this to Claire Suddath's "An Open Letter to the Totally Impractical Size Chart for Women's Clothing." The comic depicts the overwhelming choice that women confront, even when trying to purchase a pair of jeans, an article of clothing which, the salesperson in the strip points out, is meant to be "liberating."

Focusing on Yesterday, Focusing on Today
Even Ladies Can Wear Levi's! (p. 206)

Students may find this vintage Levi's advertisement a little hokey, so ask them why they think that might be the case. What about this advertisement—and the style depicted—makes it seem so old-fashioned? Ask your students if there is anything that could be added or removed from the ad to make it seem more modern.

"Everybody's Work Is Equally Important."
(p. 207)

Some of your students may have seen this more recent Levi's ad campaign in magazines and on billboards. Have students analyze the message of the ads, and ask them how the advertisements relate to the product that they are trying to sell. Unlike in the vintage ad, the jeans are not a visual focal point—how does this change the intended message? Do your students think that the ad's message is clear and effective? Why or why not? You may also want to point students to the *New York Times* article, "Levi's Features a Town Trying to Recover" (www.nytimes.com/2010/06/24/business/media/24adco.html) that discusses the campaign.

ADDITIONAL RESOURCES

1. For further reading, consult Orphira Edut's *Adios, Barbie: Young Women Write about Body Image and Identity* (1998), a fascinating collection of essays dealing with female body image cross-culturally.

2. Movies such as *Freaks, Frankenstein, The Elephant Man, Shallow Hal, The Mask, The Man without a Face, Powder, Edward Scissorhands,* and *Vanilla Sky* feature characters whose body image does not meet the ideal of beauty of the culture in which they live. Show clips from one or more of these movies to spark discussion. You could do the same with clips from TV talk shows or makeover shows that feature guests who look different from the "norm."

3. Poems that work well with essays in this chapter are "Barbie Doll" and "A Work of Artifice" by Marge Piercy, "Hanging Fire" by Audre Lourde, and "Mirror" by Sylvia Plath.

4. See Laura Fraser's *Losing It: America's Obsession with Weight and the Industry That Feeds on It* (1997), which exposes the diet industry's manipulation of its consumers, for an in-depth discussion of this subject.

5. Many of the essays in Chapter 3, "Define 'American': Reflections on Cultural Identity," work well with this chapter, such as Dinaw Mengestu's "Home at Last."

6. Katherine Heine's article "Men, Plastic Surgery's Not Just for Michael Jackson Anymore" (*Austin American-Statesman*, August 28, 2005, Life and Arts, K14), works well with the paired selections in this chapter.

7. Instructors or students can bring to class gender- or culture-specific toys, such as action figures or Barbie dolls. Working as a class or in small groups, ask students to discuss these dolls or action figures and the ways that playing with them may influence gender development, body image, and cultural self-image.

8. The *U.S. News & World Report* cover story "Makeover Nation," which accompanied the opening visual of this chapter, "American Gothic Makeover" (May 31, 2004: 53–63), provides an in-depth look at the makeover craze.

9. Alison Stein Wellner's article from the March 2004 issue of *Continental* titled "(Covert) Cosmetics: The Strange Relationship between a Modern Man and His Looks" makes an interesting pairing with Dan Barden's

"My New Nose" or Patricia McLaughlin's "Venus Envy." A telling quotation from Wellner's essay is the following: "No longer can a guy simply ignore his appearance: nine in ten men surveyed by the marketing firm Euro RSCG Worldwide say that good grooming is essential for men in the business world, and over 60 percent say that men who are attractive are more likely to get ahead in the business world than men who are, well, not."

10. A humorous take on men's appearance is Dave Barry's "The Ugly Truth about Beauty," which appeared in *Philadelphia Magazine* on February 3, 1998. Barry contends that "most men . . . think of themselves as average-looking. Men will think this even if their faces cause heart failure in cattle at a range of 300 yards. Being average does not bother them. . . . If, at the end of his four-minute daily beauty regimen, a man has managed to wipe most of the shaving cream out of his hair and is not bleeding too badly, he feels that he has done all he can, so he stops thinking about his appearance and devotes his mind to more critical issues, such as the Super Bowl."

11. Carolyn Edgar's "Black and Blue" (*Reconstruction*, volume 2.3: 1994) pairs well with Alice Walker's "Beauty: When the Other Dancer Is the Self." Edgar's essay details the battles with self-image of an African American and Native American woman as she considers her childhood, young adulthood, and future motherhood. Maya Angelou's poems "Africa" and "Phenomenal Woman" describe the resilience of both Edgar and Walker.

What Are You Trying to Say?
How Language Works

6

Few things are as intrinsic to culture as the way we express ourselves, and as this chapter illustrates, popular culture continues to expand the ways that we communicate. Because America is a multicultural society, American English is increasingly infused with words and phrases from other cultures, and new technologies are creating new means for expressing our thoughts. Chapter 6 explores traditional thinking about language as it is spoken and written by each of us every day, but it also gets students thinking about language in ways they haven't before, especially how it evolves along with popular culture. Students are asked to read essays by John J. Miller and Mindy Cameron about the threat of extinction that is faced by some very old languages and essays about new social rules that we must consider thanks to the popularity of text messaging.

Kryptos (p. 209)

The *Kryptos* sculpture remains a mystery to code breakers, and is a reminder of how powerful language can be. Have students do some quick online research into *Kryptos* and see what they find. There are hundreds of Web sites devoted to the decoding of the sculpture, with message boards and updates on any clues or breakthroughs. What do students make of these Web sites? Why do they think so many people are interested in decoding the sculpture?

Lost in Translation (p. 212)
Lera Boroditsky

The creation and experience of culture may be strongly tied to the words that come out of our mouths. Studies now indicate that the language we are speaking (or learning) influences our perception of the world. Lera Boroditsky's essay suggests that people who speak Spanish, for example, have a different perception of their external or internal realities than people who speak Japanese or Turkish, if perceptions are bound up in the varied patterns of the language being used. As we study languages and their differences, we uncover more and more about the similarities and differences of the human experience.

TEACHING STRATEGIES

Questions for Discussion

1. Do students believe that perceptions of the world are based on the languages we speak? Do they consider these shifts in our perceptions minor? Students should discuss examples given in the essay in addition to any of

their own. If the differences in perception are minor, ask students to verbalize what they feel is absolute, or always the same, about shared perceptions?

2. Do students believe it is important to learn a language other than their primary one? Why or why not? What is difficult about learning a foreign language? How is it different from or similar to learning other subjects or skills?

Group Activities

1. Ask students to converse in pairs about any foreign languages they know. Did they learn it in a school setting or at home? Have they ever been immersed in a foreign language outside the classroom? Have they had the opportunity to practice speaking or using that language over the course of their lives? Do they feel the other language (or languages) has had an effect on how they see the world or relate to other speakers? Ask each pair to talk briefly about their experiences with the class.

2. In small groups, have students examine Lera Boroditsky's discussion of how different linguistic structures influence our perception of events, using the Humpty Dumpty nursery rhyme as an example. If they change the structure of the English to reflect what is conveyed in Indonesian, Russian, and Turkish languages, for example, what is the effect on their understanding of the rhyme? After their small group conversations, students should present their findings to the class for further discussion.

Out of Class Projects

1. Ask students to compile a list of phrases in two languages that are meant to be equivalents but somehow differ in translation. If a student isn't familiar with another language, he/she can use examples from the essay. What sorts of differences do the students find? How do their findings indicate that perception of events or relationships differ between the two examples? (Another way to approach this project for someone who speaks only one language is to consider how a child, an English *learner*, might create a different word or sentence construction and explain why.)

2. The United States has brought together many people who once spoke different languages. Have students do research on the Web about different cultures in America and ask them to pick a group that once spoke a different language; they should write a brief paper on how that group's culture is influenced by the language of origin — even if the language is no longer the primary one used by those Americans of Asian, European, South American, Middle Eastern, or other descent.

Global Wording (p. 218)
ADAM JACOT DE BOINOD

Language arises from a need to communicate, but as Adam Jacot de Boinod makes clear through humorous examples in "Global Wording," some cultures need to communicate concepts that others have no need for. By pairing this essay with Mindy Cameron's "In the Language of Our Ancestors," students will be led to discuss how language and culture are frequently inseparable.

TEACHING STRATEGIES

Questions for Discussion

1. Ask the class why certain cultures have an expanded vocabulary for certain concepts or things.

2. Ask students if, in our own American culture, there are certain areas for which we have created language to define things.

Group Activities

1. Provide your students with pieces of poetry written in different languages, and ask them to translate the words as directly as possible using a foreign language dictionary. Ask students to present their translations to the class, and have the class decide whether the poem makes sense (and why or why not).

2. Divide the class into groups, assign each group one culture, and ask each group to research population, cultural traditions, economy, environment, and language for that culture. They should examine how language relates to culture and present their findings to the class.

Out of Class Projects

1. Have your students research Esperanto. They should look at the proposed purpose of this language and its success (if any).

2. Ask students to name some of the most common foreign words that the English language has "adopted." They should choose one and track its integration into our spoken and written language.

Corporate Names and Products Creep into Everyday Language (p. 222)
GENEVA WHITE

America is sometimes called a "consumer culture." Geneva White offers an example of how this might be true in the ways that we use brand names in everyday speech. White presents both sides of the argument regarding the value of this phenomenon, and students will no doubt have their own opinions and experiences.

TEACHING STRATEGIES

Questions for Discussion

1. Do your students think that using brand-name language in academic work should be allowed? Why or why not?

2. Ask your students what words they might use instead of brand names. For instance, if they didn't Google, what would they do instead? Are these alternative terms as appealing to use as brand names? Why or why not?

Group Activities

1. In small groups, have the class research the words that have been added to *Merriam-Webster's New Collegiate Dictionary* in the past year and make a chart categorizing the kinds of words they are (such as transportation related, technology related, and leisure related).

2. Direct students to look up the sales history of a product whose name has become part of the English language (such as Kleenex, Xerox, and TiVo) and trace their success compared to their competitors' success. Ask them if their chosen brand name is top in its field. They should present their findings to the class.

Out of Class Activities

1. Have students research other cultures that have their own brands that found their way into the language. They should find some examples and explain the parallels to the situation that is detailed in White's story.

2. Ask students to write a one-page story in which they use as many brand names as they can think of. Have students volunteer to read their creative efforts aloud, and ask their audience to determine who has employed the best use of brand names.

Swoosh! (p. 225)
READ MERCER SCHUCHARDT

Students possess a wealth of information about signs and symbols and their meanings within groups. Students' nonverbal exchanges are so integral to their daily activities that they may never examine the significance of symbols or even think about them as the extension of language that they are. In this essay, Read Mercer Schuchardt goes to the heart of nonverbal communication and skillfully combines it with another interest that often consumes student attention—the quest for popular name-brand apparel. His essay offers a plethora of ideas for thought-provoking discussion, from the state of literacy in the twenty-first century to the influence of the pervasive language—and representative language—of advertising.

TEACHING STRATEGIES

Questions for Discussion

1. What is Schuchardt implying when he refers to our society as "postliterate" (para. 7)? What examples can students offer to prove that our dependence on language has lessened over the past several decades? The author asserts that "language is being replaced by icons" (para. 9). Ask your class to give some specific examples. What trends do they see continuing today that reinforce or invalidate this thesis? How might the world be different one or two generations from now if the movement toward less verbal communication continues?

2. How important a factor do your students think technology is, especially computer technology, in rendering us a less literate society than we once were? Would this shift away from verbal language to symbols and icons have happened as quickly without the computer? Would it have happened at all? Some futurists predict that hard copies of such things as books, letters, and other documents will soon be found only in museums and that all of our reading and exchanging of what used to be paperwork will become computer-work. How likely is this scenario? What advantages and disadvantages would result?

Group Activities

1. Form the class into small groups, and have students brainstorm a list of icons or symbols that are widely understood by most people in our society without any text or verbal language (examples can be from outside the context of advertising). Have them choose five of these and draw them on sheets of notebook or computer paper, using a felt-tipped pen so the symbols will be clearly visible. Ask your class to take turns flashing their symbols to the other groups to see how quickly other students can identify what the icons they have selected represent. Discuss why these symbols speak so clearly without the benefit of words.

2. Divide the class in half for a debate. Ask one side to argue that all future communication should be accomplished via computers, and the other side to argue against the loss of handwritten letters, telephones, and other forms of personal communication. Students should take time to carefully plan the defense of their position. Each side will have five uninterrupted minutes to present an opening statement, after which they can take turns rebutting the position offered by the opposition. Have your class choose several spokespersons, but allow everyone on each side to participate by submitting to the speakers the points to be raised or questions to be asked.

Out of Class Projects

1. Have your class do some research about a popular advertising logo. How was it developed? By whom? How long has it been used? Did it replace an earlier symbol? Ask students to draw a picture of their selected symbol and show it to ten people on campus. How many of them can identify the product it represents? Ask students to present their drawing and research results to the class.

2. Ask your class to watch two hours of television and to keep a running list of every advertising logo, icon, or symbol that they see, not only in the commercials but during the shows as well. Students should be sure to note the date, the time, the station, and the shows that they watched. Ask students to share their results in class. How do the symbols and icons that they saw relate to the target audience for the shows that they watched and the commercials that were aired?

Deciphering the Chatter of Monkeys and Chimps (p. 230)
NICHOLAS WADE

Some of your students may be familiar with efforts to teach primates to talk, although they may not be aware of the most recent findings. This essay is a concise summary of many of the recent advances made in studying communication and language in monkeys and chimps. Although it may be somewhat disappointing to learn that we are no closer to finding an effective method for teaching chimps language—or even a concrete reason why they can't—Wade's report offers insight into the differences between language and communication and the types of things we are able to learn from studying animals' communication.

TEACHING STRATEGIES

Questions for Discussion

1. Wade points out that "with a few exceptions, teaching animals human language has proved to be a dead end" (para. 5). Why do students think that scientists continue to do this research if so little is being discovered? Do they think that the discoveries presented here are reason enough to continue scientific studies of language in animals? Why or why not?

2. Discuss with students the difference between language and communication. How do we separate these two ideas, and why do we need to? How have they interacted or communicated with animals in the past, and how do they make the distinction between this communication and the idea that animals are capable of language?

Group Activities

1. In small groups, have students discuss whether they think the "lifetime of research" Dr. Zuberbühler suggests in the article would be worth the time. Why or why not? What could the findings help humans accomplish? Move from small group discussions to a class discussion in which groups present their ideas.

2. Assign half the class to argue for the importance of the presented research, and the other half of the class to argue against it. Then pair students and have them debate each other.

Out of Class Projects

1. Assign students to do further research on a study mentioned in the essay, and write a summary of the research that elaborates on what is presented in the essay. Then have the students present their findings to the class.

2. Wade's article is an unbiased report on some of the current findings in primate language research. Have students identify what makes the essay unbiased, and then have them write their own essay, using facts from Wade's article and from additional research, that presents an argument on the subject.

How Do You Say *Extinct*? (p. 236)
John J. Miller

Students are most likely used to the idea of preservation, but perhaps not as it pertains to language. They've no doubt grown up being taught about efforts to preserve endangered species, protect the environment, and restore artifacts of historical value. John J. Miller's argument against language preservation runs counter to the idea that everything that is endangered ought to be preserved. He claims that creating more speakers of mainstream languages creates opportunities for people who have been limited by an inability to communicate with larger society.

TEACHING STRATEGIES

Questions for Discussion

1. Miller writes that "we may learn about biology if we preserve and study obscure languages—but [Crystal] seems oblivious to the reality that most people would rather eat a Big Mac than a fistful of beetle larvae" (para. 11). Ask students what this statement suggests that the writer's point of view on this subject may be and if his opinion might be controversial in any way.

2. Ask your students if they agree with UNESCO's point of view that "language diversity" is "one of humanity's most precious commodities" (para. 4)? They should explain why or why not they agree.

Group Activities

1. Break the class into two groups, and have one play the role of UNESCO and one advocate for a lingua franca. Then lead them to conduct a formal debate on the subject.

2. Divide students into groups, and provide each group with a selection from *Beowulf* in its original Old English or a piece from Chaucer's *Canterbury Tales*. Ask them to translate the selection to the best of their ability.

Out of Class Projects

1. The author uses the example of Papua New Guinea in the essay. Ask students to research this nation and the role that its diversified languages have had on shaping its culture.

2. Ask students to find and research a dying language. They should determine what bits of culture might be lost along with that language and whether they think that the loss of this culture is OK if it benefits the economic well-being of its speakers.

In the Language of Our Ancestors
(p. 241)
MINDY CAMERON

Although John. J. Miller sees certain social benefits to letting languages go extinct, here Mindy Cameron examines efforts to keep Native American languages alive. Her article provides some vivid examples of the ways that language works not only as a tool for communication but also as the conveyor of culture. Ask students to consider what might be lost if the American English language was suddenly threatened with extinction. What unique facets of American culture would also be lost?

TEACHING STRATEGIES

Questions for Discussion

1. In this essay, Cameron gives an example of education as a detrimental force for some aspects of Native American life. Ask students if they think that education can ever be detrimental and why they think so.

2. Ask students if they have ever learned a second language (at home or in school) and whether they feel that it is easier to absorb a new language at a younger age. Ask them to share their experience.

Group Activities

1. Divide students into two groups—one that represents the point of view of John J. Miller in "How Do You Say *Extinct*?" and one that represents Mindy Cameron's point of view. Conduct a class debate around the question, "Should some languages be allowed to die?"

2. In small groups, have students research a Native American folktale and present it to the class. They should explain what makes this story unique to its specific culture.

Out of Class Projects

1. Provide your students with a short story or novel excerpt from a Native American author (such as *The Lone Ranger and Tonto Fistfight in Heaven* by Sherman Alexie), and ask them to consider how tone and language play into the effectiveness of the narrative. They should look at whether this relates to the concept of "Indian English."

2. Ask students to research the concept of "language nests" and to find some successful (or unsuccessful) examples of this.

Genius in Four Frames (p. 249)
BEN SARGENT

Sargent's essay, a *Doonesbury* retrospective, points out that even after forty years the innovative comic strip still addresses the important sociopolitical issues of the day. Trudeau's characters have grown up and continue to be surrounded by the same world events as the rest of us. Trudeau has kept the strip alive even as the print newspaper has declined, and the interest in comic strips has waned with the rise of digital media.

TEACHING STRATEGIES

Questions for Discussion

1. Why do students read cartoons? What are their favorites? Do cartoons ever shape their perception of the greater political/social world around them? How so?

2. Discuss the purpose of an editorial cartoon versus a comic strip. If *Doonesbury* is in fact a "hybrid," what would students expect Trudeau to offer in every strip? Take a look at one or two of the early and modern versions of *Doonesbury* and talk about whether they meet the class's criteria.

Group Activities

1. In groups, ask students to discuss the themes Trudeau has tackled in *Doonesbury*. What political or social issues would each group like to see

raised in a comic strip? Ask students to discuss why they would like to see a particular issue in this form and then have each group present its answers to the class.

2. Ask students to compare the feel of a 1970s or 1980s *Doonesbury* cartoon with a more recent one (2000 to present). What has changed in the strip's tone or appearance over the years? What has stayed the same? In groups, ask students to write about the evolution of the comic strip based on their peer discussion.

Out of Class Projects

1. Have students explore the Web site Doonesbury.com, keeping a list of the political and social issues Trudeau takes on that they find most compelling in a cartoon strip. Then, ask students to write a short essay explaining why they feel the way they do.

2. The Pulitzer Prize is awarded to artists who work in many different categories. Have students research the history of the Pulitzer and the past winners of the prize. Ask them to explain why *Doonesbury* might be Pulitzer-worthy based on what they've learned from their research and from Sargent's article.

Doonesbury by Garry Trudeau (p. 255)

This *Doonesbury* strip shows just how overwhelming social media has become. Throughout the strip, the daughter is typing while talking as her father waits just to the side of the frame. Even though he hasn't said anything during her monologue, she accuses him of making the judgment that "social media is ruining [her] life." You may want to ask students if they have been in a similar situation. Although the comment about Myspace is now outdated, how is the strip still relevant? Can they think of ways that the strip could be updated with the advent of Twitter, Tumblr, and Google+?

Digital Information and the Future of Reading (p. 256)
ALEX PHAM AND DAVID SARNO

Students may already be comfortable with interactive reading, or "living books," as described in Alex Pham and David Sarno's piece about the transformation of texts. The authors explain how the act of reading is changing, and with it, the publishing industry. Whether one is for or against what is happening to what people read and how they read it, the revolution is here; according to Pham and Sarno, the culture of reading is already being made new.

TEACHING STRATEGIES

Questions for Discussion

1. Have students ever had the sort of experience that Emma Teitgen had with her interactive textbook? What subject did the interactive book cover? What was particularly interesting or valuable about the interactive material? Do students believe such books should be supplements (as "The Elements: A Visual Exploration" was) or as the main texts for school subjects?

2. How do students respond to the cautious statements toward the end of the article? Do they agree or disagree with those who believe new technologies will affect attention spans or leave readers with a "continuous partial attention" to information (para. 32)?

Group Activities

1. In groups, ask students to consider the statement: "The same technology enables readers to reach out to authors, provide instant reaction and even become creative collaborators, influencing plot developments and the writer's use of dramatic devices" (para. 6). Do students feel that having this sort of connection to a text is a positive or negative for the reader? Do students feel authors should have complete control over their works until they are ready to be read? What are the consequences of this sort of crossover?

2. Students may already know something about the first dramatic shift in the ordinary person's experience of reading, which began with the printing of the Gutenberg Bible (or they should be able to quickly do some research). In pairs, ask students to list how technologies changed human beings' ideas about literacy when the Bible was printed and also how technologies are changing people's ideas about literacy now. As a class, discuss if there are any connections between the two revolutions?

Out of Class Projects

1. Ask students to write a summary of a "traditional" book they've read recently. How would students feel if that book suddenly became interactive, along the lines of Anne Rice's *The Master of Rampling Gate*? What sort of digital information would students hope to see accompanying the book? Why would that deepen/add to the reader's experience of the book?

2. Have students look at a Web site that redefines a traditional book — a dictionary, for example. Are there online dictionaries that are more "interactive" than others? Can they find one they prefer as a tool for learning the meanings of words? What about for using them in context?

Focusing on Yesterday, Focusing on Today
Benjamin Franklin at His Printing Press
(p. 262)

You may want to bring in a copy of *Poor Richard's Almanac* and have students study the images that accompany the text. Ask them why they think this was such an important book in its time, and how they think books have evolved over the last three hundred years. What kinds of innovations—like the printing press and now e-books—do they think will come in the next three hundred years?

A Novel Idea (p. 263)

With the popularity of e-books and e-readers, paper books are becoming a nostalgic kitsch item, as evidenced by this "vintage book" computer cover. Ask students how they read nowadays—are they using primarily print books or e-books? Why do they think a cover like this would appeal to computer owners?

ADDITIONAL RESOURCES

1. The Web site UrbanDitionary.com provides information about new and evolving slang. Not always PG-rated, the site is nevertheless a good resource because definitions of new words are voted up or down in prominence by user consensus, with points awarded for creative usage.

2. Some films in which language plays prominently as a theme are *Babel*, *Nell*, and *The King's Speech*. Many films with heavy dialogue would also merit some analysis in class, such as Woody Allen films like *Annie Hall* and *Manhattan*. Additionally, you could show the film *Juno* and examine its witty, crisp dialogue and use of sarcasm and humor. For each film, you could discuss how language functions as a theme or how the dialogue adds texture to the rest of the movie.

3. The German Web site Language@Internet (www.languageatinternet.de) is a scholarly, peer-reviewed online journal that publishes "original research on language and language use mediated by the Internet." Although academic, it might be a useful research source for some students who wish to write on how the Internet is influencing language evolution.

4. Steven Pinker's classic text *The Language Instinct* is a wonderful supplemental reading that inspires students to think about our innate capacity for language and the way that it evolves.

5. The Internet Slang Dictionary and Translator (www.noslang.com) is a fun resource for exploring and translating the ever-growing body of acronyms

and slang generated by the Internet age. The site also features a "Netspeak Guide."

6. Michael Agger's essay "How We Read Online" on Slate.com (June 13, 2008) is a fun visual representation of the way reading is changing, and pairs well with "Digital Information and the Future of Reading."

7 Fantasies for Sale
Marketing American Culture Here and Abroad

Students may be amazed at how much they already know about advertising. They know the jingles, the slogans, the logos, and the spokespeople. What they may not know—because they have probably never been encouraged to think critically about it—is the pervasive grip that advertising has on our culture and on each of us individually. Most students can tell you what an ad is for—that is, what product is being hawked. In this chapter, they learn to ask, "What's the real message here? What is this ad *about*?" Because just about everything in our society, from sneakers to social issues, is touched by advertising, this far-ranging chapter provides widespread possibilities for discussion and writing.

America: Land of the Logos, Home of the Branded (p. 265)

This image by Shi-Zhe Yung was created for an Unbrand America ad campaign in *Adbusters*. Great for teaching visual rhetoric, it directly confronts the American consumer culture. What does this image say about the way that Americans prioritize shopping? What kind of an image might express disagreement with Yung's position?

On Sale at Old Navy: Cool Clothes for Identical Zombies! (p. 268)
DAMIEN CAVE

Clothing, culture, and conformity are the topics of Damien Cave's article, "On Sale at Old Navy: Cool Clothes for Identical Zombies!" The title says it all—Americans have bought into an anticorporate culture marketed by various chains (like Old Navy). These stores offer clothing that is branded as different and as a bargain; however, the items in all the stores (bought by millions of people) are identical, and not necessarily of good quality. Advertising and consumerism become the culture Americans participate in, as corporations stamp out the way they dress and furnish their living spaces.

TEACHING STRATEGIES

Questions for Discussion

1. How many students have shopped at the stores mentioned in Cave's essay? How many shop there on a regular basis? Do they believe (after reading this article) that they are being duped by the companies that market to them? What do they find appealing about these stores, or others like them?

2. Are students aware of advertising all around them? How much of a role do ads and branding play in their lives? Ask if they've ever felt, as Cave points out, that they are "essentially turning their rooms [or themselves] into billboards" (para. 23).

Group Activities

1. Divide the class into groups, and ask students to discuss their ideas about identity. What does it mean to have an identity? What shapes theirs? How do clothes and other material goods play into this idea of identity? Ask each group to speak briefly about their discussion.

2. Functioning as an ad team, have groups choose a product most participants feel comfortable with from a store such as Old Navy or Ikea. When they market their product to the rest of the class, have them consider the arguments Cave makes about what Americans find appealing about these stores and how they rope in their consumers. After the ad teams make their pitches, discuss as a class how the marketers were trying to draw in consumers.

Out of Class Projects

1. After reading the essay, have students watch the movie *Fight Club*—although be aware of the graphic and violent nature of the film. Alternatively, you may want to show selected, classroom-appropriate scenes relating to "Ikea boy." How do students respond to the character? What is students' relationship to stores like Ikea and Old Navy? Does watching the film after reading this essay have an effect on their perception of such stores?

2. Ask students to choose one clothing store, furniture store, or restaurant that is part of a chain found in the United States. Let them tour more than one store, or ask them to go through one physically and then research the chain on the Web or in print advertisements. What can they say about the sameness of each store and the general atmosphere the store strives to create (or the store and how it's marketed on the Web, in print, etc.)? Are the stores selling "a destination"? Why is the word *zombie* appropriate or inappropriate when used to describe the sort of customer who regularly shops there?

Sewn in Secret: Iranian Designers (p. 275)
NEWSWEEK

Fashion is changing in Iran, but very slowly, and those designers who are the trailblazers for fashion in their own country run the risk of imprisonment for subversion. The strict Islamic dress code is still the norm in Iran, and top designers have often immigrated to the West in order to maintain their safety, as well as a career. In a country like Iran, social freedoms and political freedoms are often viewed as walking hand in hand, and with a fundamentalist regime in power, most freedoms are held in check by the government.

TEACHING STRATEGIES

Questions for Discussion

1. Can changes in fashion be a threat to a government or other authorities? Have students ever thought about a change in fashion having an effect on the government in any other part of the world (besides the Middle East)?

2. How do small changes in Iranian fashion indicate the possibility of more social freedoms coming about in that country? How is the government's response to such changes indicative of the restriction of personal and social freedoms there?

Group Activities

1. Pair students together. Ask one student in each pair to argue the position of an Iranian in favor of a strict dress code (a fundamentalist or otherwise). The other student should take the position of someone who would rather not adhere to the Islamic dress code (a designer or young person, perhaps). After paired discussions, create a For and Against list on the board for comparison.

2. In small groups, have students consider the appeal of various Western fashions. What do those fashions indicate about Westerners? Why would a foreign culture find them appealing?

Out of Class Projects

1. Have students research the fundamentalist regime in Iran and write a description of President Mahmoud Ahmadinejad as a political figure. Why would changes to Islamic dress code be of concern to him?

2. Ask students to find information on designers out of Tehran. What information is available on them? What can they learn about their exile and success?

Champagne Taste, Beer Budget (p. 279)
DELIA CLEVELAND

Some students believe themselves to be free of peer influence in clothing choices. Others readily admit dressing to impress or just to fit in. Regardless of the degree to which each of us admits to being affected, all of us are constantly bombarded with "what's hot and what's not" messages. Sometimes the desire to have the latest styles can have serious consequences. In this essay, Delia Cleveland explores the fashion fallout in her own life.

TEACHING STRATEGIES

Questions for Discussion

1. To what extent do your students accept the old adage "Clothes make the man [or woman]"? How much emphasis do they think that other people really place on our appearance? Are we judged by the labels we display?

2. In Cleveland's case, her mother intervenes to break Cleveland's credit card habit. Do class members think that parents should intercede when college students make unwise financial decisions? What about in the case of other choices that parents may deem unwise?

Group Activities

1. Divide students into small groups and ask them to explain why some people are willing to compromise other areas of their lives to wear designer labels. Have them share their conclusions with the class.

2. In groups of two or three ask students to share experiences that they may have had in high school that revolved around clothing choices. Was the clothing of certain groups an issue? Was there a dress code? How rigidly was it enforced?

Out of Class Projects

1. Instruct students to locate a high-traffic spot on campus and then to sit there for fifteen minutes recording any designer clothing labels they see. Have students compare notes with others in the next class period to draw conclusions about which designers are most popular on your campus. Are the results surprising? Why or why not?

2. Ask students to interview two peers whose high schools required uniforms, two whose schools had dress codes but no specific uniforms, and two who attended schools with no dress regulations. Have students question their subjects about the influence these rules or lack of them had on the social climate and on the quality of the education they received.

The Pants That Stalked Me on the Web
(p. 283)
Michael Learmonth

If someone recently visited Zappos looking for clothing, that someone may find the articles following him or her through cyberspace, thanks to retargeting advertising now in place on the Internet. Anything examined on certain store sites may now resurface on other pages, as Michael Learmonth discovered after searching for shorts one summer. To his dismay, the shorts began to surface on every post-Zappos Web page he visited, leading him to do a little research on why the shorts were following him and how to stop the cyberstalking.

TEACHING STRATEGIES

Questions for Discussion

1. Has anyone in the class encountered retargeting campaigns like the one Learmonth writes about? Were they bothered by it? Did the students end up buying the product?

2. Do students take issue with telemarketers even if they don't feel particularly bothered by the type of advertising that Learmonth is complaining about? How many of them have signed up for a "do not call" list or something similar? Should companies not be allowed to share information with others or identify an individual's needs based on what he or she looks at on the Web?

Group Activities

1. In pairs, let students talk about whether they would opt out of retargeting ads. Do they feel that such ads are simply part of the larger world of advertising around them? Is there something more invasive about the tracking and targeting that's happening on the Internet? Why?

2. Facebook is mentioned by Learmonth as a site people use, on which they often freely give out information about themselves. In groups, ask students to express their opinions about privacy and sites like Facebook. How do they protect their privacy? How much of their detailed personal information, how many of their desires and aspirations, do they want made public? Do they make any connections between the public nature of sites like Facebook and the intrusion of advertising from a site like Zappos?

Out of Class Projects

1. Have students consider non-Internet advertising that exists all around them. What form does that advertising take? What messages are they being sent? Ask students to write down as many types of non-Internet advertising as they can, using examples from public and private life. Then ask them to arrange the advertising in terms of what they feel is most influential, and note why.

2. Suggest that students follow the path Learmonth took in his essay by beginning at Zappos (remembering that he did not put the shorts in his checkout bag) and then traveling to various sites on the Web. Does anything seem to be "following" them? If any items do begin to pop up, students should click on the banner Learmonth mentions and see if it

redirects them to Criteo. They are welcome to opt out of the retargeting campaign. After walking in Learmonth's shoes, so to speak, ask students to write about their experience. Did they feel pestered, as he did? Did anything about the experience surprise them?

Retargeting Ads Follow Surfers to Other Sites (p. 287)

MIGUEL HELFT AND TANZINA VEGA

In their *New York Times* article, Miguel Helft and Tanzina Vega reiterate many of the points made in Michael Learmonth's "The Pants That Stalked Me on the Web," but they get a sense of the general public's reaction to behavioral targeting with more extensive interviews. Consumers, they find, are noticing remarketing. What is the response of the Internet-searching public? As one digital marketing agency executive remarks, "What is the benefit of freaking customers out?" (para. 25).

TEACHING STRATEGIES

Questions for Discussion

1. Do students know that corporations have "detailed information" about them from the Web sites they browse? How else do corporations have information about consumers? Is information gathered via the Internet easier to access or more important somehow than information gathered in another way?

2. What is the benefit of retargeting for marketers in the travel, real estate, or financial services industries? Does the use of such ads by these industries feel more invasive than the use of the ads by the clothing industry? Why or why not?

Group Activities

1. Ask students to debate, in groups, whether there is any difference between seeing ads for certain products while reading a particular magazine and going to a store Web site and then watching the items you looked at as they surface on other sites.

2. In small groups, ask students to write a response to Learmonth's claim, quoted in this article, that "as tracking gets more and more crass and obvious, consumers will rightfully become more concerned about it" (para. 23). Discuss group responses as a class.

Out of Class Projects

1. Suggest that students reread Michael Learmonth's article "The Pants That Stalked Me on the Web" and then "Retargeting Ads Follow Surfers

to Other Sites." Do students notice the overlap in information between the two articles? Where are the authors saying the same things? How might Learmonth feel about his article resurfacing on a different "page" (in the "Retargeting Ads" article)?

2. In addition to asking themselves about the overlap between the articles, find out how students respond to the individual articles. Which one did they feel was most compelling, and why? Which one did they enjoy reading more? Why do they prefer one over the other?

Grand Mall Seizure (p. 292)
DANIEL ALARCON

No examination of popular culture would be complete without a discussion of mall culture. The American shopping mall, argues Daniel Alarcon, embodies many commercial representations of American values—in mall store names, mall attractions, and even mall shoppers. Alarcon's essay on the Mall of America lyrically describes how America's large shopping meccas represent the best and worst in all of us.

TEACHING STRATEGIES

Discussion Questions

1. Ask students how, according to Alarcon, the purpose of the shopping mall has changed from the Victor Gruen's original 1956 conception of an enclosed shopping mall. They should discuss the role that is played by the shopping mall in their lives.

2. Alarcon writes that Victor Gruen believed that shopping malls "not only served a community's physical needs, but its civic, cultural, and social needs as well" (para. 8). Have students discuss how a shopping mall might meet all these needs and whether they feel that shopping malls accomplish this lofty goal.

Group Activities

1. Divide the class into groups, and ask each group to think about the themes that the corridors in their mall would have, if they could design one (refer students to paras. 14 and 15 for examples from the Mall of America). Ask each group to list themes that they'd want to represent and explain how these corridors represent something important about America. Discuss each group's list as a class.

2. Alarcon references the film *Dawn of the Dead* several times in "Grand Mall Seizure." Divide students into groups, and ask them to think of other movies that they have seen where a shopping mall drives the plot. They should touch on the ways that a mall is a setting that is conducive

to furthering a plot. (Other recent mall-based films include *Observe and Report* and *Paul Blart: Mall Cop*.)

Out of Class Projects

1. Have students spend a day at the local mall and perform some ethnographic research on the people and environments that they encounter there. Ask them to compare their own experiences to Alarcon's.

2. Ask students to think about some uniquely American qualities or values that they would want to incorporate in their own shopping centers, and have them sketch out a floor plan for these retail meccas. What stores would be included, and how would the mall be decorated to convey iconic values? Ask each student to present his or her mall plans to the rest of the class.

What Is Independent Hip Hop? (p. 303)
HECTOR GONZALEZ

There is some debate about whether the underground hip hop community wishes to connect visibly with the capitalist system, linking itself with giant corporations like Toyota in order to garner attention. There is no doubt that Scion and young hip hop artists mutually benefit from a solid relationship: Scion appears "cool" and sells more cars, while the artists earn money by joining forces with the auto industry. However, many are against the relationship, saying that artists who plug Scion are selling out, allowing a corporation to put its fingerprints on their work. The question remains: Does corporate sponsorship allow artists to do their work by providing financial support or does it put a brand on an otherwise "pure" and free act of expression?

TEACHING STRATEGIES

Questions for Discussion

1. What do students think of hip hop? What words do they associate with the art form? What do they think of corporate America? What words do they associate with business? Where do those lists diverge or intersect?

2. Can an artist be independent and associated with a brand at the same time? What about an athlete? How can independence coexist with integrity, or how is it lost when buying and selling brands becomes part of the mix?

Group Activities

1. Divide students into groups to discuss how they feel about the essay's opening scenario. Do they think Hector Gonzalez is being duped into participating in a multimillion dollar campaign? How would they feel if

they were in his place? Ask students to take notes on their group discussions and present their findings to the class.

2. Do students feel that wearing a Scion shirt, listening to a CD about Toyota brands, or reading a magazine about Scions will make them more likely to buy one? Why or why not? In pairs, ask students to debate their positions.

Out of Class Projects

1. Many artistic venues and artists are sponsored by big corporations. Have students notice in their daily activities how that sponsorship is conveyed. Who owns the art venues (for music, theater, visual arts) in town? Are particular artists identified with certain brands due to sponsorship? Are there other areas or media that corporations clearly fund? Does the question of hip hop sponsorship differ from these in any way?

2. Examine advertising in print media and on television. How can you tell from an ad which group is being targeted? Make a list of several ads encountered on a regular basis and explain how you know what age, gender, or race is being courted by the ad.

Why Apple Deserves an Oscar Too (p. 307)
Abe Sauer

Product placement is everywhere: in TV shows, movies, music videos, at awards ceremonies, and even written into popular books. In this essay, Abe Sauer shows how Apple has not only perfected product placement but also successfully branded itself as an mainstay, meaning that it actually seems more forced in a movie or show if someone *isn't* using an Apple product. From *Wall-E* to *CSI*, Apple devices can be found in all facets of mainstream media entertainment. Before reading this article, ask your students if they are aware of the specifics of product placement. See if any of your students change their ideas about Apple by the end of the article.

TEACHING STRATEGIES

Questions for Discussion

1. Ask students if they are aware of product placement while they are watching television or movies. Has there been a time where they were taken out of the story because a certain product placement was so obvious it was distracting?

2. Ask students why they think product placement is or is not effective. Do they think it is more effective than traditional advertising in commercial breaks? Why or why not?

3. Recently, there has been criticism in the music industry that music videos are overrun with product placement. Do students think there are certain types of movies, shows, or videos where product placement is more appropriate? Less appropriate? How do they decide on these standards?

Group Activities

1. In groups, have students make a list of any product placements they can recall from shows or movies they watch frequently. What products are mentioned or promoted? How do these products relate to the show, if at all? Have students present their findings to the rest of the class.

2. Have small groups of students agree on a movie or television show that they are all familiar with. Then, have them brainstorm possible product placements for that show or movie. Where would these product placements be the least obvious? Where would they be most effective? Have the groups share their ideas with the class.

Out of Class Projects

1. Allow students to watch a contemporary movie of their choice—preferably one that they have seen before so they can easily follow the story while identifying product placement. As the movie is playing, have students note any product placement that they might see, from beer to soda to, of course, Apple products. Students should note the name and type of the product, and how it is featured in the movie. If the same product appears more than once, make sure students keep track of the number of appearances. Have them present their findings to the class.

2. Direct students to the Web site for Hollywood Branded, a prominent product placement company (www.hollywoodbranded.com). Have students browse the site, paying close attention to the "Case Studies" section, and write a short response to what they find. Were they surprised by any of the product placement examples provided by the company?

Hooters Translates in China (p. 314)
CRAIG SIMONS

Students are probably aware that many American businesses have gone global. From McDonald's to the Gap, these businesses spread American culture overseas and reap big profits selling the idea of America. Occasionally, these businesses must reconcile American culture and values with foreign ones that may or may not easily agree. Craig Simmons writes about the seemingly unlikely success of the Hooters restaurant chain in China and discusses how the restaurant has managed to do well in a culture that at first glance would seem to reject its use of sex to sell onion rings.

TEACHING STRATEGIES

Discussion Questions

1. Survey your students about their knowledge of Chinese culture. Make a list of the adjectives that they suggest to describe Chinese culture based on their own knowledge and this reading. Ask them if the reading adds to their understanding of Chinese culture.

2. After you have made a list of words that your students use to describe Chinese culture, ask them to suggest a list of words that characterize the Hooters restaurant chain. There will likely be little overlap in words. Discuss the differences, and ask students how effectively Simons's article connects Chinese culture and Hooters.

Group Activities

1. This article packs a punch largely because of the disconnect in Americans' perceptions of a restaurant like Hooters and Chinese culture. Divide students into groups, and ask them to come up with other popular American chains that might not seem to translate well in other countries. What about these companies makes the corporate image difficult to translate outside American culture?

2. Divide students into groups, and ask them to develop an ad campaign that promotes one of the companies from activity 1 to a foreign culture. Students will need to think about where they are pitching this company, what qualities of American culture this company embodies, and how those qualities can be used to promote the company.

Out of Class Projects

1. Ask students to pick a popular American chain and research its presence in other countries. Ask them to pick one particular country where the chain is established and find out as much as they can about how the company tailors its business to appeal to foreign culture.

2. Many places where Americans shop (particularly certain clothing stores) are not American-owned companies, yet we may not always realize it. Ask students to think of some of their favorites brands or stores and research where they are headquartered. Have them look at the corporate Web sites and think about how the image of the company as an entity differs from its American iteration. (You may suggest clothing stores like H&M, French Connection UK, or Ben Sherman.)

Focusing on Yesterday, Focusing on Today
Queen-Sized Beds and Pizza! (p. 318)

The neon sign above the motel says it best: "Clean Comfort." That's all motor travelers used to look for, but expectations have changed. Ask students if they have stayed or would stay in a motel like the one pictured. Why or why not? Why do they think roadside motels like these lost popularity?

Residence Inn, Suitcases and Grocery Sacks
(p. 319)

Hotels are no longer a stopping point between destinations, but a temporary home for many businessmen and women. Ask students to analyze the objects and the room in the advertisement—are these typically what one might find in a motel or hotel? What message do your students think the ad is trying to convey, and what kind of clientele is Marriot trying to reach? Does it differ from the clientele of the roadside motel? How so?

ADDITIONAL RESOURCES

1. Hillary Chura's November 12, 2001, essay, "Identifying a Demographic Sweet Spot: Soda Marketers Shift Focus toward Hispanic and Black Teens," is an excellent resource on targeting an audience. It appeared in *Ad Age* magazine and can be found at adage.com.

2. Bring a number of contemporary magazines to class to allow students access to numerous print ads for the activities and projects suggested.

3. Bring into class a picture that, when you stare at it for a few seconds, reveals an image behind an image. Discuss how the artistic sleight of hand is different from and similar to subliminal advertising.

4. For classic examples of subliminal advertisements, see *Media Sexploitation* and *The Clam-Plate Orgy* by Wilson Bryan Key.

5. If your university has a marketing department, invite a guest speaker to talk with your class about current issues in the marketing field.

6. Daniel Eisenberg's essay "It's an Ad, Ad, Ad, Ad World: As Conventional Methods Lose Their Punch, More Marketers Are Going Undercover to Reach Consumers" provides a fascinating look at "stealth marketing." This essay appeared in the September 2, 2002, issue of *Time* magazine.

7. Whole Foods Market Inc. spends very little on advertising and yet has grown enormously. An interesting article on the Whole Foods approach is "Whole Foods Shuns Ads, Sells Life Style," in the July 10, 2005, "Business and Personal Finances" section of the *Austin American-Statesman*.

8. *Adbusters* magazine is a great source for anti-advertising articles, as is Kalle Lasn's book *Culture Jammers*.

9. Morgan Spurlock's *Super Size Me* is a "documentary" indictment of McDonald's that students will find interesting. Spurlock also has a book, *The Greatest Movie Ever sold*, that makes a good resource for this chapter.

10. The article "Product Placement—You Can't Escape It" from USAtoday .Com (October 10, 2006) is a good supplement to "Why Apple Deserves an Oscar Too." It provides statistics and reactions to the growing number of product placement and advertisements in media.

Picture This

Reflecting Culture Onscreen

In Steve Martini's best-selling 1998 novel *Critical Mass*, the Russian character Mirnov attempts to explain the pervasive influence of Americans and their culture: "They did not conquer the world with armies, but with words, with their motion pictures and movie stars, McDonald's, and Disneyland."

Mirnov may be a fictional character, but he reaches the same conclusion that many students of history and current events also reach. America's broad cultural sweep across nations too numerous to name is fueled by an advance battalion not of soldiers but of soundtracks, not of Marines but of Bella, Edward, and Jacob, George Clooney, and the Kardashians. And this influence is felt just as strongly at home as abroad. In this chapter, authors ranging from Stephen King to Eugene Robinson examine our attraction to the movies and television shows. Students are already avid devotees of these aspects of popular culture; few can imagine—in fact, few remember—a world without Dolby sound or the Simpsons. Teaching them to think critically about something they know so much about opens up a whole new realm of possibilities. And technology enhances their learning by making it possible to show videotaped excerpts in class to illustrate all sorts of examples of television's and Hollywood's messages.

Thriller (p. 321)

The music video for *Thriller* is still one of the most iconic and recognizable music videos in their (somewhat brief) history. Show the full video to your students, and ask them why this video is still so popular and well-known. Why has it endured the the changing pop culture tide while other videos have been forgotten? You may also want to show the class clips from shows and movies featuring *Thriller* choreography, such as *Thirteen Going on Thirty* and *Glee* and discuss how modern adaptations may have helped keep *Thriller* current.

Why We Crave Horror Movies (p. 324)

STEPHEN KING

Fortunately for Godzilla, Hannibal Lector, and the likes of Freddy Krueger, we seem to crave the panic and fear that their exploits create in us. Perhaps no other author has been as prolific in his creation of horror as Stephen King. King's life would make a fascinating movie in itself: Besides being a writer, King has worked as a janitor, a mill laborer, an English teacher, and an actor (in films, and American Express credit card commercials). He owns a publishing house and a rock 'n' roll radio station in Bangor, Maine, where he lives with his writer wife, Tabitha. He also plays in a rock 'n' roll band with fellow writers including Dave Barry and Amy Tan. His published works include novels, short fiction, serials, and screenplays. But it is his ability to scare us that cements his reputation.

TEACHING STRATEGIES

Questions for Discussion

1. The modern horror story took root in three pieces of literature: Mary Wollstonecraft Shelley's *Frankenstein*, Robert Louis Stevenson's *Dr. Jekyll and Mr. Hyde*, and Bram Stoker's *Dracula*. But the horror genre has usually been forced into a subservient position in critical literary discussions. Do your students think that popular stories from the dark side deserve a place among mainstream literary works? Why? What attraction is there for serious readers and literary scholars? Why are some critics reluctant to admit the genre of horror stories into the limelight of well-respected fiction?

2. As an author who makes ordinary things like cars and dogs horrifying (for example, in *Christine* and *Cujo*), Stephen King remains unique in his ability to terrify us with the normal. Gary Williams Crawford, author of *Discovering Stephen King*, writes that King "has placed his horrors in contemporary settings and has depicted the struggle of an American culture to face the horrors within it." How does this horror that originates from the familiar compare to the horror created from something unfamiliar and strange, like Godzilla or King Kong? Which is more unsettling? Why?

3. In this essay, King asserts that watching a horror movie is like "lifting a trapdoor in the civilized forebrain and throwing a basket of raw meat to the hungry alligators swimming around in that subterranean river beneath" (para. 12). What might King mean by this? How do horror movies feed the need to see what's in the dark recesses of our civilized society?

Group Activities

1. Working in small groups, students should discuss the most frightening horror movie that they have ever seen. What made it particularly scary—the plot, the settings, the special effects, the characters and acting, or something else? Does anyone in the group avoid horror movies? Why? What attracts others to watch them?

2. In a *Sourcebook* interview, King told Keith Bellows, "The more frightened people become about the real world, the easier they are to scare." Divide the class into small groups to brainstorm a list of some things that Americans fear today. Where might these fears originate? How do reality shows like *Survivor* and *Fear Factor* exploit these fears? Could these fears be captured in a horror movie, and if so, what would the movie

be like? How might a horror movie help people to face or manage their fears?

Out of Class Projects

1. Many of the earliest versions of fairy tales were not the charming, happily-ever-after Disney stories that we are used to seeing. Ask students to do some research on the Internet and in the library about the early versions of a fairy tale like *Cinderella* or other stories written by the brothers Grimm such as *Hansel and Gretel* or *Little Red Riding Hood*. Ask them to compare and contrast the authentic original versions with the versions popular today and to share the original tales with the class. How did these early fairy tales fulfill some of the same purposes that King ascribes to horror movies?

2. Have your class watch a King horror movie and a horror movie by another director such as Alfred Hitchcock or Wes Craven. Which of the two do they find more frightening? Why? What aspects—such as special effects, lighting, or music—help to create the suspense and fear in each movie?

Exploring the Undead: University of Baltimore to Offer English Class on Zombies (p. 329)

Daniel de Vise

Students may debate the relevance of zombie studies in higher education, but Daniel de Vise's essay considers the appropriateness of such classes, one of which is being offered at the University of Baltimore. Zombies have become a pop culture phenomenon, he explains, showing up in films and literature—and now in media studies. Students may be surprised to learn how Zombies arrived in the American pop culture scene, and what de Vise says they have to teach us.

TEACHING STRATEGIES

Questions for Discussion

1. What is a zombie, exactly? What makes zombies so interesting to someone that he would catalog eighty-five zombie movies in a book (*Zombiemania*)? How do the zombies in *28 Days Later* differ from the zombies in *Dawn of the Dead*? Are the zombies in *Pride and Prejudice and Zombies* the same ones found in *The Walking Dead*?

2. The essay opens with the question, "Is *Night of the Living Dead* a simple zombie film or a subtle antiwar statement?" Have students ever thought

about how a fantasy or horror film sheds light on reality? Encourage students to discuss their knowledge of such film genres in a way that ties them to current events or reveals a psychological truth.

Group Activities

1. How do students understand the quotation (from Arnold Blumberg at University of Baltimore): "The zombie is, simply, us" (para. 8)? Break students into small groups and ask them to explain what Blumberg might mean. They should create a zombie "profile": physical and emotional characteristics, psychological traits, observations about behavior, an so on.

2. Divide the class into two groups. Ask students to poll each other on their interest in a class like Blumberg's. Why would a student be interested or not interested in taking such a class? Then group students by who would or would not choose "Media Genres: Zombies" or its equivalent, and ask each group to defend its reasons to the whole class.

Out of Class Projects

1. Ask your students to watch one of the films or read one of the books mentioned by de Vise. They should take notes on how what they see or read might be considered a commentary on our society—how we live or what we fear. Then, have them share their observations with the class, allowing them to use short film clips, read passages, and/or share photos to add to their report.

2. Students should take a look at the movies currently in cinemas and comment on whether the horror genre is still part of the "zeitgeist," as de Vise puts it. Based on what they see, do horror films still cultivate a following? If not, what types of films or storylines are most prevalent at this time?

Fade In, Fade Out: Addiction, Recovery, in American Film (p. 334)
Stefan Hall

One may wonder, given the content of movies today, if the portrayal of drug and alcohol abuse in film has ever been taboo; not everyone is aware of how that portrayal in American movies has evolved over the years. According to Stefan Hall, in the past, restrictions on a movie's content were tightened or loosened depending on American sentiment, government intervention, and current events. In many American movies from 1894 to the present, as Hall points out, drug use fueled the plot line, analyzed a weakness, upheld a moral standard, or reflected a culture.

TEACHING STRATEGIES

Questions for Discussion

1. Why is "Fade In, Fade Out" an apt title for this piece? Consider the many different ways it resonates with the subject matter under discussion. Do students feel it is a strong title or a weak title? Why?

2. Is there some way in which the addiction presented in the films Hall mentions could be construed as particularly American? Is there something about the movies mentioned that looks at addiction in a way that might be presented differently in another country? Students should discuss which aspects presented in the films are more American and which are more global.

Group Activities

1. Hall chronicles the history of addiction in American films in his essay. In groups, ask students to discuss another theme in television or movies besides addiction. How has that theme changed in these media over the years? Students should prepare a short presentation for the class that offers the highlights of their discussion.

2. Divide the class into groups and ask them to discuss, as if they are members of an audience, the possible effects of viewing the films mentioned here. Do they think they are more likely to have strengthened values after watching a film like *Reefer Madness*? Are they more likely to have looser morals if they watch Cheech and Chong? Why or why not? After the groups debate, they should present their opinions to the class.

Out of Class Projects

1. Many of the movies mentioned in Hall's essay are famous (*Reefer Madness*, *Up in Smoke*, and *Leaving Las Vegas*); some are relatively obscure (*The Mystery of the Leaping Fish*, *Weed with Roots in Hell*). Ask students to watch one of the films Hall mentions and write a response to it. Can students comment on anything else that would have strengthened Hall's argument in the essay if he had elaborated on that one particular film?

2. Ask students to research one of the events mentioned by Hall that led to change in the portrayal of drugs in the movies—either Fatty Arbuckle's manslaughter trial or the sway of the counterculture in the 1960s. Students should explore whether these events had an effect on anything besides movies and their content; based on their research, they should articulate how movies reflect greater society.

Bollywood Princess, Hollywood Hopeful: Aishwarya's Quest for Global Stardom
(p. 340)
ANUPAMA CHOPRA

Although Hollywood is by far the leading producer of film entertainment in the world, many other countries have their own thriving film industries. Anupama Chopra's "Bollywood Princess, Hollywood Hopeful" provides many points for comparison between what students know about Hollywood and the American film industry and how films are produced in India.

TEACHING STRATEGIES

Questions for Discussion

1. How well versed are students in recent foreign films? Ask those who have recently seen a foreign film to describe how much they felt the film was influenced by American cinema. They should mention the aspects of the film that seemed familiar to them.

2. As an alternative to the exercise above, select a clip from a foreign film (perhaps something from Bollywood), and screen it for the class. Ask students which film techniques reminded them of American films and which were different than typical American films

Group Activities

1. Divide students into two groups, and have each group consider the pros and cons that are raised in Chopra's article regarding the sacrifices required to achieve international stardom. Have the groups debate pro and con on this issue.

2. In small groups, ask students to list as many foreign actors as they can who have achieved stardom in America. Ask them to list as many movies as they can in which the actors in their list have starred. To what extent do they consider these actors and their roles "American"?

Out of Class Projects

1. Ask students to research the current biggest hits in a foreign country of their choice. Of these, how many of the most popular films were produced in the country in which they are popular? How many are American?

2. Ask students to come up with a list of qualities and traits that represent the American movie star, and have them create a collage from magazines of images that represent star quality. Share them as a class. Then as a class, discuss how many of these collages contain images that represent other cultures.

The Bollywood Princess Waiting for Her Prince to Come (p. 345)

This photo is from the movie *Jodhaa Akbar*, starring Aishwarya Rai Bachchan and Hrithik Roshan. Your students might be able to categorize this movie as an epic romance. What things in the image provide clues to this genre? If this were an American film, what elements in the photo might be different?

Tyler Perry's Money Machine (p. 346)
EUGENE ROBINSON

Eugene Robinson won the Pulitzer Prize for Commentary in 2009. In this column, he discusses the surge in popularity of writer and filmmaker Tyler Perry, whose films Robinson believes satisfy a dearth of entertainment targeted at the African American community. This piece provides an opportunity to discuss the issue of diversity in mainstream cinema. In any given week, how many of the top-grossing films feature minority casts and directors? Do students agree with Robinson's opinion that African Americans in American films are used as plot devices? You may want to show some examples from Perry's films to get discussion started.

TEACHING STRATEGIES

Discussion Questions

1. Eugene Robinson writes, "Perry's movies aren't great art-house films, but neither are Adam Sandler's; they succeed at what counts, which is speaking to their audience" (para. 12). Discuss with your students what they think makes a "good" film versus a "relatable" film. What are their favorite movies, and why do they like them? How did critics respond to the films that students love most?

2. Ask your students what about films appeals to us as audiences. Is it important to be able to relate to a film on the level of personal identity? Are stories truly universal, or do they require adaptation for specific audiences?

Group Activities

1. Divide students into two groups, and conduct a debate. Ask students to evaluate the pros and cons of classifying film genres according to which racial group they target.

2. Ask students to come up with a list of favorite movies that they relate to on a personal level. In small groups, have students share their lists and discuss what about the films they've chosen speaks to them.

Out of Class Activities

1. Assign students to watch any of Tyler Perry's films and play the role of film critic. Have them decide, from the standpoint of entertainment, how successful a storyteller Perry is and what signature features of his films audiences will find appealing.

2. Ask students to conduct outside research on the marketing campaigns for several of Perry's films. Have them examine how Perry has come to represent movies that are targeted at African American audiences, how he has come to be a brand name, and how the marketing for his films capitalizes on this status.

Drag Hags (p. 350)
JENNIE YABROFF

Film comedy is full of examples of men in drag. Jennie Yabroff questions the appropriateness of this convention, arguing that such portrayals may be less about lampooning male buffoonery and more about demeaning women in a number of ways.

TEACHING STRATEGIES

Discussion Questions

1. Yabroff quotes Craig Zadan, producer of the movie musical *Hairspray*, as saying, "The public loves the idea of men playing women in film, especially in a comedy" (para. 3). Do your students agree with this statement? Why or why not?

2. What do these films seem to say about women? What stereotypically feminine traits do they play up? How do the roles played in drag in these films differ in character from the roles played by real women? You may want to show clips of any of the films that Yabroff mentions to stimulate discussion.

Group Activities

1. Divide students into groups that have equal numbers of men and women. Have each group create two lists of the traits that they feel represent most men and women. Have men and women reverse genders and act out these traits for the class. How do these broad portrayals differ from reality?

2. Assign groups of students to talk about any of the roles that are discussed in Yabroff's essay, and ask them to evaluate whether they feel that the films would have been as effective if the roles had been played by women instead of men in drag. How would the films have changed?

Out of Class Activities

1. Have students pick one of the films that Yabroff discusses and watch it at home. Ask them to write a brief critique of the film as if they were Yabroff.

2. Ask students to read Eugene Robinson's "Tyler Perry's Money Machine" and watch one of Perry's *Madea* films outside of class. Have them prepare a brief response to Yabroff in which they agree or disagree with some of the criticisms that she levels at drag in mainstream film.

Virtual Humans (p. 355)
KELLY TYLER-LEWIS

When the character of Smiegol/Gollum appeared in the second *Lord of the Rings* film, reviews of the joint perfomance of actor Andy Sirkus and the CGI animators who used him as the basis for the character were so overwhelmingly positive that there was a debate over whether a virtual performance could be nominated for an Academy Award. If what many of the CGI animators prophesy in Kelly Tyler-Lewis's "Virtual Humans" comes to pass, we may eventually have to face the reality that an actor who is not exactly real might win an award.

TEACHING STRATEGIES

Discussion Questions

1. Ask students to offer some examples of films that they've seen that feature "synthespians." Were these performances convincing? Were students able to forget that the performance they were watching was created using computers?

2. Suppose that flesh-and-blood actors are becoming increasingly obsolete. Ask students how they would feel about a world in which most films are created entirely inside computers. Would they find this to be an acceptable or attractive prospect? Why or why not?

Group Activity

1. Divide the class into groups, and conduct a pro and con debate around this statement: "There is a limit to which computers should be used in films to recreate humanity."

Out of Class Projects

1. Ask students to research the Digital Emily Project at gl.ict.usc.edu/Research/DigitalEmily/. It covers in-depth the process that Image Metrics and the USC Institute for Creative Technologies Graphics Lab used to

digitize actress Emily O'Brien. Students will find videos from the project and an overview of the technology that went into creating the digital Emily. Ask students to write a brief report analyzing their own reactions to the project and share them with the class.

2. The film version of *Avatar* (2009) featured CGI versions of real actors. Ask students to view the film outside of class and to write a film review that takes into account the effectiveness of the use of CGI in the movie.

An Unlikely Commuter (p. 362)

Many of your students will recognize the character Gollum from the *Lord of the Rings* films. In this ad campaign, he's depicted in a normal urban scene as a subway passenger. To what extent does removing him from the context of a fantasy film underscore that the character is a computer-generated creation? Or does it make him seem more real? Are we getting used to having computers blur the line between real and artificial?

Left for Dead by MTV, Music Videos Rebound on the Web (p. 363)

JAKE COYLE

Many of today's students are children of the Internet, born long after the rise and fall of MTV, the channel once devoted to playing music videos and launching careers of many popular artists. Jake Coyle's article recounts the disappearance of music videos from Music Television, and MTV's replacement by Internet sites such as YouTube. Thanks to the explosion of videos on YouTube, the music video is evolving and thriving for musicians and their audiences.

TEACHING STRATEGIES

Questions for Discussion

1. Music videos, according to Coyle, were recently "on life support," but now they are experiencing a "revival" on the Web. Can students think of anything else in recent history or their experience that was on its way out but is now experiencing a similar return via the Internet or through new technologies?

2. Why do students think the music video is suited to the Web? Do students think the excitement about and incorporation of YouTube in their lives will fade out the way MTV did for its viewers? Why or why not?

Group Activities

1. Divide the class into two groups, one of MTV music video producers and one of producers of videos geared for Web viewing. Ask each group to

brainstorm about what in their videos will appeal to their viewers and why. Groups should present their ideas to the class and explain how their videos are marketed with their audience in mind and are geared to best fit their particular medium.

2. In small groups, ask students to discuss videos that "went viral" that they've watched or heard about. Why do they think these particular videos caught on? Are they familiar with the ones mentioned in Coyle's article? They should present the results of their discussions to the class.

Out of Class Projects

1. Ask students to consider the interactive nature of the Internet versus MTV. Have them explore YouTube and watch several music videos. Why did they choose the videos they did? If they didn't know exactly what they wanted to watch, were they directed in any way by their Internet search? How so? How do the comments that follow videos or the viewing of YouTube posts via social networking sites like Facebook add or detract from their experience of music videos on the Web? Have students take notes as they do this project.

2. In his article, Coyle makes a distinction between MTV-geared music videos and what he calls "Web-oriented videos." Students can analyze this difference even if they've never watched videos on MTV. Ask them to view some older MTV-era videos on the Web and compare and contrast them with the newer Internet-ready videos. Can they see the differences pointed out by Ted Leo, who is quoted as saying (of the post-MTV video): "People are actually able to present images that to them relate to the music that they're making, as opposed to feeling like they need to present images with quick cuts, flashy, hi-fi performance shots and pose-y things" (para. 23)?

Lady Gaga (p. 368)

Lady Gaga's meat dress became very controversial, not because of the message she was trying to convey, but because of the apparent animal rights violations. The statement that Lady Gaga was trying to make may not be immediately recognized. In fact, students may have concluded that she was trying to say something about animal rights or even hunger. Taken out of context and without Gaga's explanation, the dress is a curiosity, but not necessarily a powerful statement.

Here, There, and Everywhere: Television Spreading is New Directions (p. 370)
THE ECONOMIST

Television is not just about passively watching a show—in today's world, it's an interactive experience. Often shows have their own lines of merchandise to be sold to ever-eager audiences. It's not just American television that's flourishing; there's a consumer niche for overseas hit shows as well. But the most expensive television shows are being filmed in the United States, which continues to export its material to the global market.

TEACHING STRATEGIES

Questions for Discussion

1. Do students gravitate toward particular television shows? Which ones? Are there common "hit" shows being discussed? Find out what draws students to particular shows.

2. Ask students if they've ever heard of *The Price Is Right*. If so, have they ever seen it? Where do their associations come from? Have they ever played a "Price Is Right" slot machine or computer game, or encountered the show in any other way?

Group Activities

1. Divide the class into two groups. Members of each group should consider themselves committee members who will create multimedia products for their particular show. As a group, they should create a television show from scratch or model one on a popular series. Ask them to consider the content of the show, its production quality, its audience, its budget, and anything else that might influence their strategies, and they should come up with merchandise and advertising ideas that can then be presented to the class.

2. In small groups, ask students to list the things they would be interested in when visiting a television show's Web site. *The Economist* offer some ideas in paragraph 7 of the essay. Ask the small groups to go further and imagine as detailed a site as possible for a particular show. How do Web sites add another dimension to the fictions of television? Why would people find these particular extensions appealing?

Out of Class Projects

1. Ask students to do some research into Web episodes for one of the TV shows mentioned in the essay (*Lost* and *Heroes* are referenced in para. 8, but there are others). Do they agree with the assertion that "they also allow the main story, on television, to be kept fairly uncluttered—or at least less cluttered than it might have become otherwise"? In a brief paper, ask them to defend their assertion based on the evidence they find.

2. Students can test the argument made in this essay about production values for American versus foreign broadcasters by viewing dramas made by Hollywood and comparing them to a foreign-made drama. Do the experiment described in paragraph 17 and comment on the findings. Can

students tell the difference between them? Does American television appear to have noticeably more money than its counterparts? Ask them to buttress their claims based on the tests they've conducted.

Focusing on Yesterday, Focusing on Today
"I Am ... Dracula." (p. 378)

Students will most likely be familiar with the character of Dracula, but have probably never seen the classic film advertised in this poster. The image in the poster is trying to convey horror, while the *Twilight* poster is romantic. Show a clip of *Dracula* to your students and have them respond to the tone of the film. How is the film reflected in the poster? How does it differ from current vampire dramas like *Twilight*, *True Blood*, and *Vampire Diaries*? How is it similar?

Twilight, "Love Never Dies." (p. 379)

The *Twilight* books and movies spawned a new generation of vampire enthusiasts, but with a twist. While most of the older portrayals of vampires are meant to be horrifying and frightening, current vampires are mysterious and desirable, as this poster illustrates. Have students compare the two posters and ask what they would expect from the films if they had never heard of them. What kind of audience are the posters trying to appeal to? Do they think *Dracula* was intended for the same type of audience as *Twilight*? Why might the portrayal of vampires have changed since the original *Dracula*?

ADDITIONAL RESOURCES

1. A good video guide like *Leonard Maltin's 2012 Movie Guide* or *Time Out Film Guide 2012* is an invaluable resource when teaching film.

2. See Bernard F. Dick's *Anatomy of Film*, Sixth Edition (Bedford/St. Martin's, 2010), for a discussion of horror film grosses and for general information on movies. Timothy Corrigan and Patricia White's *The Film Experience: An Introduction*, Second Edition (Bedford/St. Martin's, 2009), is also an invaluable resource.

3. David Skal's *The Monster Show: A Cultural History of Horror* (Faber & Faber, 2001); *The Horror Film Reader*, edited by Alain Silver and James Ursini (Limelight Editions, 2000); and Stephen King's *On Writing: A Memoir of the Craft* (Pocket Books, 2000) are all valuable, very readable resources.

4. The film section of the Web site PopMatters.com offers thought-provoking long-form essays on film and cultural analysis. Some examples your stu-

dents might be interested in are "Trouble in Wonderland, or The Crisis of the Fairytale in Film" (May 31, 2011), and "Whedon and Company: Worlds Await" (April 15, 2011). The latter would pair well with both the Focusing on Yesterday and Focusing on Today in this chapter, as well as the essay "Exploring the Undead: University of Baltimore to Offer English Class on Zombies."

about gender roles are reflected in each image? What do the advertisements say about the roles of men and women during the two time periods?

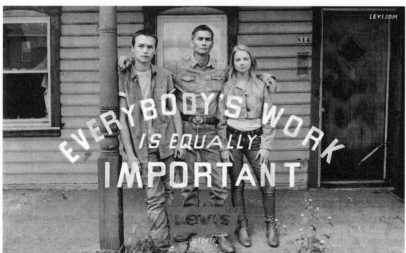

Photographs by Melodie McDaniel. Concept by Wieden+Kennedy. Courtesy Levi Strauss & Co.

"Everybody's Work Is Equally Important."

CONNECTING TO THE CULTURE

1. If, as Patricia McLaughlin ("Venus Envy," p. 168) and Dan Barden ("My New Nose," p. 181) argue, men are now more concerned than ever before with their appearance, what elements in our society are most responsible for this heightened awareness? To what extent are the media (television, movies, magazines, newspapers, and the Internet) responsible? What consequences do you expect? What changes in advertising or new products support this thesis?

2. Think about the people who have helped shape your self-image, both inner and outer. These may be people you know personally or celebrities you have never actually met. These people may have been positive role models for you, helping you to set goals for yourself, or negative influences showing you what you did not want to become. In an essay, explore how one or several of these people have influenced you.

3. Different cultures have different ideals of beauty. Do some research on another country whose beauty ideals are different from those in the United States. In an essay, examine the differences you have found and relate how the standard of beauty affects the members of the culture you selected.

4. Ideals of beauty and fashion have changed throughout history in the United States. Pick a specific historical period and research how these ideals were defined for men or women during that time. Then write an essay in which you compare the ideals of that historical period to today's ideals of beauty and fashion. Use specific examples and visuals from the time period you have researched.

What Are You Trying to Say?

How Language Works

Analyzing the Image

 When Jim Sanborn created the *Kryptos* sculpture, he did not think that parts of its code would remain unbroken for over twenty years. The sculpture rests quietly in a courtyard of the Central Intelligence Agency's headquarters in Langley, Virginia, four curved copper panels covered with an enigmatic series of letters. Thousands of professional and amateur codebreakers have labored to interpret its message. Dan Brown, author of *The Da Vinci Code* and *The Lost Symbol,* has even referred to the sculpture in his novels.

- *Kryptos* is a Greek word. What does it mean? Why is this an appropriate name for this sculpture?

- What is the significance of this sculpture being in this location?

- The third passage on the sculpture, which has been deciphered, is a paraphrased account of Egyptologist Howard Carter's first foray into King Tut's tomb. What does that moment in time share with *Kryptos?*

- What does the mystery of Sanborn's sculpture imply about the power of language?

Research this topic with TopLinks at bedfordstmartins.com/toplinks

GEARING UP   Is English your first language? Whether it is or isn't, what do you remember about learning to speak English? By whom were you taught? What early words did you use? Do you speak another language now? Would you like to be fluent in another language? Which one? Why?

For human beings, language skills may be our most significant acquisition. We learn early to be vocal to get what we want. However, short of a bout of bad laryngitis, most of us take for granted the fluency and frequency with which we employ language to communicate our needs and desires. We don't spend much time considering how words—or which words— become part of our common linguistic currency. Unlike the French government, the U.S. government bureaucracy doesn't include a committee whose sole function is to attempt to regulate the language. American English is very eclectic; we adopt words from just about everywhere. Consider the words *hors d'oeuvres, kayak, moped, zeitgeist, jihad, raccoon, queso, fjord, aardvark, sauna, kosher, phobia, Fahrenheit, kindergarten, smorgasbord, macho, chef, genre, cul-de-sac, karate,* and *apartheid.*

In spite of being so welcoming to words from other languages, we engage in animated debate over whether the native speakers of those languages should continue to use their mother tongues exclusively when they live in the United States. Should immigrants assimilate culturally and linguistically, or should they strive to retain their own culture's customs and language? Language is, after all, an innate part of cultural identity. Is bilingual education a benefit to students new to the American school system, or is it a hindrance not in their best interest? Should everyone who wants to be an American live and work and play in English?

And exactly which English would we have newcomers learn? There's the casual English with which we interact with friends, and there's the standard English our professors and bosses expect us to master. Have today's thumb-jumping text messagers lost the ability to distinguish between language for Myspace and language appropriate for someone else's space, like the classroom or the workplace? To what extent has "friending" on Facebook replaced face-to-face communication? What happens when all emotions have been reduced to emoticons? Or when we discover that humans are not alone in their ability to communicate emotion through language?

It's impossible to separate our language from our popular culture. An entire category of words bombarding our speech habits comes from advertising. When does a product name become so commonplace that is begins to represent all things of that type (Kleenex, for example)? Even parts of speech undergo metamorphosis. How many nouns have recently become verbs, not through *Merriam-Webster's,* but through daily usage? "How long have you been officed in that building downtown?" "Why don't you just Google it?" "I'll text you about the party." And although computers may not be able to replicate themselves yet, they have spawned their own vocabulary: "blogging," "virtual reality," and "surfing the Web," for example.

The selections in this chapter explore these ideas and other language-related assumptions in ways that may cause you to really think about the words you speak and those you hear.

COLLABORATING   In groups of three or four students, make a list of all the ways you can think of to communicate with another person. List the advantages and disadvantages of each method. Have each member of the group defend his or her favorite method, and then poll your classmates to see which method of communication they prefer. Brainstorm together about how communication may change over the next twenty years.

Lost in Translation

LERA BORODITSKY

Lera Boroditsky grew up in Minsk in the former Soviet Union. She is an assistant professor of psychology at Stanford University and is editor in chief of *Frontiers in Cultural Psychology.* Her article "Lost in Translation" appeared in a July 2010 edition of the *Wall Street Journal.*

> **THINKING AHEAD** Do you speak more than one language? How did you acquire this second language? Do you think in more than one language? Do you think identically in each language? What is different? What is the same? What may prevent ideas from being translated precisely from one language to another? How does the language you speak affect the way you think?

Do the languages we speak shape the way we think? Do they merely express thoughts, or do the structures in languages (without our knowledge or consent) shape the very thoughts we wish to express? 1

Take "Humpty Dumpty sat on wall" Even this snippet[1] of a nursery rhyme reveals how much languages can differ from one another. In English, we have to mark the verb for tense; in this case, we say "sat" rather than "sit." In Indonesian you need not (in fact, you can't) change the verb to mark tense. 2

In Russian, you would have to mark tense and also gender, changing the verb if Mrs. Dumpty did the sitting. You would also have to decide if the sitting event was completed or not. If our ovoid[2] hero sat on the wall for the entire time he was meant to, it would be a different form of the verb than if, say, he had a great fall. 3

In Turkish, you would have to include in the verb how you acquired this information. For example, if you saw the chubby fellow on the wall with your own eyes, you'd use one form of the verb, but if you had simply read or heard about it, you'd use a different form. 4

Do English, Indonesian, Russian and Turkish speakers end up attending to, understanding, and remembering their experiences differently simply because they speak different languages? 5

These questions touch on all the major controversies in the study of mind, with important implications for politics, law and religion. Yet very little empirical work had been done on these questions until recently. The idea that language might shape thought was for a long time considered untestable at 6

---

[1] **snippet:** A small piece.
[2] **ovoid:** Shaped like an egg.

best and more often simply crazy and wrong. Now, a flurry of new cognitive science research is showing that in fact, language does profoundly influence how we see the world.

The question of whether languages shape the way we think goes back   7
centuries; Charlemagne proclaimed that "to have a second language is to have a second soul." But the idea went out of favor with scientists when Noam Chomsky's theories of language gained popularity in the 1960s and '70s. Dr. Chomsky proposed that there is a universal grammar for all human languages—essentially, that languages don't really differ from one another in significant ways. And because languages didn't differ from one another, the theory went, it made no sense to ask whether linguistic differences led to differences in thinking.

The search for linguistic universals yielded interesting data on languages,   8
but after decades of work, not a single proposed universal has withstood scrutiny. Instead, as linguists probed deeper into the world's languages (7,000 or so, only a fraction of them analyzed), innumerable unpredictable differences emerged.

Of course, just because people talk differently doesn't necessarily mean   9
they think differently. In the past decade, cognitive scientists have begun to measure not just how people talk, but also how they think, asking whether our understanding of even such fundamental domains of experience as space, time and causality could be constructed by language.

For example, in Pormpuraaw, a remote Aboriginal community in Aus-   10
tralia, the indigenous languages don't use terms like "left" and "right." Instead, everything is talked about in terms of absolute cardinal directions (north, south, east, west), which means you say things like, "There's an ant on your southwest leg." To say hello in Pormpuraaw, one asks, "Where are you going?", and an appropriate response might be, "A long way to the south-southwest. How about you?" If you don't know which way is which, you literally can't get past hello.

About a third of the world's languages (spoken in all kinds of physical   11
environments) rely on absolute directions for space. As a result of this constant linguistic training, speakers of such languages are remarkably good at staying oriented and keeping track of where they are, even in unfamiliar landscapes. They perform navigational feats scientists once thought were beyond human capabilities. This is a big difference, a fundamentally different way of conceptualizing space, trained by language.

Differences in how people think about space don't end there. People   12
rely on their spatial knowledge to build many other more complex or abstract representations including time, number, musical pitch, kinship relations, morality and emotions. So if Pormpuraawans think differently about space, do they also think differently about other things, like time?

To find out, my colleague Alice Gaby and I traveled to Australia and   13
gave Pormpuraawans sets of pictures that showed temporal progressions (for example, pictures of a man at different ages, or a crocodile growing, or a banana being eaten). Their job was to arrange the shuffled photos on the

ground to show the correct temporal order. We tested each person in two separate sittings, each time facing in a different cardinal direction. When asked to do this, English speakers arrange time from left to right. Hebrew speakers do it from right to left (because Hebrew is written from right to left).

Pormpuraawans, we found, arranged time from east to west. That is, seated facing south, time went left to right. When facing north, right to left. When facing east, toward the body, and so on. Of course, we never told any of our participants which direction they faced. The Pormpuraawans not only knew that already, but they also spontaneously used this spatial orientation to construct their representations of time. And many other ways to organize time exist in the world's languages. In Mandarin, the future can be below and the past above. In Aymara, spoken in South America, the future is behind and the past in front.   14

In addition to space and time, languages also shape how we understand causality. For example, English likes to describe events in terms of agents doing things. English speakers tend to say things like "John broke the vase" even for accidents. Speakers of Spanish or Japanese would be more likely to say "the vase broke itself." Such differences between languages have profound consequences for how their speakers understand events, construct notions of causality and agency, what they remember as eyewitnesses and how much they blame and punish others.   15

In studies conducted by Caitlin Fausey at Stanford, speakers of English, Spanish and Japanese watched videos of two people popping balloons, breaking eggs and spilling drinks either intentionally or accidentally. Later everyone got a surprise memory test: For each event, can you remember who did it? She discovered a striking cross-linguistic difference in eyewitness memory. Spanish and Japanese speakers did not remember the agents of accidental events as well as did English speakers. Mind you, they remembered the agents of intentional events (for which their language would mention the agent) just fine. But for accidental events, when one wouldn't normally mention the agent in Spanish or Japanese, they didn't encode or remember the agent as well.   16

In another study, English speakers watched the video of Janet Jackson's infamous "wardrobe malfunction" (a wonderful nonagentive coinage introduced into the English language by Justin Timberlake), accompanied by one of two written reports. The reports were identical except in the last sentence where one used the agentive phrase "ripped the costume" while the other said "the costume ripped." Even though everyone watched the same video and witnessed the ripping with their own eyes, language mattered. Not only did people who read "ripped the costume" blame Justin Timberlake more, they also levied a whopping 53% more in fines.   17

Beyond space, time and causality, patterns in language have been shown to shape many other domains of thought. Russian speakers, who make an extra distinction between light and dark blues in their language, are better able to visually discriminate shades of blue. The Piraha, a tribe in the   18

Amazon in Brazil, whose language eschews number words in favor of terms like few and many, are not able to keep track of exact quantities. And Shakespeare, it turns out, was wrong about roses: Roses by many other names (as told to blindfolded subjects) do not smell as sweet.

Patterns in language offer a window on a culture's dispositions and 19 priorities. For example, English sentence structures focus on agents, and in our criminal-justice system, justice has been done when we've found the transgressor and punished him or her accordingly (rather than finding the victims and restituting appropriately, an alternative approach to justice). So does the language shape cultural values, or does the influence go the other way, or both?

Languages, of course, are human creations, tools we invent and hone 20 to suit our needs. Simply showing that speakers of different languages think differently doesn't tell us whether it's language that shapes thought or the other way around. To demonstrate the causal role of language, what's needed are studies that directly manipulate language and look for effects in cognition.

One of the key advances in recent years has been the demonstration of 21 precisely this causal link. It turns out that if you change how people talk, that changes how they think. If people learn another language, they inadvertently also learn a new way of looking at the world. When bilingual people switch from one language to another, they start thinking differently, too. And if you take away people's ability to use language in what should be a simple nonlinguistic task, their performance can change dramatically, sometimes making them look no smarter than rats or infants. (For example, in recent studies, MIT students were shown dots on a screen and asked to say how many there were. If they were allowed to count normally, they did great. If they simultaneously did a nonlinguistic task—like banging out rhythms—they still did great. But if they did a verbal task when shown the dots—like repeating the words spoken in a news report—their counting fell apart. In other words, they needed their language skills to count.)

All this new research shows us that the languages we speak not only 22 reflect or express our thoughts, but also shape the very thoughts we wish to express. The structures that exist in our languages profoundly shape how we construct reality, and help make us as smart and sophisticated as we are.

Language is a uniquely human gift. When we study language, we are 23 uncovering in part what makes us human, getting a peek at the very nature of human nature. As we uncover how languages and their speakers differ from one another, we discover that human natures too can differ dramatically, depending on the languages we speak. The next steps are to understand the mechanisms through which languages help us construct the incredibly complex knowledge systems we have. Understanding how knowledge is built will allow us to create ideas that go beyond the currently thinkable. This research cuts right to the fundamental questions we all ask about ourselves. How do we come to be the way we are? Why do we think the way we do? An important part of the answer, it turns out, is in the languages we speak.

EXERCISING VOCABULARY

1. Record your own definition for each of these words.

   implications (n.) (6)   indigenous (adj.) (10)
   empirical (adj.) (6)   conceptualizing (v.) (11)
   cognitive (adj.) (6)   encode (v.) (16)
   scrutiny (n.) (8)   levied (v.) (17)
   innumerable (adj.) (8)   eschews (v.) (18)
   causality (n.) (9)   hone (v.) (20)

2. In paragraph 6, the author reports that a "flurry" of new scientific re-search is taking place. With what is the word *flurry* usually associated? What does the word mean in this context?

3. If something is universal, to whom (or what) does it apply? In para-graph 8, the author refers to "linguistic universals." What type of uni-versals would these be? To what extent do these apparently exist?

4. In one language experiment, Boroditsky and Gaby showed the Porm-puraawans a series of images showing temporal progressions. What does the word *temporal* mean? What is this word's origin? How did spatial orientation affect temporal progression in this experiment?

PROBING CONTENT

1. What historically has been the problem with determining how language affects thought? What has happened to change that assumption?

2. Whose theories in the 1960s and 1970s argued against the idea that the language we speak affects our thought processes? Briefly explain this person's central theory.

3. What advantage do speakers of languages that depend on absolute di-rections have? What is one example of a language that uses absolute directions?

4. Explain the significance of the study conducted using a video of Janet Jackson's "wardrobe malfunction."

5. What kind of studies must be undertaken to prove the direct influence of language on thought patterns?

CONSIDERING CRAFT

1. The title Boroditsky chose has significant meaning for her essay. This article title is also a film title. Explain why she chose this particular title and how it relates to her thesis. What connections did Boroditsky wish her readers to make?

2. In this article, the author incorporates several scientific studies — one she conducted with a fellow researcher and two conducted by others. What effect does the inclusion of these research studies have on the reader's response to her writing? Why?

3. In paragraph 18, the author paraphrases a famous Shakespearean quotation to make her point. What is the original quotation? From which Shakespearean play does this come? What does she achieve by referring to Shakespeare?

WRITING PROMPTS

Responding to the Topic   Boroditsky notes that Charlemagne believed "to have a second language is to have a second soul" (para. 7). If you speak a second language, respond to this statement's truth or falsehood in an essay. If you do not speak more than one language, interview someone who does and use the information you gather to compose your essay. Include your interview notes when you submit your essay.

Responding to the Writer   Near the conclusion of her essay, Boroditsky writes, "the languages we speak not only reflect or express our thoughts, but also shape the very thoughts we wish to express" (para. 22). Write an essay exploring the implications of this statement for a global society. You may choose to examine politics, religion, economics, culture, or other areas of interest.

Responding to Multiple Viewpoints   Concluding her essay, Boroditsky closely relates language to the human experience: "Languages, of course, are human creations, tools we invent and hone to suit our needs" (para. 20). "Language is a uniquely human gift" (para. 23). Write an essay in which you transcribe an imaginary conversation between Lera Boroditsky and Klaus Zuberbühler (of Nicholas Wade's "Deciphering the Chatter of Monkeys and Chimps" p. 230).

For a quiz on this reading, go to bedfordstmartins.com/mirror.

Global Wording

ADAM JACOT DE BOINOD

Adam Jacot de Boinod was a researcher for the British Broadcasting Company when he noticed that the Albanian dictionary contained twenty-seven different words for eyebrows. Since then, he has obsessively researched foreign dictionaries and catalogued some the world's oddest and most precise terms. He has published two books from his findings, *The Meaning of Tingo: And Other Extraordinary Words from Around the World* (2006), *Toujours Tingo* (2007), and *The Wonder of Whiffling: And Other Extraordinary Words in the English Language* (2010). The following is an excerpt from *The Meaning of Tingo* that was republished in the March 2006 edition of *Smithsonian* magazine.

> **THINKING AHEAD** Name some words you use routinely that are not originally English words but were "borrowed" from other languages. When you use such words, are you aware that you are speaking Chinese, Arabic, or Spanish? Why or why not? How do words from languages other than English become so much a part of our everyday American speech?

One day while I was working as a researcher for the BBC quiz program 1 *QI*, I picked up a weighty Albanian dictionary and discovered that the Albanians have no fewer than twenty-seven words for eyebrows and the same number for mustache, ranging from *mustaqe madh,* or brushy, to *mustaqe posht,* or drooping at both ends. Soon I was unable to go near a secondhand bookshop or library without seeking out the shelves where the foreign-language dictionaries were kept. I would scour books in friends' houses with a similar need to pan for gold.

My curiosity became a passion, even an obsession. In time I combed 2 through more than two million words in hundreds of dictionaries. I trawled the Internet, phoned embassies and tracked down foreign-language speakers who could confirm my findings. Who knew, for example, that Persian has a word for "a camel that won't give milk until her nostrils have been tickled" (*nakhur*)? Or that the Inuits[1] have a verb for "to exchange wives for a few days only" (*areodjarekput*)? Why does Pascuense, spoken on Easter Island,[2] offer *tingo*, which means "to borrow things from a friend's house, one by one, until there's nothing left"?

---

[1] **Inuits:** Eskimos.
[2] **Easter Island:** An island in the southeast Pacific Ocean.

The English language has a long-established and voracious tendency to naturalize foreign words: *ad hoc, feng shui, croissant, kindergarten.* We've been borrowing them from other cultures for centuries. But there are so many we've missed.

Our body-conscious culture might have some use for the Hawaiian *awawa,* for the gap between each finger or toe; the Afrikaans *waal,* for the area behind the knee; or the Ulwa (Nicaragua) *alang,* for the fold of skin under the chin. Surely we could use the Tulu (India) *karelu,* for the mark left on the skin by wearing anything tight. And how could we have passed up the German *Kummerspeck,* for the excess weight one gains from emotion-related overeating? (It translates literally as "grief bacon.")

Gras bilong fes, from the Papua New Guinea Tok Pisin, is more poetic than "beard"; it means "grass belonging to the face." And how about the German *Backpfeifengesicht,* or "face that cries out for a fist in it"?

In Wagiman (Australia), there's an infinitive—*murr-ma*—for "to walk along in the water searching for something with your feet." The Dutch have *uitwaaien,* for "to walk in windy weather for fun," but then Central American Spanish speakers may win a prize for articulating forms of motion with *achaplinarse*—"to hesitate and then run away in the manner of Charlie Chaplin."[3]

In Russian, they don't speak of crying over spilled milk; they say *kusat sebe lokti,* which means "to bite one's elbows." That may be better than breaking your heart in Japanese, because *harawata o tatsu* translates literally as "to sever one's intestines." To be hopelessly in love in Colombian Spanish is to be "swallowed like a postman's sock" (*tragado como media de cartero*). That happy state may lead to dancing closely, which in Central American Spanish is *pulir hebillas* ("to polish belt buckles").

Malaysians recognize *kontal-kontil,* or "the swinging of long earrings or the swishing of a dress as one walks." Fuegian, in Chile, has a word for "that shared look of longing where both parties know the score yet neither is willing to make the first move" (*mamihlapinatapei*). But Italian has *biodegradabile,* for one "who falls in love easily and often."

Persian has *mahj,* for "looking beautiful after a disease"—which, deftly used, might well flatter (*vaseliner* in French, for "to apply Vaseline") some recovered patients. But you'd have to lay it on pretty thick for a *nedovtipa,* who in Czech is "someone who finds it difficult to take a hint."

On Easter Island, it may take two to *tingo,* but it takes only one to *hakamaru,* which means "to keep borrowed objects until the owner has to ask for them back." Of course, words once borrowed are seldom returned. But nobody is going *harawata o tatsu* over that.

---

[3] **Charlie Chaplin:** Famous star of silent movies known for his distinctive walk.

EXERCISING VOCABULARY

1. Record your own definition for each of these words.

   scour (v.) (1)   sever (v.) (7)
   combed (v.) (2)   swishing (v.) (8)
   voracious (adj.) (3)   longing (n.) (8)
   naturalize (v.) (3)   deftly (adv.) (9)
   articulating (v.) (6)

2. The expressive verb often used for searching the Internet is *to surf*. Instead, de Boinod uses "trawled the Internet" (para. 2). In what ways are these two images alike? How are they different? Why does the author choose the verb *trawled?*

3. Throughout this essay, de Boinod uses a number of expressive verbs to highlight his actions as he pursues his new passion. Locate several of these descriptive verbs and explain why he chose them and how their use enhances the tone of his essay.

PROBING CONTENT

1. What started de Boinod on his quest for unusual words and phrases? How did he feed his growing hunger for new words?

2. Choose two of the foreign phrases that catch de Boinod's attention in this essay. Explain what language they come from and what they mean. To what extent would they be useful expressions for English speakers to learn?

CONSIDERING CRAFT

1. Explain the play on words in the title. What is the word most often heard following *global* in magazines, on news programs, and in Congress? Why does de Boinod choose this association for his title?

2. Look at a number of examples of foreign phrases that de Boinod uses and translates in this essay. What do these expressions have in common? What characteristics seem to have been de Boinod's criteria for choosing his examples?

3. In an essay about foreign phrases and their meanings, the author uses quite a few idiomatic English expressions, which may be unfamiliar to some readers. For example, he explains a foreign phrase in paragraph 8 by saying that "both parties know the score," and in paragraph 9 he writes, "you'd have to lay it on pretty thick." What do these two idiomatic expressions mean? Why does he use idioms in English to explain idiomatic expressions in other languages?

WRITING PROMPTS

Responding to the Topic   Check the appendix of a collegiate dictionary to find a list of foreign words and phrases. Choose five or six that interest you. Write an essay in which you explain their meanings and discuss their usefulness as additions to English vocabulary.

Responding to the Writer   De Boinod finds it intriguing that words and phrases from foreign tongues could be helpful if added to an American English vocabulary. Other people feel strongly that English should be kept pure, not infiltrated by non-English expressions. Write an essay in which you take a position on this issue. Be sure to use specific examples to reinforce your argument.

Responding to Multiple Viewpoints   How might opponents of immigration react to the infiltration of bits of foreign language into our everyday speech? Read David Gergen's essay "A Smart Exception" (p. 93) in Chapter 3. Then write an essay exploring how our thoughts about the influx of foreign words and phrases is both similar to and different from our thoughts about the influx of immigrants.

For a quiz on this reading, go to bedfordstmartins.com/mirror.

Corporate Names and Products Creep into Everyday Language

GENEVA WHITE

Geneva White was a reporter and columnist for the *Northwest Herald* in the Greater Chicago area until 2008. In this article, which appeared in the *Northwest Herald* in 2007, White discusses all the ways we incorporate brand names into our everyday language, sometimes without even realizing we've done so.

THINKING AHEAD What brand names do you employ in your own speech to represent everything of that type (Band-Aid, for example). Make a list of these. Now add to your list other brand names used generically that you've heard on television or in movies. How do proper nouns become common nouns in our vocabulary?

We "Google" ex-boyfriends and ex-girlfriends. 1

We "Netflix" DVDs. 2

Before heading to parties, we often "Mapquest" the directions. 3

And rather than miss our favorite television shows, we "TiVo" them. 4

What has become of the English language? Linguists insist this integration of corporate names, products and services into our everyday speech is nothing new. 5

Dennis Baron, a professor of English and linguistics, points out that in the 1980s, we were "Xeroxing" copies. Older generations likely remember the days when all cameras were called "Kodaks." 6

"This is one of the ways that language naturally works," said Baron, who teaches at the University of Illinois in Champaign. "Common inventions, technologies and products become embedded in the language and extend their use to other areas. That's how language changes and spreads." 7

Scott Osmundson, 31, said he finds himself incorporating words that originated with the Internet. 8

"Yeah, I say 'Google it,'" said Osmundson, of Johnsburg. "With how big the Internet has gotten it was bound to happen." 9

Osmundson said his friends have told him to "YouTube" videos. "MySpace me" is another expression he's heard people say. 10

"We're starting to lose the English language," Osmundson said. "Especially with texting and how people abbreviate words now." 11

As the English language evolves, new words must be added to *Merriam-Webster's Collegiate Dictionary*. Among the latest words appearing in the 12 dictionary's 11th edition, set to be released this fall, are *DVR* (Digital Video Recorder), *speed dating, sudoku*[1] and *telenovela.*[2]

"Webster is constantly adding new words to the dictionary," said   13
Heather Brown, assistant chair of the English department at Woodstock High School. "If you notice, most of those are technology driven."

So far, Brown, who teaches creative writing and American literature,   14
hasn't seen students use terms such as "Googling" in their papers.

"But it's definitely in their lexicon when they're talking with each   15
other," she said.

Frequent use of a word not only helps it get into the dictionary. The prac-   16
tice can also put a product's copyright at stake.

"It's tricky for [corporations]," Baron said. "They want the names of   17
their products to be on everybody's lips, but they don't want it to be used as a generic [word]. They don't want all tissues to be Kleenex."

Ironically, just because a word ends up in the dictionary, it's still not   18
necessarily O.K. to use on school papers, college entrance exams and cover letters.

"'Ain't' has been in the dictionary for some time," Brown said. "We   19
still don't allow it."

Renee Woods of Crystal Lake said "Google" often comes up in her   20
conversations.

"My friend just 'Googled' herself," said Woods, 25. "That's weird."   21

EXERCISING VOCABULARY

1. Record your own definition for each of these words.

   integration (n.) (5)
   embedded (v.) (7)
   incorporating (v.) (8)
   lexicon (n.) (15)

2. In paragraph 17, Dennis Baron is quoted as saying that businesses want their products to be popular but don't really want the product name "to be used as a generic." What does *generic* mean? What part of speech is the word as Baron uses it? Give an example of *generic* used as a different part of speech. Why does the author add a final word in brackets that wasn't part of the original quote?

3. Who are linguists? What does the study of linguistics involve? Why are linguists' ideas important to this essay?

---

[1] *sudoku*: A puzzle completed on a grid using numbers and the application of logic.
[2] *telenovela*: Melodrama miniseries made popular in Latin America.

PROBING CONTENT

1. What is one way that language evolves, according to Dennis Baron?

2. According to Heather Brown, how much of the new Internet-inspired vocabulary is making its way into students' writing?

3. To what area are most of the new words in *Merriam-Webster's Collegiate Dictionary* related? Why is this the case?

CONSIDERING CRAFT

1. In this relatively brief selection, White quotes four sources. How does this affect your reading of her essay? What observations can you make about the credentials of White's sources? Why do you think she chose these particular sources?

2. How does White incorporate her topic into the introduction to catch the reader's attention? What can you learn from her introduction that you can apply to your own writing?

3. In this selection, what strategy does White use to prove the point that "this integration of corporate names, products and services into our everyday speech is nothing new" (para. 5)?

WRITING PROMPTS

Responding to the Topic   Write an essay in which you discuss some changes you personally have noted in the language we use daily. Elaborate on the reasons for these changes. Be sure to use specific examples to support your argument.

Responding to the Writer   Dennis Baron states, "This is one of the ways that language naturally works" (para. 7). Scott Osmundson, however, complains, "We're starting to lose the English language" (para. 11). Whose viewpoint is more accurate? Write an essay in which you defend one of these positions.

Responding to Multiple Viewpoints   Read Adam Jacot de Boinod's essay "Global Wording" (p. 218) in this chapter. Write an essay comparing and contrasting the acquisition of foreign words and phrases to the adoption of brand names as common nouns in American English. Consider frequency of use and level of acceptance of words from these two sources.

For a quiz on this reading, go to bedfordstmartins.com/mirror.

Swoosh!

READ MERCER SCHUCHARDT

Our culture lives by symbols. In fact, every day more and more of these symbols replace the words they represent. Read Mercer Schuchardt examines one of modern America's most successful icons, the Nike Swoosh, in this essay originally published in *Re:Generation Quarterly* and reprinted in the *Utne Reader* in 1997. He is currently assistant professor of media ecology and web communication at Wheaton College and has published in the *Chicago Tribune* and the *Washington Times.* He is also the publisher of Metaphilm.com, a film criticism Web site. In 2008, he edited a collection of essays about the novel *Fight Club* and its film adaptation, titled *You Do Not Talk about Fight Club.*

> **THINKING AHEAD** Think about some products whose symbols or icons are so well known that consumers recognize them without seeing the product's actual name. How did these symbols become so familiar to us? Why do we understand their meaning without the help of words? How do they work to unite us in a common understanding?

T he early followers of Christ created a symbol to represent their beliefs 1
and communicate with one another in times of persecution. The well-known Ichthus, or "Christian fish," consisted of two curved lines that transected each other to form the abstract outline of fish and tail. The word for *fish* also happened to be a Greek acronym wherein:

- Iota = Iesous = Jesus
- Chi = Christos = Christ
- Theta = Theos = God
- Upsilon = Huios = Son
- Sigma = Soter = Savior

Combining symbol and word, the fish provided believers with an integrated media package that could be easily explained and understood. When the threat of being fed to the lions forced Christians to be less explicit, they dropped the text. Without the acronym to define the symbol's significance, the fish could mean anything or nothing, an obvious advantage in a culture hostile to certain beliefs. But to Christians the textless symbol still signified silent rebellion against the ruling authorities. Within three centuries, the faith signified by the fish had transformed Rome into a Christian empire.

Today, in an electronically accelerated culture, a symbol can change the   3
face of society in about one-sixteenth that time. Enter the Nike Swoosh, the
most ubiquitous icon in the country, and one that many other corporations
have sought to emulate. In a world where technology, entertainment, and
design are converging, the story of the Swoosh is by far the most fascinating
case study of a systematic, integrated, and insanely successful formula for
icon-driven marketing.

The simple version of the story is that a young Oregon design student   4
named Caroline Davidson got $35 in 1971 to create a logo for then-
professor (now Nike CEO) Phil Knight's idea of importing and selling improved Japanese running shoes. Nike's innovative product line, combined
with aggressive marketing and brand positioning, eventually created an un-
breakable mental link between the Swoosh image and the company's name.
As Nike put it, there was so much equity in the brand that they knew it
wouldn't hurt to drop the word *Nike* and go with the Swoosh alone. Nike
went to the textless format for U.S. advertising in March 1996 and expanded it globally later that year. While the Nike name and symbol appear
together in ads today, the textless campaign set a new standard. In the modern global market, the truly successful icon must be able to stand by itself,
evoking all the manufactured associations that form a corporation's public
identity.

In the past, it would have been unthinkable to create an ad campaign   5
stripped of the company's name. Given what was at stake—Nike's advertising budget totals more than $100 million per year—what made them
think they could pull it off?

First, consider the strength of the Swoosh as an icon. The Swoosh is a   6
simple shape that reproduces well at any size, in any color, and on almost
any surface—three critical elements for a corporate logo that will be reproduced at sizes from a quarter of an inch to 500 feet. It most frequently
appears in one of three arresting colors: black, red, or white. A textless
icon, it nevertheless "reads" left to right, like most languages. Now consider the sound of the word *Swoosh*. According to various Nike ads, it's the
last sound you hear before coming in second place, the sound of a basketball hitting nothing but net. It's also the onomatopoeic[1] analogue of the
icon's visual stroke. Reading it left to right, the symbol itself actually seems
to say "swoosh" as you look at it.

However it may read, the Swoosh transcends language, making it the   7
perfect corporate icon for the postliterate[2] global village.

With the invention of the printing press, according to Italian semioti-   8
cian[3] Umberto Eco, the alphabet triumphed over the icon. But in an over-
stimulated electronic culture, the chief problem is what advertisers call

---

[1] **onomatopoeic:** Relating to a term whose name imitates the sound that it makes.
[2] **postliterate:** Occurring after the advent of electronic media.
[3] **semiotician:** A person who studies signs and symbols and the way that they operate in
    everyday life.

"clutter" or "chatter"—too many words, too much redundancy, too many competing messages. Add the rise of illiteracy and an increasingly multicultural world and you have a real communications problem. A hyperlinked global economy requires a single global communications medium, and it's simply easier to teach everyone a few common symbols than to teach the majority of non-English speakers a new language.

The unfortunate result is that language is being replaced by icons. From the rock star formerly known as Prince to e-mail "smileys" to the NAFTA[4]-induced symbolic laundry labels, the names and words we use to describe the world are being replaced by a set of universal hieroglyphs.[5] Leading the charge, as one would expect, are the organizations that stand to make the most money in a less text-dependent world: multinational corporations. With the decline of words, they now can fill in the blank of the consumer's associative mind with whatever images they deem appropriate. 9

After watching Nike do it, several companies have decided to go textless themselves, including Mercedes-Benz, whose icon is easily confused with the peace sign (an association that can only help). According to one of their print ads, "right behind every powerful icon lies a powerful idea," which is precisely the definition of a global communications medium for an accelerated culture. Pepsi's new textless symbol does not need any verbal justification because it so clearly imitates the yin-yang[6] symbol. In fact, a close look reveals it to be almost identical to the Korean national flag, which is itself a stylized yin-yang symbol in red, white, and blue. 10

Never underestimate the power of symbols. Textless corporate symbols operate at a level beneath the radar of rational language, and the power they wield can be corrupting. Advertising that relies on propaganda methods can grab you and take you somewhere whether you want to go or not; and as history tells us, it matters where you're going. 11

Language is the mediator between our minds and the world, and the thing that defines us as rational creatures. By going textless, Nike and other corporations have succeeded in performing partial lobotomies[7] on our brains, conveying their messages without engaging our rational minds. Like Pavlov's[8] bell, the Swoosh has become a stimulus that elicits a conditioned response. The problem is not that we buy Nike shoes, but that we've been led to do so by the same methods used to train Pavlov's dogs. It's ironic, of course, that this reflex is triggered by a stylized check mark—the standard reward for academic achievement and ultimate symbol for the rational, linguistically agile mind. 12

[4] **NAFTA:** North American Free Trade Agreement, an agreement that in 1994 launched the world's largest free-trade area.
[5] **hieroglyphs:** Characters in a system of picture writing.
[6] **yin-yang:** A black-and-white Chinese symbol that represents completeness by combining both halves of the universe.
[7] **lobotomies:** Surgical procedures that sever nerves in the brain and once were used to control unruly psychiatric patients.
[8] **Pavlov:** Russian scientist Ivan Pavlov (1849–1936) who experimented with predicting behavior under certain circumstances; many of his experiments used dogs as subjects.

If sport is the religion of the modern age, then Nike has successfully   13
become the official church. It is a church whose icon is a window between
this world and the other, between your existing self (you overweight slob)
and your Nike self (you god of fitness), where salvation lies in achieving the
athletic Nietzschean[9] ideal: no fear, no mercy, no second place. Like the
Christian fish, the Swoosh is a true religious icon in that it both symbolizes
the believer's reality and actually participates in it. After all, you do have to
wear something to attain this special salvation, so why not something emblazoned with the Swoosh?

EXERCISING VOCABULARY

1. Record your own definition for each of these words.

   transected (v.) (1)   transcends (v.) (7)
   emulate (v.) (3)   redundancy (n.) (8)
   innovative (adj.) (4)   mediator (n.) (12)
   arresting (adj.) (6)   stylized (adj.) (12)
   analogue (n.) (6)   emblazoned (v.) (13)

2. This essay begins with the history of an acronym. What is an acronym?
   Why are acronyms used? Give an example of an acronym that means
   something to you and explain what the letters stand for. *Scuba,* for example, stands for "self-contained underwater breathing apparatus," and
   CEO stands for "chief executive officer."

3. Schuchardt refers to the Nike Swoosh as "ubiquitous" in paragraph 3.
   How accurate is this word in describing the popularity of the Nike symbol? Name at least five different places where the Swoosh appears.

4. In paragraph 4, Schuchardt says that Nike was able to drop the word
   Nike from marketing campaigns because "there was so much equity in
   the brand." What does it mean to have equity in something? Give two or
   three examples. What does using the word *equity* here imply about the
   Nike corporation?

PROBING CONTENT

1. Why did the early Christians adopt the Ichthus symbol? What significance did it hold for them?

2. Why, according to Schuchardt, must a successful advertising icon not
   need supporting language to be clearly understood by a wide range of
   people? How do you determine whether an icon is successful as a marketing tool?

---

[9] **Nietzschean:** Referring to Friedrich Nietzsche (1844–1900), a German philosopher and
author of *Man and Superman.*

3. To what does Schuchardt attribute the success of the Nike symbol? Use specific references from the text to support your answer.

4. What does this essay describe as the conditioned or predictable response to the stimulus of the Nike Swoosh? How effective is the Swoosh in generating this response?

CONSIDERING CRAFT

1. The writer chooses a complicated introduction. How well does the Christian fish symbol work as an introduction to this topic? Why do you think Schuchardt chose this symbol to introduce his essay?

2. This essay contains a number of unfamiliar references. If Schuchardt knew that some readers would not understand these references, why did he include them? How do they improve or weaken the essay?

3. What does the final paragraph have in common with the introduction? What does the author want to accomplish by using this strategy? To what extent is he successful?

WRITING PROMPTS

Responding to the Topic   Have you noticed a surge of "textless corporate symbols" (para. 11) around you? Develop an essay exploring the influence of such symbols on your everyday life. Support your essay with numerous specific examples.

Responding to the Writer   Do you agree with Schuchardt that "language is being replaced by icons" (para. 9)? Do you agree with him that if this has happened or were to happen, the result would be unfortunate? Write an essay in which you support your position on these questions with evidence from the text, as well as additional examples that you select.

Responding to Multiple Viewpoints   Read Mercer Schuchardt writes "Language is the mediator between our minds and the world, and the thing that defines us as rational creatures" (para. 12). Write an essay in which you compare and contrast this opinion with the opinions expressed by Lera Boroditsky in "Lost in Translation" (page 212).

For a quiz on this reading, go to bedfordstmartins.com/mirror.

Deciphering the Chatter of Monkeys and Chimps

NICHOLAS WADE

Nicholas Wade is a writer for the Science Times section of the *New York Times.* Born in England, Wade attended Eton College and King's College, Cambridge. He has written several books, including *A Natural History of Vision* (2000), *Before the Dawn: Recovering the Lost History of Our Ancestors* (2007), and *The Faith Instinct: How Religion Evolved and Why It Endures* (2009). This article first appeared in the *New York Times* in 2010.

> **THINKING AHEAD** Have you ever thought about whether or how animals communicate with others of their own species? Have you ever communicated with an animal? What were the circumstances? To what extent do you believe that communication between humans and animals is possible or potentially beneficial?

Walking through the Tai forest of Ivory Coast, Klaus Zuberbühler could   1
hear the calls of the Diana monkeys, but the babble held no meaning for him.

That was in 1990. Today, after nearly 20 years of studying animal com-   2
munication, he can translate the forest's sounds. This call means a Diana monkey has seen a leopard. That one means it has sighted another predator, the crowned eagle. "In our experience time and again, it's a humbling experience to realize there is so much more information being passed in ways which hadn't been noticed before," said Dr. Zuberbühler, a psychologist at the University of St. Andrews in Scotland.

Do apes and monkeys have a secret language that has not yet been de-   3
crypted? And if so, will it resolve the mystery of how the human faculty for language evolved? Biologists have approached the issue in two ways, by trying to teach human language to chimpanzees and other species, and by listening to animals in the wild.

The first approach has been propelled by people's intense desire—   4
perhaps reinforced by childhood exposure to the loquacious animals in cartoons—to communicate with other species. Scientists have invested enormous effort in teaching chimpanzees language, whether in the form of speech or signs. A *New York Times* reporter who understands sign language, Boyce Rensberger, was able in 1974 to conduct what may be the first newspaper interview with another species when he conversed with Lucy, a signing chimp. She invited him up her tree, a proposal he declined, said Mr. Rensberger, who is now at M.I.T.

But with a few exceptions, teaching animals human language has proved   5
to be a dead end. They should speak, perhaps, but they do not. They can
communicate very expressively—think how definitely dogs can make their
desires known—but they do not link symbolic sounds together in sentences
or have anything close to language.

Better insights have come from listening to the sounds made by ani-   6
mals in the wild. Vervet monkeys were found in 1980 to have specific
alarm calls for their most serious predators. If the calls were recorded and
played back to them, the monkeys would respond appropriately. They
jumped into bushes on hearing the leopard call, scanned the ground at the
snake call, and looked up when played the eagle call.

It is tempting to think of the vervet calls as words for "leopard," "snake"   7
or "eagle," but that is not really so. The vervets do not combine the calls
with other sounds to make new meanings. They do not modulate them, so
far as is known, to convey that a leopard is 10, or 100, feet away. Their
alarm calls seem less like words and more like a person saying "Ouch!"—a
vocal representation of an inner mental state rather than an attempt to
convey exact information.

But the calls do have specific meaning, which is a start. And the biolo-   8
gists who analyzed the vervet calls, Robert Seyfarth and Dorothy Cheney of
the University of Pennsylvania, detected another significant element in primates' communication when they moved on to study baboons. Baboons
are very sensitive to who stands where in their society's hierarchy. If played
a recording of a superior baboon threatening an inferior, and the latter
screaming in terror, baboons will pay no attention—this is business as
usual in baboon affairs. But when researchers concoct a recording in which
an inferior's threat grunt precedes a superior's scream, baboons will look in
amazement toward the loudspeaker broadcasting this apparent revolution
in their social order.

Baboons evidently recognize the order in which two sounds are heard,   9
and attach different meanings to each sequence. They and other species thus
seem much closer to people in their understanding of sound sequences than
in their production of them. "The ability to think in sentences does not lead
them to speak in sentences," Drs. Seyfarth and Cheney wrote in their book
Baboon Metaphysics.

Some species may be able to produce sounds in ways that are a step or   10
two closer to human language. Dr. Zuberbühler reported last month that
Campbell's monkeys, which live in the forests of the Ivory Coast, can vary
individual calls by adding suffixes, just as a speaker of English changes a
verb's present tense to past by adding an "-ed."

The Campbell's monkeys give a "krak" alarm call when they see a leop-   11
ard. But adding an "-oo" changes it to a generic warning of predators. One
context for the krak-oo sound is when they hear the leopard alarm calls of
another species, the Diana monkey. The Campbell's monkeys would evidently
make good reporters since they distinguish between leopards they have observed directly (krak) and those they have heard others observe (krak-oo).

Even more remarkably, the Campbell's monkeys can combine two calls   12
to generate a third with a different meaning. The males have a "Boom
boom" call, which means "I'm here, come to me." When booms are followed by a series of krak-oos, the meaning is quite different, Dr. Zuberbühler says. The sequence means "Timber! Falling tree!"

Dr. Zuberbühler has observed a similar achievement among putty-   13
nosed monkeys that combine their "pyow" call (warning of a leopard)
with their "hack" call (warning of a crowned eagle) into a sequence that
means "Let's get out of here in a real hurry."

Apes have larger brains than monkeys and might be expected to pro-   14
duce more calls. But if there is an elaborate code of chimpanzee communication, their human cousins have not yet cracked it. Chimps make a food call
that seems to have a lot of variation, perhaps depending on the perceived
quality of the food. How many different meanings can the call assume?
"You would need the animals themselves to decide how many meaningful
calls they can discriminate," Dr. Zuberbühler said. Such a project, he estimates, could take a lifetime of research.

Monkeys and apes possess many of the faculties that underlie language.   15
They hear and interpret sequences of sounds much like people do. They have
good control over their vocal tract and could produce much the same range
of sounds as humans. But they cannot bring it all together.

This is particularly surprising because language is so useful to a social   16
species. Once the infrastructure of language is in place, as is almost the case
with monkeys and apes, the faculty might be expected to develop very
quickly by evolutionary standards. Yet monkeys have been around for 30
million years without saying a single sentence. Chimps, too, have nothing
resembling language, though they shared a common ancestor with humans
just five million years ago. What is it that has kept all other primates locked
in the prison of their own thoughts?

Drs. Seyfarth and Cheney believe that one reason may be that they lack   17
a "theory of mind"; the recognition that others have thoughts. Since a baboon does not know or worry about what another baboon knows, it has
no urge to share its knowledge. Dr. Zuberbühler stresses an intention to
communicate as the missing factor. Children from the youngest ages have a
great desire to share information with others, even though they gain no immediate benefit in doing so. Not so with other primates.

"In principle, a chimp could produce all the sounds a human produces,   18
but they don't do so because there has been no evolutionary pressure in
this direction," Dr. Zuberbühler said. "There is nothing to talk about for a
chimp because he has no interest in talking about it." At some point in human evolution, on the other hand, people developed the desire to share
thoughts, Dr. Zuberbühler notes. Luckily for them, all the underlying systems of perceiving and producing sounds were already in place as part of
the primate heritage, and natural selection had only to find a way of connecting these systems with thought.

Yet it is this step that seems the most mysterious of all. Marc D. Hauser,   19
an expert on animal communication at Harvard, sees the uninhibited interaction between different neural systems as critical to the development of language. "For whatever reason, maybe accident, our brains are promiscuous in a way that animal brains are not, and once this emerges it's explosive," he said.

In animal brains, by contrast, each neural system seems to be locked in   20
place and cannot interact freely with others. "Chimps have tons to say but can't say it," Dr. Hauser said. Chimpanzees can read each other's goals and intentions, and do lots of political strategizing, for which language would be very useful. But the neural systems that compute these complex social interactions have not been married to language.

Dr. Hauser is trying to find out whether animals can appreciate some   21
of the critical aspects of language, even if they cannot produce it. He and Ansgar Endress reported last year that cotton-top tamarins[1] can distinguish a word added in front of another word from the same word added at the end. This may seem like the syntactical ability to recognize a suffix or prefix, but Dr. Hauser thinks it is just the ability to recognize when one thing comes before another and has little to do with real syntax.

"I'm becoming pessimistic," he said of the efforts to explore whether   22
animals have a form of language. "I conclude that the methods we have are just impoverished and won't get us to where we want to be as far as demonstrating anything like semantics or syntax."

Yet, as is evident from Dr. Zuberbühler's research, there are many seemingly meaningless sounds in the forest that convey information in ways perhaps akin to language.   23

EXERCISING VOCABULARY

1. Record your own definition for each of these words.

   babble (n.) (1)   concoct (v.) (8)
   predator (n.) (2)   generic (adj.) (11)
   loquacious (adj.) (4)   syntactical (adj.) (21)
   modulate (v.) (7)   semantics (n.) (22)
   hierarchy (n.) (8)   akin (adj.) (23)

2. The author questions whether the language of apes and monkeys may have not yet been "decrypted" (para. 3). What is a crypt? What does it mean to decrypt something? How are these two meanings related?

3. In paragraph 16, the author discusses the relevance of the "infrastructure of language." In what context is the word *infrastructure* generally used? What does it mean to attribute infrastructure to language?

[1] **tamarins:** small South American monkey.

4. An animal communication expert, Marc D. Hauser, refers to human brains as "promiscuous" (para. 19). What does *promiscuous* mean? How can this behavior be attributed to a brain?

5. When Dr. Hauser calls the methods that humans have to explore animal language "impoverished," what does he mean? What does his use of this word indicate about why scientists haven't advanced further with research into animals' ability to communicate?

PROBING CONTENT

1. In what two ways have biologists approached the study of animals' language capacity? Which has proved more fruitful? Why?

2. Who conducted the first interview with a nonhuman animal? How was this accomplished?

3. Why do the calls made by vervet monkeys not qualify as words? What are they instead?

4. What animals communicate in ways that are closer to human speech than the articulations of vervets and baboons? How are the sounds these mammals make more advanced?

CONSIDERING CRAFT

1. Reread the first and last paragraphs of this article. How does the author use them to tie his essay together? What does Nicholas Wade accomplish in his introduction and in his conclusion?

2. Throughout this article, there is a steady progression of animals discussed. In what sequence are animals mentioned? Why does Wade choose this particular sequence? What effect does this pattern have on Wade's readers?

3. Although this is a serious article on a scientific subject, Wade occasionally injects humor. Locate and note several such instances. Why does he choose to do this, and what effect do these injections of humor have on the reader and on the article?

WRITING PROMPTS

Responding to the Topic   Sue Savage-Rumbaugh, a scientist noted for her work with language acquisition among bonobos at the Great Ape Institute, notes that "the mythology of human uniqueness is coming under challenge. If apes can learn language, which we once thought unique to humans, then it suggests that ability is not innate in just us." Write an essay exploring the implications for mankind if our current assumptions about the uniqueness of humans' language abilities are faulty.

Responding to the Writer At the end of this essay, Dr. Marc Hauser states, "I'm becoming pessimistic" about whether animals have language systems (para. 22). Nicholas Wade, the author of this article, disagrees; based on Dr. Zuberbühler's research, he believes that forest sounds may be close to language. Write an essay in which you defend the position of either Dr. Hauser or the author.

Responding to Multiple Viewpoints In his essay "How Do You Say *Extinct?*" (p. 236) John Miller writes, "Each language captures something about a way of life" (para. 16). Write an essay in which you explore how Miller would react to the research findings explored by Nicholas Wade in this essay. What implications might Miller see for the future?

How Do You Say *Extinct*?

JOHN J. MILLER

John J. Miller is a national political reporter for *The National Review*. He has also worked as a contributing editor for *Reason* and as vice president for the Center for Equal Opportunity. He is the author of *The Unmaking of Americans: How Multiculturalism Has Undermined America's Assimilation Ethic* (1998) and *A Gift of Freedom: How the John M. Olin Foundation Changed America* (2005). He is also the coauthor, with Mark Molesky, of *Our Oldest Enemy: A History of America's Disastrous Relationship with France* (2004). *The Wall Street Journal* published "How Do You Say *Extinct*?" in March 2002.

> **THINKING AHEAD** What is the relationship between language and culture? How important is it to all of us to protect languages spoken by very few people? Why? What is lost when a spoken language goes out of existence?
>
> **Paired Selection** Read this selection and the one that follows for two approaches to a similar topic. Then answer the "Drawing Connections" questions on p. 248.

When Marie Smith-Jones passes away, she will take with her a small but irreplaceable piece of human culture. That's because the octogenarian[1] Anchorage resident is the last speaker of Eyak, the traditional language of her Alaskan tribe. "It's horrible to be alone," she has said.

Yet she isn't really alone, at least in the sense of being a last speaker. There are many others like her. By one account, a last speaker of one of the world's six thousand languages dies every two weeks.

To UNESCO—the United Nations Educational, Scientific and Cultural Organization—language extinction is a disaster of, well, unspeakable proportions. Its new report warns of a "catastrophic reduction in the number of languages spoken in the world" and estimates three thousand are "endangered, seriously endangered, or dying."

In other words, children have stopped learning half the world's languages, and it's only a matter of time before their current speakers fall silent. UNESCO calls this an "irretrievable and tragic" development because "language diversity" is "one of humanity's most precious commodities."

But is it really? UNESCO's determined pessimism masks a trend that is arguably worth celebrating: A growing number of people are speaking a

---

[1] **octogenarian:** A person in his or her eighties.

smaller number of languages, meaning that age-old obstacles to communication are collapsing. Surely this is a good thing.

Except for those who believe that "diversity" trumps all else. We've heard claims like this before, in debates over college admissions and snail darters,[2] and they're often dubious. The chief problem with UNESCO's view—shared by many academic linguists—is its careless embrace of multiculturalism, or what it labels "egalitarian multilingualism." This outlook gives short shrift to the interests and choices of people in tiny language groups.

Languages disappear for all sorts of reasons, not least among them their radical transformation over time. Consider English. It helps to have a gloss handy when reading Shakespeare's plays of four centuries ago. Chaucer's Middle English may be understood only with difficulty. And the Old English of the *Beowulf* poet is not only dead but unintelligible to modern speakers.

Because languages evolve, it should come as no surprise that some expire. Michael Krauss of the University of Alaska at Fairbanks—the leading expert on the Eyak of Ms. Smith-Jones—believes that ten thousand years ago there may have been as many as twenty thousand languages spoken by a total human population of perhaps ten million, roughly 0.17 percent of our current world census. Assuming this is true, it would suggest a connection between more people and fewer languages, and between language and the technology that lets people communicate over distance.

That makes sense, because geographic isolation is an incubator of linguistic diversity. A language doesn't require more than a few hundred people to sustain it, assuming they keep to themselves. The forbidding terrain of Papua New Guinea is home to the highest concentration of languages anywhere—at least 820 different tongues in an area smaller than Utah and Wyoming combined. For UNESCO, this is a kind of Platonic[3] ideal. Its report describes Papua New Guinea as "a fitting example for other civilizations to follow."

That's an odd thing to say about a country where 99 percent of the people don't own a phone, but it's typical of the attitude of the language preservationists, who apparently would like to see tribal members live in primitive bliss, preserving their exotic customs. A thread runs through the preservationist arguments suggesting that *we* can benefit from *them*—that is, we in the developed world have much to gain if they in the undeveloped world continue communicating in obscure languages we don't bother to learn ourselves.

David Crystal makes the point unwittingly in his book *Language Death* when he describes an Australian aboriginal language "whose vocabulary provides different names for grubs (an important food source) according to the types of bush where they are found." He's trying to say that we may learn about biology if we preserve and study obscure languages—but he seems oblivious to the reality that most people would rather eat a Big Mac than a fistful of beetle larvae.

---

[2] **snail darters:** A threatened species of fish found only in the Tennessee River.
[3] **Platonic:** Characteristic of the Greek philosopher Plato.

Many linguists are deadly serious about the biological connection; they   12
would like nothing better than to join forces with environmentalists. In
Vanishing Voices, Daniel Nettle and Suzanne Romaine even write of "biolinguistic diversity," which they define as "the rich spectrum of life encompassing all the earth's species of plants and animals along with human
cultures and their languages." This invention allows them to suggest that
"the next great step in scientific development may lie locked up in some
obscure language in a distant rainforest."

Then again, it may not—and the only way to find out requires that   13
some people continue living a premodern, close-to-nature existence. The
UNESCO report and linguists everywhere say that governmental policies
of forced assimilation have contributed mightily to language extinction,
and they certainly have a point. But what they're endorsing now is a kind
of forced dissimilation, in the hope, apparently, that a cure for cancer will
one day find expression in an Amazonian dialect.

That's the fundamental mistake of the UNESCO report. "Linguistic   14
diversity is an invaluable asset and resource rather than an obstacle to
progress," it claims. Yet the most important reason some languages are disappearing is precisely that their native speakers don't regard them as quite
so precious. They view linguistic adaptation—especially for their kids—as
a key to getting ahead. This is understandable when about half the world's
population speaks one of only ten languages and when speaking English in
particular is a profitable skill. Nowadays, the difference between knowing
a lingua franca[4] and an obscure language is the difference between performing algorithms on a computer and counting with your fingers.

Linguists say that about half the world's population is already able to   15
speak at least two languages, and they insist that such bilingualism is a key to
preserving "diversity." Perhaps, but it sounds better in theory than it works
in practice. Simple verbal exchanges are one thing; communicating at high
levels of proficiency is another. If bilingual education in the United States
has revealed anything, it is that schools can teach a rudimentary knowledge
of two languages to students while leaving them fluent in neither.

Each language captures something about a way of life, and when one   16
goes mute, it is hard not to feel a sense of loss. But languages are no less
mortal than the men and women who speak them. Maybe linguists should
try to learn as much as they can about "dying" languages before they vanish completely, rather than engage in a quixotic attempt to save them.

EXERCISING VOCABULARY

1. Record your own definition for each of these words.

irreplaceable (adj.) (1)	dubious (adj.) (6)
trumps (v.) (6)	unwittingly (adv.) (11)

---

[4] **lingua franca:** Common language.

oblivious (adj.) (11)   rudimentary (adj.) (15)
assimilation (n.) (13)

2. According to Miller, UNESCO considers language extinction "a disaster of, well, unspeakable proportions" (para. 3). What does *unspeakable* mean? Why does Miller choose this particular word to describe UNESCO's reaction?

3. What is "biolinguistic diversity" (para. 12)? Why and how may it unite linguists and environmentalists?

4. Miller conveys his viewpoint about the linguists' fight to preserve vanishing languages in the final sentence of his essay. Who is Don Quixote? How does Miller's use of the word *quixotic* reveal his viewpoint?

PROBING CONTENT

1. What trend defies UNESCO's pessimistic observations? According to Miller, why is this advantageous?

2. What are some of the reasons that languages expire? What role may native speakers play in their extinction or retention?

3. According to Miller, how effective has bilingual education proven to be in the United States? Why?

CONSIDERING CRAFT

1. What is ironic about the title of this essay? How does the use of irony in the title set the tone for this selection?

2. The author quotes UNESCO's report to note that three thousand languages are "endangered, seriously endangered, or dying" (para. 3). With what is the word *endangered* usually associated? What might this report have hoped to accomplish by linking the word *endangered* to languages?

3. Explain Miller's statement that "geographic isolation is an incubator of linguistic diversity" (para. 9).

WRITING PROMPTS

Responding to the Topic   How many of your friends and acquaintances speak more than one language? From your own experience, write an essay examining the benefits of personal linguistic diversity.

Responding to the Writer   Write an essay taking a position on whether the extinction of languages spoken by small populations should be a serious concern for all of us.

Responding to Multiple Viewpoints   How would Alex Pham and David Sarno ("Digital Information and the Future of Reading," p. 256) regard Miller's conclusion in the final paragraph of "How Do You Say *Extinct*?" Write an essay in which you explore their possible response in detail, using text from both essays to support your answer.

For a quiz on this reading, go to bedfordstmartins.com/mirror.

In the Language of Our Ancestors

MINDY CAMERON

Mindy Cameron is a freelance writer based in Sandpoint, Idaho. She was formerly an editor for the *Seattle Times,* and she received that paper's Publisher's Circle Award for Executive of the Year. "In the Language of Our Ancestors" first appeared in *Northwest Education Magazine.* In it, she chronicles efforts to save dying Native American languages, making important arguments about the ties between language and culture.

> **THINKING AHEAD**   Should people who move to another country learn the language of that country's native residents? Why?
>
> **Paired Selection**   Read this selection and the one before it for two approaches to a similar topic. Then answer the "Drawing Connections" questions on p. 248.

S tudents in Eva Boyd's class are typical teenagers. They fidget, wisecrack, talk to friends, and only occasionally pay attention. 1

But when asked why they are in this class, they speak with one voice: We are losing our language; we want to preserve our heritage. The presence of these Salish teens in this classroom, along with Eva Boyd, a tribal elder, is testimony to that singular desire to save a culture by saving the language. 2

Across Indian Country, many efforts to revive and revitalize Native American languages are under way. And none too soon. Estimates vary, but of the hundreds of languages that existed here before the arrival of white settlers, as many as two-thirds may have disappeared. Of those that remain, many could die along with the elders, the dwindling brain trust of tribal language. 3

Boyd's story shows why so many of these languages disappeared, why some survived, and how they might be saved. 4

The Toll of Assimilation

From the late-nineteenth century until the mid-twentieth century, the national policy regarding American Indians and Alaska Natives was assimilation. After decades of removing indigenous people from their land to reservations, the federal government sought to mainstream them into American society. 5

Education was a critical aspect of the assimilation policy. It was believed that through education, Native Americans would learn the white man's language and culture and develop the skills to function effectively in 6 white man's society. By 1887 the federal government had established more than two hundred Indian schools to carry out this mission.

Like many of her tribal contemporaries, Boyd was sent to an Indian   7
boarding school. At the typical boarding school, children were punished for speaking their traditional language. Some were made to stand in the corner, others had their knuckles rapped or rags tied around their mouths. Many children eventually forgot their tribal language, and those who remembered were often ashamed to use it.

Eva Boyd managed to escape that fate. She was a willful 10-year-old   8
when she went to boarding school. Decades later, she explains simply, "I didn't like it, so I left." Three days after she arrived, Boyd walked out and hitchhiked back home to the Camas Prairie area of the Flathead Reservation in Western Montana. There, her grandmother raised her in the language of their ancestors.

Boyd, a former foreign language instructor at Salish Kootenai College,   9
came out of retirement to teach three Salish language classes at Ronan High School. For her, it's a simple matter of tribal survival. "If we don't keep the language alive our tribe is going down. Without the language we won't be Indians any more."

Students in her class understand that and struggle to learn the language.   10
A difficult task is made more difficult by a lack of resources. The sole text is a Salish storybook, *The Story of a Mean Little Old Lady,* with English translation.

"We have to do the best we can," says Boyd. Like her students, Boyd   11
wishes Native language instruction could start earlier, at an age when learning a new language is not so difficult.

Julie Cajune agrees. She is Indian Education Coordinator for the Ronan-   12
Pablo School District. She admires and values what Eva Boyd is doing. "A teacher such as Eva is one way to make the school more reflective of the community," she says, "but we are doing language at the wrong end."

"Go to Nkwusm," Cajune insists.   13

Starting Early

Thirty miles down the road at Arlee, in a former bowling alley that also   14
houses a casino, is Nkwusm. It's a tribal-run language immersion school for preschoolers.

Five little ones squirm on the floor at the feet of two elders, Pat Pierre   15
and Stephen Small Salmon. Like Boyd, the adults are fluent in Salish and committed to keeping the language alive, even if it means coming out of retirement, as Pierre has done.

On this damp and chilly day, he is reviewing the Salish names for   16
months, days of the week, and numbers. The children vigorously recite the words. They follow Pierre to the window where he points to the sky, the ground, and the distant hills. It is a short lesson in Salish about the weather.

Pierre explains, "The power and wisdom of language is what has kept   17
our people together so that we can do meaningful things. If I can teach the
little ones the language, then we keep our identity."

The research is clear about learning languages. A second language is   18
more easily acquired early on as children develop their language skills,
rather than at a later stage. That has great importance for indigenous people
facing the extinction of their ancestral language. Language is more than
words and rules of usage. It is the repository of culture and identity.

Using Language Nests

In Nkwusm, the Salish are replicating what has worked elsewhere to revive   19
indigenous languages; they are using what's called a "language nest." As the
name implies, a language nest is more than just another language program. It
is language immersion for the youngest members of a Native population.

When the Maoris of New Zealand faced the extinction of their lan-   20
guage more than twenty years ago, they created language nests. Hawaiians
soon adopted the Maori model and, in the mid-1990s, a similar program
was established on the Blackfeet Reservation in Northwest Montana.

Language nests are seen by many as a key to reviving tribal languages.   21
Last year Hawaii Senator Daniel Inouye proposed an amendment to the
Native American Languages Act of 1990. If passed, it would provide federal
government support for Native American survival schools, including language nests. The 1990 act establishes as national policy the government's
responsibility to "preserve, protect, and promote the rights of Native
Americans to use, practice, and develop" their Native languages.

Last May, at a U.S. Senate hearing on the proposed amendment, a del-   22
egation representing the Blackfeet Nation stressed the difference between
Native American language survival schools and public schools. "The academic outcomes of Native American language survival schools are as strong
as, or stronger than, public education systems and students become speakers
of their Native language," they said.

The Blackfeet Native language school in Browning, Montana—   23
Nizipuhwasin—has become a model for Nkwusm and for other communities that hope to develop programs for young speakers of tribal languages.

Few tribes, however, can sustain such schools indefinitely. Founders of   24
Nkwusm, which is now supported by grants and the Salish-Kootenai tribe,
hope eventually to be self-sustaining. They also seek to have an endowment, run a K–12 school, and provide distance learning for the Flathead
Reservation.

As important as tribal programs such as Nizipuhwasin and Nkwusm   25
are, the current reality is that most Native youth are educated in public
schools, not tribal-run classrooms. Native educators say if traditional languages are to be saved, public schools will have to play a key role.

Integrating Language

In Washington's Marysville School District, Tulalip Elementary offers one   26
example of how to develop an integrated curriculum of language, literature, and culture with Lushootseed—the language of the Tulalip tribe—at
the center.

The program began several years ago at the school, which is about 70   27
percent American Indian. Tribal members and district staff worked together
to develop a Tulalip-based classroom in the fourth grade. A non-Native
teacher teamed with a tribal language teacher to create a new curriculum,
which has now evolved into Lushootseed language and culture instruction
at every grade level.

Any curriculum introduced in schools today must meet state standards   28
and the requirements of the federal No Child Left Behind Act. The Tulalip-
based curriculum in Marysville has managed to do that.

One of many challenges for schools that already have—or would like   29
to start—Native language programs is finding qualified teachers. Some
states have responded to that need by authorizing alternative certification
for Native language teachers. In Montana, Washington, Oregon, and Idaho,
the authority for granting certification to these teachers has been delegated
to tribal authorities. (In Alaska, this authority is reserved for each school
board or regional educational attendance area.)

Once a tribe has determined an applicant is fluent enough to qualify, he   30
or she is recommended for certification to the State Board of Education.
Upon certification, Native language teachers, usually tribal elders, get the
same pay and benefits and must meet the same requirements for continuing
education as other certified teachers.

There have been some issues involving classroom management. "[That's]   31
no small matter in a room with more than a dozen teenagers," notes Julie
Cajune. Even so, she thinks it's a good move. Without certification, Native language teachers, who were paid at the level of teacher aides, were
devalued.

The Montana Board of Public Education adopted its policy for alterna-   32
tive certification, called Class 7 Specialist Certificate for Native American
Languages, in 1995. At that time one tribe identified only five elders who
were fluent in their Native language. Today, there are 112 Class 7 teachers
in Montana.

Washington state adopted its alternative certification in 2003. It is a   33
three-year pilot program with the purpose of contributing "to the recovery,
revitalization, and promotion of First Peoples' languages." By the end of
the first year, seven teachers had been certified under the program.

Indian English

Teaching Native American children, whether the subject is reading, math,   34
or their indigenous language, presents a unique set of circumstances. While
very few Native youngsters speak the language of their ancestors, their first
language is not necessarily the English of their white classmates, either. The
first language of two-thirds of American Indian youth today is Indian
English, according to a research report by Washington state's Office of the
Superintendent of Public Instruction and the Evergreen Center for Educational Improvement at Evergreen State College in Olympia.

Authors of the report, Magda Costantino and Joe St. Charles of Ever-   35
green, and Denny Hurtado of OSPI, describe Indian English as English dialects used by American Indians that do not conform in certain ways to
standard English. Despite the differences, however, the dialects "are nonetheless well-ordered and highly structured languages that reflect the linguistic competencies that must underlie all languages."

In *American Indian English,* W. L. Leap provides important context for   36
the restoration of Native languages. He writes that distinctive characteristics
of Indian English—what he calls "codes"—"derive, in large part, from their
close association with their speakers' ancestral language traditions. In many
cases, rules of grammar and discourse from that tradition provide the basis
for grammar and discourse in these English codes—even in instances where
the speakers are not fluent in their ancestral language."

It can be argued, then, that Indian English serves as a language bridge   37
between the past and present. Understanding the role and importance of
Indian English, however, may not be as big a hurdle as the larger issues and
prevailing attitudes about language use and instruction. Many people believe that because English is the dominant language, instruction should be
in English and all students should learn its proper usage. Disagreement
about the role and importance of bilingual education is a fact of life in
many school districts, tossing up one more barrier to public school efforts
to become involved in Native language revival.

What Research Shows

Advocates of Native language revival programs point to research that   38
shows academic advantages for children who speak two languages. Gina
Cantoni, a language pedagogy[1] professor at Northern Arizona University,
has written of "abundant evidence" that teaching the home language does
not interfere with the development of English skills. To the contrary, she
notes, instruction that "promotes proficiency in one's first language also
promotes proficiency in the second language."

Cantoni contends that "mastery of more than one linguistic code re-   39
sults in a special kind of cognitive flexibility." Unfortunately, she notes, the

---

[1] **pedagogy:** The art and science of teaching.

"special" abilities related to mastery of more than one language are not covered by most tests used to measure academic achievement.

Research reinforces the argument for expanding Native language instruction. Even more compelling are the voices of Native American advocates, from the students in Eva Boyd's class to the elders teaching youngsters at Nkwusm and to longtime Montana educator Joyce Silverthorne.   40

Silverthorne, a member of the Salish tribe of the Flathead Reservation in Montana, has been a classroom teacher, college instructor, school board member, program administrator on the reservation, and member of the Montana Board of Public Education, where she worked for passage of the Montana Class 7 certificate.   41

While language and culture are linked in all societies, "what is unique to Native Americans is that this is our homeland," says Silverthorne. "There is no 'old country' to return to. When language dies here, it dies forever."   42

Nkwusm founder and teacher Melanie Sandoval is committed to seeing that doesn't happen. Now 28, she says she has been trying to learn the language of her tribe as long as she can remember. She now learns along with the children, thanks to the two elders who come into the classroom six hours a day, five days a week. After years of formal study, she is now learning useful, everyday phrases like "blow your nose" and "jump down off that."   43

What's happening at the school is more than preserving the language. Sandoval observes that preservation "is like having a bottle on the shelf. We want to breathe life into the language, to speak it, and pass it on to the next generation."   44

EXERCISING VOCABULARY

1. Record your own definition for each of these words.

singular (adj.) (2)	replicating (v.) (19)
revitalize (v.) (3)	competencies (n.) (35)
indigenous (adj.) (5)	discourse (n.) (36)
immersion (adj.) (14)	advocates (n.) (40)
repository (n.) (18)	

2. Why does Cameron call tribal elders "the dwindling brain trust of tribal languages" (para. 3)? What is a brain trust? What does this imply about the status of the elders?

3. What is the denotative meaning of the word *assimilation*? How does one group of people become assimilated into another group? Is the connotative meaning of this word positive or negative as Cameron uses it in this essay?

4. Gina Cantoni believes that comprehending multiple languages results in "a special kind of cognitive flexibility" (para. 39). What does the term *cognitive* mean? What does "cognitive flexibility" imply?

PROBING CONTENT

1. What was the government's policy toward American Indians and Alaska Natives from the late nineteenth century until the mid-twentieth century? What was a primary tool in executing this policy?

2. What makes Eva Boyd's task more difficult? What might make language learning less difficult? What research supports this idea?

3. Explain the "language nest" concept. Name several ethnic groups that have used language nests successfully. Why may language nest instruction alone not be enough to save disappearing languages?

4. What is the first language of many American Indian youth? What are some characteristics of this language?

CONSIDERING CRAFT

1. What is the author's purpose in writing this essay? Defend your answer with text from the essay.

2. In this essay, Cameron uses quite a few Indian names, the pronunciation of which will not be familiar to most readers. What effect does their inclusion have on your reading of this essay? How does their use support Cameron's purpose?

3. Cameron does not specifically state her own opinion about preserving native languages, but her opinion is evident throughout the essay. Cite phrases and sentences from the text that reveal clearly her position on her topic. What does she accomplish by having the reader infer her position rather than stating it bluntly?

WRITING PROMPTS

Responding to the Topic   Cameron states that language "is the repository of culture and identity" (para. 18). Write an essay in which you examine the truth of this statement from your own experience.

Responding to the Writer   Eva Boyd says, "Without the language we won't be Indians any more" (para. 9). Cameron notes that we may "save a culture by saving the language" (para. 2). Write an essay in which you take a position on the necessity of preserving a language in order to preserve a culture.

Responding to Multiple Viewpoints   Using the other essays in this chapter as source material, formulate ten questions about the extent to which all citizens of the United States should be fluent in standard English. Interview five people using your questions, and then write an essay detailing your findings.

For a quiz on this reading, go to bedfordstmartins.com/mirror.

DRAWING CONNECTIONS: PAIRED SELECTIONS

1. How would John Miller ("How Do You Say *Extinct*?" p. 236) react to the concept and advisability of language nests as described by Cameron ("In the Language of Our Ancestors")? Support your answer with evidence from both selections.

2. How would Cameron regard the following statement by John Miller: "A growing number of people are speaking a smaller number of languages, meaning that age-old obstacles to communication are collapsing. Surely this is a good thing" (para. 5, "How Do You Say *Extinct*?"). Support your answer with evidence from both texts.

3. Why is the language preservation ideal in Papua New Guinea that John Miller discusses ("How Do You Say *Extinct*?") not possible for Native Americans?

Genius in Four Frames

BEN SARGENT

Ben Sargent, born in 1948, is a Pulitzer Prize–winning American editorial cartoonist who began drawing for the Texas–based *Austin American-Statesman*
in 1974. His article about fellow cartoonist Garry Trudeau appeared in the
Statesman on October 17, 2010. Although Sargent retired from the *Statesman* as a cartoonist in 2009, his cartoons, like Trudeau's, are distributed by
Universal Press Syndicate.

> **THINKING AHEAD** Have you read the comic strip *Doones-
> bury*? Do you consider yourself a fan? Why or why not? To what
> extent can significant statements about American culture be com-
> municated in a comic strip?

That first strip was a modest affair. 1

In the initial *Doonesbury* strip on Oct. 26, 1970, Walden College 2
quarterback B.D. meets his new roommate, self-appointed chick magnet
Mike Doonesbury of Tulsa, Oklahoma, and concludes there are "still a few
bugs" in the computerized roommate selection system.

The minimalist drawing style and busy dialogue have a whiff of Jules 3
Feiffer's hip, spare, often wordy cartoons of the '50s and '60s, but the first
Doonesbury still has the feel of a campus newspaper strip just taking its
first step into grown-up syndication—which, at the time, it was.

Forty years later, after more than 14,000 daily and Sunday strips, a 4
Pulitzer Prize, a Broadway musical, an animated TV special, Oscar and
Grammy nominations, a wide-ranging website and nearly 80 published collections and books (including a massive new 40th anniversary retrospective), Garry Trudeau's *Doonesbury* has clearly risen from mere comic strip
to a permanent and influential part of the American cultural pantheon.

Doonesbury evolved from a strip called *Bull Tales*, which undergradu- 5
ate Trudeau began contributing to the *Yale Daily News* in 1968, comment-
ing on local and campus issues. Soon, however, two phenomena intervened
to lift the strip from the college paper's back pages to media stardom.

One was Jim Andrews, who with John McMeel had just founded Uni- 6
versal Press Syndicate and was looking for material that would catch the
eyes of newspaper editors. The other was the dawn of the politically turbu-
lent 1970s, a time when, Trudeau wrote in introducing his retrospective
collection, "there were so many banners afield, so many movements afire."

Universal signed the strip, now named after its main character, as its 7
first syndicated offering, and Trudeau's characters plunged into the era's

social and political battlefields as few comic strips had ever done before, powered by the cartoonist's uncanny gift for spotting and spoofing the cultural currents of the day.

Doonesbury's unabashed hybrid of the editorial cartoon and the comic strip, said comics historian Jerry Robinson, placed it "in a pivotal place in the development of comics. It really established the comic strip as viable commentary for political and social satire. It challenged a lot of conventional thought and comic strip taboos, and was very courageous." 8

The political frankness of the strip soon led many newspapers (the first in 1973) to run it on their opinion pages rather than the comics page, and Trudeau's relentless exploration of the boundaries of acceptable comic strip behavior started a long, long list of *Doonesbury* controversies over politics, sexual mores,[1] language, taste and timing. Each dust-up,[2] Robinson said, "almost always led to papers dropping the strip in protest, but 95 percent of them always came back." 9

Lee Salem, who came to Universal in 1974 and is now the syndicate's president and editor, has run interference for *Doonesbury* for almost all of its four-decade run, and though he said it's a misapprehension that he spent his whole syndicate career dealing with skittish *Doonesbury* clients, "at times it was intense." (He recalled, for example, a full week dealing with Frank Sinatra's lawyers over a *Doonesbury* sequence pointedly speculating on the crooner's mob ties, until the lawyers "said they weren't going to sue us because we just wanted the publicity.") 10

Doonesbury's overt serving up of opinion attracted almost immediate attention. 11

President Gerald Ford told the Radio and Television Correspondents' Association in 1975 that "there are only three major vehicles to keep us informed as to what is going on in Washington: the electronic media, the print media and *Doonesbury,* and not necessarily in that order." In the same year, *Doonesbury* became the first comic strip to win the Pulitzer Prize for editorial cartooning. Trudeau was just 26. 12

At the time, the Association of American Editorial Cartoonists sourly condemned the award and urged the Pulitzer board to rescind it, joining the editors who continued to be jumpy about a comic strip with a point of view. 13

"People said you can't do that in comics," said Lucy Caswell, curator of the Billy Ireland Cartoon Library and Museum at Ohio State University, "and, of course, that's ridiculous. From the beginning, people have told serious stories in comics." 14

Nonetheless, *Doonesbury* has been exceptional, she said, in that "one of the things Garry has done is to show us it's possible to have sustained narrative and meaningful content in a comic strip, at a time when many people said the comic strip was dead. At a time when people said it couldn't be done, people like Garry Trudeau continue to engage us." 15

---

[1] **mores:** Moral attitudes.
[2] **dust-up:** Fight.

"Sustained narrative," in Caswell's phrase, has played as much a part   16
as pointed political satire in making *Doonesbury* such an extraordinary
success.

From B.D. and Mike Doonesbury in that first strip, the cast of characters   17
in the *Doonesbury* world has grown to more than 75, which even Trudeau
writes could be "challenging for longtime readers and intimidating for late-
comers—sort of like opening a Russian novel in the middle." (*Doonesbury*
still lags behind the other great character-driven cultural phenomenon "The
Simpsons" and its more than 100 characters, but there's still time.)

The strip follows its characters and their experiences in more-or-less   18
real time, giving them a credible flesh-and-blood existence even as it winds
them in and out of various current-events-driven plot lines.

The original cast of characters seemed eternally rooted as undergradu-   19
ates at the fictional Walden College until Trudeau took an unheard-of (for
cartoonists at the time) sabbatical[3] in 1983 and '84, and they returned graduated and launched into baby-boomer careers and family lives, which have
continued at a fairly realistic pace, right down to the subtle displacement of
the strip's central character, Mike Doonesbury, by his daughter Alex.

Often, as regular readers know, the strip's cast expands to include real-   20
life political figures, sometimes represented by a floating icon (Bill Clinton
as a waffle, George W. Bush as a battered warrior's helmet, etc.) and always
dead-on[4] in Trudeau's ability to capture the cadences of their speech and
the habits of their thoughts.

One group of characters that has had particular resonance in recent   21
years, and which observers such as Pulitzer Prize–winning cartoonist Signe
Wilkinson have said moved *Doonesbury* "to a whole new level," has been
Trudeau's military and veteran characters, who have brought readers face-
to-face with a searingly authentic and empathetic experience of those
who've fought in America's recent wars.

Starting with B.D. himself, who loses a leg in combat in Iraq, these   22
characters have been as diverse as Leo "Toggle" DeLuca, who returns state-
side with a brain injury, and Spc. Melissa Wheeler, a helicopter mechanic
dealing with command rape in Afghanistan.

In an e-mail interview, Trudeau said he developed "a bit of a follow-   23
ing" among soldier-readers during the first Iraq war and was invited to the
front by Army Chief of Staff Gen. Gordon Sullivan. At first there were visa
problems getting into Saudi Arabia, after a series of *Doonesbury* strips
ridiculing the lavish lifestyles of the Saudi ruling class.

But two months later, Col. Bill Nash, a tank-brigade commander, told   24
Trudeau to come anyway, and managed to spirit him, visa-less, past Saudi
customs and into Kuwait. "He wanted me to see the difference between the
mismatched conscripts[5] he'd wrangled as a young lieutenant in Vietnam and
the professional all-volunteer force he'd led into battle in Kuwait," Trudeau

---

[3] **sabbatical:** Time away from a normal routine.
[4] **dead-on:** Exactly correct.
[5] **conscripts:** People who are forced to serve.

wrote. "So, for a week, I talked to soldiers, trying to get into their heads, discover what military culture had become."

His visit led to an ongoing correspondence with many soldiers, and when he returned to cartooning about war with the second Iraq invasion (and B.D.'s wounding), the Department of Defense wanted him to visit the wounded, to help him get the details right. "Initially, I went into Walter Reed (Army Medical Center) under a USO protocol," Trudeau said, "but after a while, people got used to me, and I had basically unlimited access. Then I made my way downstream—visiting VA hospitals, vet centers, etc. It's been an extraordinary opportunity—and privilege."   25

For all of *Doonesbury*'s deep and rich creativity, of course, it is still a comic strip, and like all comic strips, is inextricably embedded in the printed newspaper medium where the comic strip was born in the 1890s. The audience has fled in the last two decades from the communal experience of traditional media to the fragmented individual experience of digital media, and comic strips, like the newspapers where they live, no longer enjoy the all-pervasive claim they once had on the public's attention.   26

Newspaper comics, Trudeau said, "barely work at all" today in comparison to their influence 40 years ago. "Animation—and to a lesser degree, comic books and graphic novels—are really the only fields that offer a future to cartoonists. The carnage seems worse for editorial cartoonists, but comic strip artists, who've always played a zero-sum game,[6] are being squeezed out of existence."   27

"I'm one of the lucky ones," he said. "I have a big enough client list (about 1,200, compared with 1,400 at its peak) so that I'll be one of the guys who's asked to turn out the lights. But it's pretty grim out there."   28

"On the other hand," Trudeau wrote, "I'm deeply aware of how fortunate I've been to have such a long run. If I have to pack it in tomorrow, I'd have no reason to complain."   29

Doonesbury has made a leap to the new media, with a well-developed website, doonesbury.com. And for a 21st-century comic strip, said Lee Salem, "a non-print component is mandatory to complement the print medium."   30

Lucy Caswell insists that the verdict isn't in on whether comic strips are a viable medium on the Web. "The Web's a comic-friendly platform," she said, "but it's different. The reader seeks it out much more intentionally, and that's a real difference."   31

Whatever the future holds for the traditional comic strip, of course, the monumental effect of *Doonesbury* on American social and political commentary over its 40-year run is real and undeniable.   32

Said Salem, "I think *Doonesbury* is that giant rock thrown into the pond with ripples still being felt. It opened up subject areas, treated characters as if they were in a novel, had a steady skeptical eye on politics and culture, and had lots of readers who loved it or despised it. Not bad for 60 or so words a day with pictures."   33

---

[6] **zero-sum game:** A gain for one side equals a loss for the other side.

And Garry Trudeau, what are your thoughts about where the strip goes   34
from here?

"I have exactly none," he wrote. "If you have any ideas before 3 p.m.   35
next Tuesday, I'd be most grateful if you'd send them along."

Spoken like a true cartoonist.   36

EXERCISING VOCABULARY

1. Record your own definition for each of these words.

   minimalist (adj.) (3)
   whiff (n.) (3)
   syndication (n.) (3)
   retrospective (n.) (4)
   evolved (v.) (5)
   uncanny (adj.) (7)
   unabashed (adj.) (8)
   hybrid (n.) (8)
   taboos (n.)(8)
   frankness (n.) (9)
   skittish (adj.) (10)
   misapprehension (n.) (10)

   overt (adj.) (11)
   rescind (v.) (13)
   curator (n.) (14)
   cadences (n.) (20)
   resonance (n.) (21)
   searingly (adv.) (21)
   empathetic (adj.) (21)
   wrangled (v.) (24)
   inextricably (adv.) (26)
   carnage (n.) (27)
   component (n.) (30)

2. The author refers to Mike Doonesbury as a "self-appointed chick magnet" (para. 1). What does it mean to be self-appointed? What does the slang expression "chick magnet" mean?

3. In paragraph 3, Sargent writes that the *Doonesbury* strip has become a meaningful standard in "the American cultural pantheon." What is the origin of the word *pantheon*? What does the word mean in this context?

4. The fact that *Doonesbury* maintains a "sustained narrative" has been cited as one reason for the strip's success. Explain what is meant by sustained narrative and how this technique operates in *Doonesbury*.

5. *Doonesbury* author Garry Trudeau believes that he will be "one of the guys who's asked to turn out the lights" (para. 28). What does this metaphor mean? Why will this action be necessary? Why may this task fall to Trudeau?

PROBING CONTENT

1. When was the *Doonesbury* comic strip first published? What happened in that first strip? What two factors contributed to the strip's rise to fame?

2. What topics did Trudeau approach in the comic strip that led to the strip's being dropped numerous times by some of the newspapers that published it? Why did this not eliminate the strip from circulation?

3. What significant award did *Doonesbury* win in 1975? How did editorial cartoonists and newspaper editors react to the award? Why?

4. Explain how Trudeau became so involved with the American military. Describe some of his experiences.

5. What steps has Trudeau taken to try to ensure the future of *Doonesbury?*

CONSIDERING CRAFT

1. Explain the title of this essay. What aspect of the essay does the title emphasize?

2. At numerous points in this article, Sargent quotes the opinions of others about *Doonesbury* and the strip's success. Why does Sargent choose to rely so heavily on others' opinions? What characteristics mark the other sources he quotes? What is the effect of their inclusion on the article?

3. How does Sargent conclude his essay? Why do you think he chooses this strategy? How effective is his conclusion? Why?

WRITING PROMPTS

Responding to the Topic   Choose an influential, long-running comic strip other than the one discussed in this article. In an essay, discuss its history and analyze its influence on and representation of American culture.

Responding to the Writer   Ben Sargent asserts that "Garry Trudeau's *Doonesbury* has clearly risen from mere comic strip to a permanent and influential part of the American cultural pantheon" (para. 4). Write an essay supporting or denying Sargent's assertion.

Responding to Multiple Viewpoints   In paragraph 26, Sargent writes that "the audience has fled in the last two decades from the communal experience of traditional media to the fragmented individual experience of digital media." Compare this analysis of Americans' interaction with reading to the analysis offered by Alex Pham and David Sarno in "Digital Information and the Future of Reading" (p. 256).

For a quiz on this reading, go to bedfordstmartins.com/mirror.

Analyzing the Image

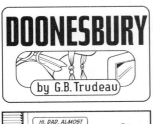

This *Doonesbury* cartoon first appeared in 2009 and is an excellent example of Trudeau's determination to tackle current social phenomena head on.

- What is the theme of the daughter's monologue?

- What purpose do the words "Clik! Clik!" serve in every frame but the final one? Why are they omitted there?

- How does the reader's vantage point change from frame to frame? Why? Why does only the second panel feature a silhouette?

- What is the role of the father in this strip? What is ironic about the dialogue in the last frame?

Digital Information and the Future of Reading

ALEX PHAM AND DAVID SARNO

Alex Pham and David Sarno are reporters for the *Los Angeles Times.* They created a series for the *Times* on the future of reading, exploring the evolution of the book as reading is transformed by new technologies in the twenty-first century. The essay that follows appeared as an article called "Electronic Reading Devices Are Transforming the Concept of a Book" on July 18, 2010.

> **THINKING AHEAD** If publishers decide in the future that digital technology has erased the need for hard copies of books, what would be gained? What would be lost? On what should their decision be based?

Emma Teitgen, 12, thought the chemistry book her teacher recommended would make perfect bedside reading. Perfect because it might help her fall asleep. 1

Then she downloaded "The Elements: A Visual Exploration" to her iPad. Instead of making her drowsy, it blossomed in her hands. The 118 chemical elements, from hydrogen to ununoctium, came alive in vivid images that could be rotated with a swipe of the finger. Tapping on link after link, Teitgen was soon engrossed in a world of atomic weights and crystal structures. Three hours later, the seventh-grader looked up to see that it was 11 p.m., way past her bedtime. 2

"It was like a breath of fresh air compared to my textbook," said Teitgen, who lives in Pittsford, N.Y. "I was really amazed by all the things it could do. I just kept clicking so I could read more." 3

More than 550 years after Johannes Gutenberg printed 180 copies of the Bible on paper and vellum[1] new technologies are changing the concept of a book and what it means to be literate. Sound, animation and the ability to connect to the Internet have created the notion of a living book that can establish an entirely new kind of relationship with readers. 4

As electronic reading devices evolve and proliferate, books are increasingly able to talk to readers, quiz them on their grasp of the material, play videos to illustrate a point or connect them with a community of fellow readers. 5

The same technology enables readers to reach out to authors, provide instant reaction and even become creative collaborators, influencing plot 6

---

[1] **vellum:** Lambskin or calfskin especially prepared to be written on.

developments and the writer's use of dramatic devices. Digital tools are also making it possible for independent authors to publish and promote their books, causing an outpouring of written work on every topic imaginable.

If the upheaval in the music industry over the last decade is any guide,   7 the closing of more bookstores and a decreasing demand for physical books will force authors and their publishers to find new ways to profit from their work. "There is not a single aspect of book publishing that digital won't touch," said Carolyn Kroll Reidy, chief executive of Simon & Schuster.

The Master of Rampling Gate, a novella[2] by Anne Rice published in   8 1991 as a paperback, illustrates some of the possibilities. The work tells the story of a brother and sister who inherit a remote mansion occupied by the undead.

The out-of-print title was given new life in March, when it was reis-   9 sued in digital form by Vook, an Alameda, Calif., startup that sells titles for the iPad and iPhone. As a $4.99 application sold through Apple's iTunes store, *The Master of Rampling Gate* comes with video interviews with Rice and others. Rice speaks about her inspiration for her works and about the Gothic genre in which she writes.

Within the text are links to Web pages that elaborate on events and   10 places in the story—a description of the Mayfair neighborhood in London where the protagonists live or a history of the Black Death plague, which plays a key role in the fourth chapter.

"For me, this is a way to communicate with my readers, establish a   11 connection with them and build a community around them," Rice said in an interview.

Vook (the name is a mash-up of "video" and "book") has published   12 more than two dozen titles, including *Reckless Road*, which describes the early days of heavy metal band Guns N' Roses. *Reckless Road* weaves in dozens of videos of the L.A. band's early performances and interviews with band members and groupies.

Tim O'Reilly, whose O'Reilly Media in Sebastopol, Calif., is at the   13 forefront of designing and distributing digital books over the Internet and on mobile devices, said technology has the power to "broaden our thinking about what a book does."

Owners of *iBird Explorer*, a digital book produced for the iPhone by   14 field guide publisher Mitch Waite Group, can play the songs of more than 900 bird species. Using microphones, it can also capture the chirps and warbles of wild birds and match them against a database of bird sounds to help the "reader" identify the species.

In addition to displaying pages from a book, digital e-readers can read   15 them aloud, opening up a literary trove for the blind and the visually impaired who have long had only a thin selection of audio and Braille books to choose from. Devices made by Amazon.com Inc. and Intel Corp. are able to convert text into speech.

---

[2] **novella:** A short novel.

Digital technology is also morphing reading from a solitary experience   16
into a social one.

The newest generation of readers—the texting, chatting, You Tubing   17
kids for whom the term "offline" sounds quaint—has run circles around
the fusty[3] publishing process, keeping its favorite stories alive online long
after they're done reading the books. At online fan communities for popular
fantasy series like *Harry Potter* and *Twilight*, young enthusiasts collaborate
on new story lines involving monsters, ghosts and secret crushes.

Fans in other forums, blogs and chat rooms weave alternative endings   18
or side plots for their favorite works. One site, FanFiction.net, features hundreds of short stories based on a series of young adult novels by Scott
Westerfeld called *Uglies*.

"They're extending the world by creating new characters," Westerfeld   19
said. "That's what good readers do. They take apart the narrative engine
and, examining the different parts, they ask how things could have been
different."

On Scribd.com, writers and digital pack rats are building a huge swap   20
meet for written works of every length, many of which once existed on
paper. Visitors can browse digital versions of novels and nonfiction
books—some by established authors, others by complete unknowns—along
with recipes for spinach calzones[4] and 1950s manuals for building transis-
tor radios.

As in many places online, free content is the rule. Roughly 15 percent of   21
more than 20 million documents is for sale. The prices, which are set by
publishers, range from $1.99 for *The Dark Dreamweaver*, a fantasy novel
about an 11-year-old who ventures into a land of dreams, to a $27.99 book
published by O'Reilly Media for designing Web pages. Scribd takes a 20
percent cut of those sales, but gets most of its revenue by selling advertising
on the site.

Trip Adler, a 26-year-old entrepreneur who started developing the site   22
as a Harvard undergraduate, says it's on the verge of being profitable.

"It's like having a huge library at your fingertips, but with stuff you'd   23
never think to look at," said Helen Black, a mother of five in Portland, Ore.

The proliferation of amateur content poses a conundrum for publishers,   24
who must find a way to make a profit in a sprawling marketplace increasingly filled with free content. And some people worry that new technologies
will diminish the classic reading experience.

Whereas printed texts often are linear paths paved by the author chapter   25
by chapter, digital books encourage readers to click here or tap there, launching them on side journeys before they even reach the bottom of a page.

Some scholars fear that this is breeding a generation of readers who   26
won't have the attention span to get through *The Catcher in the Rye*, let
alone *Moby-Dick*.

---

[3] **fusty:** Old-fashioned.
[4] **calzones:** Baked turnovers of pizza dough stuffed with various fillings.

"Reading well is like playing the piano or the violin," said poet and critic Dana Gioia, former chairman of the National Endowment for the Arts. "It is a high-level cognitive ability that requires long-term practice. 27

"I worry that those mechanisms in our culture that used to take a child and have him or her learn more words and more complex syntax are breaking down," Gioia said. 28

But Larry Rosen, a psychology professor at Cal State University, Dominguez Hills, said it was a mistake to conclude that young people learned less simply because "they are flitting around all over the place" as they read. 29

"Kids are reading and writing more than ever," he said. "Their lives are all centered around words." 30

Dr. Gary Small, director of the Center on Aging at UCLA and author of *iBrain*, said using the Internet activated more parts of the brain than reading a book did. 31

On the other hand, online readers often demonstrate what Small calls "continuous partial attention" as they click from one link to the next. The risk is that we become mindless ants following endless crumbs of digital data. 32

"People tend to ask whether this is good or bad," he said. "My response is that the tech train is out of the station, and it's impossible to stop." 33

EXERCISING VOCABULARY

1. Record your own definition for each of these words.

   engrossed (v.) (2)
   evolve (v.) (5)
   proliferate (v.) (5)
   outpouring (n.) (6)
   upheaval (n.) (7)
   genre (n.) (9)
   protagonists (n.) (10)
   weaves (v.) (12)

   trove (n.) (15)
   morphing (v.) (16)
   verge (n.) (22)
   proliferation (n.) (24)
   sprawling (adj.) (24)
   diminish (v.) (24)
   linear (adj.) (25)
   cognitive (adj.) (27)

2. Where does the name "Vook" come from? How is *Reckless Road* a fitting example of the name's significance?

3. Trip Adler, who developed the Scribd Web site, is described in this article as an "entrepreneur." What is the origin of this word? To whom does it refer? Why does Adler merit being called an entrepreneur?

4. Pham and Sarno note that the "proliferation of amateur content poses a *conundrum*" (para. 24). What is a conundrum? To what specific conundrum are the authors referring? Who faces this conundrum? Why?

PROBING CONTENT

1. How has new digital technology altered the relationship between readers and authors? How has it influenced who can become an author?

2. How is the Vook edition of Anne Rice's *The Master of Rambling Gate* different from editions of the novella first published in 1991? According to Rice, why is this significant?

3. How has the new technology impacted the lives of those with visual disabilities?

4. According to Scott Westerfield, what do good readers do? Where do they do this?

CONSIDERING CRAFT

1. How do Pham and Sarto begin their essay? How effective is this introduction?

2. Reread paragraph 5. In this section, the authors personify electronic reading devices and books, noting that they "evolve and proliferate," "talk to readers, quiz them," and "play videos." What do the authors accomplish by attributing human actions to these inanimate objects? How does this use of language influence the reader?

3. Pham and Sarno observe in paragraph 24 that "some people worry that new technologies will diminish the classic reading experience." Readers may define "a classic reading experience" differently. Why do the authors not define the concept here?

4. The quotation with which this essay concludes — "the tech train is out of the station, and it's impossible to stop" — would seem to indicate that debate about the values inherent in digital reading is pointless. Why did Pham and Sarno choose this quotation to conclude their essay? What effect does this conclusion have on the reader?

WRITING PROMPTS

Responding to the Topic Write an essay in which you support or reject the viewpoint of Dana Gioia that reading digital books is detrimental to the skills learned by reading hard-copy books. You may reference the other experts cited in this essay, but expand your research to include other voices and other aspects of the argument.

Responding to the Writer Write an essay in which you explore the positive and negative aspects of digital technology's opening access to publication and widespread distribution to anyone with access to the Internet.

Responding to Multiple Viewpoints   Write an essay in which you apply John J. Miller's argument about allowing obscure languages to die out naturally (How Do You Say *Extinct?"* p. 236) to the issue raised in this essay by Pham and Sarno about the potential loss of the printed word as we know it.

For a quiz on this reading, go to bedfordstmartins.com/mirror.

Wrapping Up Chapter 6

Focusing on Yesterday, Focusing on Today

How information is distributed has certainly changed since Benjamin Franklin's day. By 1728, when Franklin opened his own printing office in Philadelphia, it took a room filled with equipment and hours of hard labor just to print copies of one book. Franklin's most famous publication, *Poor Richard's Almanac,* frequently featured cartoons and illustrations along with the text of articles. Why were these graphics so important? Why was the printing press such a significant innovation?

Benjamin Franklin at His Printing Press

In the twenty-first century, newspapers and books are being chased from the public eye by the billions of bytes available on a computer screen. In an ironic twist, a company called Twelve South markets a laptop cover designed to resemble an old book. The zipper tag even appears to the casual observer to be a bookmark. Why is this laptop cover ironic? Why would anyone want a laptop to be mistaken for an old book? How is the caption, "A Novel Idea," a play on words?

A Novel Idea

CONNECTING TO THE CULTURE

1. Choose a blog and participate in its online conversations for at least a week. Write an essay in which you describe your experiences, including what kind of people you met online, what the topics of discussion were, what rules and etiquette seemed to govern the participants, and what you learned about online communication and language.

2. Choose a language other than English and research how new words become part of that language. Is there a governmental process, or do new words just appear when popular usage introduces them? Write an essay in which you explain the process and compare it with the way new words become part of American English.

3. Research the issue of bilingual education and then write an essay in which you take a position on its effectiveness for helping non-native speakers become fluent in English. Be sure to include specific examples to support your ideas.

4. Select one group of people who use their own jargon. This might be doctors, rappers, athletes, computer programmers, or some other group. Investigate the language they use to communicate within the group, including an interview with several group members, and then write an essay detailing how that specialized language functions within the select group. Be sure to support your ideas with numerous specific examples.

5. Choose one significant textless symbol like the Nike Swoosh to research. How did it originate? How and where is it used? How widely is it recognized? Develop your findings into an informative essay.

Analyzing the Image

How prevalent have logos become in advertising here and abroad? To what extent have they replaced traditional written language? Has the advertising industry succeeded in taking America hostage and transforming its consumers into logo-obsessed shoppers?

This eye-catching version of a revered American icon, the Stars and Stripes, was created by Shi-Zhe Yung for the 2000 Creative Resistance Contest sponsored by *Adbusters,* a "watchdog" publication whose goal is to reveal the ways in which the advertising industry markets fantasy to consumers in the guise of truth.

- Describe your initial reaction to this image. Why did you react the way you did? Why do you think the artist chose to render the American flag in this way?

- How many of these logos do you or your classmates recognize?

- What does this logo recognition say about the impact of advertising in America today?

- What message is *Adbusters* sending to viewers of this visual?

- What effect does the text appearing on the lower-left corner have on you and your classmates? Compare it to the Pledge of Allegiance.

Research this topic with TopLinks at bedfordstmartins.com/toplinks.

GEARING UP   Make a list of all the brand-name products you have used, worn, or eaten since you got up this morning. Briefly describe commercials or advertisements for some of these products. How did this advertising influence your decision to buy or use them? Try to honestly evaluate why you made these choices. How much are your habits as a consumer influenced by advertising?

I remember the exact day. I was thirteen, and I saw this big billboard on Decatur Street, not far from my house, had this big, lean black guy, really good-looking, with his jeans rolled up, splashing water on a beach, cigarette in one hand and a slinky black chick on his back. All smiles. All perfect teeth. Salem menthols. What great fun. I thought to myself, Now there's the good life. I'd like to have some of that. So I went home, went to my drawer, got my money, walked down the street, and bought a pack of Salem menthols.

The speaker is Angel Weese, a young character in John Grisham's best-selling novel *The Runaway Jury*. Our own encounters with advertising may not cause such immediate and direct responses, but we do respond. Most of us want what Angel wants—some of the good life. And if those jeans, that flat screen, that car, that iPod, or those sneakers help get us to the good life, we're there. Advertising is so much a part of our lives that we may not notice its pervasive, subtle effect. How are ads created? What messages are ads sending? Why do some ad mascots like the Geico gecko, the Energizer Bunny, and the AFLAC duck become our friends? Why do some jingles or famous ad phrases—like "Just do it," "For everything else, there's Master-Card," "Can you hear me now?" or "Maybe she's born with it. Maybe it's Maybelline."—stay in our heads? How do ad agencies find the perfect pitch, the best "hook," the winning slogan?

What do the ads that get our attention and send us to the stores—whether real or virtual—say about us as consumers? We are advertising targets not just as individual consumers but also collectively. Of the groups you belong to—college students, men or women, particular racial or ethnic backgrounds—which ones seem to have been targeted by manufacturers' ad campaigns? One size never fits all in strategic advertising. When we move beyond asking what product an ad is selling and instead demand to know what the ad is really saying about ourselves and our culture, both here and abroad, we may be surprised by the insights we gain and the savvy consumers we become.

COLLABORATING   In groups of three or four students, list five phrases, symbols, jingles, or slogans associated with widely advertised products. Collect these lists and play an Advertising IQ game based on the *Jeopardy* model. Choose a host to read the clues aloud and to call on teams to guess the product. For example, if the clue read aloud is "I'm lovin' it," the correct response would be "What is an advertising slogan for McDonald's?"

After the game, discuss why you can easily supply questions for these advertising answers when it's so difficult to remember other things — like historical dates or the Periodic Table of the Elements.

On Sale at Old Navy:
Cool Clothes for Identical Zombies!

DAMIEN CAVE

Damien Cave, a *New York Times* correspondent, holds a BA from Boston University and an MS from Columbia University's Graduate School in Journalism. Before joining the *New York Times,* he worked as staff writer and contributing editor for *Rolling Stone* magazine and Salon.com. In 2000, he held a Robert Novak Journalism Fellowship from the Phillips Foundation, awarded to "working print and online journalists supportive of American culture and a free society." His essay "On Sale at Old Navy: Cool Clothes for Identical Zombies!" appeared on Salon.com in 2010.

> **THINKING AHEAD** To what extent are you attracted to trendy, popular clothing styles? Do you wear what's "in" or what you personally prefer? Do you dress to stand out or to blend in? List your three favorite places to buy clothes and explain why you chose each one.

Thomas Frank walks by the candy-cane-adorned displays of Old Navy, passing the sign exclaiming "priced so low, you can't say no," and into the chain's San Francisco flagship store. The all-devouring Christmas rush hasn't started yet, but it's clear from the frown on Frank's face that he's not being seduced by the cheap but stylish clothes, the swirling neon and the bass-heavy hip-hop pounding in his ears. 1

"Oh God, this is disgusting," Frank says. This reaction isn't surprising. The bespectacled[1] Midwesterner is a pioneering social critic — one of the first writers to document how, starting in the '60s, American businesses have co-opted cool anti-corporate culture and used it to seduce the masses. His arguments in the *Baffler,* a pugnacious review Frank founded in 1988, and in 1997's *The Conquest of Cool* read like sermons, angry wake-up calls for consumers who hungrily ingest hipper-than-thou ("Think Different") marketing campaigns without ever questioning their intent. 2

Old Navy and other cheap but tasteful retailers provide perfect fodder[2] for Frank's critique. Their low prices and hip-but-wholesome branding strategy are supposed to present a healthy alternative to the conspicuous consumption of a Calvin Klein. But critics like Frank and Naomi Klein, 3

---

[1] **bespectacled:** Wearing eyeglasses.
[2] **fodder:** Material that supplies a strong demand.

author of *No Logo,* argue that the formula is really nothing more than the wolf of materialism wrapped in cheaper sheep's clothing.

Consumers are being scammed, says Klein, arguing that stores like Old   4
Navy and Ikea are duping millions, inspiring mass conformity while pretending to deliver high culture to the masses. "It's this whole idea of creating a carnival for the most homogeneous fashions and furniture," says Klein. "It's mass cloning that's being masked in a carnival of diversity. You don't notice that you're conforming because everything is so colorful."

Klein and Frank say that few consumers recognize just how conformist   5
their consumption habits have become. And certainly, it's hard to argue that Ikea's and Old Navy's items haven't become icons of urbanite and suburbanite imagination. Watch MTV, or rent *Fight Club,* to see Ikea's candy-colored décor, then truck down[3] to your local Old Navy flagship store. When you arrive, what you'll find is that hordes of people have beaten you there. At virtually every opening of Old Navy's and Ikea's stores—in the New York, Chicago and San Francisco areas, for example—tens of thousands of people appeared in the first few days. Even now, long after the stores first opened, lines remain long.

What's wrong with these people? Nothing, say defenders of the com-   6
panies. The popularity of brands like Ikea and Old Navy, they argue, derives from the retailers' ability to offer good stuff cheap. "They provide remarkable value," says Joel Reichart, a professor at the Fordham School of Business who has written case studies on Ikea. "They're truly satisfying people's needs."

Despite his irritation with the way companies like Old Navy market   7
themselves, Frank acknowledges that businesses have always sought to offer cheap, relatively high-quality merchandise and concedes that there is some value in their attempts. He even admits that consumerism is good for the economy.

But he and other critics argue that in the end we're only being conned   8
into thinking that our needs are being satisfied. What's really happening, they argue, is that clever marketers are turning us into automatons who equate being cool with buying cheap stuff that everyone else has. Under the stores' guise of delivering good taste to the general public, any chance we have at experiencing or creating authenticity is being undermined. Ultimately, our brave new shopping world is one in which we are spending more time in the checkout line than reading books, watching movies or otherwise challenging ourselves with real culture.

"Shopping is a way of putting together your identity," laments *No-*   9
brow author John Seabrook. And the "homogenized taste" of today's Old Navy and Ikea shoppers proves, he says, that Americans either are consciously choosing to look and live alike or are determined not to notice that that is what they're doing.

---

[3] **truck down:** Slang for "go to."

Consider the numbers. Old Navy now has 580 stores nationwide and   10
is still expanding. The Gap, Old Navy's parent company, remains convinced that people want more, and it seems to be right. In 1998, when Old
Navy opened its first store in downtown Chicago, more than 10,000 people
lined up hours before the doors opened. When the San Francisco flagship
store opened in 1999, the rush was equally astounding. There were give-
aways, rock bands and rabid, clothes-carrying crowds fighting their way to
the registers. Never mind that Old Navy carries far fewer pieces of apparel
than other comparably sized stores. And never mind that half the clothes
are just knockoffs of items available at the Gap. After all, deals are to be
had—and shopping at Old Navy is just so cool!

Ikea is an even bigger phenomenon. More than 320 million people   11
worldwide walked through one of the Swedish company's stores last year.
That's more than seven times the number of people who visited all four of
Disney's theme parks.

Shoppers can claim that they're just being good consumers—that buy-   12
ing a $179 Poang chair at Ikea is actually ecofriendly. Old Navy shoppers
might say they're just frugal. Not so, according to critics like Christine
Rosen, a professor in the Haas School of Business at UC-Berkeley. According to Rosen, people who fill their closets, homes and lives with Old Navy
and Ikea—or Pottery Barn or a host of other slick stores—are simply new
examples of the trend toward conformity that started when the first
"brands" appeared in the 1910s and '20s. "We're Pavlovianly trained[4] to
respond to this," she says.

And we're also just too damn lazy. That's the theory floated by Packard   13
Jennings, an anti-consumerism activist who says that stores like Old Navy
are designed to numb the brain and remove all semblance of creativity from
the purchasing process. "Ikea pre-arranges sets of furniture in its stores,
thereby lessening individual thought," he says. Once people are in the store,
they can't resist. "Entire households are purchased at Ikea," he says.

Indeed, Janice Simonsen, an Ikea spokeswoman, confirmed that a large   14
part of the chain's demographic consists of "people who come in and say, 'I
need everything.'" Meanwhile, those who don't want everything usually
end up with more than they need, says Fordham's Reichart. "The way they
design their stores"—with an up escalator to the showroom and no exit
until the checkout—"you end up going through the entire store," he says.

Old Navy plays by the same sneaky rules. When Frank and I entered   15
the San Francisco store, clerks offered us giant mesh bags. Ostensibly, this
is just good service, but since the bags are capable of holding at least half a
dozen pairs of jeans and a few shirts, it's obvious that they're also meant to
encourage overconsumption.

Frank called the bags "gross" but not out of line with other state-of-the-   16
art retailing practices. But according to Klein, the sacks, in conjunction

---

[4] **Pavlovianly trained:** Predisposed to give a predictable response; so named for Ivan Pavlov,
a Russian physiologist who discovered the conditioned response.

with Old Navy's penchant for displaying T-shirts in mock-1950s super-market coolers, prove that the company is aiming to do something more. The idea behind this "theater for the brand" architecture is to commodify the products, to make them "as easy to buy as a gallon of milk," Klein says.

"The idea is to create a Mecca[5] where people make pilgrimages to their brand," Klein says. "You experience the identity of the brand and not the product."   17

Disney, which opened its first store in 1987, was the first to employ this strategy. And since then others have appeared. Niketown, the Body Shop, the Discovery Store—they all aim to sell products by selling a destination.   18

Old Navy and Ikea, however, are far more popular than those predecessors—and, if you believe the more pessimistic of their critics, more dangerous. Not only are the two chains remaking many closets and homes into one designer showcase, says Klein, but they are also lulling consumers to sleep and encouraging them to overlook some important issues.   19

Such as quality. People think they're getting "authenticity on the cheap," says David Lewis, author of "The Soul of the New Consumer." But the truth may be that they're simply purchasing the perception of quality and authen-ticity. "Because [Ikea and Old Navy] create these self-enclosed lifestyles," Klein explains, "you overlook the fact that the products are pretty crappy and fall apart." Adds Jennings, "Things may be cheaper, but you keep going back to replace the faulty merchandise."   20

Then there is the trap of materialism. Survey after survey suggests that people who place a high value on material goods are less happy than those who do not, says Eric Rindfleisch, a marketing professor at the University of Arizona. The focus on bargains, incremental purchases and commodifi-cation plays to a uniquely American blind spot.   21

"We operate with a duality," explains Rindfleisch, who has conducted studies linking materialism with depression. "Americans know that money doesn't buy happiness, but most people somehow believe that increments in pay or goods will improve our lives. It's a human weakness—particularly in America."   22

The most insidious danger may be more abstract. The anti-consumerism critics argue that by elevating shopping to cultural status, we are losing our grip on real culture. We live in a time where college kids think nothing of decorating their rooms with Absolut vodka ads and fail to realize that they're essentially turning their rooms into billboards. Meanwhile, museum stores keep getting larger, Starbucks sells branded CDs to go with your coffee and because Ikea and other stores now look like movie theaters or theme parks, we don't just shop, "we make a day of it," as Klein puts it.   23

This only helps steer us away from other endeavors. When people spend so much time buying, thinking and talking about products, they don't have   24

---

[5] **Mecca:** City in Saudi Arabia that is a pilgrimage site for the Islamic faith; any location sought by people with a common purpose.

time for anything else, for real conversations about politics or culture or for real interaction with people.

Ultimately, the popularity of Old Navy, Ikea and their ilk[6] proves that we're stuck in what Harvard professor Juliet Schor calls "the cycle of work and spend." Breaking that cycle may not be easy, but if one believes critics like Frank, it's essential if we are to control our own culture, instead of allowing it to be defined by corporations.   25

The cycle may not be possible to break. Frank, for one, is extremely pessimistic about our chances for turning back the tide of conformity and co-opted cool. Maybe that's one reason why he wanted to get out of Old Navy as fast as he could.   26

But I'm not so sure. When "Ikea boy," Edward Norton's character in *Fight Club*, watched his apartment and his Swedish furniture explode in a blaze of glory, I wasn't the only one in the theater who cheered.   27

EXERCISING VOCABULARY

1. Record your own definition for each of these words.

   pioneering (adj.) (2)   laments (v.) (9)
   co-opted (v.) (2)   ecofriendly (adj.) (12)
   pugnacious (adj.) (2)   frugal (adj.) (12)
   ingest (v.) (2)   semblance (n.) (13)
   scammed (v.) (4)   ostensibly (adv.) (15)
   duping (v.) (4)   penchant (n.) (16)
   homogeneous (adj.) (4)   predecessors (n.) (19)
   hordes (n.) (5)   lulling (v.) (19)
   concedes (v.) (7)   incremental (adj.) (21)
   guise (n.) (8)   duality (n.) (22)

2. In paragraph 1, Cave refers to Old Navy's "San Francisco flagship store." What is the origin of the expression "flagship store"? What does this reference indicate about this particular Old Navy store?

3. Cave describes the shoppers attending the opening of the San Francisco Old Navy store as "rabid, clothes-carrying crowds" (para. 10). What does *rabid* mean? How is this word usually used? What does Cave mean in this context?

4. In paragraph 14, Ikea spokesperson Janice Simonsen discusses Ikea's *demographic*. What does this term mean? Why is understanding its demographic so vital to Ikea and other companies?

5. What does it mean for Old Navy to "*commodify* the products" (para. 16)? What is the company's objective?

[6] **ilk:** Kind.

PROBING CONTENT

1. Describe the Old Navy store visited by Thomas Frank. Identify and then explain Frank's reaction to this environment.

2. Explain what Naomi Klein means when she accuses companies like Old Navy and Ikea of "mass cloning that's being masked in a carnival of diversity" (para. 4). According to Klein and Frank, why is this marketing strategy so effective? How do the companies explain their success?

3. Cave notes several explanations from various viewpoints about why shoppers flock to Old Navy. What reasons do shoppers themselves give? What is Christine Rosen's explanation? How does Packard Jennings explain this trend?

4. Explain the strategy of companies that "aim to sell products by selling a destination" (para. 18). Name several of those companies in addition to Ikea and Old Navy.

CONSIDERING CRAFT

1. Examine the title of this essay. What is a zombie? Explain the irony in this title. How does the title forecast Cave's position on his topic?

2. In paragraph 8, Cave discusses the adverse effects of "our brave new shopping world." What reference is he making here? What image do the words *brave new world* evoke? How does this reference reinforce Cave's thesis?

3. To give the reader an idea of the volume of Ikea's business, Cave compares the number of people worldwide who visited Ikea in a certain year to the number of people who visited all four Disney theme parks during that same time period. Why does Cave select this particular comparison?

4. In his concluding paragraph, Cave references a movie with an Ikea connection. How does this example relate to the rest of the article? Why does Cave choose this type of conclusion? What are the advantages and risks of this approach?

WRITING PROMPTS

Responding to the Topic   Cave writes in paragraph 2 that Thomas Frank documents "how, starting in the '60s, American businesses have co-opted cool anti-corporate culture and used it to seduce the masses." Write an essay in which you examine how one American corporation not mentioned in Cave's article has done this.

Responding to the Writer   In paragraph 25, Cave asserts that we are close to allowing American culture to be "defined by corporations." Write an essay in which you support or reject this idea and the notion that Americans are "losing our grip on real culture" (para. 23). Use specific examples to support your thesis.

Responding to Multiple Viewpoints   Write an essay examining how Hector Gonzalez ("What Is Independent Hip Hop?" p. 303) would react to Damien Cave's concerns about corporations overly influencing American culture.

For a quiz on this reading, go to bedfordstmartins.com/mirror.

Sewn in Secret: Iranian Designers

NEWSWEEK

"Sewn in Secret: Iranian Designers," which appeared in the international edition of *Newsweek* in September 2009, describes the world of fashion that exists underground in Iran in defiance of the hard-line Islamic government. The hidden fashion culture is an exercise of creative freedom, but it can be construed as an act of protest. As one designer notes, "If we get social freedoms, then political freedoms will happen." Due to the sensitive politics mentioned in the article, the names of the writers were not included at publication.

> **THINKING AHEAD** Has anyone ever tried to restrict your clothing choices? What were the circumstances? What authority did this person or group have to do this? How did you react? What does being able to dress as you choose mean to you?

M odels strutted down the catwalk[1] in high heels to the blare of Persian pop, while chatty women gawked at wispy dresses showing off shoulders, legs, and arms—sometimes all at once. The fashion show, held in the ballroom of a Tehran apartment complex last month, would be pedestrian in the West. But by just attending the surreptitious event, the 275 women there were committing a crime.

While Iran's strict Islamic dress code requires women to wear the form-hiding manteau[2] overcoat and a hijab[3] that covers the hair, there is a quietly growing demand for homegrown haute couture.[4] Despite an unprecedented security crackdown following the summer's disputed presidential election, a network of high-end underground fashion designers, photographers, and models continue their subversive work, sketching, cutting patterns, conducting fittings, and strutting the catwalk in secret locations. "In the post-election situation, everything has gotten worse," says Hassan Rezaian, a fashion photographer in his mid-20s. "I don't want to call [what we do] protesting, but we are standing our ground." (For security, names have been changed.)

The mere existence of this hidden world of fashion is a slap to the fundamentalist regime. During President Mahmoud Ahmadinejad's first term, the mullahs[5] tried unsuccessfully to stamp out Western fashion influences

---

[1] **catwalk:** A fashion show's runway.
[2] **manteau:** A loose cloak or robe.
[3] **hijab:** Head covering traditionally worn by Muslim women.
[4] **haute couture:** Exclusive, often trend-setting fashion.
[5] **mullahs:** Muslims trained in religious law and doctrine.

by arresting hundreds of women for wearing manteaus deemed too short, showing too much hair, or even choosing overly colorful dresses. "Those who have indecent appearances are sent by the enemy," declared Ahmadinejad in 2007. Even so, knockoffs of high-end Western imports have been flooding the market, and the government appears increasingly aware that large swaths of the country's youth, raised on satellite TV and the (filtered) Internet, have rejected Islamic dress in favor of tight jeans, low-cut tops, and strapless dresses. Lacking the manpower to crack down on this barrage of Western clothing, authorities have zeroed in on local designers—especially female ones—whom they consider a greater threat to the values of the theocratic regime than racy imports like Victoria's Secret lingerie or Manolo Blahnik pumps.

So local fashionistas[6] have headed underground, working out of private backroom studios and warehouse galleries. Their designs include evening gowns with plunging décolletage[7] and slinky sleeveless blouses banned in public, as well as chic manteaus. "If the government knows an Iranian designer is designing [Westernized] clothes, the problems will start," says Roya Parsa, a designer in her late 20s who organized the ballroom fashion show last month.

She is one of perhaps a dozen top designers in the country, many of whom were trained in the West but ultimately returned to Iran. Her dresses, including classic dresses and wedding gowns, as well as more experimental designs fusing Western and Persian elements, fetch between $2,000 and $6,000, a princely sum only the country's elite can afford. Unlike their counterparts who stayed in the West—most notably menswear titan Bijan Pakzad, as well as upstarts like Nima Behnoud, Behnaz Kanani, and Masih Zad—these Tehran designers operate within exclusive circles of friends and friends-of-friends who commission one-of-a-kind creations, order from catalogs censored for security reasons, or select their dresses during secretive seasonal shows. Indeed, their very safety depends on their obscurity.

Parsa, who returned from graduate school in Europe last year to help inject an Iranian spirit into high fashion, says she finds inspiration from everyday life, however difficult. One of her new designs, for instance, is a tattered blouse with detachable sleeves and shoulder straps—a reference to the common practice of going to a private party and removing one's restrictive outerwear to expose something more revealing.

Her show last month had been postponed since June by the post-election violence. Like most progressive 20-somethings, she took to the streets, demonstrating several times a week even after "Bloody Saturday," when dozens of protesters were gunned down following a threatening speech by the Supreme Leader, Ayatollah Ali Khamenei. Although she speaks of democracy, she cites the "hijab problem"—meaning the strict dress code—as perhaps the largest stumbling block to change. "You have to work on the culture

---

[6] **fashionistas:** People who are extremely interested in fashion.
[7] **décolletage:** Low-cut neckline.

first," she says. And while most designers would much rather talk fabric patterns than politics, they see their counterculture fashion styles as a form of attack on the hard-line regime. "We don't want a revolution," says Zarina Afshar, a 45-year-old designer. "People here want step-by-step reform. If we get social freedoms, then political freedoms will happen."

Afshar designs mostly outerwear, spending her days trying to evade the scrutiny of the fashion police. One of her recent manteaus failed to sell because it was semitransparent and too yellow—infractions that could land its wearer in court. Afraid of the same fate, she omits names, descriptions, contact info, and often faces in her catalogs. "Always you are at a risk," she says.   8

Still, there is a sense among local designers that their time is coming. Authorities grudgingly tolerate un-Islamic dress in neighborhoods far away from the regime's conservative strongholds. Fashions have changed even in Qum, the power base of the ruling clerics and Iran's most conservative city. Today, vendors hawk revealing blouses in a rainbow of gaudy colors to worshipers leaving the city's holy shrine. Frustrated designers would do well to remember that just a few years ago, selling a simple white T-shirt was illegal.   9

EXERCISING VOCABULARY

1. Record your own definition for each of these words.

   strutted (v.) (1)   fusing (adj.) (5)
   gawked (v.) (1)   obscurity (n.) (5)
   wispy (adj.) (1)   tattered (adj.) (6)
   surreptitious (adj.) (1)   evade (v.) (8)
   subversive (adj.) (2)   scrutiny (n.) (8)
   swaths (n.) (3)   infractions (n.) (8)
   barrage (n.) (3)   grudgingly (adv.) (9)
   racy (adj.) (3)   strongholds (n.) (9)
   pumps (n.) (3)   hawk (v.) (9)

2. In the first paragraph, the author explains that the unusual fashion show held in Tehran, Iran, would be "pedestrian in the West." In what sense is the word *pedestrian* generally used? What does the word mean when used as an adjective in this context? How are the two meanings related?

3. In paragraph 3, the author identifies Iran as a "theocratic regime." What kind of government is a theocracy? In what major ways does this type of government differ from a democracy?

4. Roya Parsa came back to Tehran from Europe "to help inject an Iranian spirit into high fashion" (para. 6). What kinds of things are usually injected? For what purpose? What does this verb imply as it is used here?

PROBING CONTENT

1. Describe the Islamic dress code for women in Iran. Why are some designers operating outside this mandatory dress code? Why is their choice so dangerous?

2. What has influenced young Iranian women to adopt Western styles of dress? How has the Iranian government reacted? Why has the clothing rebellion not been fully suppressed?

3. How is shopping for the clothes made by these Tehran designers different from clothes shopping in the United States? Who buys these designers' clothes? Why?

CONSIDERING CRAFT

1. How does the author use the first paragraph to capture the reader's interest? How does this paragraph predict the author's viewpoint on this topic?

2. In this article, the author only indirectly states his/her own opinion about the topic. Why does the author not state his/her own feelings directly? Locate and write down several phrases in this article that reveal the author's own thoughts.

3. Explain the point the author is making in the last sentence of the concluding paragraph. Why is this an appropriate conclusion for this article?

WRITING PROMPTS

Responding to the Topic   Write an essay in which you explain how the accepted dress in a country other than Iran reflects that country's morals, values, and culture. Choose a specific country or section of a country and use sufficient examples to support your thesis.

Responding to the Writer   One of the designers quoted in this article states, "We don't want a revolution" (para. 7). However, the freedom of dress that she and her fellow designers advocate would surely create upheaval if widely adopted. Write an essay in which you examine the possible impact of such a relaxation of clothing restrictions on the culture of Iran.

Responding to Multiple Viewpoints   Write an essay in which you explore what the Iranian fashion designers discussed and quoted in "Sewn in Secret" would have to say to the Old Navy customers targeted by Thomas Frank in Damien Cave's essay "On Sale at Old Navy: Cool Clothes for Identical Zombies!" (p. 268).

For a quiz on this reading, go to bedfordstmartins.com/mirror.

Champagne Taste, Beer Budget

DELIA CLEVELAND

Have you ever bought something you couldn't afford and regretted it later? In "Champagne Taste, Beer Budget," Delia Cleveland recounts her own experiences as a victim of the advertising machine. The following essay first appeared in the March 2001 issue of *Essence* magazine. Cleveland wrote this essay while attending New York University as a media studies major and has had her work published in *Black Elegance* and *Spice* magazines.

> **THINKING AHEAD**   Have you ever been obsessed with owning something, going somewhere, or doing some particular thing? How did this obsession affect you? How did you achieve the object of your desire? To what extent did reaching your goal satisfy you?

My name is Dee, and I'm a recovering junkie. Yeah, I was hooked on the strong stuff. Stuff that emptied my wallet and maxed out my credit card during a single trip to the mall. I was a fashion addict. I wore a designer emblem on my chest like a badge of honor and respect. But the unnatural high of sporting a pricey label distorted my understanding of what it really meant to have "arrived."

At first I just took pride in being the best-dressed female at my high school. Fellows adored my jiggy style; girls were insanely jealous. I became a fiend for the attention. In my mind, clothes made the woman and everything else was secondary. Who cared about geometry? Every Friday I spent all my paltry paycheck from my part-time job on designer clothes. Life as I knew it revolved around a classy façade. Then slowly my money started getting tight, so tight I even resorted to borrowing from my mother. Me, go out looking average? Hell no! I'd cut a class or wouldn't bother going to school at all, unable to bear the thought of friends saying that I had fallen off and was no longer in vogue.

Out of concern, my mother started snooping around my bedroom to see where my paycheck was going. She found a telltale receipt I'd carelessly left in a shopping bag. Worse, she had set up a savings account for me, and I secretly withdrew most of the money—$1,000—to satisfy my jones.[1] Then I feverishly charged $600 for yet another quick fashion fix.

"Delia, you're turning into a lunatic, giving all your hard-earned money to multimillionaires!" she screamed.

"Mama," I shrugged, "you're behind the times." I was looking fly,[2] and that was all that mattered.

---

[1] **jones:** A craving for something.
[2] **fly:** Cool; fabulous.

Until I got left back in the tenth grade.   6

The fact that I was an A student before I discovered labels put fire un-   7
der my mother's feet. In her eyes, I was letting brand names control my life,
and I needed help. Feeling she had no other choice, she got me transferred
to another school. I had screwed up so badly that a change did seem to be
in order. Besides, I wanted to show her that labels couldn't control me. So
even though everyone, including me, knew I was "smart" and an excellent
student, I found myself at an alternative high school.

Meanwhile, I began looking at how other well-dressed addicts lived   8
to see where they were headed. The sobering reality: They weren't going
anywhere. In fact, the farthest they'd venture was the neighborhood corner or a party—all dressed up, nowhere to go. I watched them bop around³
in $150 hiking boots—they'd never been hiking. They sported $300 ski
jackets—never went near a slope. I saw parents take three-hour bus trips to
buy their kids discount-price designer labels, yet these parents wouldn't
take a trip to make a bank deposit in their child's name. Watching them, I
was forced to look at myself, at my own financial and intellectual stagna-
tion, at the soaring interest on my overused credit card.

That's when it all became clear. At my new high school I attended   9
classes with adults—less emphasis on clothes, more emphasis on work.
Although the alternative school gave me invaluable work experience, I
never received the kind of high-school education I should have had—no
sports, no prom, no fun. I realized I had sacrificed an important part of my
life for material stuff that wasn't benefiting me at all.

That was twelve years ago. Today I'm enjoying a clean-and-sober life-   10
style. Armed with a new awareness, I've vowed to leave designer labels to
people who can truly afford them. I refuse to tote a $500 baguette⁴ until I
can fill it with an equal amount of cash. I'm not swaggering around in over-
priced Italian shoes till I can book a trip to Italy. On my road to recovery, I
have continued to purchase clothing—sensibly priced. And every now and
then, the money I save goes toward a Broadway play or a vacation in the
sun. I'm determined to seek the culture my designer clothes once implied I
had. I no longer look the part—because I'm too busy living it.

EXERCISING VOCABULARY

1. Record your own definition for each of these words.

paltry (adj.) (2)	tote (v.) (10)
façade (n.) (2)	swaggering (v.) (10)
stagnation (n.) (8)	

---

³ **bop around:** To go freely from place to place.
⁴ **baguette:** A handbag shaped like a loaf of French bread.

2. Examine the title. What does the phrase "champagne taste" imply? How would such taste be in conflict with a "beer budget"? How well does this title work for this essay?

3. Cleveland comments that in high school she couldn't bear the thought of not being "in vogue" (para. 2). What does it mean to be in vogue? How could being in vogue in one area of the United States mean being hopelessly out of fashion in another area? Give several examples to illustrate your answer.

PROBING CONTENT

1. What was the author's obsession in high school? What effect did this have on her life?

2. How did Cleveland's mother find out about her daughter's problem? How did her mother's reaction to this discovery change Cleveland?

3. What event finally caught Cleveland's attention? What action did her mother take? Why was this an unexpected decision?

4. What important realizations did the author reach? How did she arrive at these conclusions?

5. What evidence does Cleveland offer to confirm that she has recovered from her addiction?

CONSIDERING CRAFT

1. When you begin reading this essay, you might think that Cleveland's obsession is going to be with drugs. What language does she use to encourage this misdirection? Cite several specific examples. Why does the author deliberately allow the reader to be misled in this way? How does her use of such language affect the way you read the essay?

2. Throughout her essay, Cleveland sprinkles slang that may be unfamiliar to you. Cite several examples of such language. Why would the author include these expressions if many readers might not be familiar with them and most dictionaries do not include them? What would be lost if they were to be omitted or replaced by standard English?

WRITING PROMPTS

Responding to the Topic To what extent do you identify with Cleveland's willingness to invest most of her money in clothes? Does the fact that her decisions caused her to miss much of the fun of high school make you sympathize with her? Did you know people like Delia Cleveland in high school, or do you know them now in college? What advice would you offer them?

Responding to the Writer   Cleveland admits to being a recovering "fashion addict" who once "wore a designer emblem on [her] chest like a badge of honor and respect" (para. 1). To what extent should consumers blame the advertising industry for their own harmful shopping habits? What steps should consumers take to make sure that they do not become victims of misleading advertising?

Responding to Multiple Viewpoints   Based on your reading of the essays in this chapter, write an essay in which you identify the most effective advertising strategies used by marketers today. Consider the role of the Internet, celebrity endorsements, and the Green movement.

For a quiz on this reading, go to bedfordstmartins.com/mirror.

The Pants That Stalked Me on the Web

MICHAEL LEARMONTH

Michael Learmonth is digital lead at the prominent journal *Advertising Age,* which offers the latest news and analysis on marketing and media issues. Learmonth's column "The Pants That Stalked Me on the Web" calls attention to the newest methods of online advertising, raising questions about consumer privacy and the potential for federal regulations. Thanks to online store Zappos's relationship with retargeting firm Criteo, says Learmonth, after he browsed clothing on the Web, he was "stalked by a pair of pants. Short pants, actually, and several of them."

THINKING AHEAD   Do you shop for clothes online? What are the advantages and disadvantages? Do you head directly to favorite stores' sites, or do you browse for the item and see what sites appear? Why? Have you ever been followed around the Web by a site you visited? How did you respond to this pursuit?

Paired Selection   Read this selection and the one that follows for two approaches to a similar topic. Then answer the "Drawing Connections" questions on p. 291.

There's a lonely section on old Route 66 between Seligman and King-   1
man, Arizona, where re-creations of once-ubiquitous Burma-Shave[1] signs fly by: You Can Drive A/ Mile A Minute/ But There Is No/ Future In It.

Those ads know where you're going, and they know where you've been.   2
I thought of them this week as I was stalked by a pair of pants. Short pants, actually, and several of them.

There's a heatwave in New York City, as you may have heard, and I   3
found myself in need of shorts appropriate for polite company, and not just painting the kitchen. I hate trying on clothes at stores, so I surfed over to my favorite apparel website, Zappos, now a part of Amazon.

After a few clicks, Zappos' recommendation engine went to work and   4
started offering me the selections that people who looked at the same shorts I did ultimately bought—a cool idea and a feature that has been useful to me in the past.

Then, I abandoned the search and did something else. That's when the   5
weirdness started.

---

[1] **Burma Shave:** Men's shaving cream that was marketed by short phrases on a series of signs along major highways.

In the five days since, those recommendations have been appearing just   6
about everywhere I've been on the Web, including MSNBC, Salon, CNN
.com and The Guardian. The ad scrolls through my Zappos recommendations: Hurley, Converse by John Varvatos, Quicksilver, Rip Curl, Volcom.
Whatever. At this point I've started to actually think I never really have to
go back to Zappos to buy the shorts—no need, they're following me.

I realize I'm considered by marketing folk to be at some place they call   7
the "purchase funnel," if you can really say that with a straight face about a
$55 pair of shorts. As a media professional covering online advertising,
among other things, I know why I'm getting these ads. But as a consumer I'd
be creeped out by it, and definitely a little annoyed, kind of like the morning
my Facebook connections started popping up on sites around the web.

It so happens these ads are some of the most transparent I've ever seen   8
on the Web. There's a "Why are you being shown this banner?" link on the
bottom, which takes you to the source, Criteo, which takes you to a
comprehensive opt-out page. Criteo is a re-targeting firm whose pitch[2] to
e-commerce sites is "re-engage with lost prospects via personalised banners
across the Internet." They charge on a per-click basis, so Zappos/Amazon
are only paying for clicks, not on a CPM basis. Since I've leaved through
my recommendations a couple times, Criteo earned a few pennies from retargeting me.

The Criteo ads are keeping my shorts "top of mind," but at what cost   9
to Zappos, whose brand is emblazoned across the ads themselves? As
tracking gets more and more crass and obvious, consumers will rightfully
become more concerned about it. There's a big difference between serving
an auto ad to someone who's visited Edmunds.com[3] in the last month and
chasing them around the web with items once in their shopping cart. (For
the record, I was just browsing and never even loaded a cart).

If the industry is truly worried about a federally mandated "do not track"   10
list akin to[4] "do not call" for the Internet, they're not really showing it. As ads
become more persistent and more customized, consumers are going to demand one place to opt out of everything, and not to have to check boxes at
Criteo, Yahoo, Google, Blue Kai or whoever else is targeting them that day.

Those ads on Route 66 are retro novelty, but imagine a Web where   11
you're just pestered by persistent ads. If that's where we're headed, I'll be
taking the next exit.

EXERCISING VOCABULARY

1. Record your own definition for each of these words.

ubiquitous (adj.) (1)	ultimately (adv.) (4)
engine (n.) (4)	transparent (adj.) (8)

[2] **pitch:** A sales presentation.
[3] **Edmunds.com:** A Web site devoted to the valuation of vehicles.
[4] **akin to:** Like.

emblazoned (v.) (9)   persistent (adj.) (10)
crass (adj.) (9)   customized (adj.) (10)
mandated (adj.) (10)

2. In paragraph 7, Learmonth writes that the reminders from Zappos might have caused him to be "creeped out." What does this expression mean? Why does the author *not* have this predictable reaction?

3. The author writes that Criteo has "a comprehensive opt-out page" (para. 8) and later states that "consumers are going to demand one place to opt out of everything" (para. 10). What does it mean to "opt out"? Why is this option significant?

PROBING CONTENT

1. What happens to the author after he shops for a pair of shorts on the Web? How does he react to this?

2. Learmonth identifies himself as being at "the purchase funnel" in paragraph 7. He does not explain this term, but given the context, explain what you think it means.

3. Learmonth identifies Criteo as a "re-targeting" firm. What is the purpose of such a firm? How does Criteo make money?

4. How would a "do not track" list for the Internet function? What existing list would it resemble? Why might the ability to be on such a list appeal to consumers?

CONSIDERING CRAFT

1. In his title, Learmonth uses figurative language to introduce his topic. Identify the type of figurative language used and explain why this approach is effective here.

2. Reread the first and last paragraphs of this essay. What technique does Learmonth use to tie the beginning and the end together? How effective is this technique?

3. In paragraph 7, Learmonth identifies himself as "a media professional." What effect does his professional knowledge have on his writing? How does knowing the author's background impact your reading of this essay?

4. In paragraph 11, the author uses an oxymoron to enforce a point about the Burma Shave ads. What is an oxymoron? What is the one used in this last paragraph? Explain why the author uses it.

WRITING PROMPTS

Responding to the Topic   Write an essay in which you explore an advertising technique like retargeting that really annoys, puzzles, or attracts you. Be sure to use specific examples to reinforce your point of view.

Responding to the Writer   Learmonth notes that the advertising industry does not seem to be concerned about a "federally mandated 'do not track' list." Write an essay in which you explore the effect such a list might have on Internet advertising and sales. Include reasons that you personally would or would not opt to be on such a list.

Responding to Multiple Viewpoints   Read "An Open Letter to the Totally Impractical Size Chart for Women's Clothing" by Claire Suddath (p. 202). Write a letter in which Learmonth responds to Suddath's complaint.

For a quiz on this reading, go to bedfordstmartins.com/mirror.

Retargeting Ads Follow Surfers to Other Sites

Miguel Helft and Tanzina Vega

Miguel Helft and Tanzina Vega are *New York Times* reporters. Vega is a media reporter and multimedia journalist, and Helft covers Internet companies for the Business Desk of the *New York Times*. They wrote "Retargeting Ads Follow Surfers to Other Sites" following the appearance of Michael Learmonth's column, "The Pants That Stalked Me on the Web," in *Advertising Age*. Helft and Vega's article examines a similar topic, outlining the pros and cons of behavioral targeting. Overwhelmingly, the consumer response they have gathered seems to be in line with that of Alan Pearlstein, chief executive of Cross Pixel Media, who asks, "What is the benefit of freaking customers out?"

> **THINKING AHEAD** Do you enjoy surfing the Internet? Why or why not? How much time do you devote to this? What do you gain from the time you spend online? Have you considered what information about yourself you reveal as you move from site to site — and who might be reviewing that information? What might those unknown recipients be doing with your information?
>
> **Paired Selection** Read this selection and the one before it for two approaches to a similar topic. Then answer the "Drawing Connections" questions on p. 291.

T he shoes that Julie Matlin recently saw on Zappos.com were kind of cute, or so she thought. But Ms. Matlin wasn't ready to buy and left the site. 1

Then the shoes started to follow her everywhere she went online. An ad for those very shoes showed up on the blog TechCrunch. It popped up again on several other blogs and on Twitpic. It was as if Zappos had unleashed a persistent salesman who wouldn't take no for an answer. 2

"For days or weeks, every site I went to seemed to be showing me ads for those shoes," said Ms. Matlin, a mother of two from Montreal. "It is a pretty clever marketing tool. But it's a little creepy, especially if you don't know what's going on." 3

People have grown accustomed to being tracked online and shown ads for categories of products they have shown interest in, be it tennis or bank loans. 4

Increasingly, however, the ads tailored to them are for specific products that they have perused online. While the technique, which the ad industry 5 calls personalized retargeting or remarketing, is not new, it is becoming more pervasive as companies like Google and Microsoft have entered the field. And retargeting has reached a level of precision that is leaving consumers with the palpable feeling that they are being watched as they roam the virtual aisles of online stores.

More retailers like Art.com, B&H Photo, Diapers.com, eBags.com and the Discovery Channel store use these kinds of ads. Nordstrom says it is considering using them, and retargeting is becoming increasingly common with marketers in the travel, real estate and financial services industries. The ads often appear on popular sites like YouTube, Facebook, MySpace or Realtor.com.

In the digital advertising business, this form of highly personalized marketing is being hailed as the latest breakthrough because it tries to show consumers the right ad at the right time. "The overwhelming response has been positive," said Aaron Magness, senior director for brand marketing and business development at Zappos, a unit of Amazon.com. The parent company declined to say whether it also uses the ads.

Others, though, find it disturbing. When a recent *Advertising Age* column noted the phenomenon, several readers chimed in[1] to voice their displeasure.

Bad as it was to be stalked by shoes, Ms. Matlin said that she felt even worse when she was hounded recently by ads for a dieting service she had used online. "They are still following me around, and it makes me feel fat," she said.

With more consumers queasy about intrusions into their privacy, the technique is raising anew the threat of industry regulation. "Retargeting has helped turn on a light bulb for consumers," said Jeff Chester, a privacy advocate and executive director of the Washington-based Center for Digital Democracy. "It illustrates that there is a commercial surveillance system in place online that is sweeping in scope and raises privacy and civil liberties issues, too."

Retargeting, however, relies on a form of online tracking that has been around for years and is not particularly intrusive. Retargeting programs typically use small text files called cookies that are exchanged when a Web browser visits a site. Cookies are used by virtually all commercial Web sites for various purposes, including advertising, keeping users signed in and customizing content.

In remarketing, when a person visits an e-commerce site and looks at say, an Etienne Aigner Athena satchel on eBags.com, a cookie is placed into that person's browser, linking it with the handbag. When that person, or someone using the same computer, visits another site, the advertising system creates an ad for that very purse.

Mr. Magness, of Zappos, said that consumers may be unnerved because they may feel that they are being tracked from site to site as they

---

[1] **chimed in:** Expressed an opinion.

browse the Web. To reassure consumers, Zappos, which is using the ads to peddle items like shoes, handbags and women's underwear, displays a message inside the banner ads that reads, "Why am I seeing these ads?" When users click on it, they are taken to the Web site of Criteo, the advertising technology company behind the Zappos ads, where the ads are explained.

While users are given the choice to opt out, few do once they understand how the ads are selected for them, said Jean-Baptiste Rudelle, the chief executive of Criteo.   14

But some advertising and media experts said that explaining the technology behind the ads might not allay the fears of many consumers who worry about being tracked or who simply fear that someone they share a computer with will see what items they have browsed.   15

"When you begin to give people a sense of how this is happening, they really don't like it," said Joseph Turow, a professor at the Annenberg School for Communication at the University of Pennsylvania, who has conducted consumer surveys about online advertising. Professor Turow, who studies digital media and recently testified at a Senate committee hearing on digital advertising, said he had a visceral negative reaction to the ads, even though he understands the technologies behind them.   16

"It seemed so bold," Professor Turow said. "I was not pleased, frankly."   17

While start-ups[2] like Criteo and TellApart are among the most active remarketers, the technique has also been embraced by online advertising giants.   18

Google began testing this technique in 2009, calling it remarketing to connote the idea of customized messages like special offers or discounts being sent to users. In March, the company made the service available to all advertisers on its AdWords network.   19

For Google, remarketing is a more specific form of behavioral targeting, the practice under which a person who has visited NBA.com, for instance, may be tagged as a basketball fan and later will be shown ads for related merchandise.   20

Behavioral targeting has been hotly debated in Washington, and lawmakers are considering various proposals to regulate it. During the recent Senate hearing, Senator Claire McCaskill, Democrat of Missouri, said she found the technique troubling. "I understand that advertising supports the Internet, but I am a little spooked out," Ms. McCaskill said of behavioral targeting. "This is creepy."   21

When *Advertising Age*, the advertising industry publication, tackled the subject of remarketing recently, the writer Michael Learmonth described being stalked by a pair of pants he had considered buying on Zappos.   22

"As tracking gets more and more crass and obvious, consumers will rightfully become more concerned about it," he wrote. "If the industry is truly worried about a federally mandated 'do not track' list akin to 'do not call' for the Internet, they're not really showing it."   23

---

[2] **start-ups:** New businesses.

Some advertising executives agree that highly personalized remarket- 24
ing not only goes too far but also is unnecessary.

"I don't think that exposing all this detailed information you have 25
about the customer is necessary," said Alan Pearlstein, chief executive of
Cross Pixel Media, a digital marketing agency. Mr. Pearlstein says he supports retargeting, but with more subtle ads that, for instance, could offer
consumers a discount coupon if they return to an online store. "What is the
benefit of freaking customers out?"

EXERCISING VOCABULARY

1. Record your own definition for each of these words.

   persistent (adj.) (2)   phenomenon (n.) (8)
   perused (v.) (5)   queasy (adj.) (10)
   palpable (adj.) (5)   virtually (adv.) (11)
   roam (v.) (5)   allay (v.) (15)
   hailed (v.) (7)   connote (v.) (19)

2. In paragraph 2, the authors note that Ms. Matlin's situation felt as though
   "Zappos had *unleashed* a persistent salesman." What does the verb *unleashed* mean? What is the origin of the word used in this context? What
   does it imply about a person or thing to talk about its being unleashed?

3. Professor Joseph Turow stated that he experienced a "visceral negative
   reaction" to the online ads (para. 16). Define *visceral*. How intense would
   such a reaction be?

PROBING CONTENT

1. What exactly is "personalized retargeting"? What is another name for
   it? If this technique is not new, how has it changed?

2. What does Zappos have to say about retargeting? With what larger
   company is Zappos affliated?

3. What is a "cookie"? When are cookies exchanged? How are they used?
   How common is this usage?

4. What advertising technology company is behind the Zappos ads? What
   steps does this company take to ensure that consumers are not alarmed?
   How often do consumers opt out when given that option?

CONSIDERING CRAFT

1. Throughout this essay, the authors rely on quotations from a variety of
   experts to address their topic. How effective is this strategy as support
   material for their essay?

2. In paragraph 2, Helft and Vega write "Then the shoes started to follow her everywhere she went online." What type of figure of speech is being used? What effect does its use have on your reading?

WRITING PROMPTS

Responding to the Topic   Write an essay in which you support or reject the right of the federal government to intervene to regulate retargeting advertisements on the Internet.

Responding to the Writer   In paragraph 10, the authors quote the executive director of the Center for Digital Democracy: "[Retargeting] illustrates that there is a commercial surveillance system in place online that is sweeping in scope and raises privacy and civil liberties issues, too." Write an essay in which you identify and discuss the civil liberties and privacy issues involved.

Responding to Multiple Viewpoints   Write an essay in which you examine the implications of retargeting for someone like Delia Cleveland, author of "Champagne Taste, Beer Budget" (p. 279).

For a quiz on this reading, go to bedfordstmartins.com/mirror.

DRAWING CONNECTIONS: PAIRED SELECTIONS

1. Compare and contrast the aftermath of Matlin's online shoe search ("Retargeting Ads Follow Surfers to Other Sites") to the repercussions of Learmonth's ("The Pants That Stalked Me on the Web," p. 283) attempt to shop for shorts. How do their experiences seem similar? How are their attitudes different?

2. Michael Learmonth and the two authors of "Retargeting Ads Follow Surfers to Other Sites" choose very different approaches to support their contentions. Explain the differences in the supporting material used in the two essays. Which do you find more effective? Why? Which essay allows you to more readily grasp the opinion of the author?

Grand Mall Seizure

DANIEL ALARCON

Daniel Alarcon is an associate editor for *Etiqueta Negra,* a magazine published in Lima, Peru. He is a visiting scholar at the Center for Latin American Studies at the University of California, Berkeley. His novel *Lost City Radio* (2007) appeared on the best-of-the-year lists in the *Washington Post,* the *Los Angeles Times,* and the *Chicago Tribune.* He is also the author of a short story collection, *War by Candlelight* (2005). In "Grand Mall Seizure," published on *Alternet* in 2004, Alarcon chronicles his visit to the Mall of America, the largest shopping center in the country.

> **THINKING AHEAD**   How much do you like shopping at a mall? As a middle school or high school student, how often did you go to the mall just to hang out? What did you buy there? What rituals did you observe? Now that you're older, how have your thoughts about malls changed?

It is Saturday at the Mall of America, the nation's largest shopping center, and the crowds are thick and expectant. A small brass band of high school students parades by, playing a cheerful version of "Sunshine of Your Love." Above the glass atrium, a bank of heavy clouds bruises the Midwestern sky. Inside, it is incongruously bright and warm. I sit on a bench and take it all in. A group of teenage boys with piercings and baggy black jeans pass me, one wearing a red T-shirt that reads, "I Have No Idea What's Going On." A fat woman trundles[1] by carrying an enormous bouquet of colorful cellophane balloons, literally dozens of them — cartoon characters, hearts, smiley-faces. Her own smile is easy and unforced, and I'm struck for a moment with the image of her floating, the whole of her, above this sprawling panorama, upwards to the steel girders that crisscross the Mall's glass ceiling, and then beyond.

Two older gentlemen sit amidst the din and controlled madness of Camp Snoopy, the Mall's indoor amusement park, focusing on the matter at hand: a game of checkers.

I share my bench with a large human size statue of Snoopy, and it isn't long before a group of women asks me politely if I wouldn't mind moving. "It's for my granddaughter!" one of them says, posing for a photograph with an arm draped affectionately over Snoopy, both human and canine smiling broadly. Cameras flash. I sit again, but every five minutes or so another group poses with the big white smiling dog. Eventually I give up my seat for

---

[1] **trundles:** Moves as if on wheels.

good. A rollercoaster roars overhead. There are whistles and screams, the ambient[2] noise of fun all around.

The men play checkers.   4

Robert is retired and lives in Bloomington. He comes most Satur-   5
days to play. His partner Juma is a darker-skinned, more ragged version of Henry Kissinger,[3] and seems unwilling or unable to answer my questions. Though his English isn't good, I understand he comes every Saturday and Sunday to play checkers. "From 10 to 4," he says, without looking up from the game. When he speaks, I can see that he has only a few teeth still holding on.

They do not banter or chat. They tolerate my questions for a moment,   6
but it isn't long before I can sense their patience waning. Robert explains they've been playing together for close to four years. Both claim to do very little actual shopping at the Mall. Do you bring the checkers set, I ask. They do not. They play on a cloth set provided by Camp Snoopy Outfitters, next to a sign that says brightly, "Checkers set on sale inside!"

They are, in other words, living advertisements for a store.   7

To understand the Mall of America, it is helpful to know how this all be-   8
gan. Southdale, the first enclosed shopping [mall] in the United States opened in Edina, Minnesota, to great fanfare in 1956. It is still in operation today, not even a half hour from the present site of the Mall of America. Its architect was a man named Victor Gruen, an Austrian Jew who fled the Nazi invasion of 1938 and arrived in the United States with $6 in his pocket. A man of European sensibilities, Gruen's Southdale was inspired by the covered pedestrian galleries of Milan and Venice. He saw the enclosed mall, with its walkways and open spaces, as a hedge against the corrosive suburban sprawl that was then just beginning to overwhelm the American landscape. He wrote of shopping centers that not only served a community's physical needs, but its civic, cultural, and social needs as well. In describing Southdale, he grandiosely and unselfconsciously evoked the Greek agora[4] and the medieval city centers of old Europe.

All over the country the Southdale model was replicated, simplified,   9
and the money came in hand over fist. Developers bought farmland at the junctions of highways and the building frenzy began in earnest. By 1964, when Gruen wrote *The Heart of Our Cities: Urban Crisis*, he had watched his creation grow like a hydra and spiral away from its original intent. He blamed local governments and unscrupulous developers for the decay of America's cities. More to the point, he refused to accept any credit or blame for the invention of the enclosed shopping center. "I have been referred to in some publications as The Father of the Mall. I want to take this opportunity to disclaim paternity once and for all."

---

[2] **ambient:** Present on every side.
[3] **Henry Kissinger:** Former American secretary of state.
[4] **agora:** Marketplace in ancient Greece.

Gruen left his adopted country in 1968, and returned to Vienna, where   10
he died twelve years later.

Unlike Gruen, the immigrant developers of the Mall of America, four   11
Iranian-born Canadian brothers surnamed Ghermezian, never seemed at
all torn about the purposes of their project. They are not urban designers,
city planners, or architects. They are showmen. The Ghermezians are mer-
cenary capitalists, no less visionary than Gruen, but certainly less thoughtful. And the Mall of America was created to fulfill their baroque[5] visions of
festive shopping, where commerce and entertainment would come together
in a profitable union. In 1986, when the Mall was still in its planning stages
and meeting resistance, Nader Ghermezian spoke as if he couldn't understand his opponents, as if he were baffled by their short-sightedness: "You
will have all the shoppers from New York, Rome, Los Angeles, and Paris
coming here," he proclaimed at a press conference. "I bring you the moon
and you don't want it?"

He was only partially exaggerating. The sheer numbers are staggering.   12
It cost $650 million to build. With 4.2 million square feet, the Ghermezian
brothers' behemoth[6] includes 520 stores on four levels. It has four food
courts, two health clinics, a university, a post office, a police station, and a
store that sells Christmas ornaments year-round. It hosts a weekly church
service, and is the home of Camp Snoopy, a seven-acre indoor amusement
park. The Mall is staffed by more than 11,000 year-round employees, visited by some 600,000 to 900,000 shoppers each week, depending on the
season. On an average weekend, the Mall is the third largest city in the state
of Minnesota. If you were to spend only ten minutes in each of the stores, it
would take you more than eighty-six hours to complete your circuit.

Would you like to purchase a decorative ceramic of a smiling cow? Or a   13
sexy dress for your overweight teenager? Perhaps you have come to buy a
CD recording of wind chimes that recall "the long, lazy days of summer"?
Is it leprechaun[7] shoes you want or a microwave bacon tray? A portrait of
the Virgin of Guadalupe in a gold-colored wood frame?

Shoppers laden with bags stroll down each of the themed corridors,   14
past boutiques, in and out of department stores. There are stores called
Stamps Away, Bead It!, Hat Zone, Calido Chili Traders, stores whose names
announce their particular niche in the market economy. Each of the four
corridors of the Mall has a different feel, by design. West Market, with its
gray tiled floors, painted steel benches, and a metallic silver roof above, is
the least attractive, not unlike an airplane hangar with balconies. There are
gaudy golden lamps along the columns, and small ornamental plants. North
Garden has a more traditional feel, with wooden benches, wrought iron
lampposts, small trees in planters, and lots of natural light streaming in

---

[5] **baroque:** Extravagant; excessive.
[6] **behemoth:** Something of enormous size.
[7] **leprechaun:** A mischievous elf from Irish folklore, the toes of whose shoes curled upward.

through the glass ceiling. This is the kind of design element that would have made Victor Gruen proud: without leaving the climate-controlled environs of the Mall, one has the impression of changing neighborhoods, of crossing boundaries, when, in fact, you are simply walking in circles.

Indeed, I only notice these design elements because I look for them.   15
Most shoppers I talk to seem completely unaware of their surroundings; none expressed any particular attachment to North Garden over West Market, or East Broadway as opposed to South Avenue. It's all the same, and it's all shopping, mostly, though not exclusively, for the kinds of items we could all do without. And so, after an hour or two of wandering, it is with some amazement that I stand to gather my breath in front of the display of hammers at Sears. Shoes, hats, clothes, perfumes, gadgets, jewelry are available in hedonistic[8] excess at the Mall—but hammers? They seem out of place, a wrinkle in the climate-controlled fantasy, a blip[9] in the Mall's matrix[10] of eternal leisure: hammers imply work, imply effort and sweat and all those things that do not exist at the Mall, at least not for the shopper. And yet, there they are: fifty-seven different types of hammers. I count. Fifty-seven varieties of this Stone Age tool, with ergonomic[11] handles and rubber grips, in every size and weight and color scheme. So much commercial esoterica,[12] and perhaps what is most out of place here is a tool.

In his 1986 book *The Malling of America,* sociologist William Kowinski   16
observes that spending any time in contemporary shopping centers is like walking through 3-D television. If this was true then, it is even more true today—the mall today is quite deliberately the physical representation of television's immanent consumer visions.

Television is everywhere, the glow of it calling you. I stroll down the   17
North Garden to Nordstrom's, where Donny Osmond, host of a game show called *Pyramid,* is scheduled to put in an appearance later in the day. In the meantime, a kind of star search is underway: a soundstage, a diverse crowd, looking at once expectant and bored, a slick Osmond look-alike emcee chatting onstage with potential contestants for exactly thirty seconds each before the game began (Two questions: 1. Where do you live? 2. What do you do?). The eager would-be contestants come and go in pairs, leaving us with one sentence summaries of their lives: "I'm Kurt from Bloomington and I'm a janitor," says a man whose tiny legs dangle five inches above the floor. The host smiles enthusiastically and turns to Kurt's partner. The game is played, they lose. We groan and then applaud. Three minutes later, Kurt is replaced by Dee from Apple Valley, mother of two beautiful daughters, who has recently welcomed a Swedish exchange student into her home. The crowd cheers. When Dee's team loses, we all welcome Jody, a claims

---

[8] **hedonistic:** Seeking pleasure as the greatest good.
[9] **blip:** An interruption.
[10] **matrix:** Something from which other things originate.
[11] **ergonomic:** Designed to physically benefit the people using the object.
[12] **esoterica:** Items understood and appreciated only by a small group.

administrator, who announces proudly that she has been here since 5:30 in the morning.

Black and white, Asian and Latino, fat and thin, tall and short, they   18
step up for their chance to be on television. The host's enthusiastic smile shows no signs of flagging. Every now and then, a pair wins and is selected for the next round. Applause, banter, game show: the myth machine hitting on all cylinders.

To criticize the Mall for being unreal is to miss the point entirely. *Of course*   19
it is unreal: a banner at the entrance blithely reads LOSE YOURSELF. Literal disorientation begins the moment you step into the cavernous mall. The Mall extends outward from your person in every direction, a seeming infinity of shopping possibilities. And what a place to be lost! It is clean, eternally prosperous, a safe, climate-controlled vision of Eden. And then the more narcotic meanings of the phrase LOSE YOURSELF come into play: it is undiluted fantasy, a beating heart of commerce. This is the language of addiction: we gather near it to feel the pulsating warmth of capitalism. We melt into its embrace.

And yet, somewhere outside the Mall of America, the real world does   20
exist. Hundreds of workers spent years building the complex. And all is not well. The day I visit the Mall the local headlines were of a shooting at an area high school and a government report on rising poverty. Minnesota has been spared the worst of the current economic doldrums,[13] and the Mall itself operates as if they didn't exist at all.

Michael Silsby is twenty years old, from Topeka, Kansas. He has a thin,   21
pale face, and dark brown hair pulled back in a ponytail. He finished a two-year program in graphic design in Omaha, Nebraska, and moved to Minneapolis, looking for work. Michael looked for work at computer firms, design companies, but even in Minneapolis, a job isn't easy to come by. "I never thought I'd wind up working at a mall," he says. "I hate malls."

Michael draws portraits on the eastern second floor balcony. When I   22
approach him, he's working on a portrait of his brother, drawing carefully from a glossy headshot. His boss, Kehai, is a Chinese immigrant who has run the stand for only a few months. "Business is slow," Kehai says. People walk by constantly, a few are curious enough to examine the charcoal images of Michael Jordan, Jack Nicholson, and Marilyn Monroe, but most continue on. Michael works a forty-hour week without a fixed salary, earning commission on each portrait. It works out to around minimum wage, without benefits.

It is hardly back-breaking labor, at least not in the Third World sense,   23
and there are far worse jobs in the Mall. A veritable army of custodial and security staff keeps the place gleaming evenings, weekends, and holidays. In any case, Michael doesn't foresee that he will be here very long. He doesn't mind drawing with people looking over his shoulder; it's the noise

---

[13] **doldrums:** Periods of inactivity or downturns.

that gets him. And it's true: the perpetual buzz from Camp Snoopy below is maddening, bells going off at regular intervals, shrieks of delight from the log flume,[14] the nauseating music of the carousel. They coalesce into a wall of sound, so that as we talk, we are both nearly shouting. I sit with him for nearly an hour while he draws my portrait. I listen to him talk about *Star Trek*, about his brother, who is looking for work in commercials. People stream by, looking first at the portrait in progress, then at me, and snicker. It is a humiliating experience.

From the western third floor Food Court, the gleaming neon heart of Camp Snoopy is on display. There are giant cartoon characters suspended from the ceiling; pterodactyls[15] built of Legos hover just above. Below, children scurry about through thickets of trees, along ponds and over streams heavy with coins and forgotten wishes. But we, on this level, are above it all: it is evening, the lights are low, and romance is in the air. Couples share a bite of Japanese food before heading to the movie theatre. Everywhere there is hushed conversation over a burrito or a burger, or two straws poking from the same oversize cup of soda. I watch a young man approach the railing, arm around his girlfriend, whose eyes are shut tightly. "Now look," he says. 24

She opens her eyes and it's there: the lights snaking upwards, the elegant Ferris wheel, the pastoral[16] green of the indoor garden. "It's soooo huge!" she says. "Soooo huge!" 25

This, I believe, is the essential calculus of American capitalism: bigger is better. It explains why the Mall's developers are Canadian Iranians, who seized the opportunity to sell Americans their own oversized dreams. It explains why it attracts, according to the *New York Times,* more annual visitors than Disney World, Graceland, and the Grand Canyon combined. In the American imagination, there is nothing quite like the allure and romance of being the biggest. Size is glory and relevance. Chartered buses ply the route from the airport directly to the Mall. Its size makes it a destination. 26

In one very important respect, size apparently does not matter: the spectacular size of the Mall of America has not been matched by spectacular profits. By some accounts, the Mall is now worth about $550 million, or $100 million less than its original development cost. Many observers say that the era of the mega-mall has passed. Construction of large, enclosed malls is down 70 percent since 1996. But this is only part of the story: while no new enclosed shopping centers have been built in the Minneapolis area since the opening in 1992 (and more than a few have closed), those that remained have survived through growth, the retail equivalent of an arms race. Southdale, Victor Gruen's creation, has expanded by 30 percent, to nearly 2 million square feet. By the end of this year, there will be seven 27

---

[14] **log flume:** An amusement park roller coaster that travels through water.
[15] **pterodactyls:** Prehistoric birdlike creatures of the Late Jurassic period.
[16] **pastoral:** Reminiscent of rural life.

enclosed malls with over 1 million square feet of retail space in the Greater Minneapolis area. In 1990, there were only two.

The shopping center is America's great safe haven, and it embodies the promise of the American dream. The Mall attracts foreign tourists of course, but also immigrants from all continents who have made new homes in the Minneapolis area: I see women in Arab dress, families of Africans in bright head-wraps, Latin Americans from every corner of our continent. Buying little, they wander around the Mall and inhale its scent. What better place to understand your new country than here? Consumption is a dearly held American right, a pastime and tradition.

Nowhere is this more acutely observed than in *Dawn of the Dead*, George A. Romero's 1978 zombie movie. In the film, a quartet of survivalists flee Philadelphia in a stolen helicopter, escaping the living dead who have overrun all the cities. After a few false starts, they find safety in the relative luxury of an abandoned suburban shopping mall. It has everything they might need: food, clothes, furniture, television, guns. Unfortunately the mall too is seething with zombies, stumbling along the corridors, stiff-legged, gangly, lethal. The intrepid refugees lock themselves inside a closed department store, before clearing the mall in a paroxysm[17] of violence.

Then, once safe, they celebrate by shopping, choosing new watches, trying on clothes, grinding fresh coffee, going ice skating with new skates. They parade around their liberated mall with beaming smiles, loaded with new gear and gadgets. They lose themselves to festive shopping.

In the subdued light of morning, the Mall is a thoughtful place. It is Sunday, before the stores open, and I wander the empty corridors of the Mall at rest. There are a few resolute elderly walkers, a man reading the newspaper at the open coffee shop, but mostly there is the shuttered quiet of a vacant place of commerce.

I am here for church. Each Sunday at 10:00 AM, the River Church has a service in the rented space of the Great Lakes Ballroom in the southwest corner of Camp Snoopy. I arrive early and watch the eager participants get everything ready. There are twenty or so people milling[18] around, musicians onstage, a technician putting the finishing touches on a PowerPoint presentation about today's sermon. The mood is earnest, yet informal, and everyone, it seems, is under forty.

More people arrive and the lights dim, and the band launches into a Thelonious Monk[19] tune, with agile soloists and swinging drums. I'm tapping my feet. After a few songs, a white man with a pudgy face asks us to bow our heads for fellowship. "God," he says serenely, shutting his eyes to address Him. "You are an awesome God."

For the past few Sundays, Pastor Chris Reinerston's sermons have been breaking down the Lord's Prayer, phrase by phrase. Today he will focus on

---

[17] **paroxysm:** A sudden action.
[18] **milling:** Wandering.
[19] **Thelonious Monk:** Famous American jazz musician (1920–1982).

"Your Kingdom come, Thy Will Be Done, On Earth as it is in Heaven." The last two phrases, he says, are pretty self-explanatory, so he asks our permission to concentrate on the first: God's Kingdom.

Reinerston describes a world of plenty, where children's bellies are 35 bloated not from malnutrition, but from eating so many of God's wondrous fruits and vegetables. "God will blow our minds!" Reinerston announces enthusiastically. He gains momentum as he speaks: everything will be provided for, the stock market will go up and up, and there will be no single-parent homes. "It will be," he says at one point, "like everyone sitting around, watching TV, just loving each other!" I can't do it justice of course, because Reinerston means everything he says, means it intensely, fervently. But when he says that in God's Kingdom there will be "no more run-down buildings, no more cracked sidewalks, no more graffiti," that "everything will be new!" I can't help but wonder if the place he is describing isn't actually the Mall of America, with all its abundant, excessive newness. Imagine the Mall, full of God's Elect lounging at the Bose Audio Store, watching DVDs of the latest releases, frolicking on God's trampoline, trying on clothes straight off the Macy's rack. "Imagine," he says later, voice quavering, "a world without poverty. Imagine never seeing another one of those commercials for starving children in Third World countries!"

Ultimately, what Reinerston has described is the contemporary Ameri- 36 can condition: a rarified vantage point, where it is not poverty we decry, but the televised representation of it, as if the real thing were too far, too distant and abstract to pierce this pretty, pretty bubble. Poverty, of the American variety, is on the rise, or so the newspapers are saying. But here?

After the service, I ask Pastor Chris about some of these things. He is an 37 energetic man in his mid thirties, a father of four, he tells me proudly, and eager to talk. Why a service in the Mall of America, I ask him. "It wasn't my idea," he says, "It was God's." Bart Holling, another River Church leader, joins our conversation, and he puts it this way: "The Mall of America is a river of life. People come here looking for stuff to fill their hearts with. We believe there is a God-size hole in each person's heart, and they're always trying to fill it with other stuff, but we're here to help them fill it with God." I am not convinced. What about Jesus throwing the money-changers out of the temple? Haven't you brought the temple to the money-changers? In response, Pastor Chris re-interprets his sermon as anti-consumerist; referencing commercials, he says, is just a way to connect with people.

After the service, I wander into Camp Snoopy and run into Juma, looking 38 uneasily at the empty checkers table. He wears the same clothes as yesterday. His partners haven't come. It is past 11:00 AM, and he is itching to play. He recognizes me and all but drags me to the checkers set.

I am a disappointment. He beats me in a flurry of decisive moves. We 39 set up and he beats me again. In between, I ask him where he is from, and listen over the rising noise of the Mall as he evokes in halting English a faraway African city: Kampala, Uganda. He owned a fabric store in Kampala, before Idi Amin, the murderous, self-aggrandizing dictator, expelled him thirty-one years before. "I have four sons here," he says proudly. "They study." He chose to leave. Here, in the comfort of the Mall of America, Juma doesn't seem to regret his decision—and why would he? "The Mall is good," he says. "No problems."

No war at your front step. No landslides or floods, droughts, strikes, or coup[20] attempts. The Mall banishes all worldly problems, man-made or natural. It is no wonder that so many people come not only to the Mall but to the United States: to be near so much power, so much money is to believe in the possibility of earthly tranquility.   40

Is it too simple to say that the whole world wants in? In one memorable scene in *Dawn of the Dead,* the four heroes stand triumphant on the second floor balcony, decked out with guns, jewelry, and resplendent fur coats. Below are the bodies of zombies, and beyond that the doors of the shopping center, where hundreds more living dead claw and press against the glass, trying desperately to get in. "What do they want?" one of the survivalists asks. Another answers thoughtfully: 41

They're after the place. They don't know why, they just remember they want to be in here.   42

What the hell are they?   43

They're us, that's all.   44

EXERCISING VOCABULARY

1. Record your own definition for each of these words.

expectant (adj.) (1)	undiluted (adj.) (19)
incongruously (adv.) (1)	veritable (adj.) (23)
sprawling (adj.) (1)	gleaming (adj.) (23)
waning (v.) (6)	coalesce (v.) (23)
grandiosely (adv.) (8)	allure (n.) (26)
replicated (v.) (9)	ply (v.) (26)
unscrupulous (adj.) (9)	embodies (v.) (28)
mercenary (adj.) (11)	intrepid (adj.) (29)
visionary (adj.) (11)	resolute (adj.) (31)
baffled (v.) (11)	agile (adj.) (33)
staggering (adj.) (12)	frolicking (v.) (35)
niche (n.) (14)	rarified (adj.) (36)
immanent (adj.) (16)	decry (v.) (36)
flagging (n.) (18)	self-aggrandizing (adj.) (39)
cavernous (adj.) (19)	resplendent (adj.) (41)

2. Victor Gruen decided to construct "a hedge against the corrosive suburban sprawl" that had begun to engulf his adopted country (para. 8). Of what is a hedge usually made? What purpose does a hedge serve? What

---

[20] **coup:** Sudden and highly successful action; often used with the overthrow of a government.

effect does something corrosive have? In what sense can this be applied to suburban building patterns? Rewrite this phrase in your own words.

3. Describe an atmosphere of "din and controlled madness" (para. 2). What does *din* mean? How does this early reference to the Mall of America's atmosphere set the stage for Alarcon's entire essay?

4. In paragraph 9, Alarcon notes that Victor Gruen watched his first mall idea "grow like a hydra." What is a hydra? How does a hydra grow? To what extent is this simile appropriate for the proliferation of malls across America?

5. In paragraph 27, Alarcon likens the struggle of malls to survive as "the retail equivalent of an arms race." What was the arms race? Who participated in it? How was this like the battle each mall undertakes to survive economically?

PROBING CONTENT

1. What is ironic about the location of the first enclosed shopping mall in the United States? Who was responsible for its creation? Where did he get the idea?

2. Who is responsible for the Mall of America concept? Why do you think they chose that name? How successful has their dream become?

3. Why does Alarcon feel that hammers are "a blip in the Mall's matrix" (para. 15)? What is significant about the hammers? Why do they capture the author's interest?

4. Why is the Mall of America so popular with immigrants? What do they gain from wandering past its stores, even if they buy very little?

CONSIDERING CRAFT

1. The title of this selection is a play on words. What is the more commonly heard phrase? To what does it refer? What imagery does Alarcon invoke in the reader by using this title?

2. What does Alarcon accomplish in the first paragraph of this essay? What mode of writing does he use? How effective is his opening? Why?

3. What is the purpose of the occasional one-sentence paragraphs that Alarcon uses? Locate several and discuss their function in the essay. How effective is this strategy?

4. In paragraph 18, Alarcon describes the TV show filming in the Mall as "the myth machine hitting on all cylinders." To which myth is he referring? What ordinary object does the phrase "hitting on all cylinders" evoke? What does Alarcon accomplish by including this phrase here?

5. Why does Alarcon include the description of scenes from *Dawn of the Dead?* How does referencing this movie further his purpose for this essay? Why does he choose to end with a quotation from this movie?

WRITING PROMPTS

Responding to the Topic   Does being in a mall open up for you "the promise of the American dream" (para. 28)? In an essay, describe in detail a recent mall experience you have had. If you haven't been to a mall lately, spend several hours in one. Did you experience any of the feelings Alarcon mentions? What did you see, taste, smell, hear, and touch?

Responding to the Writer   Alarcon asserts that the Mall of America represents "the essential calculus of American capitalism: bigger is better" (para. 26). To what extent does this axiom hold true in America's economy? Take a position agreeing or disagreeing with this assertion. Defend your own position with numerous examples.

Responding to Multiple Viewpoints   Write an essay in which you explore the symbolism of the mall culture and compare the degree of fantasy offered by an online virtual universe, such as Second Life or the Sims, with that offered by the universe of the American mall.

For a quiz on this reading, go to bedfordstmartins.com/mirror.

What Is Independent Hip Hop?

HECTOR GONZALEZ

Hector Gonzalez came to the United State in 1989 as a refugee from El Salvador. He grew up in San Jose, California, and is currently living in Los Angeles with his fiancé and their son. He works in the social services sector as a child and family specialist and is also heavily involved in the underground hip hop movement. His work has appeared in the *San Jose Mercury News,* the *Oakland Tribune,* and the *Miami Herald.* This essay is from the online magazine *Silicon Valley De Bug* and originally appeared in 2004.

> **THINKING AHEAD** Do you listen to hip hop? What has made hip hop such a phenomenon in American culture? In what areas besides music have hip hop artists had an impact?

A while back, I was the opening act at a hip hop show that featured underground MCs from San Jose and Los Angeles. The show took place in a small theater venue in downtown San Jose. As I walked off the stage after performing my set, I kept my head down, thinking that no one had paid to see my performance. 1

But outside was a group of people playing the role of groupies. They asked me to stand next to a car so they could take my picture. In return, they gave me a magazine and a CD. Suddenly, I felt like a superstar. 2

Little did I know this was only the beginning of a multimillion dollar campaign Toyota was setting up to sell its new product line, Scion, to younger drivers. 3

Since then, Scion has been making its presence known in the underground hip hop community. In and around San Jose, Calif., where I live, Scion paraphernalia can be found at most hip hop venues. Toyota's marketing strategy makes it clearer than ever that underground urban culture is a sought-after commodity. 4

Corporations have long used urban culture to market their products. I remember a McDonald's commercial where a circle of black youth were rapping about a Big Mac. Anyone who knew anything about MCing could tell you that those MCs were pretty whack, and that the idea of rappin' about how McDonald's burgers make you feel better was pretty corny. There's also the commercial that features a guy in K-Swiss tennis shoes break dancing. But in the hip hop scene, K-Swiss is labeled a "preppy"[1] shoe by everyone I know. 5

---

[1] **preppy:** A style of dress characterized by classic fashions and a neat appearance.

But unlike McDonald's or K-Swiss, Scion has been doing a good job in   6
maintaining its street credibility while selling its product. In 2003, Toyota
sold about 11,000 of the newly introduced vehicles. In 2004, they sold
close to 100,000.

Scion's secret is that they don't use fake gimmicks; they stick with the   7
real deal. They produce a monthly magazine that features some of the hot-
test underground hip hop heads from the Bay Area to London. Half of the
magazine focuses on urban trends in fashion, art, digital media, etc. The
other half is nothing but Scion ads.

The magazine can be compared to *URB* magazine, one of the most   8
dominant urban magazines in the world. This is no accident. The people
behind *URB*—a marketing firm called Rebel Organization—are also responsible for Scion's marketing strategy. Rebel Organization has also run
successful marketing campaigns for Reebok and T-Mobile.

Apparently, they've learned from the mistakes other corporations have   9
made in trying to tap into urban culture. "Scion doesn't attach itself to big
stars," says Josh Levine, president of Rebel Organization and a lead sculp-
tor of Scion's marketing plan. "Instead, it captures the local scenes, because
that's where urban culture really takes place."

In the local market of San Jose, Scion sponsors and supports many hip   10
hop functions. In return, the company asks that Scion banners be put up and
Scion merchandise—hats, shirts, CDs and magazines—handed out.

The latest Scion magazine asks the question, "What Is Independent?"   11
and features DJ J Boogie from San Francisco, legendary Graffiti writer Sabe,
and rapper Guru from Gang Star, among others. Underground hip hop
culture in general is based on "keepin' it real," and hip hoppers have always
questioned the integrity of others by asking them if they're "keepin' it real."
But what happens when a corporation is the one asking you that question?

Some underground artists say that going corporate means selling out,   12
while others say companies such as Scion could now be contributors to the
culture.

Tommy Aguilar—the events coordinator of the Movimiento Arte Cul-   13
tural Latino Americana, which hosts regular hip hop events—is one of the
leaders of the San Jose hip hop scene. He can usually be found downtown,
wearing a newspaper-boy hat and reporter-style glasses, promoting the hip
hop events he puts together through his independent collective Universal
Grammar.

Aguilar is responsible for bringing such acts as Crown City Rockers,   14
Lyrics Born and DJ Questlove to San Jose—all with the help of Scion. Aguilar says having Scion sponsorship does not infringe on the authenticity of
the functions. "The money they give us doesn't change our program," he
says—"it's simply put to good use."

Five years ago, Aguilar says, he saw the issue of corporate sponsorship in   15
a less positive light. His newer understanding of the business aspect of hip
hop is representative of a growing understanding in the underground scene
that artists need to be getting paid in order for the culture to maintain itself.

Kenny May is on the opposite end of the spectrum. May is the founder   16
of Funk Lab Productions, a promoting collective that has dominated the
break dancing scene in San Jose for the past decade. May has never received sponsorship from Scion. Even when the corporation offers the hip
hop community financial support, he says, "they are still taking advantage
of us, because the corporations will always get the upper hand."

When I ask Josh Levine what he thinks about people saying that Scion   17
is just another corporation trying to take advantage of artists, he uses hip
hop to frame his response.

"It's no different than an MC. Although some people would like to see   18
the MC come up, you'll always have tons who want to see that MC fail."

EXERCISING VOCABULARY

1. Record your own definition for each of these words.

   venue (n.) (1)   integrity (n.) (11)
   paraphernalia (n.) (4)   infringe (v.) (14)
   commodity (n.) (4)   authenticity (n.) (14)
   corny (adj.) (5)

2. What does Gonzalez mean in paragraph 6 when he writes that Scion has managed to achieve "street credibility"? Define *credibility.* How does one earn street credibility? By whom are those with this attribute respected?

3. In paragraph 16, Gonzalez writes that "Kenny May is on the opposite end of the spectrum." What is a spectrum? Give an example. What does Gonzalez's use of this expression tell the reader about Kenny May?

PROBING CONTENT

1. How did Gonzalez first become involved with Toyota Scion's new advertising campaign? What was his initial reaction to his experience? What does Gonzalez learn later about Toyota's motivation for this encounter?

2. How well has Toyota's marketing campaign for the Scion succeeded? What statistics validate this success? Why has this campaign been successful?

3. Explain the relationship between the Scion marketing campaign and *URB* magazine. Why is this relationship significant?

4. What does Gonzalez identify as the basis for understanding hip hop culture? How do corporations like Toyota fit into this basic premise?

CONSIDERING CRAFT

1. What does the title lead the reader to expect from this essay? To what extent is this expectation fulfilled? Explain the relationship between the title and the essay's thesis.

2. Reread paragraphs 1–3. What type of introduction does Gonzalez choose for this essay? What does his introduction accomplish?

3. Most of this essay is written in standard English, but occasionally Gonzalez introduces slang terms: "those MCs were pretty whack" (para. 5); Toyota stays "with the real deal" (para. 7); and "some people would like to see the MC come up" (para. 18). What does the inclusion of such phrases convey about the target audience for this essay? How does their inclusion affect your reading?

WRITING PROMPTS

Responding to the Topic   Identify another aspect of American culture that has been exploited by a large corporation to sell a product. Write an essay in which you examine in detail the marketing strategy, the target audience, and the effectiveness of the marketing campaign.

Responding to the Writer   "Some underground artists say that going corporate means selling out, while others say companies such as Scion could now be contributors to the culture" (para. 12). Write an essay in which you use multiple examples to support one side or the other of this debate.

Responding to Multiple Viewpoints   Both the fashion designers in "Sewn in Secret" (p. 275) and the hip hop artists identified in "What Is Independent Hip Hop?" are part of underground movements that exist outside the everyday experience of the mainstream population in their respective countries. Write an essay in which you compare and contrast these two underground cultures.

For a quiz on this reading, go to bedfordstmartins.com/mirror.

Why Apple Deserves an Oscar Too

ABE SAUER

Abe Sauer is a regular contributor to the online magazine *The Awl,* which is known for its sarcastic approach to current events. Sauer carries this snarky tone over to his own political humor blog at www.abramsauer.com.

> **THINKING AHEAD** When you are watching television, how aware are you of the make of car the hero drives? The type of soda the characters drink? The brand of phone the heroine uses for text messages? If you do notice, are you likely to be influenced to purchase that same product? Why or why not?

A vatar is in contention for an Oscar because it dominated its field, both technologically and financially. But another cinematic player was even more dominant last year: Apple. In the 44 films in 2009 that topped the box office for at least one weekend, an Apple logo or device could be seen in at least 18 of them. (That's almost 41%.) In some, Apple products even eclipsed their human scene partners. This high appearance rate does not include the heap of mass-market films from 2009 that did not own a weekend but also featured Apple product placement. [1]

Just to name a few of those? That list includes *Drag Me to Hell, Orphan, I Love You, Man, Duplicity, Crank 2: High Voltage, Ghosts of Girlfriends Past, Imagine That, Sorority Row, Answer Man, Post Grad, I Love You Beth Cooper, All About Steve, Hurt Locker, New York, I Love You, It's Complicated, Road Trip: Beer Pong, Law Abiding Citizen, Fantastic Mr. Fox, Funny People* and *Couples Retreat.* [2]

These numbers also don't include the mountain of other films and TV shows, from Macs on *Regis and Kelly* and Jimmy Fallon's desks to the Mac grotesquerie[1] of *The Office* and *30 Rock.* Fruity logo out front, advertisement aglow. [3]

For one month in 2009, product placement tracking service Nielsen IAG noted 62 total "occurrences" of Apple products, more than any other brand, including AT&T (59), Coca-Cola (55) or Ford (41). *Playboy,* even with a whole show crafted around its brand name, logged a comparatively paltry 21 occurrences. [4]

This is a downturn from 2008, when Apple appeared in exactly half of the 40 #1 films. This achievement comes at the end of a decade-long climb for Apple. [5]

---

[1] **grotesquerie:** Something that is fanciful or absurd.

Last year, Apple's product placement plan finally topped the heap as well—with Apple appearing in more #1 films than any other brand, including Ford and Pepsi, which had held the most appearances for every year going back to 2001 (except 2003, when the #1 was Cadillac). 6

Brandchannel.com's weekly product placement tracking feature Brandcameo shows that Apple has appeared in 102 of the 302 weekly number one U.S. box office films from 2001 to 2009—more than 33% of them. Apple's number is actually higher when period and fantasy/scifi films, in which Apple could not appear, are removed (the *Lord of the Rings* trilogy, *Star Wars* prequels, *3:10 to Yuma*, etc.). 7

Measured against Apple's real market share, there is a deeply inauthentic nature to many of Apple's appearances, particularly films set in administrative halls where the brand is rarely found, whether hospitals (*Scrubs*) or government offices (*24*, *Law Abiding Citizen*). Apple's "accomplishment" is made all the more extraordinary considering how automobile brands, like Ford, so easily and inconsequentially appear in a film (taxis in films are almost always Fords). Meanwhile, Apple products have to be very deliberately placed by a set designer. 8

Hamish Purdy, the assistant set decorator for *Watchmen* (which featured an Apple "Easter egg"[2]) explains, to some degree, how this happens. "One thing we often have to deal with is 'clearance' to use a product on a set. If the item has been 'product placed,' clearance is inherent. Apple has always been willing to provide product for sets without too much hassle." 9

Yeah, just so that is clear: Apple does not pay for any of this exposure. 10

As for how Apple products in scenes don't always lend realism, Purdy said, "With shows like *CSI*, the number one place people 'learn' about FBI work and police stations, the truth of it is horribly and inaccurately dramatized. Because the public feels this is what a police station looks like, other shows have to at least take a page from that design so that it registers with the public. We have created our own monster. A real police station would just look too boring and even 'fake.'" 11

Apple products have become so expected onscreen that things have gotten bizarre. The 2007 hit film *Wild Hogs* featured a character getting an Apple logo tattoo despite an earlier scene with him not even using an Apple computer. The television show *Worst Week* attempted to pass off an iPod Touch as an IPhone and when the show *Knight Rider* went out of its way to use a no-brand prop phone (clearly a Sony Xperia) the show was criticized: "Knight Rider Clones the iPhone, Poorly." That is to say, a show that did not use an Apple product was disparaged for not just using an Apple product. 12

Even the latest *Star Trek*, which features no Apple products, had some calling the starship design a "super duper Apple store," an "Internal Apple store of tomorrow," "looks like the SS Apple Store," "an Apple Store 10 years in the future," and "Would you like a tour of the iBridge?" [All sic.] 13

---

[2] **Easter egg:** A surprise hidden inside a computer game or software.

(Interestingly enough, in 1999, *Star Trek* director J.J. Abrams told *Entertainment Weekly* of his then-hit show *Felicity*'s many Mac placements, "For me, this is strictly a cultural phenomenon. There's something human and friendly and optimistic about Macintosh."

Apple's rich history of product placement reaches back to the Mac's   14
original era of market dominance, appearing in many 1980s films like *Short Circuit* and *Real Genius*. The 1990s saw Apple make a active effort to highlight its film roles, openly advertising its *Mission Impossible* and *Independence Day* tie-ins. Apple was also hyper-aggressive, with product placing legend Suzanne Forlenza pushing Mac infiltration into television shows such as *Veronica's Closet, Seinfeld, Ally McBeal, Buffy the Vampire Slayer, Dharma & Greg, Felicity, The Drew Carey Show, X-Files, Real World* and *Just Shoot Me* and films *You've Got Mail* (obviously) and *Jurassic Park*.

So it's notable that Apple now makes the same active effort to *not* draw   15
attention to its outlandish level of product placement. The brand recently even disabled its official "Starring Apple" webpage that highlighted the Apple's many cinematic achievements. In character, Apple declined to comment for this piece or about the fate of that page.

Apple is essentially like Hollywood itself, beautiful, expensive and not   16
at all representative of reality. And just like disbelief is suspended when Angelina Jolie or Brad Pitt portray normal people, Apple product placement is dismissed as creative license.

So the greater question is, how does all this product placement benefit   17
Apple? Does it at all? Apple computer sales have spiked in recent years. The reasons for this range from "people are learning the truth" to a halo effect created by the iPod and the iPhone.

Comparing Apple's product placement numbers since 2001 with its   18
sales and market share, there appears to be an overall increase, though certainly nothing concrete. If anything, initial data show the increase in Apple onscreen placements (the vast majority of which are computers) to be linked to the explosion of the iPod, which also happened to be the explosion of Apple's Q Rating.

Tim Aikin, founder and CEO of Boxwish, a site that creates a com-   19
munity of product placement spotters who solve the great quandary of how products can take advantage of their placements, says that as the Apple brand, having always polarized consumers, "has grown its market share from niche player to mass producer, thanks to the iPod, Intel-based Macs, iTunes and now the iPhone, they need to soften this polarization without losing their core audience and still maintaining a certain sense of exclusivity."

Aikin said that Apple's product placement is a success because it coun-   20
teracts the boring sameness inherent in becoming a mass-market leader. "Apple is able to keep the brand 'cool' by having the stars of the movie use the products most overtly and then also throw in the 'Easter eggs' to maintain a connection with the core audience that gave Apple so much success in its early years."

As you can tell, product placement is notorious for having no solid   21
criteria to benchmark success. Like the Brandchannel and Nielsen IAG
numbers, most product placement data cite "occurrences" and few results
outside the pathetically overly-cited, such as *E.T.* and Reese's Pieces.

A 2009 study of household computer ownership found that "approxi-   22
mately 12 percent of all U.S. computer-owning households own an Apple
computer, up from 9 percent in 2008." While 12 percent representation in
the real world is nowhere near its 50 percent onscreen rate, it still possible
that, in conjunction with iPhone and iPod halo effects, all of the free Apple
product placement benefits the brand. It's essentially the Head On "apply
directly to the forehead" approach of repetition; see Apple after Apple after
Apple after Apple after Apple after Apple after Apple in everything everywhere onscreen and a person becomes much more open to considering one
of those Macs he's hearing so much about.

Then there are the brain scans.   23

For his latest book, *Buyology: Truth and Lies About Why We Buy,*   24
Martin Lindstrom conducted scanning to investigate unconscious brain
activity in response to marketing, including product placement. When it
comes to Apple and product placement, Lindstrom says Apple is maybe the
most sophisticated player in the market: "What we know today is that a
cognitive link between the storyline and the actual brand often scares the
consumers away; it simply is too much 'in your face.' Non-conscious links
therefore will be the future. The best example of such synergy[3] is what we
witness in *Wall-E* where the Apple logo never is present." Lindstrom says
that even though the Apple "brand" is rare in *Wall-E,* audiences make an
unconscious value transfer from the movie to the brand. "Such value transfer is, according to the *Buyology* study, most prominent when the viewer
isn't aware of the product placement at the rational level in the brain and
only at a non-conscious level."

More odd is that Apple's increasingly conspicuous product placement   25
dominance draws few complaints when compared to the lesser efforts of
brands like Pepsi, General Motors, or Starbucks. The full spectrum of product placement oppositionists, from those who reject the practice because it
"compromises art" to those who see it as manipulative marketing, seem to
be far more upset about the occasional McDonald's placement than a
brand that has appeared in more than one third of all box-office hits since
2001. A great illustration of this phenomenon is the show *30 Rock,* which
has been taken to task for its product placements, especially its McDonald's McFlurry episode, even while the same show's pornographic Mac and
iPhone appearances pass with little comment.

About Apple's Teflon status, Aikin says that Apple's placements are   26
often used in context, such as fulfilling an action in a movie, and aren't "just
an overt Pepsi truck going through a scene." He also says: "The products
look good. The increasing popularity of our site serves to show that many

[3] **synergy:** Combined action.

movies act almost like a how-to guide to being contemporary and relevant. Our audience wants to be inspired by movies and Apple, arguably an inspirational brand, fits this well."

Leander Kahney, author of *Inside Steve's Brain, The Cult of Mac* and   27
The Cult of iPod and author of the blog Cult of Mac, says of Apple product placement: "Apple revels in this kind of thing. Apple has always been overrepresented in movies and TV shows. Its profile far exceeds its market share. But there's never been a backlash and there never will. People are more likely to aspire than revolt."

The *Buyology* study might nail the reason why Kahney is right. Lind-   28
strom points to how preconceived notions about the Apple brand lend it a cloak of immunity against criticism. "You're left second guessing if Apple had paid for the placement or not. Apple is not perceived as one of the bad guys-brands such as BP, McDonald's and Microsoft often are, either because they're seen as being the companies destroying the environment, being unhealthy or greedy." And sure enough *Buyology* showed that part of what makes Apple's product placements immune from criticism is that it isn't seen as a product at all. "Apple has steered clear of this reputation because the brand is more a religion than anything else," said Lindstrom. "[The study] showed a clear correlation between the brand Apple and the faith of Christianity. And due to such status, people rarely will question the presence of the brand, just as they wouldn't question why various religions are featured in movies."

But how long will audiences, and especially prop managers, continue   29
to think differently about Apple and its product placement? As Apple becomes more mass market it may find its culture role increasingly difficult, which in turn may endanger all of its free onscreen exposure.

There is evidence this is already happening. In small increments, Apple   30
product placement that might have been is being stifled by producers camouflaging the glowing fruit with any number of tricky set props. A pencil jar here; a yellow stickie note there.

Apple's product placement pace will remain strong in 2010, with Apple   31
placements already confirmed in the films *Book of Ell, When in Rome, Kick Ass, Chloe, The Killers, Wall Street 2, City Island, She's Out of My League, The Joneses, The Spy Next Door, Percy Jackson: Lightening Thief, Valentine's Day, The Bounty Hunter* and *Toy Story 3*. But the fat years of being a film darling may be on the decline. Even Madonna eventually got married and had kids.

EXERCISING VOCABULARY

1. Record your own definition for each of these words.

eclipsed (v.) (1)	disparaged (v.) (12)
paltry (adj.) (4)	infiltration (n.) (14)
inauthentic (adj.) (8)	outlandish (adj.) (15)

quandary (n.) (19)
niche (adj.) (19)
inherent (adj.) (20)
overtly (adv.) (20)
notorious (adj.) (21)
pathetically (adv.) (21)
conjunction (n.) (22)

cognitive (adj.) (24)
spectrum (n.) (25)
revels (v.) (27)
backlash (n.) (27)
correlation (n.) (28)
increments (n.) (30)

2. Explain what is meant by the term *product placement*. How is this marketing strategy both different from and similar to other forms of advertising?

3. Director J. J. Abrams explained the frequent appearance of Mac products on his show as "strictly a cultural phenomenon" (para. 13). What is a phenomenon? What is required for something to become a cultural phenomenon?

4. What does Sauer mean in paragraph 17 when he lists "the halo effect" as a possible reason for Apple's increase in sales? From what is this expression derived?

5. In paragraph 26, the author refers to "Apple's Teflon status." What is Teflon? Where is it usually found? How does this apply to Apple?

PROBING CONTENT

1. What does Sauer mean in the first paragraph when he refers to films that "did not own a weekend"? Why is this designation significant?

2. Prior to the rise of Apple, what two brands previously dominated product placement statistics? Why are Apple products more difficult than these two brands to place in films and television episodes?

3. In what types of films do Apple products *not* appear? Why?

4. Explain what Sauer means in paragraph 22 when he writes that Apple utilizes "the Head On 'apply directly to the forehead' approach of repetition." What is the desired end result of this marketing technique?

5. Why are "product placement oppositionists" (para. 25) opposed to this marketing strategy? Why does Apple seem to be immune to such opposition?

CONSIDERING CRAFT

1. Explain Sauer's choice of a title for this essay. How effective is this title? Why?

2. Sauer notes that those who study product placement often reference a classic example, "*E.T.* and Reese's Pieces" (para. 21). Why does Sauer

include this and other examples that may not be familiar to many readers?

3. Paragraphs 10 and 23 consist of only one sentence each. Why does the author choose this approach for these paragraphs? What effect does this writing strategy have on the reader?

4. Reread the final two sentences of this essay. What point is Sauer making? How effective is this conclusion? Why?

WRITING PROMPTS

Responding to the Topic   Write an essay in which you explore similarities and differences in product placement and subliminal advertising. You will first need to research subliminal advertising. Use specific examples of both product placement and subliminal advertising to support your main ideas.

Responding to the Writer   In paragraph 26 Sauer quotes Tim Aiken, CEO of Boxwish, an online community of product placement locators: "The increasing popularity of our site serves to show that many movies act almost like a how-to guide to being contemporary and relevant." Write an essay in which you agree or disagree with Aiken's statement about the influence of movies. Support your thesis with relevant, specific examples.

Responding to Multiple Viewpoints   In "Grand Mall Seizure (p. 292)," Daniel Alarcon analyzes the cult of the American mall. Write an essay in which you compare and contrast mall culture as described by Alarcon to the Apple culture discussed by Sauer in "Why Apple Deserves an Oscar Too."

For a quiz on this reading, go to bedfordstmartins.com/mirror.

Hooters Translates in China

CRAIG SIMONS

American businesses are highly visible throughout the world, but sometimes, as this essay shows, particularly iconic businesses can be reinterpreted by different world cultures. Craig Simons covers the region from India to Japan for Cox News Service. His particular focus is China, where he first lived as a Peace Corps volunteer from 1996 to 1998. Since then, he has been a regular contributor to *Newsweek* and an editor and a reporter in the Singapore bureau of Reuters news service. His writing has also appeared in the *New York Times* and the *International Herald Tribune*. "Hooters Translates in China" was published through the Cox syndicate in February 2006.

> **THINKING AHEAD**   What do you know about the Hooters restaurant chain? Have you ever been to a Hooters restaurant? What was your primary reason for choosing that restaurant? If you've never been, would you go if given an opportunity? Why?

Zhou Shouya is a textbook example of how a simple idea can appeal across cultures. 1

Dressed in a tight tank top and hip-hugging orange shorts—the uniform worn by Hooters Girls around the world—the twenty-three-year-old law student paused from delivering sandwiches and plates of buffalo wings at China's first Hooters franchise to say that many of her customers are regulars. 2

"Some people come every day. It's like a home to them," she said. "I guess they feel relaxed here." 3

That's one way to explain the Shanghai restaurant's success. Since opening in October 2004, "business has been consistently profitable," marketing director Xu Fan said, adding that between 250 and 300 customers visit daily. 4

The owners paid Atlanta-based Hooters of America an undisclosed amount of money to franchise the brand and expect to open a second Shanghai location in April. Plans are in the works to open one or two Beijing branches by the end of the year. 5

"We think there's a good growth potential in China," Xu said. 6

If Hooters does develop from its small beginnings behind a Shanghai mall into a Chinese food and beverage force, it would take a page from the company's U.S. history. 7

"Hooters was appropriately incorporated on April Fool's Day, 1983, when six businessmen with absolutely no previous restaurant experience got together and decided to open a place they couldn't get kicked out of," a Web site set up by the original founders said. 8

314

The owners—a painting contractor, a liquor salesman, a retired ser-   9
vice station proprietor, a real estate executive, a mason and the co-manager
of a painting business—"found a little dive in Clearwater," Florida, and
devised a "creative menu" that "combined nicely with the most important
element, the beautiful and vivacious Hooters Girls," the site said.

The founders soon found partners that helped the company grow far   10
beyond that original restaurant. It now has more than four hundred restaurants including thirty-six foreign franchises in cities such as Lima, Peru;
Interlaken, Switzerland; and Singapore.

"It's a pretty steep learning curve to take an all-American concept like   11
Hooters and take it international," Hooters of America marketing vice
president Mike McNeil said. "But we see the future as very, very bright
internationally."

Shanghai marketing director Xu agreed.   12

While most of the customers at the Shanghai franchise are Westerners,   13
increasing numbers of Chinese are patronizing the eatery.

"Hooters isn't just a restaurant," she said. "It's also American culture,   14
and that appeals to many Chinese."

Chinese acceptance of the brand owes as much to a loosening of Chi-   15
nese views on sexuality over the past decades as it does to the market savvy
of the "Hooters Six."

During the Cultural Revolution[1] in the 1960s and '70s, Chinese women   16
who wore revealing clothing or grew their hair long were often punished
for failing to uphold the socialist[2] state's image of a model worker. Even in
the 1990s, shorts and miniskirts were rarely worn in many parts of China.

"The younger generation is very different from our parents," Xu said.   17
"There has been a big change in Chinese values."

While the use of female sexuality as a marketing tool has provoked   18
anger among some Americans, McNeil said, Chinese businesses routinely
hire attractive young women to sell products. Many Chinese companies
require applicants to submit recent photographs when applying for jobs.

"It's natural for employers to hire good-looking people to deal with   19
the public," Xu said, adding that the Shanghai franchise had never received
a complaint about the waitresses' uniforms.

"Hooters is a very fun and clean environment," Xu said. "Hooters Girls   20
are like cheerleaders."

Zhou, who uses the English name Lucky and was named "China Hoot-   21
ers Girl of the Year" last year, actually is a cheerleader. Besides studying at
Shanghai's Fudan University and working twenty hours a week at Hooters,
she cheers for the Shanghai Sharks, the basketball team that Houston
Rockets center Yao Ming once played for.

---

[1] **Cultural Revolution:** Attempt by Chairman Mao Zedong to reassert his influence on China's
people.
[2] **socialist:** Advocating community or government ownership of means of production and
all goods.

Zhou likes the job because she can improve her English, make new 22 friends, and earn several hundred dollars a month.

"And working at Hooters has taught me a lot about American cul- 23 ture," she said, before delivering another plate of buffalo wings.

EXERCISING VOCABULARY

1. Record your own definition for each of these words.

franchise (n.) (2)
consistently (adv.) (4)
undisclosed (adj.) (5)
proprietor (n.) (9)
mason (n.) (9)

vivacious (adj.) (9)
patronizing (v.) (13)
uphold (v.) (16)
provoked (v.) (18)

2. Simons opens his essay with this statement: "Zhou Shouya is a textbook example of how a simple idea can appeal across cultures." You know what a textbook is. How can a person serve as a textbook example? What qualities would such a person have?

3. According to Simons, the success of Hooters didn't depend solely on "the market savvy" of the men who started Hooters (para. 15). What does the noun *savvy* mean? Which market is being referred to here? What is "market savvy"?

PROBING CONTENT

1. When and how was the Hooters restaurant chain created? What is significant about the date?

2. Who are the "Hooters Six"? Why are they unlikely restaurant owners?

3. Why does visiting Hooters appeal to many Chinese? What attitudes in China had to shift for Hooters to be successful there?

4. Describe Zhou Shouya. Why does she work at Hooters? How suited is Zhou to her job?

CONSIDERING CRAFT

1. Why does Simons select this title for his essay? In what sense is the word *translates* a play on words?

2. What does Simons accomplish by focusing on just one Hooters server instead of interviewing several? Why does he select Zhou Shouya? To what extent is his strategy successful?

3. Simons writes, "If Hooters does develop from its small beginnings behind a Shanghai mall into a Chinese food and beverage force, it would

take a page from the company's U.S. history" (para. 7). Explain the figure of speech Simons uses here and comment on its effectiveness.

WRITING PROMPTS

Responding to the Topic Mike McNeil, marketing vice president for Hooters of America, argues that "it's a pretty steep learning curve to take an all-American concept like Hooters and take it international" (para. 11). Which other "all-American" concepts have been successful internationally? Write an essay in which you review another American business that has been successful internationally. Describe what you believe accounts for its success.

Responding to the Writer Xu Fan, Shanghai marketing director of Hooters, notes that "Hooters isn't just a restaurant. It's also American culture, and that appeals to many Chinese" (para. 14). Zhou Shouya feels that working at Hooters "has taught [her] a lot about American culture" (para. 23). To what extent does Hooters represent American culture? Write an essay in which you take a position on this question and support it with evidence from this essay and from other sources that you incorporate.

Responding to Multiple Viewpoints Compare the obstacles faced by companies mentioned in Tara Parker-Pope's essay "Custom-Made" (p. 117) in Chapter 4 with those faced by Hooters in its bid for widespread acceptance in China.

For a quiz on this reading, go to bedfordstmartins.com/mirror.

Wrapping Up Chapter 7

Focusing on Yesterday, Focusing on Today

Both the neon signs and the advertisements are designed to lure travelers to a particular hotel, but what is required to attract the weary visitor has certainly changed. Driving by the Thunderbird Motel on Route 66 in the 1950s, motorists saw that this establishment offered "Clean Comfort," "Queen Size Beds," and even "Pizza." Those charms may have been sufficient to have the on-the-road salesman or the off-to-see-grandma family turn in for the night. Most travelers from this era saw the motel as a stopover; one or two nights, and they were gone again.

Today's road warrior is much more demanding, and many more hotel chains are vying for his or her attention. The complete kitchen and full bags of

Queen-Sized Beds and Pizza!

groceries in the Residence Inn ad suggest a long stay. Today's hotel room needs to function not as a quick stopover but as a "home away from home," even for short-stay visitors.

- What message is conveyed by the Thunderbird's logo and signage? What message about Residence Inn does this Marriott ad convey?
- Describe the characteristics of the target clientele for each of these hotels.
- Why have the expectations for the services a hotel provides changed so much over the last several decades?

Residence Inn
Inn®
Marriott

Residence Inn, Suitcases and Grocery Sacks

CONNECTING TO THE CULTURE

1. Locate at least five different ads that try to sell products or fashions by using the same hook. Consider sex, celebrities, unusual art, shock value, children, or animals as possible hooks. Analyze each ad and explain how the same advertising angle is used differently to sell each product or brand. Explore the real message each ad sends to consumers. Review Chapter 2, "Deconstructing Media: Analyzing an Image," to help you organize your essay.

2. Choose one group of people (for example, Latinos, the elderly, teenagers, women, parents, gays, or African Americans) and develop a hypothesis about how they are portrayed in advertising. Then go to magazines, television, or the Internet to locate ads featuring that group. If the evidence you find supports your hypothesis, you have a thesis. If the evidence contradicts your hypothesis, develop a new thesis based on the evidence. Write an essay using specific examples to fully support your thesis.

3. Watch a movie or several television shows and make notes about all the product and fashion brands that are featured or mentioned. Are these brands essential to the plot or to character development? Why are they used? What message does their use convey to viewers?

4. Invent a product or a fashion brand and create an advertising campaign for it. Include details such as who the target audience will be, how the print and Web ads will look, where the print ads will be placed, how a short script for a television ad will read, who will star in the commercials, and what background music will play in the ads.

5. Think about what kind of fashion consumer you are. What do you spend your money on and why? Do you feel pressured to buy — or to avoid — certain brands? Write an essay in which you examine your consumer habits and what they say about you and the culture in which you live.

Analyzing the Image

 Produced in 1983, Michael Jackson's *Thriller* still holds the record for the most iconic music video of all time, and proof is everywhere today. This publicity photo features the King of Pop wearing a shiny red jacket that sold for an astounding $1.8 million in 2011. The fourteen-minute video, directed by John Landis, was inducted into the National Film Registry of the Library of Congress in 2009, the first music video to be so honored. And Michael Jackson's celebrity lives on beyond his untimely death at the age of fifty that same year. Fans still play his music, watch his videos, and imitate his style and dance moves. Many YouTube videos feature bridal parties performing their own renditions of *Thriller* for their delighted guests. Millions of fans were glued to their television screens for the 2011 post–Super Bowl *Glee* episode. It featured a halftime show in which cheerleaders, jocks, and geeks dressed as zombies sang and danced to a rousing mash-up of the Yeah Yeah Yeahs's "Heads Will Roll" and Jackson's immortal song.

- Describe what you see in this visual. Note the body positions and clothing of the performers.

- Where is Michael Jackson positioned in relation to the other zombies? Why?

- In the original photograph, Jackson is wearing a red jacket while the other zombies are wearing black and white. Why?

- Describe the facial expressions of the performers in this visual. How do their expressions affect your viewing experience?

- In what ways does this image recall different kinds of media and the onscreen experience? Think about times you have seen zombies or Michael Jackson onscreen. How did you react?

Research this topic with TopLinks at bedfordstmartins.com/toplinks.

GEARING UP   If you could assume the life of any character in a film, television show, or video, whose life would you choose? What would be the advantages and disadvantages of being this character?

COLLABORATING   In groups of three or four, discuss your routine on-screen experiences. How much time do you spend in front of a screen on a daily basis? How do you spend that time? Watching television? Videos? Films? Real-time chatting?

Think about the ways in which you watch material on-screen. What do you watch? How much of it is on a television set, on a computer, in a movie theater, or on a smartphone? How do these different kinds of screens affect your viewing experience? Which do you prefer? Why?

How has technology impacted the way in which we view videos? Have the changes been primarily positive or negative?

Why We Crave Horror Movies

STEPHEN KING

An old English prayer — "From ghoulies and ghosties, long-leggedy beasties, and things that go bump in the night, Lord God protect us" — suggests that people have worried about "things that go bump in the night" for a long time. If ghouls and ghosts frighten us so, why do so many of us love scary movies? The famous author of this essay provides us with the answer to this question. Horror master Stephen King needs no introduction to either readers or film buffs around the world. He is the creator of such frightening tales as *Carrie* (1973), *The Shining* (1977), *Misery* (1987), *The Eyes of the Dragon* (1987), *Bag of Bones* (1998), *Hearts in Atlantis* (1999), and *Riding the Bullet* (2000), an e-book available only on the Internet. King repopularized the serial novel with *The Green Mile*, published in six installments from March through August 1996. He has also authored many short stories and screenplays and has played cameo roles in several films based on his works. The king of horror's prolific writing career nearly came to an end in 1999, when he was struck by a van and critically injured while walking near his summer home in western Maine. The author chronicles this painful period of both his personal and professional life in *On Writing: A Memoir of the Craft* (2000). His most recent books are *Under the Dome* (2009) and *Full Dark, No Stars* (2010), a collection of five stories. "Why We Crave Horror Movies" is King's attempt to explain why we love it when he scares us to nightmares. The essay was first published in *Playboy* in December 1981.

> **THINKING AHEAD**   Do you like horror movies? Which ones terrify you? Why? If they frighten you, why do you watch them?
>
> **Paired Selection**   Read this selection and the one that follows for two approaches to a similar topic. Then answer the "Drawing Connections" questions on p. 333.

1 think that we're all mentally ill; those of us outside the asylums only hide it a little better — and maybe not all that much better, after all. We've all known people who talk to themselves, people who sometimes squinch their faces into horrible grimaces when they believe no one is watching, people who have some hysterical fear — of snakes, the dark, the tight place, the long drop . . . and, of course, those final worms and grubs that are waiting so patiently underground.

2 When we pay our four or five bucks and seat ourselves at tenth-row center in a theater showing a horror movie, we are daring the nightmare.

3 Why? Some of the reasons are simple and obvious. To show that we can, that we are not afraid, that we can ride this roller coaster. Which is not

to say that a really good horror movie may not surprise a scream out of us at some point, the way we may scream when the roller coaster twists through a complete 360 or plows through a lake at the bottom of the drop. And horror movies, like roller coasters, have always been the special province of the young; by the time one turns forty or fifty, one's appetite for double twists or 360-degree loops may be considerably depleted.

We also go to reestablish our feelings of essential normality; the horror movie is innately conservative, even reactionary. Freda Jackson as the horrible melting woman in *Die, Monster, Die!* confirms for us that no matter how far we may be removed from the beauty of a Robert Redford or a Diana Ross, we are still light-years from true ugliness.

And we go to have fun.

Ah, but this is where the ground starts to slope away, isn't it? Because this is a very peculiar sort of fun indeed. The fun comes from seeing others menaced — sometimes killed. One critic suggested that if pro football has become the voyeur's version of combat, then the horror film has become the modern version of the public lynching.

It is true that the mythic, "fairy-tale" horror film intends to take away the shades of gray. . . . It urges us to put away our more civilized and adult penchant for analysis and to become children again, seeing things in pure blacks and whites. It may be that horror movies provide psychic relief on this level because this invitation to lapse into simplicity, irrationality, and even outright madness is extended so rarely. We are told we may allow our emotions a free rein . . . or no rein at all.

If we are all insane, then sanity becomes a matter of degree. If your insanity leads you to carve up women like Jack the Ripper or the Cleveland Torso Murderer, we clap you away in the funny farm (but neither of those two amateur-night surgeons was ever caught, heh-heh-heh); if, on the other hand, your insanity leads you only to talk to yourself when you're under stress or to pick your nose on your morning bus, then you are left alone to go about your business . . . though it is doubtful that you will ever be invited to the best parties.

The potential lyncher is in almost all of us (excluding saints, past and present; but then, most saints have been crazy in their own ways), and every now and then, he has to be let loose to scream and roll around in the grass. Our emotions and our fears form their own body, and we recognize that it demands its own exercise to maintain proper muscle tone. Certain of these emotional muscles are accepted — even exalted — in civilized society; they are, of course, the emotions that tend to maintain the status quo of civilization itself. Love, friendship, loyalty, kindness — these are all the emotions that we applaud, emotions that have been immortalized in the couplets of Hallmark cards and in the verses (I don't dare call it poetry) of Leonard Nimoy.[1]

---

[1] **Leonard Nimoy:** An actor who played Commander Spock in television's original *Star Trek* series.

When we exhibit these emotions, society showers us with positive rein- 10
forcement; we learn this even before we get out of diapers. When, as children, we hug our rotten little puke of a sister and give her a kiss, all the
aunts and uncles smile and twit and cry, "Isn't he the sweetest little thing?"
Such coveted treats as chocolate-covered graham crackers often follow. But
if we deliberately slam the rotten little puke of a sister's fingers in the door,
sanctions follow—angry remonstrance from parents, aunts, and uncles—
instead of a chocolate-covered graham cracker, a spanking.

But anticivilization emotions don't go away, and they demand periodic 11
exercise. We have such "sick" jokes as "What's the difference between a
truckload of bowling balls and a truckload of dead babies?" (You can't un-
load the truckload of bowling balls with a pitchfork . . . a joke, by the way,
that I heard originally from a ten-year-old.) Such a joke may surprise a
laugh or a grin out of us even as we recoil, a possibility that confirms the
thesis: If we share a brotherhood of man, then we also share an insanity of
man. None of which is intended as a defense of either the sick joke or insanity but merely as an explanation of why the best horror films, like the
best fairy tales, manage to be reactionary, anarchistic, and revolutionary all
at the same time.

The mythic horror movie, like the sick joke, has a dirty job to do. It 12
deliberately appeals to all that is worst in us. It is morbidity unchained, our
most base instincts let free, our nastiest fantasies realized . . . and it all happens, fittingly enough in the dark. For those reasons, good liberals often
shy away from horror films. For myself, I like to see the most aggressive of
them—*Dawn of the Dead*, for instance—as lifting a trapdoor in the civilized forebrain and throwing a basket of raw meat to the hungry alligators
swimming around in that subterranean river beneath.

Why bother? Because it keeps them from getting out, man, it keeps them 13
down there and me up here. It was Lennon and McCartney who said that all
you need is love, and I would agree with that.

As long as you keep the gators fed. 14

EXERCISING VOCABULARY

1. Record your own definition for each of these words.

   grimaces (n.) (1)   status quo (n.) (9)
   depleted (v.) (3)   sanctions (n.) (10)
   innately (adv.) (4)   remonstrance (n.) (10)
   voyeur (n.) (6)   recoil (v.) (11)
   penchant (n.) (7)

2. At the end of paragraph 11, King asserts that really good horror movies
   "manage to be reactionary, anarchistic, and revolutionary all at the same
   time." Define these three adjectives. Usually these words have a political
   meaning and are used to refer to governments. Explain their meaning
   when King applies them to horror movies.

3. In paragraph 12, King describes the "mythic horror movie" as "morbidity unchained." Define *morbidity* and explain King's use of it here.

PROBING CONTENT

1. To what is King referring when he mentions "those final worms and grubs that are waiting so patiently underground" (para. 1)? How does this reference contribute to the main point of this essay? How does it establish the author's tone?

2. How is watching a horror movie "daring the nightmare" (para. 2)? Why, according to King, do we do this?

3. In what sense, according to the essay, do horror movies encourage us to think like children? Why might adults want an opportunity to think like children again?

4. Which emotions does King say "tend to maintain the status quo of civilization itself" (para. 9)? Why are these emotions so important to society?

5. What "dirty job" does King think horror movies perform for us? Why is it important that something assume this job?

6. What do "the hungry alligators" in paragraph 12 represent? How do horror movies feed these alligators?

CONSIDERING CRAFT

1. Does King literally "think that we're all mentally ill," as he says in paragraph 1? Why does he write this? What does such a statement add to King's essay?

2. Locate two single-sentence paragraphs in the essay. Describe the effect of these paragraphs. How does this effect aid the overall impact of each point? How does it aid the essay's main idea?

3. Some of the language and references deliberately chosen by King are not polite — "to pick your nose" (para. 8), "rotten little puke of a sister" (para. 10), and the joke about dead babies in paragraph 11. What do you expect audience reaction to these references to be? What is your own reaction? Why does King include these?

WRITING PROMPTS

Responding to the Topic   From your own experience, evaluate King's explanation of why we like horror movies. How accurate is it to assume that a dark side is lurking in each of us just beneath our civilized skins?

What difference does it make in your relationships with other people if you accept or reject this notion?

Responding to the Writer   Write an essay in which you agree or disagree with King's argument that horror films allow a safe release for what would otherwise be expressed as insane or even criminal behavior. You may extend your argument to include other forms of "dangerous" leisure-time activities, such as playing violent video or computer games, watching violent television shows or videos, reading violent novels, or listening to violent music.

Responding to Multiple Viewpoints   In "Tyler Perry's Money Machine" (p. 346), Eugene Robinson writes, "Nielsen calls African Americans a 'high-growth, high-potential audience.' African Americans are 'embracing and using the newest technologies at rates that exceed the national average,' including high-definition television and movies-on-demand, Nielsen reports" (para. 10). Based on the reading you have done in this chapter, write an essay in which you consider how a film director like Stephen King ("Why We Crave Horror Movies"), the director of a zombie film like George Romero ("Exploring the Undead: University of Baltimore to Offer English Class on Zombies," p. 329), or the television director of a "multimedia phenomenon" like *The Price Is Right* ("Here, There, and Everywhere," p. 370) might attract more African American audience members.

For a quiz on this reading, go to bedfordstmartins.com/mirror.

Exploring the Undead: University of Baltimore to Offer English Class on Zombies

DANIEL DE VISE

Daniel de Vise is a *Washington Post* staff member who writes mainly about higher education. A graduate of Wesleyan and Northwestern Universities, de Vise has worked as a journalist for over 20 years with various newspapers including *San Diego Union Tribune* and *Miami Herald.* His article "Exploring the Undead: University of Baltimore to Offer English Class on Zombies" appeared in the *Washington Post* on September 10, 2010, and chronicles the focus on zombies in pop culture.

THINKING AHEAD   What are zombies? Would you take a course to study them? Why or why not? What would you expect to learn in such a class? In what ways could such a course be beneficial in your general curriculum?

Paired Selection   Read this selection and the one before it for two approaches to a similar topic. Then answer the "Drawing Connections" questions on p. 333.

1   Is *Night of the Living Dead* a simple zombie film or a subtle antiwar statement? Precisely when did viral pandemic supplant nuclear radiation as the leading cause of zombification? And which sort of animated dead has the greater potential to frighten: Shambler[1] or sprinter?

2   Those questions and others will be laid to rest—and then grotesquely revivified—in a new course at the University of Baltimore called "Media Genres: Zombies."

3   Arnold Blumberg, a lifelong enthusiast of popular culture in general and zombie films in particular, is among the first university professors to devote a semester to study of the reawakened dead. His course, and recent offerings at Columbia College, Rice University and Georgia Tech, share a common interest in the zombie movie as an expression of the zeitgeist.[2]

4   Zombies have clawed their way to the center of pop culture over the past decade in several big-budget mainstream films.

5   There was *28 Days Later,* a 2002 British production that revived the genre with hip London zombies that were supremely athletic if not, strictly

[1] **shambler:** One who shambles or shuffles; one who walks slowly and awkwardly.
[2] **zeitgeist:** Spirit of the age.

speaking, dead. And *Dawn of the Dead,* a 2004 remake of a George A. Romero classic. And *Shaun of the Dead,* the definitive satire. And *Zombieland,* the slightly less-definitive satire.

And *Pride and Prejudice and Zombies,* the 2009 literary mash-up[3] that has intermittently outsold the Jane Austen original. And *The Walking Dead,* the comic awaiting rebirth as an AMC TV series. And annual zombie walks in fashionable urban centers.   6

"Right now we're in a massive surge of zombie entertainment," said Blumberg, whose University of Baltimore course is English 333, a number that is—numerologists, take note—exactly half of 666.   7

"On the most basic level, zombies are probably one of the most potent horror icons, one of the closest to us in terms of identification factor, in terms of reflecting ourselves," he said. "The zombie is, simply, us."   8

Blumberg is curator of Geppi's Entertainment Museum, a shrine to popular culture at Baltimore's Camden Yards. He has degrees from the University of Baltimore and the University of Maryland Baltimore County and co-wrote the book *Zombiemania,* a scholarly interest possibly surpassed only by his love for the venerable British science fiction series *Dr. Who.* He teaches a UMBC course on the comic book as literature.   9

Zombiemania examines 85 zombie movies "to die for." The zombie course covers a mere 16 "classic" titles, from the 1932 Bela Lugosi vehicle *White Zombie* through last year's *Zombieland,* the highest-grossing zombie film to date.   10

"We're looking at how the character of the zombie changes and evolves over the years and how it reflects our culture," Blumberg said.   11

Even before zombie films became self-aware and artsy, they betrayed the great societal fears of their times. Early zombies obeyed evil voodoo priests and seemed to channel the United States' unresolved issues with race. Nuclear waste spawned Cold War zombies. Romero's gore reminded 1960s viewers of the nightly televised carnage in Vietnam. Millennial zombies—not actually dead, but hungry and cranky because of viral mutation—mirror the post-September 11 obsession with pathogen.[3]   12

Blumberg pitched the course just as the university was rolling out a new minor in pop culture.   13

"We were trying to think of some interesting course to kick it off with," said Jonathan Shorr, director of the School of Communications Design. "And 20 minutes later, Arnold wrote to me and said, 'Are you interested in a zombie course?'"   14

The class has 45 spaces and is nearly full, with a fairly even distribution of men and women, zombie buffs and neophytes.[4]   15

"It's not about zombies. It's about how ideas in society express themselves," said Matthew Williams, 35, a junior who is taking the course toward a bachelor's degree in corporate communications.   16

---

[3] **mash-up:** Combination.
[4] **pathogen:** Any disease-producing agent, especially a virus or bacterium.
[5] **neophytes:** People who are new to and thus unfamiliar with a subject or situation.

Collegiate zombie study is not without precedent. Brendan Riley, an 17
English professor at Columbia College in Chicago, introduced a course called
"Zombies in Popular Media" in 2007, a bit earlier in the national zombie
revival. He thinks his was the first all-zombie course. It is a perennial entry
on lists of oddest college classes.

"It was kind of a fight to get it as a recognized course at the school," 18
Riley said. "Because at first, it appears to be kind of a frivolous topic."

Students have responded with stirring interdisciplinary projects. One 19
music major, Riley said, "rewrote the libretto for *Oklahoma!* to be all about
zombies."

Steven Schlozman, a Harvard Medical School professor who has writ- 20
ten, only half-jokingly, on the neurophysiology[4] of zombies, regards the
awakened dead as perhaps the only cinematic monsters truly deserving of
their own collegiate course—the zombie as a sort of horror-movie everyman,
ill-defined and unpredictable. Werewolves and vampires seem positively one-
dimensional by comparison.

"There's this kind of raging debate about what are the more appropriate 21
zombies to discuss, the slow-moving zombies, as in *Night of the Living Dead,*
or the fast-moving zombies, as in *28 Days Later* or *I Am Legend,*" Schlozman said. "How do you define consciousness? How do you define human?
There's whole philosophy classes on it."

EXERCISING VOCABULARY

1. Record your own definition for each of these words.

   pandemic (n.) (1)
   supplant (v.) (1)
   revivified (v.) (2)
   genre (n.) (5)
   definitive (adj.) (5)
   intermittently (adv.) (6)
   potent (adj.) (8)
   curator (n.) (9)
   surpassed (v.) (9)
   venerable (adj.) (9)

   evolves (v.) (11)
   channel (v.) (12)
   spawned (v.) (12)
   carnage (n.) (12)
   millennial (adj.) (12)
   perennial (adj.) (17)
   frivolous (adj.) (18)
   libretto (n.) (19)
   raging (adj.) (21)

2. In paragraph 7, de Vise points out that numerologists will be interested
   in the course number of Blumberg's zombie course. What does a nu-
   merologist study? What is the significance of the course number 333?

3. The writer calls Geppi's Entertainment Museum a "shrine to popular
   culture" (para. 9). What is a shrine? Why do people establish shrines?
   How can a museum be a shrine?

[4] **neurophysiology:** The study of the functions of the nervous system.

4. De Vise writes that Professor Brendan Riley notes that students have responded to his course with "stirring interdisciplinary projects" (para. 19). What does the word *interdisciplinary* mean? What would characterize an interdisciplinary course project?

5. Paraphrasing Steven Schlozman, the writer refers to a zombie as a "horror-movie everyman" (para. 20). What are the characteristics of an everyman? How then can a zombie be considered an everyman?

PROBING CONTENT

1. Why is Professor Blumberg teaching a course on zombies? What is his rationale for such a course?

2. How have zombie films mirrored society's fears? Give three specific examples.

3. Who claims to have taught the first course on zombies? How did people react to his course?

4. Who is Steven Schlozman? What does he think about zombies?

CONSIDERING CRAFT

1. The author begins his essay with three questions. How effective is this strategy? Why?

2. In paragraph 2, the author states, "Those questions and others will be laid to rest — and then grotesquely revivified." How does personification function in this sentence? How do the phrases "laid to rest" and "grotesquely revivified" relate to zombies? Why are these phrases particularly appropriate in this context?

3. Much of this essay is devoted to quotations from Arnold Blumberg, Brendan Riley, and Steven Schlozman. Why does the author focus on the comments of these three men? How do their comments support the essay's purpose?

WRITING PROMPTS

Responding to the Topic   Pick a popular culture horror icon like zombies, vampires, or werewolves. Design a course focusing on this icon. Write a syllabus in which you include the goals of the course and the required texts, including both books and movies. Also describe specific assignments like journals, essays, and presentations.

Responding to the Writer   Write an essay arguing for or against the retention of Professor Blumberg's course "Media Genres: Zombies" in the curriculum. Make sure that your argument is clearly articulated and persuasive. Include as many examples as possible.

Responding to Multiple Viewpoints   In paragraph 8, de Vise quotes Arnold Blumberg: "On the most basic level, zombies are probably one of the most potent horror icons, one of the closest to us in terms of identification factor, in terms of reflecting ourselves. The zombie is, simply, us." Drawing from other essays in this chapter, compose an essay in which you argue that other icons of film, television, or videos provide reflections of ourselves and our culture. Make sure to provide specific examples and supporting evidence to convince your audience.

For a quiz on this reading, go to bedfordstmartins.com/mirror.

DRAWING CONNECTIONS: PAIRED SELECTIONS

1. In "Why We Crave Horror Movies (p. 324)," Stephen King writes, "I like to see the most aggressive of them [horror films] — *Dawn of the Dead,* for instance — as lifting a trapdoor in the civilized forebrain and throwing a basket of raw meat to the hungry alligators swimming around in that subterranean river beneath" (para. 12). How would Arnold Blumberg, Brendan Riley, and Steven Schlozman, all quoted in "Exploring the Undead," respond to King? Provide textual evidence to support your position.

2. According to Stephen King ("Why We Crave Horror Movies"), "It is true that the mythic, 'fairy-tale' horror film intends to take away the shades of gray. . . . It urges us to put away our more civilized and adult penchant for analysis and to become children again, seeing things in pure blacks and whites" (para. 7). Write an essay in which you answer the following question: Would Professor Blumberg agree with King's statement? Why or why not?

Fade In, Fade Out: Addiction, Recovery, in American Film

STEFAN HALL

Stefan Hall is an assistant professor of communication and media studies at Defiance College and a former arts and entertainment columnist for *Phi Kappa Phi Journal,* in which the following essay first appeared in the 2010 summer issue. He is also a PhD candidate in the Critical Studies in Film, Media, and Culture track within the American Culture Studies program at Bowling Green State University. His dissertation, " 'You've Seen the Movie, Now Play the Game': Recoding the Cinematic in Digital Media and Virtual Culture," looks at how digital media has established and affected the relationship between film and video games.

> **THINKING AHEAD** Think of the three most memorable films you have seen in which drug use figures prominently. What were the messages of these films? What about each of these films made an impression on you?

C inematic depictions of addiction have been a feature of American movies since their beginning. From early silent films to recent blockbusters, treatment shifts to reflect societal values at the time of their release. An addict in American movies has moved from foreign invader to social problem to hedonistic[1] goof to average citizen. 1

Practically from the moment of its inception in 1891, cinema served witness to the perils of drugs. In 1894, W. K. L. Dickson, who worked for Thomas Edison's motion picture camera company, made *Chinese Opium Den* for the penny arcades. All that remains of the film is a single still, yet its viewpoint compelled Billy Bitzer to revisit the topic in *Rube in an Opium Joint* in 1905. As Ian Christie observes in *The Last Machine: Early Cinema and the Birth of the Modern World* (1994), it illustrates a theme in early American cinema: a stereotypic country bumpkin[2] threatened, often comically, sometimes maniacally, by an urban menace, in this case, opium. Like *A Chinese Opium Joint* (1898) and *Fun in an Opium Joint* (1903), it outlined what had become a dangerous tourist trap staffed by exotic Asians who were regarded by many as a "yellow plague." 2

Productions about cocaine and morphine arose as American drugs of choice shifted in the early 20th century. *For His Son* (1912), directed by 3

---

[1] **hedonistic:** Vain; egotistical.
[2] **country bumpkin:** A naïve person who is easily taken advantage of.

legendary D. W. Griffith, was one of the first, writes Maurizio Viano in "An Intoxicated Screen: Reflections on Film and Drugs," from the 2002 collection of essays, *High Anxieties: Cultural Studies in Addiction*. The movie was loosely based on the issues surrounding Coca-Cola after passage of the 1906 Pure Food and Drug Act that, among other stipulations, required drugs—including alcohol, cocaine, heroin, morphine, and cannabis[3]—be labeled with contents and dosages in order to continue to be legally sold. In the silent film, a physician develops Dopokoke, a cocaine-infused drink, to raise money for his shiftless son. The drink is a hit, but the son becomes addicted to it and loses his fiancée while wasting away. Interestingly, Coca-Cola was involved in legal proceedings not only because of cocaine in the product but also because of the amount of caffeine.

The Harrison Narcotics Tax Act of 1914—regulating and taxing the   4
production, importation, and distribution of opiates and cocaine—resulted in a spike of anti-drug films. (These drugs had been mostly unregulated and readily available to consumers, even through venerable American institutions like the Sears, Roebuck catalog.) *Narcotic Spectre* (1914), *The Drug Traffic* (1914), and *Cocaine Traffic* (1914), plus other "socially conscious dramas," addressed the problem, Kevin Brownlow notes in *Behind the Mask of Innocence: Sex, Violence, Crime: Films of Social Conscience in the Silent Era* (1992). For instance, in *The Secret Sin* (1915), Blanche Sweet plays twin sisters who become addicted to opium and morphine, doubling the horror—twice, or even four times. And *The Devil's Needle* (1916) follows an up-and-coming young artist whose travails[4] with a socialite drive him to cocaine addiction and recovery.

Not all films sounded the alarm. *The Mystery of the Leaping Fish* (1916),   5
a bizarre comedy written by eccentric Tod Browning, starred Douglas Fairbanks, Sr., as a detective who, like Sherlock Holmes, relies on drugs to solve crime. Coke Ennyday, as he's called, gleefully uses just about any that come his way.

The occasional light treatment would virtually disappear with the Mo-   6
tion Picture Production Code in 1930. Fearful of federal regulation in the wake of the manslaughter trial of star comedian Roscoe "Fatty" Arbuckle; the murder of prolific director William Desmond Taylor; and the drug-related deaths of popular actors Wallace Reid and Alma Rubens, plus performers Olive Thomas, Barbara La Marr, and Jeanne Eagels, the Motion Picture Producers and Distributors Association adopted this censorious Code of acceptable and unacceptable content for U.S. movies. The Code upheld moral standards and opposed crime, wrongdoing, evil, or sin. Moviemakers dutifully followed the rules.

---

[3] **cannabis:** Any of the various parts of the plant from which hashish, marijuana, and similar hallucinogenic drugs are made.
[4] **travails:** Painfully difficult exertion.

They partly focused on marijuana, which had been left out of the Harrison Act. Exploitation films[5] tried to scare audiences straight, particularly susceptible teens. For instance, in *Reefer Madness* (1936), high school students light up (and listen to jazz music), then spiral into a hit-and-run accident, manslaughter, suicide, rape, and insanity. *Assassin of Youth* (1937) largely concerns a young woman up for an inheritance tied to a morals clause and greedy relatives scheming to use marijuana to discredit her.   7

Such exaggerated cautionary tales also anticipated or reflected the Marihuana Tax Act of 1937, which criminalized cannabis and, in the process, legitimized the slang word. The poster for *Marihuana: Weed with Roots in Hell* (1936)—about a youth who, after trying marijuana at a beach party, becomes pregnant and eventually turns to drug pushing—shows intravenous drug use with vials labeled "lust," "crime," and "sorrow," among others, while larger font advertises "Weird Orgies," "Wild Parties," and "Unleashed Passions!" This propaganda echoes earlier productions that attacked opiates, particularly in the intent to scare off usage in the first place, but overblown depictions remove many from serious consideration.   8

Other films during the Code era tackled addictions more thoughtfully, as Michael Stark documents in *Cocaine Fiends and Reefer Madness: An Illustrated History of Drugs in the Movies* (1982). For example, *The Man with the Golden Arm,* (1955), directed by Otto Preminger, showcased Frank Sinatra as a heroin addict and wannabe drummer who gets clean in prison but struggles after release with renewed drug use and a gambling problem. Reviewers hailed Sinatra's nuanced characterization. *Monkey on My Back* (1957) was a fact-based biopic about World War II veteran and professional boxer Barney Ross and his addiction to morphine. A tag line declared, "[SHOCK by SHOCK] it jabs like a hopped-up needle!" As noted in Norman Denzin's 1991 *Hollywood Shot by Shot: Alcoholism in American Cinema,* the hazards of alcoholism were epitomized in the melodramas *The Lost Weekend* (1945), which trailed a struggling writer, recently sober, on his devastating bender—and earned Academy Awards for best picture, actor (Ray Milland), director (Billy Wilder) and screenplay—and director Blake Edwards' *Days of Wine and Roses* (1962), about a boozy adman (played by Jack Lemmon) who introduces a secretary and his future wife (Lee Remick) to drinking, causing the dissolution of their marriage.   9

The film rating system replaces the strict Code in 1968, partly because of challenges to the Code (including from *The Man with the Golden Arm*), increasing competition from more open-minded foreign films, and changing social attitudes via the counterculture. One result: slapstick comedies poked fun of pot and considered it less a criminal activity, more a "harmless" diversion, and sometimes a mandatory rite for the in-crowd.   10

The satiric writing/performing duo Cheech (Marin) and (Tommy) Chong topped this marquee. Their first film, *Up in Smoke* (1978), established the template: marijuana-fueled high jinks from appealing doofuses, in this   11

---

[5] **exploitation films:** Films that exploit or use disturbing subject matter, often to deliver a strong message to their audience.

case, stoners smuggling a van, made almost entirely from marijuana, from Mexico to Los Angeles, while being pursued by inept law enforcement.

Cheech and Chong influenced many films, for instance, writer/director Richard Linklater's *Dazed and Confused* (1993), in which small-town Texas high schoolers look to get wasted (or drunk) on graduation day in 1976; the cameo-filled *Half Baked* (1998), in which dumb stoner roommates raise bail money for their luckless jailed friend by selling pot stolen from a research lab; and *Harold & Kumar Go to White Castle* (2004) and its sequel *Harold & Kumar Escape from Guantanamo Bay* (2008), the first about how the nerdy-cool little characters (the former an investment banker and the latter a would-be medical student) get the munchies one Friday night after inhaling, the second about how they are incarcerated when mistaken for terrorists but eventually share a joint with President George W. Bush.

The repeal of the Code also augured[6] a mindful, worldly understanding of addictions that gained momentum in the late 1980s with the major releases *Barfly* (1987), *Clean and Sober* (1988), and *Drugstore Cowboy* (1989) and became a main theme in the 1990s with *Jacob's Ladder* (1990), *Naked Lunch* (1991), *Bad Lieutenant* (1992), *Pulp Fiction* (1994), *Drunks* (1995), *Permanent Midnight* (1998), and *Fear and Loathing in Las Vegas* (1998). The flush[7] economy made drugs affordable and the fin de siècle[8] made Americans question themselves; thus, cinematic depictions of addiction and recovery were frank, creative, or otherwise intense.

For instance, in *Rush* (1991), a rookie cop (played by Jennifer Jason Leigh) and undercover veteran (Jason Patric) fall in love with each other and their stash while infiltrating a drug ring. And director Danny Boyle's *Trainspotting* (1996) dissects the disturbing charisma of young heroin addicts in impoverished Edinburgh. Plus, the sense of loss permeating performances—such as Nicolas Cage's Academy Award for *Leaving Las Vegas* (1995) as a broke Hollywood writer determined to drink himself to death—partly reflected angst[9] at the loss of the century. It also symbolized an American promise that had not been realized, as in director Darren Aronofsky's *Requiem for a Dream* (2000). Based on the novel of the same name by Hubert Selby, Jr., who co-wrote the script with Aronofsky, it starkly examines four interconnected addicts whose fixations span not only drugs but also food; fame; and red, white and blue values.

What are the coming attractions for the 21st century regarding addiction in American film? In this age of media saturation, maybe the most pervasive narcotic of all is information. From watching YouTube clips on cell phones to hunching in front of solitary monitors in cubicles, our collective screens form contemporary nickelodeons[10] only a click away. What of ourselves is reflected there?

12

13

14

15

---

[6] **augured:** Predicted; forecast.
[7] **flush:** Wealthy.
[8] **fin de siècle:** French for "end of the century."
[9] **angst:** Anxiety; concern.
[10] **nickelodeons:** Early storefront theaters that charged a nickel admission.

EXERCISING VOCABULARY

1. Record your own definition for each of these words.

   depictions (n.) (1)   cautionary (adj.) (8)
   inception (n.) (2)   hailed (v.) (9)
   maniacally (adv.) (2)   nuanced (adj.((9)
   stipulations (n.) (3)   epitomized (v.) (9)
   shiftless (adj.) (3)   dissolution (n.) (9)
   spike (n.) (4)   mandatory (adj.) (10)
   venerable (adj.) (4)   template (n.) (11)
   eccentric (adj.) (5)   incarcerated (v.) (12)
   gleefully (adv.) (5)   charisma (n.) (14)
   prolific (adj.) (6)   impoverished (adj.) (14)
   censorious (adj.) (6)   permeating (v.) (14)
   susceptible (adj.) (7)   pervasive (adj.) (15)
   discredit (v.) (7)

2. In paragraph 2, the author writes that all that remains of the film *Chinese Opium Den* is a "single still." What does it mean to be still? What is a "movie still"? Since the word *movie* is short for *moving picture,* how could the term "movie still" be considered an oxymoron?

3. In his essay Stefan Hall states, "In this age of media *saturation,* maybe the most pervasive narcotic of all is information" (para. 15). Describe the process of saturation. What do we usually think of when we hear the word *saturation?* What then is media saturation?

4. In paragraph 9, the author describes the film *Monkey on My Back* as a biopic. Break down the word *biopic* into its two parts. For what two words are "bio" and "pic" shortened forms? What then is a biopic? Give two examples of biopics with which you are familiar.

PROBING CONTENT

1. How long have American films featured the theme of drug addiction? What did the Harrison Narcotics Tax Act of 1914 regulate? How did this act affect films that featured addiction?

2. What did the 1930 Production Code monitor? How did the Production Code affect drug use onscreen?

3. How did the repeal of the Production Code affect the depiction of drug use in movies? What part did Cheech and Chong play in films after this repeal?

4. In the late 1980s and the 1990s, how did films present addiction? Give some examples of specific films. Discuss how each portrays addiction.

CONSIDERING CRAFT

1. Reread the title of the essay. What is the double meaning of "Fade In, Fade Out" given the subject of the essay? How does the title reflect the essay's content?

2. Hall uses several examples of specialized film language, or jargon, with which you may be unfamiliar, like "biopic" (para. 9). Find three examples of such specialized language. How does their inclusion affect your reading?

3. The author does not include films from the first decade of the twenty-first century even though his essay dates from summer 2010. Why do you think he decided to stop his discussion at 2000? Did this create a problem for you as a reader? Why or why not?

4. How did the writer's inclusion and description of so many films affect your reading? Did he include too many films or too many plot points? Defend your answer.

WRITING PROMPTS

Responding to the Topic   Write an essay in which you continue Hall's history of addiction and recovery in the movies. Begin your essay at the turn of the twenty-first century, the point in time when the author concludes. Give examples of films that deal with drug use in your paper. Aim for an interesting variety of films from various genres such as dramas, comedies, and documentaries.

Responding to the Writer   In paragraph 15, the author writes, "From watching YouTube clips on cell phones to hunching in front of solitary monitors in cubicles, our collective screens form contemporary nickelodeons only a click away. What of ourselves is reflected there?" In an essay, answer the question posed here.

Responding to Multiple Viewpoints   In the final paragraph of "Fade In, Fade Out: Addiction, Recovery, in American Film," Hall writes, "In this age of media saturation, maybe the most pervasive narcotic of all is information." How might the author of "Here, There, and Everywhere" (p. 370) react to this statement? Using examples and quotations from this essay, write a paper in which you describe the ways in which your chosen author(s) would agree or disagree with Hall's pronouncement.

For a quiz on this reading, go to bedfordstmartins.com/mirror.

Bollywood Princess, Hollywood Hopeful: Aishwarya's Quest for Global Stardom

ANUPAMA CHOPRA

Anupama Chopra is a book and film critic for *India Today*, India's largest English-language magazine, and for NDTV, New Delhi Television Limited. In 2007, she published *King of Bollywood: Shah Rukh Khan and the Seductive World of Indian Cinema.* "Bollywood Princess, Hollywood Hopeful" was published in the *New York Times* in 2008. In it, the author examines what it takes for an actor in India's Bollywood film industry to make the leap to international stardom in Hollywood.

> **THINKING AHEAD** Think about any foreign films that you have seen. Where were the films made? What was your reaction to these films and to the actors in them?

Last October Aishwarya Bachchan grappled with a tough choice. The 1 Bollywood star could either stay in Los Angeles to pursue a lead role in Will Smith's new film, *Seven Pounds,* or she could return home to Mumbai to celebrate Karva Chauth, a daylong ceremonial fast that some married Hindu women observe as a prayer for their husband's health and long life. (The observance is a new one for Ms. Bachchan; in April she married Abhishek Bachchan, an actor and the son of the Indian film star Amitabh Bachchan, a union that prompted *Time* magazine to describe the three as "Bollywood's Father, Son and Holy Babe.")

Ultimately Ms. Bachchan chose to return to Mumbai and starve with a 2 smile. National television channels covered her first Karva Chauth as headline news. Two months later she shrugged off her loss in an interview. "You do what you have to do," she said. "Feeling torn and thereby unhappy, confused or guilty is not something I want to feel. So you make your choices and go with it. You get some and some you don't."

This month Ms. Bachchan brings some of that clarity and traditional- 3 ism to a role she was born to play: that of Queen Jodhaa in the sumptuous-looking historical drama *Jodhaa Akbar.* The $10 million film is one of Bollywood's biggest productions this year. It will be released worldwide on Friday, in more than 115 theaters in the United States alone, making it the biggest American release ever for a Hindi[1] film.

[1] **Hindi:** The most widely spoken language in India, spoken mostly in the north; Hindi and English are the two official languages of India.

Jodhaa Akbar focuses on that quintessentially Indian subject: arranged   4
marriage. Set in the sixteenth century, it explores the marriage between the
great Mughal Emperor Akbar, a Muslim, and his Hindu wife Jodhaa.

Historians have described the union as a political alliance, but in the   5
hands of Ashutosh Gowariker, the film's director, the story has become "an
epic romance with its share of battles, harem politics and intrigue," he said
in a telephone interview. Mr. Gowariker, whose 2001 period film,[2] *Lagaan:
Once Upon a Time in India,* was nominated for an Oscar for best foreign
film, isn't claiming factual accuracy but insists that the film is "embedded
in historical truth."

He cast Ms. Bachchan as the queen (a figure some Indian historians   6
dispute ever existed) because, he said, "Aishwarya is a comic book princess with a certain dignity, elegance and sense of purity." For the role of
Akbar, Mr. Gowariker wanted someone with "the physique of a warrior
and the face of a romantic," and selected another Bollywood superstar,
Hrithik Roshan.

Mr. Gowariker described it as a dream cast, which, at least as far as box   7
office appeal goes, seems accurate. Both actors, to steal the phrase Pauline
Kael invented to describe Michelle Pfeiffer, are "paradisically beautiful,"
and are consummate superstars. With their ethnically indeterminate looks
and impeccable English, Ms. Bachchan and Mr. Roshan could be India's
first international movie stars.

Ms. Bachchan has already made considerable progress in that direc-   8
tion. She is the international face of L'Oréal[3] and Longines,[4] as well as a
consistently glamorous presence at the Cannes Film Festival; in 2003 she
became the first Bollywood actress to serve on the jury. In 2004 she made
Time magazine's list of the 100 most influential people in the world.

So far Ms. Bachchan's international projects — *Bride & Prejudice, The*   9
Mistress of Spices and *The Last Legion* — have sputtered commercially and
critically, but with her high-profile marriage, A-list brand endorsements
and plum Hindi film projects, she continues to generate global attention.

Mr. Smith, who wanted to cast her in *Hitch,* but couldn't, because of   10
scheduling conflicts, remains an ardent admirer. "She has this powerful
energy where she doesn't have to say anything; do anything; she can just
stand there," he said in a February 2006 interview with BBC News. "Anything she's making, I'll be there."

Next February Ms. Bachchan will be seen in *Pink Panther 2,* in which   11
Inspector Clouseau, played by Steve Martin, teams up with a squad of
international detectives to catch a thief with a penchant for historical
artifacts.

As it happens, her *Jodhaa Akbar* co-star, Mr. Roshan, thirty-three, re-   12
jected a role in the same film because it wasn't important enough.

---

[2] **period film:** A film set in a specific historical period.
[3] **L'Oréal:** Company that produces beauty products and perfumes.
[4] **Longines:** Swiss manufacturer of luxury watches.

In an interview in Mumbai, Mr. Roshan made it clear that while he is   13
"actively pursuing Hollywood" he would not "do a film just because it's
Hollywood."

Hollywood and Mr. Roshan have been flirting with each other since he   14
burst into Bollywood with a film called *Kaho Na Pyar Hai* (*Say You Love
Me*) in 2000. The film, directed and produced by his father, Rakesh Roshan,
was a blockbuster and catapulted the newcomer to superstar status in India.

In 2002 the American edition of *GQ* ran a profile headlined "The most   15
famous person you've never heard of," and rumors of a project with Tarsem
Singh, the Indian-born director of *The Cell,* and Jennifer Lopez swirled in
the Indian press. It didn't happen, nor did a series of other proposed projects that for various reasons Mr. Roshan declined. But last October he took
his first concrete step toward a Hollywood career by signing with Brillstein
Entertainment Partners in Los Angeles.

Despite their global stardom—Bollywood has an estimated annual   16
worldwide audience of 3.6 billion—Ms. Bachchan and Mr. Roshan will
not find it easy to break into Hollywood. The two film industries are forging closer ties (last year Sony Pictures Entertainment released its first Hindi
production, *Saawariya*), and a few Indian names like Mira Nair, Kal Penn
and Shekhar Kapur diversify the Hollywood landscape. Still, for a variety
of reasons, no actor has successfully made the transition from Bollywood
to Hollywood.

Schedules and expectations are difficult to match. Bollywood superstars   17
are generally unwilling to play supporting roles in American movies, and
there just aren't many movies coming out of Los Angeles that feature Indians as leads.

"You don't want to sacrifice your own kingdom to set up somewhere   18
else," Mr. Gowariker said. "But an international star can only be in the English
language."

If Ms. Bachchan and Mr. Roshan do cross over, they could be Holly-   19
wood's most old-fashioned stars. Until she married at thirty-three, Ms.
Bachchan (now thirty-four), lived with her parents, which both Oprah
Winfrey and David Letterman noted when she appeared on their shows in
2005. ("We don't need to take appointments with our parents to meet for
dinner," she replied cheekily to Mr. Letterman.) Now that she is married,
Ms. Bachchan lives with her husband at his parents' house in Mumbai.

As for Mr. Roshan, he is married to his childhood sweetheart. They are   20
expecting their second child this year, and they also continue to live with
the senior Roshans.

Unlike Ms. Bachchan, Mr. Roshan has yet to find a Hollywood film that   21
fits his taste and schedule. Currently he is "breaking the ice," which means
reading two scripts a week and giving feedback so that he and his Hollywood managers can "get to know each other."

He said he is hopeful that *Jodhaa Akbar* will be a first step in expand-   22
ing the traditional fan base, and UTV Motion Pictures, the co-producer

and worldwide distributor of the film, is pushing hard to make sure that it does. Theatrical trailers were released globally as early as September.

"Of course we are relying on South Asian viewers," said Siddharth Roy Kapur, the director of UTV, in a telephone interview. "But this is the perfect film for anyone who is curious about Bollywood. It has scale, stars, drama, song and dance."

EXERCISING VOCABULARY

1. Record your own definition for each of these words.

   grappled (v.) (1)

   sumptuous (adj.) (3)

   quintessentially (adv.) (4)

   epic (adj.) (5)

   harem (adj.) (5)

   consummate (adj.) (7)

   indeterminate (adj.) (7)

   impeccable (adj.) (7)

   plum (adj.) (9)

   penchant (n.) (11)

   artifacts (n.) (11)

   swirled (v.) (15)

   forging (v.) (16)

   cheekily (adv.) (19)

   scale (n.) (23)

2. Chopra writes, "So far Ms. Bachchan's international projects — *Bride & Prejudice*, *The Mistress of Spices* and *The Last Legion* — have sputtered commercially and critically . . ." (para. 9). What does it mean when we say something "sputtered" in a literal sense? What kinds of things sputter? What does Chopra's figurative use of the term *sputter* reveal here about Bachchan's films?

3. In paragraph 22, Chopra writes that "theatrical trailers were released globally." What are theatrical trailers? To what are they attached? In what other contexts is the word *trailers* used? What do these other trailers and film *trailers* have in common?

4. Hrithik Roshan's film *Kaho Na Pyar Hai* "catapulted the newcomer to superstar status" (para. 14). What is a catapult? What does Chopra's use of this verb indicate about the actor?

PROBING CONTENT

1. Why did Aishwarya Bachchan turn down a role in Will Smith's new film? What did she do instead?

2. What role is Aishwarya Bachchan playing in the film *Jodhaa Akbar*? Does the author believe that this is a fitting role for the actor? Why?

3. Who may be the next two international film stars from India, according to Chopra? Why?

4. According to the writer, what is the current relationship between Bollywood and Hollywood? What are some of the problems that Indian actors face if they attempt to cross over from one system to the other?

CONSIDERING CRAFT

1. Look at the title and subtitle of the essay. Then read the title aloud. Why do you think Chopra chose this particular title?

2. Chopra quotes actor Will Smith and director Ashutosh Gowariker in the essay. Why does the author choose these two people?

3. In paragraph 14, Chopra notes that "Hollywood and Mr. Roshan have been flirting with each other" for some time. By choosing this expression, what does the author reveal about the relationship between Hollywood and the actor?

WRITING PROMPTS

Responding to the Topic   Write an essay in which you discuss your experience with foreign film. Detail which foreign films, if any, you have seen. If you have not seen any films produced in another country, explain why you have not chosen to see any. What have you learned — or do you think you could learn — about another culture by watching the films of that culture?

Responding to the Writer   Do you agree with Aishwarya Bachchan's decision to place her personal moral code above her career? How could this affect her professional opportunities? In an essay, explain why you agree or disagree with her position and the impact that you think her moral code will have on her career.

Responding to Multiple Viewpoints   Read Eugene Robinson's essay "Tyler Perry's Money Machine" (p. 346). What advice might Tyler Perry give Aishwarya Bachchan about her attempt to cross over into mainstream Hollywood? Write an essay in the form of a letter from Perry to Bachchan.

For a quiz on this reading, go to bedfordstmartins.com/mirror.

Analyzing the Image

The Bollywood Princess Waiting for Her Prince to Come

In this film image, called a movie still, from the epic romance *Jodhaa Akbar*, some would say we see Bollywood Princess Aishwarya Rai Bachchan dreaming of her Prince Charming, played by Bollywood superstar Hrithik Roshan. The film was released worldwide in 2008 and in 115 theaters in the United States, thus making history as the largest Hindi release in this country. This lush historical epic from director Ashutosh Gowariker traces the complicated relationship between the great Mughal emperor Akbar, a Muslim, and Jodhaa, a Hindu beauty who becomes his wife. Although the historical basis of the epic is disputed, it is clear that these two Indian actors have a chance of becoming the first truly global Bollywood superstars.

- What do you first notice about this movie still?

- What do you think Jodhaa and Akbar are thinking about?

- Why are the two figures different sizes?

- How do the stars' clothing and positioning indicate the sixteenth-century Indian setting of this film?

- In the original visual, the colors gold, red, and white predominate. What significance might these three colors have in an epic romance?

- Does this visual make you want to see the film *Jodhaa Akbar*? Why?

Research this topic with TopLinks at bedfordstmartins.com/toplinks.

Tyler Perry's Money Machine

EUGENE ROBINSON

Eugene Robinson is an assistant managing editor for the *Washington Post* and writes a twice-weekly column. In his career at the paper, he has also worked as a city hall reporter, city editor, and foreign correspondent. He is the author of *Coal to Cream: A Black Man's Journey beyond Color to an Affirmation of Race* (1999), *Last Dance in Havana: The Final Days of Fidel and the Start of the New Cuban Revolution* (2004), and *Disintegration: The Splintering of Black America* (2010). In 2009, he was awarded the Pulitzer Prize. "Tyler Perry's Money Machine," which appeared in the *Washington Post* on October 16, 2007, discusses the phenomenal success of African American writer, actor, and filmmaker Tyler Perry.

> **THINKING AHEAD** Think about African Americans that you have seen on-screen, either on television or in the movies. What roles do you remember African Americans portraying? In which films or shows? Which African American directors, actors, films, and television shows do you like? Why?

George Clooney is a big-time movie star. Cate Blanchett is a big-time 1 movie star. But Tyler Perry's new movie did more box-office on its opening weekend than Clooney's and Blanchett's new movies combined, which makes Perry a big-time movie star, too, and also a phenomenon.

Perry's *Why Did I Get Married?*—which features singers Janet Jackson 2 and Jill Scott—ruled the weekend with $21.5 million in sales. Clooney's thriller *Michael Clayton* struggled to earn half that much, while Blanchett's costume drama[1] *Elizabeth: The Golden Age* barely broke $6 million.

What makes this worth noting? According to Perry's distributor, Lions 3 Gate Films, around 90 percent of the audience for *Why Did I Get Married?* was African American. The ensemble cast is African American, too.

A playwright, actor and filmmaker—based not in Hollywood but in 4 somewhat less glamorous Atlanta—Perry is making a habit of pulling this kind of stunt. Last year his *Madea's Family Reunion* opened with a $30 million weekend. Critics find Perry's films formulaic, but clearly he has found a formula that works. And he has found an untapped audience that literally can't wait to see itself on the big screen.

In his plays and movies, Perry shows African Americans as they . . . well, 5 I was about to say he shows us as we really are, but that's not true. Reality

---

[1] **costume drama:** A film set in a historical period and employing authentic costumes of the period.

is for documentaries; Perry's characters are unsubtle, his humor is broad, and his plots are soaked with melodrama. Among his big themes are love, fidelity and the importance of family, and his movies usually have religious overtones.

What Perry does is depict black Americans as people relating to other people—not as mere plot devices and not as characters defined solely by how they relate to the white world. The rest of the movie industry would do well to take note.   6

In depicting African Americans, mainstream Hollywood still struggles to leave behind the "magic Negro" paradigm[2]—the idea, epitomized by *Driving Miss Daisy,* that black characters exist solely to teach valuable lessons to white characters. We still don't get a lot of films in which black characters bestow their moral wisdom on one another. Even in *The Pursuit of Happyness,* Will Smith's character was only secondarily a lesson-giver to his son; mostly, his role was to teach and uplift the audience.   7

There's nothing wrong with a little inspiration. But African American moviegoers who want to see their own concerns and struggles—their own lives, even if rendered in broad outline—projected at the cineplex still aren't getting much love from Hollywood.   8

The same is true on the small screen. A new Nielsen report says that there has been a remarkable convergence of white and black television viewing habits; for the first time in years, lists of the top twenty shows among whites and blacks are largely the same. But that is at least partly due to the fact that UPN and WB, which used to carry a lot of black-oriented programming, were merged into one network, which meant jettisoning a number of shows popular with black viewers. And it's at least partly due to the dominance of *American Idol, Dancing with the Stars* and other reality shows that choose their contestants with diversity in mind.   9

Nielsen calls African Americans a "high-growth, high-potential audience." African Americans are "embracing and using the newest technologies at rates that exceed the national average," including high-definition television and movies-on-demand, Nielsen reports.   10

But black viewers still won't watch *Desperate Housewives*. They'd rather watch *Girlfriends* instead.   11

Perry's movies are based on his stage plays, which play to packed audiences around the country. *Why Did I Get Married?* is about the black middle class. It's about relationships, the universal subject of date movies. Perry's movies aren't great art-house films,[3] but neither are Adam Sandler's; they succeed at what counts, which is speaking to their audience.   12

Tom Ortenberg, president of Lions Gate Films, told the *Los Angeles Times* that Perry's "message of family values and personal redemption   13

[2] **paradigm:** A set of assumptions, concepts, values, and practices that constitutes a way of viewing reality for the community that shares them.
[3] **art-house films:** Movies intended to be primarily artistic works rather than commercial films of mass appeal.

speaks very strongly to people who are not frequent moviegoers." He added, "My strong hunch is that this is the last time anybody will underestimate Tyler Perry."

"African Americans have learned to flex their market muscle," Nielsen said in its report, noting that African American buying power will top $900 billion within a few years.   14

If the pattern from his earlier films holds true, *Why Did I Get Married?* will probably drop off next weekend—black audiences anticipate his films and rush out to see them as soon as they open. That eagerness suggests a hunger that others might want to try to satisfy. That is, if they want to make money.   15

EXERCISING VOCABULARY

1. Record your own definition for each of these words.

   phenomenon (n.) (1)
   formulaic (adj.) (4)
   melodrama (n.) (5)
   overtones (n.) (5)
   epitomized (adj.) (7)
   bestow (v.) (7)

   rendered (v.) (8)
   convergence (n.) (9)
   jettisoning (v.) (9)
   universal (adj.) (12)
   hunch (n.) (13)

2. In paragraph 14, Robinson quotes the Nielsen report, which says that "African Americans have learned to flex their market muscle." What does it mean to flex a muscle? How does a group develop "market muscle"? What would result from flexing that market muscle?

3. The author writes that Tyler Perry "has found an untapped audience that literally can't wait to see itself on the big screen" (para. 4). What does it mean to tap someone or something? Give some examples of people or things that can be tapped. What does Robinson's description of the audience for Perry's films indicate?

PROBING CONTENT

1. According to Robinson, how are African Americans depicted in Tyler Perry's plays and films? What are his major themes?

2. How does mainstream Hollywood depict African Americans? What is the "'magic Negro' paradigm" (para. 7)? How does Hollywood handle it?

3. Who is Tom Ortenberg? What is his opinion of Tyler Perry's work? Why does he hold this opinion? Why is his opinion significant?

4. What has recently become notable about "white and black television viewing habits" (para. 9)? To what does Robinson attribute this change?

CONSIDERING CRAFT

1. Why does Robinson begin his essay with statistics about movies? Why did he pick the films that he did? How does this opening introduce his purpose in this essay?

2. The author uses informal conversational language in his essay on several occasions. Find two such examples and explain how they affect the tone of the essay.

3. What does the Nielsen report measure? Why does Robinson cite the Nielsen report in his essay? Is this an effective strategy? Why?

WRITING PROMPTS

Responding to the Topic   Why do you go to the movies? According to Robinson, many people go to see themselves on the big screen. Is this the reason you and your friends attend movies? In an essay, detail your personal reasons for choosing the films you do. Support your ideas with numerous specific examples.

Responding to the Writer   Robinson believes that one reason for the success of Perry's films is that they move beyond showing African Americans only as "they relate to the white world" (para. 6). What will it take for any film that depicts a minority group to have broad appeal outside that population? Write an essay in which you take a position on this issue and provide examples of films that support your thesis.

Responding to Multiple Viewpoints   In "Tyler Perry's Money Machine," Robinson argues that Perry's movies are especially popular with African American audiences. Stephen King, in "Why We Crave Horror Movies" (p. 324), writes, "And horror movies, like roller coasters, have always been the special province of the young" (para. 3). Based on your reading of these essays and others in this chapter, write an essay in which you consider the advantanges and disadvantages of producing movies that target specific audiences. Provide examples to support your position.

For a quiz on this reading, go to bedfordstmartins.com/mirror.

Drag Hags

JENNIE YABROFF

Jennie Yabroff writes movie and book reviews, as well as features on women in pop culture, for publications such as *Newsweek*, the *New York Times*, the *San Francisco Chronicle*, and *Salon*. The following essay, "Drag Hags," was first published in *Newsweek* in July 2007. In it, Yabroff examines some recent comedies in which male actors have portrayed women and raises an interesting point: In an America that is so attuned to being sensitive to others' identities, is gender still a blind spot?

> **THINKING AHEAD** Which movies, plays, or television shows have you seen in which men dress as women? Why did the men dress this way? How did this affect your entertainment experience?

Edna Turnblad has a weakness for pink-sequined dresses, a passion for her husband and a triple-E bra. Edna also has a secret. Edna is a man. To be precise, her character in *Hairspray* has always been played by a man: drag queen Divine in the original John Waters film, gruff-voiced Harvey Fierstein in the Broadway musical and, starting this week, John Travolta in the movie musical. Just as Peter Pan is almost always played by a woman, it's impossible to imagine a *Hairspray* in which Edna isn't hiding a stubble under her pancake makeup. The obvious reason is that more-is-more is part of the *Hairspray* ethos, from the hairstyles to the musical numbers. Having a man play the plus-size Edna makes her funnier and adds a wink-wink knowingness to the depiction of an archetype[1] of maternity.

But what is that wink all about? Edna is hardly the only iconic female character who's really a he. Tyler Perry has made a career of playing the overweight, overbearing grandmother Madea, while both Eddie Murphy and Martin Lawrence strapped on fat suits and wigs in recent films. Despite decades-long careers, Dustin Hoffman's and Robin Williams's most beloved alter egos[2] are arguably Tootsie and Mrs. Doubtfire. "Jack Lemmon doing the tango with Joe E. Brown in *Some Like It Hot* was hilarious, but you can't tell me there wasn't the further charge of what it was representing," says Richard Barrios, a film historian and author of *Screened Out: Playing Gay in Hollywood from Edison to Stonewall*. "It's a blurring of differences between masculinity and femininity." But lots of conventions of drama don't fly anymore. A white actor wouldn't dare put on dark makeup

---

[1] **archetype:** An original model; a prototype or ideal example.
[2] **alter egos:** Personas; second selves.

to appear black today—Angelina Jolie took a lot of heat for slightly darkening her complexion to play Mariane Pearl in *A Mighty Heart*. A non-Asian actor would never get away with taping his eyes and assuming a silly accent to sound Chinese, as Mickey Rooney did in *Breakfast at Tiffany's* (1961). Even fat activists complain when actors don fat suits for laughs, as Gwyneth Paltrow found out when she artificially bulked up for *Shallow Hal*. So it would seem logical that drag today, especially when the man playing the part is straight, is both misogynistic (notice how the "women" in these movies are always awkward and ugly) and homophobic (notice how they also flutter and flounce like a stereotypical gay man). So why is it still OK for male actors to wear dresses?

The convention of men playing women dates back to ancient Greece   3
and also has roots in Japanese Kabuki theater. Men played all the roles in Shakespeare's day, heightening the gender confusion in plays such as *As You Like It,* where Rosalind, originally played by a male actor, disguises herself as a man to win her lover's heart. Men wearing dresses have been a comedy staple in both Britain and America since the 1892 play *Charley's Aunt,* which was first made into a film in 1915. Bugs Bunny has even dolled himself up to outwit (and mock-seduce) Elmer Fudd. As long as women have worn dresses, male actors have been borrowing them to get a laugh. "There have been surveys of movies in which men play women, and they were all successes," says Craig Zadan, executive producer of *Hairspray*. "The public loves the idea of men playing women in film, especially in a comedy."

Take Martin Lawrence. In the *Big Momma* movies, Lawrence follows a   4
time-honored tradition of male characters who are forced to go "undercover" as women, either to elude the bad guys or to win the heart of a real, yet surprisingly clueless woman. This wolf-in-sheep's-clothing ruse powers *Some Like It Hot, Tootsie* and countless fraternity films in which the brothers depilate[3] and rouge themselves (ineptly, of course) to pass as women. In the more thoughtful movies, drag can be a vehicle for personal growth for the men, who, after initial outrage at the way they are treated as women, remain sensitized even after they wipe off their lipstick. However, the women in these films never experience the same fulfilling character arc. It's the men who emancipate them from their second-class status; in *Tootsie,* Michael's alter ego, Dorothy, lobbies for gender equality in the workplace. Though much of the visual comedy comes from the man's struggle to adopt "feminine" ways, the female love interest never seems to question the gender of her new best friend, and accepts the switch unquestioningly once the "gal pal" unmasks himself as a potential suitor. In *Some Like It Hot,* when Josephine reveals that he is really Joe, Sugar (Marilyn Monroe) shrugs off his concerns that she'll feel betrayed, saying, "I told you. I'm not very bright." Though some critics laud *Some Like It Hot* for lampooning[4]

---

[3] **depilate:** To remove hair by shaving or waxing.
[4] **lampooning:** Satirizing; ridiculing.

gender stereotypes, the message of the film could also be that a woman isn't nearly as bright as a man in a dress.

Tyler Perry's Madea, Eddie Murphy's Rasputia and Travolta's Edna, on the other hand, never appear on screen as men. So why not just cast a woman in the roles in the first place — Rosie O'Donnell would have made a great Edna. "It seems not only are we to be made fun of and demeaned in films, but we are also being put out of work," says writer Jill Nelson. "If Martin and Eddie can dress up and be us, why do the studios need to make an effort to hire black women? It's like they're killing us two ways." Travolta has been called out by gay activists who claim Edna is an iconic gay role (Waters and Fierstein are gay, as was Divine), and therefore should be played by a gay man. While blackface[5] is universally reviled, drag is trickier: some gays embrace it as an important aspect of alternative culture, while others believe it perpetuates tired stereotypes of gay men as secretly wanting to be women. Most agree, though, that drag's charge, negative or positive, is neutralized when a straight man does it. When Waters cast Divine, a flamboyant gay man and real-life drag queen, as a traditional loving mother, it underscored the film's message of acceptance. But that nuance is lost when Edna is played simply for laughs. And Travolta's Edna is as straight as they come.

Yet Zadan says he never considered any women for Edna, choosing to honor the tradition begun by Waters when he created the role for Divine. "Why would you put up boundaries for what an actor's capable of accomplishing in film?" asks Zadan. "With visual effects, makeup, so many things at our disposal, there's no limit to what you can accomplish." Prosthetically enhanced gender swapping, Travolta style, may be the drag of the future. His Edna has more in common with Mike Myers's Fat Bastard, Jim Carrey's Grinch or Paltrow's Rosemary Shanahan than Divine. When actors such as Travolta, Murphy or Lawrence take on these roles, they actually downplay any gender confusion; Travolta has said he didn't want to portray Edna as a "drag joke." Instead, these macho actors brag about the physical discomfort required to transform themselves into wig-topped Jabba the Huttettes.[6] "Good drag is used knowingly for its transgressive[7] qualities," says Barrios. "But films like *Big Momma* and *Hairspray* don't want to be attuned to whatever transgressiveness they may contain. Drag is just an easy way to get laughs without extending themselves beyond putting on some latex." And when drag becomes more about latex than subtext, it's not funny at all.

[5] **blackface:** The practice of white actors playing black roles while wearing dark makeup; a conventionalized comic travesty of black people, especially in a minstrel show.
[6] **Jabba the Huttettes:** Refers to the film character Jabba the Hutt, a grotesquely overweight alien who was a criminal overlord in George Lucas's *Star Wars* saga.
[7] **transgressive:** Exceeding or overstepping a limit.

EXERCISING VOCABULARY

1. Record your own definition for each of these words.

   ethos (n.) (1)
   iconic (adj.) (2)
   overbearing (adj.) (2)
   misogynistic (adj.) (2)
   staple (n.) (3)
   elude (v.) (4)
   ruse (n.) (4)
   ineptly (adv.) (4)
   lobbies (v.) (4)

   shrugs (v.) (4)
   laud (v.) (4)
   demeaned (v.) (5)
   reviled (v.) (5)
   nuance (n.) (5)
   prosthetically (adv.) (6)
   downplay (v.) (6)
   attuned (v.) (6)

2. Yabroff writes that drag seems "homophobic" (para. 2). What does it mean to be phobic? Name some common phobias and the words that describe them. Look up the prefix *homo* in the dictionary. What does it mean when used in a term like *Homo sapiens*? What then does it mean to be homophobic?

3. In the final sentence of her essay, Yabroff states, "And when drag becomes more about latex than subtext, it's not funny at all." What does the prefix *sub* mean? What are some words of which it is a part? What then is a subtext?

4. Yabroff describes Divine as "a flamboyant gay man" (para. 5). Look up the word *flamboyant*. From what language does it derive? How is it related to the word *flame*? What does the author mean when she calls Divine a "flamboyant" gay man? How does knowing the origin of the word add to your understanding and to the word's descriptive quality?

PROBING CONTENT

1. How long have men played women's roles? Why have men dressed in women's clothing to play these roles?

2. How does Yabroff feel about men dressing as women? Does she approve? Why?

3. In which other situations is it unacceptable for one person to pretend to be another? What reasons does Yabroff give?

4. What effect does male actors' dressing in drag have on women? On female actors? On gay men?

CONSIDERING CRAFT

1. Examine the title of the essay. What is unique about it? How effective is this title?

2. Yabroff includes several questions in her essay. Find four examples where she does so. Why does Yabroff use this writing strategy?

3. The author provides a multitude of examples in her essay. Why does she include examples other than men playing women's roles? Locate three of these and comment on why Yabroff includes them.

4. The essay begins and ends with mentions of John Travolta's role in *Hairspray*. Why does Yabroff use this strategy? How effective is it?

WRITING PROMPTS

Responding to the Topic   What films have you seen in which men dress as women or women dress as men? In an essay, detail how these "drag" roles affected your opinion of the film. To what extent do you believe there was a subtext or larger message in these roles? Make sure that you provide specific examples from the films.

Responding to the Writer   In the final line of her essay, Yabroff states, "And when drag becomes more about latex than subtext, it's not funny at all." Write an essay in which you take a position on this statement. Provide adequate examples to support your stance.

Responding to Multiple Viewpoints   Yabroff claims that "Tyler Perry's Madea, Eddie Murphy's Rasputia and Travolta's Edna . . . never appear on screen as men. So why not just cast a woman in the roles in the first place — Rosie O'Donnell would have made a great Edna" (para. 5). Would Eugene Robinson, author of "Tyler Perry's Money Machine" (p. 346), agree with Yabroff that it would be advantageous to cast women in roles like Madea's, Rasputia's, and Edna's instead of casting men? Write an essay in which you answer this question. Provide adequate detail and examples to prove your position.

For a quiz on this reading, go to bedfordstmartins.com/mirror.

Virtual Humans

KELLY TYLER-LEWIS

Kelly Tyler-Lewis is a producer for PBS's *Nova.* She coproduced the program "Special Effects of *Titanic* and Beyond" and is also an associate producer for the large-format film unit, working on projects such as *Stormchasers* (1995), *Special Effects* (1996), *Island of the Sharks* (1999), and *The Endurance: Shackleton's Epic Journey* (2001), which won an Emmy for Best Historical Documentary. Tyler-Lewis is also the author of *The Lost Men: The Harrowing Saga of Shackleton's Ross Sea Party* (2006). In "Virtual Humans," written for Nova Online, she discusses the realistic computer-generated characters made possible by new advances in technology.

> **THINKING AHEAD** Which films that use virtual actors are you familiar with? What do you think of these computer-generated actors? What are the benefits of using them? What are the disadvantages? How do computer-generated actors compare to human ones?

After millions of years of natural selection, human beings have some serious competition for their lofty perch on the evolutionary ladder—and the challenger has only been evolving for less than a decade. Some computer artists contend that anything we can do, "virtual humans" can do better, and they're poised to revolutionize moviemaking with a new species that doesn't require an astronomical salary, works around the clock without complaint, and lives quietly on a hard drive between death-defying stunts.

A generation of computer-generated (CG) characters, called "synthespians" or "vactors," is attracting notice in Hollywood. Some insiders envision a future when digital stars compete for roles with the flesh-and-blood variety. While a photoreal digital actor has yet to carry a major motion picture, synthespians have captured supporting roles for some time now, whenever the going gets too tough or too expensive. Synthespians serve as doubles for breathtaking stunts too dangerous for mortal stars: a girl leaping from a skyscraper in *The Fifth Element,* Sylvester Stallone chasing through the skies on an airborne motorcycle in *Judge Dredd,* and a luckless attorney becoming tyrannosaur fodder in *Jurassic Park.* And producers cut costs on the "cast of thousands" by using digital extras to stand in for the legions of troops in *Hamlet,* mobs of Washington demonstrators in *Forrest Gump,* and passengers aboard the doomed *Titanic.*

Fooling the Eye

The leap from extra to starring role for synthespians is a big one, since it invites heightened scrutiny from the viewer. Human beings have a finely tuned ability to recognize their kind, an ability that is thought to be both innate and learned, and that ups the ante for filmmakers seeking to fool them with a synthetic stand-in. Creating convincing movement is particularly difficult. Animators can take the perceptual challenge head-on and painstakingly create movement for their characters frame by frame from scratch, or they can use the real thing. A technique called motion capture allows actual movement to be recorded and applied to digital characters. An actor wears reflective markers at key body joints, and surrounding cameras record the motion of reflected infrared light in the computer. Later, this motion data is transferred to the digital character.   3

The human face presents an even more daunting challenge. Ed Catmull, a computer graphics pioneer since the late 1970s and a founder of Pixar (*Toy Story, A Bug's Life*), regards it as a central issue in character animation.   4

"The human face is a unique problem," he says. "We are genetically programmed to recognize human faces. We're so good that most people aren't even aware of it while they think about it. It turns out, for instance, that if we make a perfectly symmetrical face, we see it as being wrong. So we want things to be not quite perfect, have a lot of subtlety, but if they're too imperfect, then we think that they're strange."   5

For Scott Ross, president of Digital Domain, the problem is more intangible: "One of the things that I'm mostly concerned about in terms of virtual actors is that there's been millions of years of experience in our genetic code. And I'm concerned that when you create a close-up of a virtual actor and look into its eyes, that it will take real skill to be able to give that virtual actor soul. And I've not yet seen that."   6

The Silicon Rush

The quest to create virtual actors is comparatively recent; the first interactive computer graphics program was only developed in 1961. Designed by Ivan Sutherland at the Massachusetts Institute of Technology, Sketchpad generated simple geometrical line drawings for design and engineering applications. These simple operations required a state-of-the-art TX-2 defense computer to run.   7

The silicon[1] rush in Hollywood began in 1985, when a knight sprang from a stained glass window and handily dispatched a human opponent in *Young Sherlock Holmes,* courtesy of computer animation. A virtual stampede of digital characters followed: the water creature of *The Abyss,* the   8

---

[1] **silicon:** The material used as the base for most integrated circuits; hardware, especially integrated circuits or microprocessor-based computer systems.

quicksilver[2] T-1000 of *Terminator 2: Judgment Day,* the menagerie of *Jumanji,* and the dinosaurs of *Jurassic Park.* In 1995, *Toy Story* was released, the first CG film in history, populated entirely by digital characters in a world made of bits and bytes.

The reason for this explosion? Jim Blinn, an early computer graphics   9
innovator who created the well-known *Voyager* fly-by animations for the Jet Propulsion Laboratory, credits the decreasing cost of computer memory. "In my lifetime, the cost of the basic tools of my trade — of making images with a computer — has gone from about $500,000 to about $2,000," he says. "It's a factor of two hundred or three hundred to one." A corresponding inverse growth in computer power and memory has equipped CG Pygmalions[3] to cope with the high degree of complexity and detail inherent in living creatures. Today's microcomputers have roughly four hundred times more memory and operate about five thousand times faster than the TX-2 used by Sutherland.

Scott Ross projects continuing growth in hardware capability, spurring   10
increasingly sophisticated animation. "The concept of Moore's law states that the processing power of computing doubles every year," he says. "We're seeing that in terms of what we're doing today in the film industry."

Building a Better Human

With this enhanced technology, animators have turned from fantasy characters and extinct animals to a new digital grail: photorealistic *Homo sapiens.* Ellen Poon, a visual effects supervisor for Industrial Light and Magic who has been involved with such films as *Jumanji* and *Men in Black,* is optimistic, but sees technical challenges ahead.   11

"I think we are very close to creating a realistic-looking virtual person," she says. "There are a few things that have to be right, and we're still in the process of researching them. And those elements are hair, skin, clothing, movement, and facial expressions."   12

The problem of hair has bedeviled animators for years. There are thousands of hairs on the human head, which vary in color, light reflectance, and texture and can move either singly or together. The lion in *Jumanji* required the modeling of one million individual hairs for the mane alone. Nadia Mangenat Thalmann of Miralab, a computer research center at the University of Geneva, tackled similar complexity as she developed clothing for digital characters.   13

"Fabric is very difficult," says Thalmann. "The computer has to know   14
every moment where the wrinkles are that are created by the movement of the fabric. We used two or three hours of calculation for one single frame

---

[2] **quicksilver:** Liquid silver; mercury.
[3] **Pygmalions:** Creators; refers to Pygmalion, who, according to Greek legend, sculpted a woman named Galatea out of ivory, fell in love with her, and convinced Venus to bring her to life.

of animation to get it right—and there are twenty-four frames in one second of film."

Questioning the Digital Grail

Hurdles notwithstanding, the advantages of a virtual actor are appealing. 15
A child synthespian won't have temper tantrums or work hours mandated by labor laws. A vactor will never be busy when it's time for re-shoots after a film has wrapped. A virtual human never grows old. And, to the delight of producers, a digital superstar won't require a $20 million salary, a deluxe trailer and a coterie of bodyguards, masseuses and aromatherapists to get the job done.

For the animators at Miralab, it's only a matter of time and computing 16
power before icons of the past take the limelight again. Thalmann has developed a virtual Marilyn Monroe. She is uncannily realistic, but the illusion loses its photorealistic quality in close-up. Continuing technical advances raise the possibility that there may someday be stars who truly will live forever.

Even so, many in the special effects industry question whether silicon 17
actors will ever pose a real threat to the carbon-based variety. Dennis Muren, visual effects supervisor for Industrial Light and Magic and nine-time Oscar winner, is skeptical of the creative benefits.

"What's the point?" he wonders. "If you want to put Marilyn Monroe 18
in a movie, you could get a terrific actress, give her a great make-up artist, six months of studying and voice training, and she could do a better Marilyn Monroe than we could ever do."

Jim Blinn questions whether synthespians make economic sense: "A 19
dinosaur doesn't exist, so it's practical to simulate it. With human beings, however, having a staff of twenty people all working on the lighting, the modeling, and the motion might not be a great trade-off, because you can replace that whole team with one human actor who can do what the director wants."

To the Future . . . and Beyond

Thalmann contemplates taking virtual humans to a new level. "I'm not so 20
much interested to see pictures, which you watch passively," she says. "My ultimate goal is to be able to live in the virtual worlds, and to meet virtual humans that are collaborators," says Thalmann.

Thalmann is not alone. Computer game developers have begun ex- 21
perimenting with artificial intelligence[4] (AI), endowing game characters with the capacity to learn and interact with their environment and the game player.

---

[4] **artificial intelligence:** The ability of a computer or other machine to perform those activities that are normally thought to require human intelligence; the branch of computer science concerned with the development of machines having this ability.

John Lasseter, director of *Toy Story*, is charting a different course. "I'm   22
interested in creating a film with characters that people obviously know
don't exist," he says. "But then they look at it and say, 'It seems so real. I
know it doesn't—but wait. I know those toys aren't alive, but it looks so
real. No, they can't be alive, no. Are they?' So I think that's one of the really
exciting things that computer animation can give you: a combination of
fantasy and the photorealistic which has never been seen before."

With the latest generation of talent and tools at their disposal, visual   23
effects filmmakers see a wide range of possibilities in the future, with or
without virtual humans. "I think we can do just about anything right now
if we had the time and money," says Dennis Muren. "It's really like your
imagination has no boundaries at the moment. . . . I'd rather put the work
into something that's unique and new, and you haven't seen anywhere before, and there's no way a person could do it."

EXERCISING VOCABULARY

1. Record your own definition for each of these words.

fodder (n.) (2)	innovator (n.) (9)
legions (n.) (2)	inverse (adj.) (9)
scrutiny (n.) (3)	inherent (adj.) (9)
innate (adj.) (3)	spurring (v.) (10)
synthetic (adj.) (3)	bedeviled (v.) (13)
perceptual (adj.) (3)	tackled (v.) (13)
daunting (adj.) (4)	hurdles (n). (15)
genetically (adv.) (5)	mandated (v.) (15)
symmetrical (adj.) (5)	coterie (n.) (15)
intangible (adj.) (6)	uncannily (adv.) (16)
handily (adv.) (8)	passively (adv.) (20)
dispatched (v.) (8)	collaborators (n.) (20)
menagerie (n.) (8)	

2. In paragraph 3, Tyler-Lewis writes that our human ability to instinctively
   recognize other humans "ups the ante for filmmakers" who would de-
   ceive us. What is the source of the expression "ups the ante?" How
   does the author use the expression here?

3. In paragraph 11, Tyler-Lewis calls "photorealistic *Homo sapiens*" "a new
   digital grail." From which language does the term *Homo sapiens* originate? What do the two parts of the term mean? What is the Holy Grail?
   Who sought it? Why was it so sought after? Why is "a photorealistic
   Homo sapiens" the "new digital grail" for computer animators?

4. The author writes, "it's only a matter of time and computing power before icons of the past take the limelight again" (para. 16). What is an
   icon? How can an actor be an icon? What is a limelight? In the theater,

what does it mean to take the limelight? How does this meaning relate to Tyler-Lewis's use of the phrase?

5. In paragraph 22, Tyler-Lewis writes that John Lasseter, the director of *Toy Story,* "is charting a different course." With what context is the phrase "charting a different course" normally associated? What does the author mean here?

PROBING CONTENT

1. What are some reasons that directors choose to cast synthespians over real actors in their films?

2. What is motion capture? How does it work?

3. Who are Ed Catmull and Scott Ross? According to them, why is portraying the human face digitally so difficult?

4. When did the surge in CG films begin? What was responsible for the "silicon rush"?

5. What strategies must a production team use to achieve box-office success, given the obviously fictitious storylines and cast of CG films?

CONSIDERING CRAFT

1. In the opening paragraph, Tyler-Lewis writes, "After millions of years of natural selection, human beings have some serious competition for their lofty perch on the evolutionary ladder." Describe how the figurative language used here works in this sentence to introduce the topic.

2. Tyler-Lewis uses several headings in her essay. Examine each one and then comment on the ways in which they affect your reading and understanding. Would you substitute another title for any of the author's headings? How would this make the essay more effective?

3. Find five places in the essay in which the author uses examples from specific films. Not every reader will have seen the movies she cites as examples. Why then does she do this?

4. In her essay, Tyler-Lewis quotes several different people. Locate four such examples. Which kinds of people does she cite? Why did she choose these individuals?

WRITING PROMPTS

Responding to the Topic   Describe your experience viewing a film containing one or more synthespians. If you have not seen a movie with vactors, rent or borrow one from the library. How would the experience differ if the director had cast live actors? Did the film contain any specific scenes or stunts that would have to be cut from the shooting script had they not been performed by vactors?

Responding to the Writer   Should digital actors be cast in roles previously envisioned for flesh-and-blood actors? How far will this technological "evolution" go? Will vactors ever replace human actors? Why? To what extent are the benefits of synthespians worth exploring and developing? After considering the positions of others like Dennis Muren, Nadia Thalmann, and Jim Blinn, write an essay in which you detail your own position. Provide specific examples from films to support your argument.

Responding to Multiple Viewpoints   What would Stephen King ("Why We Crave Horror Movies," p. 324) think of virtual actors? How might vactors be especially useful in the horror genre of film? What kinds of parts could they play? What would be the benefits and drawbacks of using synthespians instead of human actors?

For a quiz on this reading, go to bedfordstmartins.com/mirror.

Analyzing the Image

An Unlikely Commuter

Who is that strange little creature sitting next to two ordinary commuters on a New York City subway train? It's Gollum, the computer-generated character from Peter Jackson's *The Lord of the Rings* film trilogy, based on the fantasy novels of British writer J. R. R. Tolkien. Gollum's presence in this photograph is part of an inspired publicity campaign for the second film, *The Lord of the Rings: The Two Towers* (2002). This campaign transformed the subway into the "Middle-Earth Shuttle" by decorating the trains with Middle-Earth creatures, vines, moss, and stones to celebrate the November 18, 2003, DVD and VHS release of the Special Extended Edition of *The Lord of the Rings: The Two Towers.*

- Where is your eye drawn first when you look at this visual? Why?

- How would you describe the expressions on the faces of the two human commuters?

- How would you react to seeing a life-size replica of the virtual actor Gollum as you go about your daily activities?

- What else in the visual forms part of the publicity campaign? Why is it there?

- How successful do you think this publicity campaign was and why?

Research this topic at TopLinks at bedfordstmartins.com/toplinks.

Left for Dead by MTV, Music Videos Rebound on the Web

JAKE COYLE

Jake Coyle is an Associated Press entertainment writer. "Left for Dead by MTV, Music Videos Rebound on the Web," published on September 9, 2010, examines the music video's recent comeback via the Internet. According to Coyle, "It wasn't long ago that the music video was on life support," but through the Internet, most notably YouTube, the video has changed and re-made itself into something that has reentered the world's consciousness. Coyle quotes those who believe "we're entering another golden era for music videos."

> **THINKING AHEAD**   How often do you watch music videos? Which kinds of media do you use to watch these videos? Which artists' videos do you watch? Why?

I t wasn't long ago that the music video was on life support. 1

MTV—which will hold its 27th annual Video Music Awards on 2 Sunday—phased out videos in favor of reality programming and other shows that attracted better ratings. At the same time, the music industry was collapsing and slashed budgets no longer had room for elaborate clips.

But recently, the music video has had a revival. Watching music videos 3 has become a central aspect of Internet usage. Music blogs and social media have greased the channels, facilitating the quick, easy spreading of videos, especially those with arresting or controversial visuals. People even buy clips on iTunes.

Lady Gaga and Beyoncé go on a scantily clad murderous rampage with 4 the nearly 10-minute *Telephone*; MGMT wanders through the desert with a digitally created creature in *Congratulations*; Erykah Badu strips while strolling the path of President John Kennedy's assassination in *Window Seat*; MIA depicts a war on terror against redheads in *Born Free*.

All of these videos exploded on the Internet and became water-cooler 5 moments. Cee-Lo's recent and unprintable hit (titled "Forget You" for radio) went viral with a video of only its lyrics. And Beyoncé's *Single Ladies*; became so iconic it spawned countless imitators and even had then President-elect Barack Obama imitating the hand choreography.

"We're entering another golden era for music videos," says Saul Aus- 6 terlitz, the author of *Money for Nothing: A History of the Music Video from the Beatles to the White Stripes*. "They've become part of the cultural discourse again in a way that's reminiscent of the heyday[1] of the music video, from the early '80s to the mid '90s."

Today's audiences can be enormous. Shakira, who last year debuted a music video on Facebook, was "blown away" when her video for the official song of the World Cup, "Waka Waka (This One's for Africa)"—a colorful mix of dancing and soccer star cameos[2]—was nearing 100 million views on YouTube.

"It can take on a life of its own online," says Shakira. "And it inspires us artists to be even more creative. With access to so many videos, we need to challenge ourselves to surprise our fans."

The video, which was distributed by the music video and live music website Vevo, has gone on to be watched by more than 173 million people, good enough for the fourth most-viewed video ever on YouTube.

In fact, four of the five most-viewed clips on Google Inc.'s YouTube site are music videos released in the last year. (Justin Bieber and Lady Gaga top the charts.) Though that's partly because Vevo (which shares a small percentage of advertising revenue with YouTube) tabulates view counts across platforms, it's still a striking example of the music video's dramatic comeback. It's a long way beyond the novelty videos of OK Go that followed YouTube's debut in 2005.

"If it wasn't for YouTube, the online video space would not be where it is today," says David Kohl, executive vice president of sales and customer operations at the Sony and Universal co-owned Vevo.

At the center of [the] music video's earlier, headier times was Hype Williams, who—often with his trademark fisheye lens—created much of the iconography of hip-hop. Several of his videos are typically considered among the form's best, like Missy Elliott's *The Rain (Supa Dupa Fly)* and Busta Rhymes's *Put Your Hands Where My Eyes Could See.*

But he grew disillusioned with the commercialization of music videos and the recycling of imagery. Williams was coaxed back into music video by Kanye West and has remained active, including recently directing Jay-Z's *Empire State of Mind*, watched by nearly 60 million and nominated for three VMAs.

"It's a different time," says Williams. "It's an opportunity to find it all over again. I didn't really think that was possible until recently, seeing things like this Arcade Fire clip. It shows you that it can be more."

Released last week, the Arcade Fire video is titled *The Wilderness Downtown* and set to the band's song "We Used to Wait." It's a new kind of video, a kind particularly suited to the medium of the Web.

"It speaks volumes about where music video is going," says Williams, who's happy to pass the torch. "It's a young man's game."

At the website dedicated to the film (www.thewildernessdowntown .com), a viewer inputs his or her childhood home address. The film starts

---

[1] **heyday:** Prime time; the peak of success.
[2] **cameos:** Minor parts played by a prominent performer in a single scene of a film.

with a hooded figure running down golden suburban streets. Another browser window opens full of fluttering birds. Others pop open, too, that use Google Street View and Google Maps to show the old neighborhood. At the end of the film, the viewer is urged to write a letter to his or her young self.

Within days, the site received some 20 million hits and 3 million unique views.   18

The video, made possible by the Web programming language HTML, was directed by Chris Milk, who has previously done more traditional videos for Gnarls Barkley, West and others. He has been thinking about using the interactivity of the Web for music videos and earlier this year released *The Johnny Cash Project*, a Web-only video that gathers portraits of Cash submitted by fans and sets them to the song "Ain't No Grave."   19

"Because we're in this transitional moment, we've all been making music videos as if we're making them for a television broadcast," says Milk. "But really the Web is a totally different canvas from broadcast. It allows for a whole different set of rules."   20

Many of the new, Web-oriented videos are made possible financially because of advancements in technology, especially DSLR cameras, which are relatively inexpensive and provide excellent production value. The comedian Tom Sharpling used such a camera to shoot the recent Ted Leo and the Pharmacists' video for "Bottled in Cork," a parody of jukebox musicals[3] made for less than $7,000.   21

The video premiered not on a music blog, but the comedy site Funny or Die. It's been watched by more than 105,000, which Leo notes is several times more than those who have bought his latest album, *The Brutalist Bricks*.   22

"People are actually able to present images that to them relate to the music that they're making, as opposed to feeling like they need to present images with quick cuts, flashy, hi-fi performance shots and pose-y things that for a while were dictated by wanting to get played on MTV," Leo says.   23

Music videos haven't completely vanished from television. They can still be seen on Fuse, VH1, MTV and Palladia, the high-definition channel owned by MTV Networks. Van Toffler, president of MTV Networks Music and Logo Group, says MTV networks together play more videos—about 600 hours worth a week—than MTV did in its video heyday.   24

MTV puts its focus on blending music video into its programming, and having its online properties—which brought in more than 53 million unique visitors in August—work in tandem with its broadcast.   25

"The notion of infamy on multiple screens has given music videos a shot in the arm," says Toffler.   26

Williams goes further: "I don't know why anyone would watch a music video anywhere other than the Internet."   27

---

[3] **jukebox musicals:** A play or musical that uses previously popularized music for its musical score.

EXERCISING VOCABULARY

1. Record your own definition for each of these words.

   arresting (adj.) (3)　　　　　　tabulates (v.) (10)
   scantily (adv.) (4)　　　　　　　iconography (n.) (12)
   rampage (n.) (4)　　　　　　　　disillusioned (adj.) (13)
   viral (adj.) (5)　　　　　　　　　parody (n.) (21)
   discourse (n.) (6)　　　　　　　tandem (n.) (25)
   reminiscent (adj.) (6)　　　　　infamy (n.) (26)

2. Reread the title of the essay. What does the word *rebound* mean? In which context have you heard the word? What does it mean here?

3. According to the author, Beyoncé's *Single Ladies (Put a Ring on It)* "became so iconic it spawned countless imitators" (para. 5). What does the word *spawned* mean? What kinds of things are spawned?

4. In paragraph 26, the author quotes Tofffler as saying, "The notion of infamy on multiple screens has given music videos a shot in the arm." Why do people get shots? Then what does it mean to give music videos "a shot in the arm"?

PROBING CONTENT

1. According to the author, what has recently happened to the music video? Where do most people now watch music videos?

2. How have music videos been affected by no longer being viewed primarily on television? Cite some specific examples.

3. Who is Hype Williams? What part did he play in early music videos? Why does he say that "it's a different time" for music videos? How does he feel about this?

4. Describe the music video entitled *The Wilderness Downtown*. How is it representative of the "new" kind of music video?

CONSIDERING CRAFT

1. The essay begins with a one-sentence paragraph. Why does Coyle choose to begin his essay with a paragraph only one sentence long? Find two other examples of similar paragraphs in the essay. What effect does the author achieve by using only one sentence in some paragraphs? How do these paragraphs affect your reading?

2. The first sentence of the essay contains a metaphor. What is a metaphor? What does the writer mean when he says that the music video was "on

life support"? Find another metaphor in the essay. What is the effect of this figure of speech on your reading?

3. Coyle mentions several music artists and even quotes some of them in this essay. Why does he do this? Is this an effective writing strategy? Why?

WRITING PROMPTS

Responding to the Topic   Write an essay in which you describe in detail how, and where, you listen to music. Why is this your preference? Explain the role of music in your life.

Responding to the Writer   Coyle claims that music videos have "become part of the cultural discourse again in a way that's reminiscent of the heyday of the music video, from the early '80s to the mid-'90s" (para. 7). Do some research on earlier music videos. Then write an essay in which you agree or disagree with Coyle's argument.

Responding to Multiple Viewpoints   Reflect on the essays you have read in this chapter. Pick one of the media you have read about like television shows, music videos, or films. Then, using specific examples from the chapter and from your personal experience, write an essay in which you discuss the impact — both positive and negative — on the culture of your chosen medium.

For a quiz on this reading, go to bedfordstmartins.com/mirror.

Analyzing the Image

Lady Gaga

On the night of the 2010 MTV Video Music Awards, Lady Gaga, known for her outrageous outfits, may have even topped herself. This photograph shows the infamous meat dress she wore to accept the Moon Man for the Video of the Year for "Bad Romance." According to *USA Today* (December 28, 2010), the outfit, complete with purse, hat, and boots, was composed of 40 pounds of flank steak. Designed by Franc Fernandez, this was one of three outfits donned by Gaga at the VMAs, where she won eight awards. In a television interview with Ellen De-Generes following the awards show, Lady Gaga told Ellen that she had been escorted to the Nokia Theater in Los Angeles by members of the U.S. military who had been discharged from service due to the "Don't Ask, Don't Tell" policy. Lady Gaga said, "It is a devastation to me that I know my fans who are gay . . . feel like they have govern-mental oppression on them. That's actually why I wore the meat to-night." She added, "If we don't stand up for what we believe in and if we don't fight for our rights, pretty soon we're going to have as much rights as the meat on our own bones. And, I am not a piece of meat."

- What do you first notice when you look at this visual? Which details do you notice next?

- What is your reaction to Lady Gaga's dress? Why?

- If you had not read Lady Gaga's explanation, what statement would you have assumed that she was trying to make by dressing in flank steak?

Research this topic at TopLinks at bedfordstmartins.com/toplinks.

Here, There and Everywhere: Television Is Spreading in New Directions

THE ECONOMIST

The Economist is a London-based magazine that publishes stories on weekly news and international affairs. It was founded in 1843 by James Wilson, and in 2009 the magazine reported a circulation of about 1.6 million per issue. The magazine does not include bylines for its stories, and so the authorship of specific pieces remains largely anonymous.

> **THINKING AHEAD** How do you watch television? Do you watch it in real time? Do you record shows for later viewing? Do you ever watch television shows on a computer or on a smartphone? In what way do you prefer to watch TV?

The *Price Is Right* was looking a bit long in the tooth[1] when Fremantle Media bought it in 1996. The game show, which invites contestants to "come on down" and guess the value of various consumer goods, had first appeared on television 40 years earlier. Since 1972 it had been hosted by one man, Bob Barker. Its audience was aged. When Mr. Barker announced his retirement, one talk-show host joked that when he started watching *The Price Is Right* he knew he was getting too old to keep working.

These days the show is a multimedia phenomenon. It has been turned into computer games and slot machines. Perhaps inevitably, there is an iPhone app, which has been bought more than half a million times. Bally's, a casino in Las Vegas, puts on a theatrical version of the competition five days a week. Now with a new host, the show is chugging along[2] on daytime television, not doing at all badly.

"Once people fall in love with a brand, they want to interact with it in all sorts of ways," says Tony Cohen, the head of Fremantle Media. This would be true even without prodding from media firms. *Winter Sonata*, a South Korean soap opera, sent honeymooners flocking to the places where it had been filmed. There are plenty of unofficial tours of famous TV locations in New York and Los Angeles. Media firms have learned to capture more of this demand and profit from it. About one-third of Fremantle's revenues now come from consumer goods and other spin-offs.

---

[1] **long in the tooth:** Old.
[2] **chugging along:** Proceeding in a deliberate manner.

Popular TV shows routinely spawn DVDs, toys, websites, computer   4
games, board games and comics. Germany's *Gute Zeiten, Schlechte Zeiten*
soap has an eveningwear collection. Indeed, the point of the television
business is no longer simply to make shows but to create branded entertainment franchises made up of many products of which television shows
are merely the most important. And promoters no longer wait to see
whether a program becomes popular before turning it into a merchandising machine.

A good example is *Isa TKM*, a Venezuelan *telenovela*[3] about a schoolgirl   5
obsessed with a dishy[4] musician. The show, made by Viacom and Sony,
became a hit soon after it was launched in Latin America in 2008. It was
subsequently sold to television networks in more than 50 countries. In
view of its growing international popularity, actors from Argentina, Co-
lombia and Mexico have been drafted for a second series, *Isa TK+*.

From the beginning *Isa* has been a multi-platform franchise—a kind of   6
Hispanic answer to *Hannah Montana*, Disney's tween pop colossus. The
show appeared with an entourage of Facebook and MySpace pages. There
are websites in Spanish, Portuguese and, for American Latinas, Spanglish (a
sample: "When he's not *mirándose en el espejo*, Rey pasa el tiempo working
out"). Fans can buy mobile-phone ringtones and videos. The cast of *Isa* has
launched an album which topped the music charts in three countries.

These days you can hardly watch a TV show aimed at young people   7
without being invited to visit a website. Find out what music is playing in
the background! See some footage that did not make it into the final version! Discuss the show with other fans! And, of course, see some more advertisements. The websites of big-budget American dramas are dense and
well designed. The shrewdest producers have realized that this profusion of
spin-offs opens up a new approach to storytelling.

One of the buzzwords in Hollywood these days is "transmedia." It re-   8
fers to a kind of storytelling that goes beyond both a single platform and a
single narrative. Big-budget TV shows like *Lost* and *Heroes* pioneered the
use of web episodes to flesh out minor characters. The *Heroes* website
hosts cartoons, subsequently printed and bound into graphic novels, that
go off on tangents to the main story. Such extensions create deeper, more immersive experiences for fans. They also allow the main story, on television,
to be kept fairly uncluttered—or at least less cluttered than it might have
become otherwise: by its third or fourth season *Lost* was quite complicated
enough.

It is not yet clear that transmedia storytelling is profitable in its own right.   9
Its value is not measured in advertising dollars but in audience engagement.
Web episodes keep viewers interested during the summer when broadcast
shows go off-air. They especially please dedicated fans, who can evangelize
for the show. "The fans might be few in number but they are extremely

[3] *telenovela*: Spanish-language soap opera.
[4] *dishy*: Attractive; sexy.

vocal," says Nathan Mayfield of Hoodlum, an Australian firm that has created online content for *Lost* and *Emmerdale*, a British soap opera.

Have Content, Will Travel

When a TV show goes off the air for the last time, the online community 10
that had gathered around it tends to vanish. The games and the CDs stop
selling, too. Television brings audiences to all these other activities and
gives them life. It is also an excellent vehicle for carrying stories and characters to other countries, where the whole merchandise-rich ecosystem can
get going all over again. Indeed, it is almost the only means of doing so.

"The Internet is not multilingual yet," notes Sir Howard Stringer, Sony's 11
boss. Television and film travel much better. Shows and movies can be dubbed
and subtitled—and, in any case, it is not clear that *The Girls Next Door* or
Transformers: Rise of the Machines are greatly improved by explanation.
These days Hollywood depends on income from cinemas outside America.
Sony's films earned $1.5 billion at the American box office in 2009 but made
a record $2.1 billion outside the country. It is the same with television.

The rising middle class in Brazil, China and India needs cars and hair- 12
care products, and television advertising for such things is growing. Sir
Martin Sorrell, head of WPP, a large global ad agency, says the rise of TV
advertising outside North America and western Europe more than compensates for the drift to the Internet of marketing expenditure in those regions. But the best thing about middle-class consumers in emerging
markets, from the perspective of the international media firms, is that they
are increasingly prepared to pay for television.

In America nine out of ten homes with televisions already subscribe to 13
multi-channel TV, leaving little room for growth. In Asia and eastern Europe the proportion is less than half, and in Latin America it is less than a
quarter. SNL Kagan reckons that pay-TV revenues outside America and
western Europe will rise steeply in the next few years. Just as important,
consumers in countries such as India are acquiring second and third television sets. This provides an opening for teen-oriented fare, which otherwise
might not get a look-in. "If you have only one television in the house, the
patriarch controls it," says Philippe Dauman of Viacom.

Overseas markets are the healthiest, fastest-growing part of the televi- 14
sion business. Discovery Communications, which ventured abroad early, now
derives a third of its revenues from outside America. It helps that Discovery
produces a lot of documentaries and natural-history shows: programs with
voice-overs can be readied for export simply by recording a new narration.
Fox International Channels, News Corporation's overseas arm, turned
over more than $1 billion in the fiscal year 2008–09. Five years earlier it
had brought in less than $200 million.

In many countries the strongest competition for channels launched 15
by international media firms comes from local outfits. Knowledgeable,

Plenty of Growth Left

Multichannel-TV revenue forecasts; 2007–2014

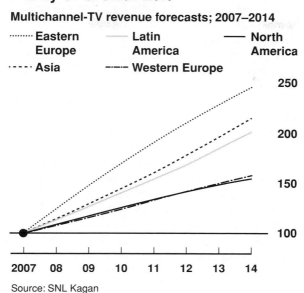

········ **Eastern Europe**   ── **Latin America**   ── **North America**

---- **Asia**   ──── **Western Europe**

Source: SNL Kagan

well connected and often protected by foreign-ownership rules, they have an advantage over the new entrants. Some, like the BBC, have a guaranteed source of income. Others have exploited historical and linguistic connections overseas. France's Canal Plus has a channel in Vietnam; Brazil's Globo is doing well in Angola, like Brazil a former Portuguese colony.

A few have even sneaked hits into America. The Spanish-language *telenovelas* that Mexico's Televisa supplies to Univision frequently draw bigger prime-time audiences than English-language shows. Europeans dominate the worldwide reality-TV business. FremantleMedia, which is owned by Bertelsmann, produces *American Idol*. Endemol, a Netherlands-based firm, churns out the kind of reality shows that Americans love to complain about—and love to watch. But these are localized versions of imported formats. Most Americans probably do not realize that *American Idol* or *Dancing with the Stars* originated in Britain. Only Hollywood routinely exports its shows unaltered. 16

An International Beauty Contest

To see why the big studios are so successful at selling overseas, conduct a test. Get hold of a copy of a drama made by Hollywood for American broadcast TV—*CSI*, *Glee* or *Heroes* will do fine—and, at a random moment, press the pause button. What do you see? Handsome actors, no doubt. But also a well-composed shot that resembles a photograph, 17 with the actors well positioned within the frame. The shot will be well lit, too. Now do the same for a show made by a foreign broadcaster. The result? Probably less impressive.

Finely crafted television like this is expensive. It costs more than $3 million for an hour of drama that is good enough to pass muster[5] on an American broadcast network. The visual acuity of Hollywood's best shows is a big reason why they can compete against homegrown products that are more culturally relevant. Their advantage is growing as households across the world invest in bigger, sharper televisions. And Hollywood is less ashamed of its role as global storyteller than it used to be.   18

A few years ago there was much talk of localizing television shows. Stung by charges of cultural imperialism, which were particularly loud in France, the big media conglomerates encouraged their foreign subsidiaries to develop their own programming. Although some still do so, it is no longer the rule. MTV India, for example, is dominated by local acts but MTV Poland is a vehicle for international music.   19

These days MTV International is run "more like a global multinational," says Bob Bakish, its president. It produces local content where there is demand for the stuff. But it is also a co-ordinated distribution engine for American programming. Series like *Jersey Shore*, an oddly compelling show that trails Italian-American youths around beaches and bars, are now released simultaneously outside America. When Michael Jackson died, MTV quickly assembled a reel of the singer's performances and dispatched it around the world. A truly decentralized outfit could not have done that.   20

Television companies have gained more leeway in part because worries about cultural imperialism have shifted from Hollywood to Silicon Valley. It was Twitter, not CNN, that was blamed for sparking protests in Iran in 2009. Google has tangled with the Chinese government and has been accused of impoverishing national newspapers. Television has lost its monopoly over the creation of cultural anxiety, and more besides.   21

EXERCISING VOCABULARY

1. Record your own definition for each of these words.

prodding (n.) (3)	reckons (v.) (13)
revenues (n.) (3)	fare (n.) (13)
spawn (v.) (4)	patriarch (n.) (13)
subsequently (adv.) (5)	exploited (v.) (15)
tangents (n.) (8)	linguistic (adj.) (15)
ecosystem (n.) (10)	unaltered (adj.) (16)
compensates (v.) (12)	acuity (n.) (18)

---

[5] **pass muster:** To meet someone's approval.

conglomerates (n.) (19)
subsidiaries (n.) (19)
decentralized (v.) (20)
leeway (n.) (21)

sparking (v.) (21)
impoverishing (v.) (21)
monopoly (n.) (21)

2. In paragraph 6, the author calls Hannah Montana "Disney's tween pop colossus." Look up the word *colossus.* What does it mean? What was the Colossus of Rhodes? Is it an overstatement to describe Hannah Montana as a colossus? Why or why not?

3. The writer states that "Big-budget TV shows like *Lost* and *Heroes* pioneered the use of web episodes to flesh out minor characters" (para. 8). What do you think of when you think of pioneers? What then does the verb *pioneered* mean in this sentence?

4. In paragraph 9, the author discusses "dedicated fans, who can evangelize for the show" of their choice. What is an evangelist? What kind of work does an evangelist do? How can a TV fan "evangelize" for a show. What would he or she do? Why?

PROBING CONTENT

1. How do advertisers turn a television show into a "merchandising machine"? Why do they do this? Why is *Isa TKM* a good example of this marketing strategy?

2. What is transmedia storytelling? Why is it used? How profitable is it?

3. How successful are big TV studios at marketing overseas? Why? Give some specific examples.

4. What kinds of television programs have been imported into America from abroad? Why are they popular here?

CONSIDERING CRAFT

1. Examine the title and two subheadings of the essay. Describe the language used in the title and the subheadings. How do they guide your reading? How effective are they?

2. This essay begins with an example of one television show. Reread the first two paragraphs. How effective is this opening?

3. The author uses numerous examples of television shows from the United States and from abroad. How does the inclusion of these examples, many of which you may not be familiar with, affect your reading?

4. How would you describe the tone of this essay? Cite specific lines from the essay that support your opinion.

WRITING PROMPTS

Responding to the Topic   Write an essay in which you explore your relationship to television. Honestly evaluate the ways in which TV plays a role in your life. Exactly how has this role changed throughout the years? Which kinds of shows do you prefer? Do you try to emulate your favorite television stars? Do you adopt their fashion, behavior, or language? Do you seek out further information about the stars, storylines, locations, or music featured in the shows? Do you join chat rooms to discuss the TV shows? Does your television watching enhance or detract from your interactions with other people? Feel free to consider other questions while planning your essay.

Responding to the Writer   Pick one television show that you believe is what the author calls a "multimedia phenomenon" (para. 2) like *The Price Is Right.* Write an essay in which you describe the ways in which the show you have chosen is a multimedia phenomenon. Then analyze the reasons behind this phenomenon. You may find it useful to interview your friends to gather information for this assignment.

Responding to Multiple Viewpoints   How would Anupama Chopra ("Bollywood Princess, Hollywood Hopeful: Aishwarya's Quest for Global Stardom," p. 340) respond to the idea of "cultural imperialism" in media discussed in *The Economist*'s "Here, There, and Everywhere: Television Is Spreading in New Directions"? Write an essay in which you answer this question. To strengthen your argument, you may wish to research Aishwarya's career since the publication of Chopra's essay, focusing on the ways in which her career has spanned the globe and what she and others have had to say about her multinational media presence.

For a quiz on this reading, go to bedfordstmartins.com/mirror.

Wrapping Up Chapter 8

CONNECTING TO THE CULTURE

1. Either on the Web or at your university library, watch an episode of one of the foreign television shows mentioned in "Here, There, and Everywhere" (p. 370). Take careful notes while you are watching the episode. You may also choose to do some additional research on your chosen show on the Web. Then write a review of the show you have watched. In your review, you may wish to compare it to similar English-language television shows.

2. Using the essays in this chapter, as well as your own observations and experiences, write an essay in which you discuss how the self-image of men or women is handled or mishandled in movies, television shows, or music videos. Include several specific examples from films, TV shows, or videos you have seen. You may also refer to other essays in this book, such as those in Chapters 3, 5, and 7.

3. Write an essay in which you argue for the iconic status of one particular movie, television show, or music video. You may wish to refer to "Fade In, Fade Out: Addiction, Recovery, in American Film" (p. 334), "Here, There, and Everywhere" (p. 370), or "Left for Dead by MTV, Music Videos Rebound on the Web" (p. 363). First consider what qualifies as an iconic movie, television show, or music video. Then make a list of at least five films, TV shows, and music videos, past or present, that could be the subject of your essay. Make your final choice, watch the movie, TV show, or music video, and take notes as you watch it. You may also wish to consult Internet sources such as IMDb.com (Internet Movie Database) or the Web site for the film, television show, or music video you have chosen.

4. Go to a Web site like YouTube and watch a film by a director of your choice. Take notes as you watch the film. Then write a review of it. Consult IMDb.com (Internet Movie Database) for examples of reviews by trusted reviewers such as Roger Ebert, James Berardinelli, or Peter Travers.

5. Choose a film whose story line deals with an ethnic group other than your own. You might choose a film like Paul Haggis's *Crash* that focuses on the interactions among characters from several different groups or a film like Tyler Perry's *Why Did I Get Married?* that focuses on a single group. Watch the film and take notes on it. Then write an essay in which you examine the ways in which ethnicity is presented in the film. You may wish to refer to "Tyler Perry's Money Machine" (p. 346) in this chapter as you write your paper.

Focusing on Yesterday, Focusing on Today

Movie posters are often both beautiful works of art and eye-catching advertisements. They send powerful messages to potential moviegoers. In the past, people saw these posters outside movie theaters, which were often "movie palaces" that could seat up to 5,000 patrons. Today, posters appear outside multiplexes and on the Web at popular sites such as the Internet Movie Database (IMDb).

These posters represent two iconic vampire films. Tod Browning's *Dracula* was first released on Valentine's Day, 1931, and was so wildly popular that it helped secure Universal Studio's success during the Golden Age of Hollywood. The first installment of Stephenie Meyers's *Twilight* saga burst onto the screen in 2008 and created a devoted fan base called Twihards. Both *Twilight and Dracula* were blockbusters that spawned a host of highly anticipated sequels.

These two movie posters were originally printed in color. In the *Dracula* poster, the couple is surrounded by a golden halo of light that radiates into red. Mina's hair is blonde, and Dracula's is brown. The film title appears in bright gold letters against Dracula's black cape. The *Twilight* poster is much more muted in tone. Edward wears a dark gray jacket, and his hair is dark

"I Am . . . Dracula."

brown; Bella is wearing a blue denim jacket, and her hair appears auburn. Their skin is luminous, although his is lighter, and their lips are red.

Examine these two posters closely as both artistic photographs and carefully crafted advertisements. Even if you have not seen either one of the films, you can infer important information from each visual.

- Compare the two couples on the posters. Study their expressions, their body language and positions, and their clothing. Note both similarities and differences. What can you infer about the two relationships as they are captured at this moment?

- How does the text relate to the visual component of each poster? Where is the text positioned? How big is it? How much text is used on each movie poster? What message about the film does the text convey?

- What is it about each poster that would convince someone to view the film it is advertising? What is the target audience for each poster (age group, gender, ethnicity)?

- How does each movie poster reflect the time period in which the film it advertises was produced? What details reveal the different times? Which poster "speaks" to you in a more powerful manner? Why?

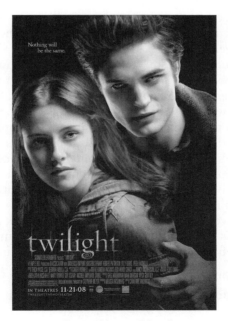

"Love Never Dies."

Evaluating and Documenting Sources

When you research topics of interest in popular culture, you are going to want to augment your own thoughts and ideas with credible sources that support your position. You may think that it will be difficult to locate such sources. On the contrary, for most topics, you'll find a wide array of potential material to incorporate into your work. You won't be able to use everything, so you will have to make some important choices in order to focus on the most legitimate and persuasive evidence.

As you begin, remember two important things. First, because popular culture involves what's popular, it changes rapidly. Remember 98 Degrees? Old news, right? Consequently, the more recent your source, the more valuable that source is to your research. A *Rolling Stone* article on current music trends isn't current if it was written in 1997, although it may still be useful if you are seeking a historical perspective.

Second, all sources are not created equal. Some publications or Web sites are created specifically to further the writer's own views. Material on the Internet is often posted without being evaluated. Let the researcher beware. You will want to establish certain basic information about any source you plan to rely on for information—for example, its date of posting or publication or the person or organization that is responsible for the veracity of the site's or the magazine's content. Learning to recognize and evaluate the bias embedded in some potentially useful material may require a little detective work, but it is essential to the authenticity and credibility of your own research.

In Chapter 2, we suggested a list of questions to ask as you deconstruct media images. Let's start with a similar list of questions to help you learn to evaluate the usefulness of possible electronic and print sources:

1. Where is the source material located?
2. What is the date of the publication, posting, or update?
3. Who is the author?
4. When the material was written or posted, who was its intended audience?
5. Is the material a primary source or a secondary source?

Just as we do when deconstructing a visual image, let's take the most easily answered questions first.

WHERE IS THE SOURCE MATERIAL LOCATED?

The first important question to ask about potential source material is "Where is it located?" If the article or advertisement is in print form, in which magazine, newspaper, or journal does it appear? What can you find out about this publication? How long has it been in circulation? Who publishes the book, newspaper, or magazine? Who sponsors this Web site? What's the purpose of the Web site or print source? Check the titles of other articles listed in the table of contents. What patterns or similarities do you see? Are different viewpoints represented?

Answers to most of these basic questions can usually be found on a page near the front of the publication. Journals, whose articles are generally closely scrutinized by editors and reviewers before they are published, are even more likely than magazines to provide such particulars. Remember that scholarly journals, unlike popular magazines, are published less frequently, are peer reviewed, and are often written for a select audience of professionals.

If your source is electronic, you may not find this information as readily. Some Internet sources are affiliated with journals, magazines, newspapers, or professional organizations. These sites are generally reliable and may include relevant dates, biographical information about the author, and general information about the site itself. However, remember that anyone can host a Web site and post whatever he or she chooses, whether or not it is accurate. Wouldn't it be embarrassing to find out that you've quoted a seventh grader's Lindsay Lohan site in a college paper? You'll want to reference only reliable Web sources that clearly reveal ownership and other factual documentation.

WHAT IS THE DATE OF THE PUBLICATION, POSTING, OR UPDATE?

How recently was this online information written and published? Magazines and journals usually print a date on the cover. Weekly publications give you more current information about popular culture topics than monthly ones do, and daily newspapers stay ahead of both. Some journals are published only once or twice a year, but they may still provide important background for your research.

Articles on the Internet may have the date of the site's creation or most recent update or may not have any date. You might have to use clues to judge how recently the information has been gathered. Check the information against other dated sources. Read carefully for dates and events mentioned within the article itself.

WHO IS THE AUTHOR?

Book authors' names are readily available, and sometimes a note on the book jacket will list important biographical data. Periodical authors who have established reputations will be identified by name either near the beginning or end of the article. A few lines about the author—other articles or books written, current position held, any literary recognition received, or other specific information that makes the author more credible than others on that subject—may also be included. Tiger Woods's writing about the best golf courses, for example, would automatically carry more clout than the average weekend golfer's. Journals generally offer a great deal of specific information about their authors' professional accomplishments and affiliations.

On the other hand, many magazine articles are written by staff writers who work full-time for the publication, providing material on whatever topic they are assigned. Still other articles are written by freelance writers who are hired by the publication or Web host to contribute one article on one particular topic at a time. Such authors may or may not be named. Whatever you can learn about authors, famous or not, will help you to read the articles more accurately and alert you to any particular bias or viewpoint. Clues about the author's angle and tone may also present themselves in the writing. An author who professes in the opening paragraph of a review to be a great fan of Julia Roberts is not likely to be truly impartial about one of her movies.

Internet sources should list at least the author's name. We suggest treating with caution any Internet article that lists no author at all. Be diligent in trying to find the author of an Internet source. You may need to go back to the home page if the author's name does not appear just before or just after the essay.

As your research on a popular culture topic progresses, chances are good that a few authors' names will appear as references in several different sources. This is testimony to the author's credibility and an indication that this author's thoughts and opinions on this topic are generally sought after and respected.

WHEN THE MATERIAL WAS WRITTEN OR POSTED, WHO WAS ITS INTENDED AUDIENCE?

Do readers of the source belong to a particular age group, ethnicity, interest group, or occupational group? *Teen Magazine*, for example, is clearly marketed toward a certain age group, as is *AARP: The Magazine*, one of the publications of the American Association of Retired Persons. Perhaps the publication or site is intended for a special-interest group. Publications like *Dog World* fit this category. Some magazines, such as *Time, Newsweek, People*, and *Reader's Digest*, are written to appeal to a much wider audience. Knowing the target audience for a publication will help you evaluate any common knowledge, vocabulary, values, and beliefs that its writers expect most readers to share.

Journals tend to be directed to specific target audiences, which frequently consist of people in the same profession. Often in such publications the language and style used will be baffling to the outsider yet easily understood by members of the profession. The medical terminology used in the *American Journal of Nursing* may sound like unintelligible jargon to someone outside the field of medicine. Remember, if you don't understand what you are reading, that material may have little value to you as a source.

In some cases, if the specifics of a complicated journal article are important to your research, you may want to consult a specialized dictionary. These references will help you decipher language unique to one field of study—like law, psychology, or engineering.

IS THE MATERIAL A PRIMARY SOURCE OR A SECONDARY SOURCE?

Determining whether material is a primary or secondary source may not be as easy as finding the date of publication or the author's name, but this distinction isn't difficult. When you see *Star Wars, Episode III: Revenge of the Sith* and then describe in a paper how George Lucas employs technology to develop the character of Yoda, you are using a primary source—the movie itself. When you read an article that compares George Lucas's use of technology in the *Star Wars* trilogy and in the prequels in *Entertainment* magazine and then quote the author of that article in your own work, you are using a secondary source—the article about the movies.

Let's take one more example. If you watch a television interview with Denzel Washington about the role of black actors in American films and refer to that interview in your research, that is a primary source. You saw the interview yourself. However, if you miss the television show and read a review of it in the next day's Life and Arts section of your local newspaper, then you'll be using a secondary source when you incorporate information from the review in your paper.

With primary sources, you are in direct contact with the music, film, novel, advertisement, or Web site. You develop your own interpretation and analysis. With secondary sources, someone else is acting as a filter between you and the CD, the play, the short story, or the painting.

Both types of sources are valuable. After all, not many of us saw the Beatles' last live concert in person. But with secondary sources you will want to be alert for any bias or viewpoint of the author's that could affect the credibility of the source material.

Practice in applying these five questions will help you to become confident about the value and validity of the sources you use to support your own ideas.

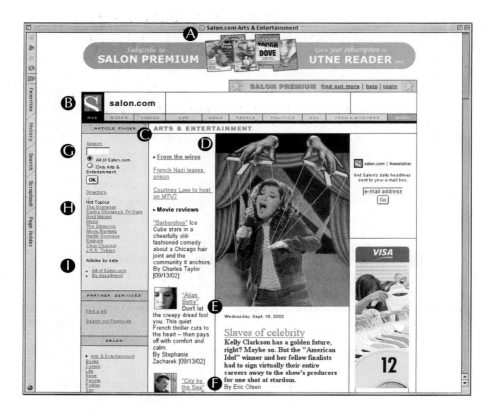

Here is an example of a Web page you might consult during your research into a popular culture topic:

- Item A identifies the group as a company (.com), not a school (.edu), an organization (.org), or a government agency (.gov).
- Item B offers a link to the Web site's home page.
- Item C provides a heading to let you know what part of the site you are viewing.
- Item D uses an engaging graphic image that is related to the subject matter of a general topic.
- Item E provides a date for the issue.
- Item F provides the name of the author below an article title.
- Item G allows for a search function.
- Item H provides links to other topics within the site that might be of interest.
- Item I provides links to additional articles.

EXERCISE

After closely examining the Web screen shot, answer the following questions:

1. Who is the intended audience for this Web page? What aspects of this site provide clues to help you identify its audience?

2. What elements of this Web site indicate the reliability or unreliability of its information?

3. What aspects of this site let you know that this Web-based company wants its audience to return to the site often?

Documenting Electronic and Print Sources

Now we are ready to take those sources for which we have established relevance and the proper credentials and think about using them in a paper or other research project.

Attention, please! Always write out a complete citation for any piece of material that you are seriously considering as a source for your research. That way, days after you put the bound volume of periodicals back on the shelf, you won't have to go through all fifty volumes to locate one article that contains just the right quotation or statistic. Also, always print out a hard copy of anything from the Internet that you consider using. The fact that you knew the URL today doesn't mean you'll know it a week from now or that the same information will be posted again in exactly the same place.

Here are some examples of the correct ways to document your sources in the body of your paper. We also provide examples of the correct ways to document your sources in your Works Cited page at the end of your paper. This is a brief listing and isn't meant to be the only reference you should consult. If you need additional information on documenting sources, ask your professor to recommend a text or go to *Research and Documentation Online* at dianahacker.com/resdoc. All the citations here follow the 2009 Modern Language Association (MLA) format. Before writing any paper, check with your instructor to see which format is required.

MLA FORMAT FOR IN-TEXT CITATIONS

You should provide an in-text citation every time you quote from, paraphrase, or summarize an outside source. Your citation should directly follow the sentence or sentences in your paper that refer to the source information. Consult the following models when you cite sources within your essay.

Books or Periodicals

When you use a quotation and do not name the author within your text, you must put both the author's name and the page number in parentheses at the end of the quotation. The complete citation that identifies the book's title, date, and place of publication will be found in the list of Works Cited:

"The fact is that much of advertising's power comes from this belief that advertising does not affect us. The most effective kind of propaganda is that which is not recognized as propaganda" (Kilbourne 27).

If a work has four or more authors, list all of their last names, or list the first author's name followed by et al., which means "and others":

"In another scenario, where a woman gives birth to her own clone, would she be her child's mother or twin sister with a different age?" (Borem et al. 83).

If you mention the author's name in your text, then only the page number needs to be in parentheses at the end of the quotation:

Kilbourne states that "much of advertising's power comes from this belief that advertising does not affect us" (27).

If an article or a Web page does not have an author, either use the complete title in the text or use a short form of the title within the parentheses before the page number. Use quotation marks around titles of essays and other short works.

Fashion companies hope that "by making an ordinary product 'exclusive' they can add a note of urgency to splurge spending" ("Putting a Limit on Labels" 12).

If you *paraphrase*, or express in your own words, an idea from a source, you must still include a citation:

Every day, the average American spends nearly an hour watching, listening to, or reading advertisements (Jacobson and Mazur 193).

Before Title IX's implementation in 1972, fewer than 300,000 high school girls played competitive sports. By 1997, that number had increased to 2.4 million (U.S. Department of Education).

MLA FORMAT FOR WORKS CITED

At the end of your essay, you must provide a list of the sources from which you quoted, paraphrased, or summarized. Put the entire list in alphabetical order using the author's last name and the title as it appears on the title page of the source. If your source has no author, alphabetize it by the first main word of the title. Double-space your Works Cited page, and indent the second line of each entry five spaces. MLA prefers that the titles of books, movies, record albums, television programs, and so on be italicized to clearly distinguish the title from surrounding words.

Books

One Author

Kilbourne, Jean. *Can't Buy My Love: How Advertising Changes the Way We Think and Feel.* New York: Touchstone, 1999. Print.

Two or More Authors

Borem, Aluizio, Fabricio R. Santos, and David E. Bowen. *Understanding Biotechnology.* Upper Saddle River: Prentice Hall, 2003. Print.

Jacobson, Michael F., and Laurie Ann Mazur. *Marketing Madness: A Survival Guide for a Consumer Society.* Boulder: Westview, 1995. Print.

Periodicals

Signed Magazine Article

Will, George F. "Electronic Morphine." *Newsweek* 25 Nov. 2002: 92-93. Print.

Unsigned Magazine Article

"Women's Dissatisfaction with Body Image Greater in More Affluent Neighborhoods." *Women's Health Weekly* 21 Mar. 2002: 12. Print.

Signed Newspaper Article

Barnes, Steve. "In a World Where Sex Sells, One Group Isn't Buying." *Austin American-Statesman* 5 June 2005: K1 + K9. Print.

Unsigned Newspaper Article

"Putting a Limit on Labels." *Wall Street Journal* 14 June 2002: W12. Print.

Signed Editorial

Cohen, Adam. "America's Favorite Television Fare? The Normals vs. the Stigmatized." Editorial. *New York Times* 2 June 2002: WK18. Print.

Journal Article

Birmingham, Elizabeth. "Fearing the Freak: How Talk TV Articulates Women and Class." *Journal of Popular Film and Television* 28.3 (2000): 133–39. Print.

Electronic Sources

Entire Web Site

Denver Water Conservation. Denver Water, 2011. Web. 21 June 2011.

Short Work from a Web Site with Author

Ladd, Andrew. "A Billion Wicked Assumptions." *The Good Men Project*. The Good Men Project, 16 May 2011. Web. 17 June 2011.

Short Work from a Web Site with No Author

"Ansel Adams." *American Experience*. PBS Online, 2002. Web. 22 June 2011.

Article in an Online Magazine

Miller, Laura. "Spamazon." *Salon.com*. Salon Media Group, 21 June 2011. Web. 22 June 2011.

Other Sources

Published Interview

King, Stephen. "Ten Questions for Stephen King." *Time* 1 Apr. 2002: 13. Print.

Broadcast Interview

Tarantino, Quentin. Interview by Charlie Rose. *Charlie Rose*. PBS. WGBH, Boston. 26 Dec. 1997. Television.

Personal Interview

Salomon, Willis. Personal interview. 14 Apr. 2001.

Print Advertisement

T Mobile BlackBerry. Advertisement. *U.S. News & World Report* 23 May 2005: 23. Print.

Television Advertisement

Nike. Advertisement. NBC. 7 June 2005. Television.

Sound Recording

U2. *How to Dismantle an Atomic Bomb*. Universal, 2004. CD.

Television Program

"Daddy Knows Best." *Cold Case Files*. Narr. Bill Kurtis. A&E. 6 Sept. 2004.
    Television.

Radio Program

"Natural Santa Claus." *All Things Considered*. Narr. Robert Siegel. Natl. Public
    Radio. WGBH, Boston. 29 Nov. 2004. Radio.

Film

Star Wars, Episode III: Revenge of the Sith. Dir. George Lucas. Perf. Ewan
    McGregor, Natalie Portman, Hayden Christensen, Ian McDiarmid, Samuel L.
    Jackson, and Christopher Lee. Lucasfilm, 2005. Film.

Speech or Lecture

Mahon, Maureen. "This Is Not White Boy Music: The Politics and Poetics of
    Black Rock." Stanford University, Stanford. 30 Jan. 2002. Lecture.

ACKNOWLEDGMENTS

Text

Tanzila Ahmed. "100% Indian Hair" appeared on *Wire Tap* on February 8, 2006. Copyright © 2006 by Tanzila Ahmed. Used by permission of the author.

Daniel Akst. "America: Land of Loners?" from the Summer, 2010 issue of *The Wilson Quarterly.* Copyright © 2010, The Woodrow Wilson International Center for Scholars. Used by permission of the author.

Daniel Alarcon. "Grand Mall Seizure" posted on *Alter Net* on December 20, 2004. Copyright © 2004 by Daniel Alarcon. Reprinted by permission of the author.

Lorraine Ali. "Do I Look Like Public Enemy Number One?" Originally published in *Mademoiselle.* Copyright © 1999 Condé Nast Publications, Inc. All rights reserved. Reprinted by permission.

Julia Alvarez. "Picky Eater" copyright © 1998 by Julia Alvarez. From *Something to Declare,* published by Plume, an imprint of Penguin Group (USA), in 1999 and originally in hardcover by Algonquin Books of Chapel Hill. First published in *We Are What We Ate,* Harcourt Brace and Company, 1998. By permission of Susan Bergholz Literary Services, New York, NY and Lamy, NM. All rights reserved.

Dan Barden. "My New Nose" originally published in *Gentleman's Quarterly,* May 2002. Copyright © 2002. Reprinted with permission of Dan Barden. Dan@danbarden.com.

Lera Boroditsky. "Lost in Translation" from *The Wall Street Journal,* July 24, 2010. Copyright © 2010 by Dow Jones & Company, Inc. Reproduced with permission of Dow Jones & Company, Inc., in the format textbook via Copyright Clearance Center.

David Brooks. "People Like Us" from *Atlantic Monthly Online.* Copyright ©2003 by The Atlantic Monthly. Reproduced with permission of The Atlantic Monthly in the format Textbook via Copyright Clearance Center.

Ray B. Browne. "Conversations with Scholars of American Popular Culture: Professor Ray B. Browne" interview conducted by Leslie Kreiner Wilson in *Americana: The Journal of American Popular Culture,* Fall, 2002. Copyright 2002 Americana: The Institute for the Study of American Popular Culture. Reprinted by permission of Leslie Kreiner Wilson.

Frank Bruni. "An Expert's Theory of Food Television's Appeal" from *The Atlantic Monthly,* August 1, 2010. Copyright © 2010 by The Atlantic Monthly. Reproduced with permission of The Atlantic Monthly in the format textbook via Copyright Clearance Center.

Mindy Cameron. "In the Language of Our Ancestors." Originally published in *Northwest Education Magazine,* Spring 2004. Copyright © 2004 Northwest Regional Education Laboratory. Reprinted with permission of NWREL. All rights reserved. www.nwrel.org.

Damien Cave. "On Sale at Old Navy: Cool Clothes for Identical Zombies!" from *Salon.com* November 23, 2000. Reprinted by permission of the author.

Michelle Jana Chan. "Identity in a Virtual World" from *CNN.com* at http://edition.cnn.com/2007/TECH/06/07/virtual_identity/index.html. Posted June 14, 2007. Copyright © 2007 by CNN Image Source. Used by permission of CNN Image Source. Atlanta, GA.

Anupama Chopra. "Bollywood Princess, Hollywood Hopeful: Aishwarya's Quest for Global Stardom from *The New York Times,* February 10, 2008. Copyright © 2008 The New York Times. All Rights Reserved. Used by permission and protected by the Copyright Laws of the United States. The printing, copying, redistribution or transmission of the material without express written permission is prohibited.

Delia Cleveland. "Champagne Taste, Beer Budget." Originally appeared in *Essence* magazine, March 2001. Adapted from an essay published in *Starting with "I"* (Persea books, 1997). Reprinted by permission of the author.

Jake Coyle. "Left for Dead by MTV, Music Videos Rebound on the Web." Used with permission of The Associated Press. Copyright © 2011. All rights reserved

Julie Dash. "Rice Culture" from *Through the Kitchen Window,* by Arlene Voski Avakian. Copyright © 1997 by Arlene Voski Avakian. Reprinted by permission of Beacon Press, Boston.

The Editors of *The Economist..* "Here, There and Everywhere: Television Is Spreading in New Directions" from *The Economist,* April 29, 2010. Copyright 2010 The Economist Newspaper Limited (London). Reprinted by permission via Rightslink.

Bruce David Forbes. "Mickey Mouse as Icon: Taking Popular Culture Seriously" from *Word & World,* Volume 23, Number 3. Copyright © 2003. Reprinted by permission.

David Gergen. "A Smart Exception" copyright © 2010 by David Gergen. Initially published in *Parade Magazine,* June 13, 2010. All rights reserved. Reprinted by permission of Parade Magazine.

Art

Before © Dan Winters Photography.   **185**: Losing the Trauma: After © Dan Winters Photography.   **205**: Cathy Comic: Options 2010. CATHY © 2010 Cathy Guisewite. Reprinted with permission of UNIVERSAL UCLICK. All rights reserved.   **206**: Even Ladies Can Wear Levi's Courtesy Levi Strauss & Co. Archives.   **207**: Everybody's Work is Equally Important Photo: Melodie McDaniel, concept: Wieden+Kennedy. Courtesy Levi Strauss & Co.   **209**: Kryptos © Adrian Gaut / Art + Commerce.   **255**: Doonesbury © 2010 G. B. Trudeau. Reprinted with permission of UNIVERSAL UCLICK. All rights reserved.   **262**: Benjamin Franklin at his Printing Press. Library of Congress.   **263**: A Novel Idea. BookBook advertisement courtesy Twelve South LLC.   **265**: Unbrand America Flag. Courtesy of www.adbusters.org.   **266**: Unbrand America Flag. Courtesy of www.adbusters.org.   **318**: Thunderbird Motel © Car Culture/Corbis.   **319**: Achieving Balance Reprinted with permission of Marriott International, Inc.   **321**: Thriller © MCA/Universal / Courtesy Everett Collection.   **322**: Thriller © MCA/Universal / Courtesy Everett Collection.   **345**: The Bollywood Princess Waiting for Her Prince to Come © UTV Motion Pictures.   **362**: An Unlikely Commuter © Mario Tama/Getty Images.   **368**: Lady Gaga in Meat Dress © Kevin Winter/Getty Images.   **378**: Dracula Poster © Universal Pictures/Courtesy Everett Collection.   **379**: Twilight "Love Never Dies" © AF archive / Alamy.

Index of Authors
and Titles